AA

WEEKEND WALKS
IN
BRITAIN

INTRODUCTION BY PAUL STERRY

Produced by AA Publishing

Copy Editor: Penny Hicks
Designers: Design 23

Contributors: Steve Ashton, Chris Barber, Jackie Bates, Kate Chevalier, Paddy Dillon, Heather Freeman, Susan Gordon, Des Hannigan, Leigh Hatts, Tony Hopkins, Charlie Hurt, Peter Lambley, Helen Livingston, Cameron McNeish, Andy Murray, Brian Pearce, Ben Perkins, Mark Richards, Erica Schwarz, Roger Smith, Roland Smith, Rebecca Snelling, Colin Speakman, Donald Stokoe, Clive Tully

Published by AA Publishing (a trading name of Automobile Association Developments Limited, whose registered office is Norfolk House, Priestley Road, Basingstoke, Hampshire RG24 9NY; registered number 1878835).

ISBN
Ringbinder 0 7495 0915 5
Paperback 0 7495 0969 4
Hardback 0 7495 1464 7

A CIP catalogue record for this book is available from the British Library.

Colour Separation by Daylight Colour Art Pte, Singapore
Printed by Brepols Turnhout, Belgium

Acknowledgements

All photographs are held in the Automobile Association's own photo library (AA PHOTO LIBRARY). The Automobile Association wishes to thank the following photographers for their assistance in the preparation of this book.

P Baker 20; **V & S Bates** 22, 36, 37, 38, 54, 55, 56, 61, 62, 63, 64, 116a, 117, 118, 119, 120, 121,170; **J Beazley** 173; **M Birkitt** 64, 71, 98; **I Burgum** 110a, 110b, 111a, 112a, 112b, 113a, 113b, 114, 115, 116b, 126a, 127a, 127b, 128, 129; **J Carnie** 189; **D Croucher** 51, 53a, 53b, 122, 123, 124, 125, 130, 131, 132a, 132b, 133, 134, 135, 136a, 136b, 138, 139; **P Davies** 75b; **S Day** 190a, 190b, 191, 192, 193a, 193b, 198; **P Eden** 33, 34; **A Edwards** 100; **E Ellington** 194b, 195, 196, 197, 199, 200; **D Forss** 18, 19, 21a, 21b, 39, 40, 41, 42a, 42b, 43, 44, 45a, 45b, 46, 47, 48, 49, 50, 52, 65, 66, 67, 68, 69, 70, 71, 72, 73, 74a, 74b, 75a, 76, 77, 78, 79, 80, 81a, 81b, 82, 83, 84, 85, 86a, 87, 96, 99, 101a, 101b, 141, 142, 143b, 147, 148a, 148b; **P Goodrum** 2, 3a, 3b, 4, 5, 6a, 6b, 9a, 9b, 10a, 10b, 11a, 11b;
A Hopkins 158a, 158b, 159, 160a, 160b, 161, 163a, 163b, 164, 165, 166, 167, 168, 169a, 169b; **J Ingram** 7a, 7b, 8a, 8b, 14; **A Lawson** 13b; **S & O Mathews** 24b, 162; **C Mellor** 88a, 88b, 90a, 90b, 95a, 95b, 97; **C Molyneux** 126b; **J Morrison** 144, 145, 146, 149a, 149b, 150, 151, 152, 153, 154a, 154b; **K Paterson** 171, 172, 174a, 174b, 175a, 175b, 176a, 176b, 177, 178, 179a, 179b, 180, 181, 182, 183, 184a, 184b, 185a, 185b, 186a, 186b, 187, 188a, 188b; **N Ray** 12, 13a, 15, 16, 17a, 17b, 25, 26; **P Sharpe** 156, 157, M Short 23, 24a, 27, 28, 29a, 29b, 30, 31, 32, 57, 58, 59a, 59b, 60;
A Stonehouse 1; **M Trelawny** 143a, **A Tryner** 91, 93, 109, 140; **W Voysey** 32, 35; **R Weir** 194a.

Section titles: The West Country, Central England and East Anglia: **P Baker**; Northern England: **J Morrison**; Wales and the Marches: **R Newton**; South and South-east England: **D Noble**; Scotland: **R Weir**.
Front cover: a) **A Baker**; b) **A Besley**; c) **A Greely**
Back cover: **D Croucher**

Artwork by Andrew Hutchinson
Introduction artwork by Richard Draper and Ann Winterbotham

Essential Information for Walkers

Map Symbols

———	Main road
–––––	Other road
- - - - -	Footpath
———	Railway
▬ ▬ ▬	Route of walk
▬ ▬ ▬	Detour/alternative route of walk
	Urban area
	Woodland
	Marsh
	Sand
	Shingle
	Mud
	Rocks/cliff
	Escarpment
Å	Camp site
⌖	Caravan site
△	Youth Hostel
♜	Castle
⛪	Church or chapel
i	Information centre
⍭	Lighthouse
✖	Windmill
P	Parking
▲	Spot height in metres
⚇	Viewpoint
★	Other place of interest
⚐	Picnic site
START	Start
➡	Walk direction

The routes in this book have been carefully researched, but despite our best efforts to ensure accuracy, changes may occur at any stage during the lifetime of the book. Please remember that landscapes do change, and features mentioned as landmarks may alter or disappear completely. The changing seasons can also affect the walks, and paths may become muddy, or overgrown during the summer months.

It is important to note also that some of the routes pass close to dangerous features in the landscape and need care, especially if children are with you. Our walks follow public rights of way and established paths, tracks and bridleways wherever possible, but the routes sometimes include stretches along a road. Even small country lanes can be deceptive, so please walk so that you can see any approaching traffic in good time.

Some of the routes are around the coast. Please remember that, although exciting places to visit, cliffs are by their very nature dangerous. Stay well away from the edge because the cliff-top soil is often loose and slippery, even though plants may be growing in profusion; there may also be an overhang. Walking on the seashore, be aware of the state of the tide – on shallow beaches, it can rise with surprising speed. When seas are rough, keep away from the water – freak waves can sweep people off their feet.

The walks, mostly round trips, have all been carefully selected to take you through attractive and varied areas of the British countryside, and to be enjoyable both for experienced and occasional walkers. Most walks are between two and four miles long, and the approximate distance is always stated, but the time taken to do the walk will vary with the individual. Generally speaking, it is safe to think in terms of two miles an hour.

Do wear sensible clothes, and remember that in this country the weather is notoriously changeable, so it is sensible to take a waterproof. You will also need comfortable footwear that will withstand wet and possibly muddy or slippery conditions.

With the information for each walk, we give an indication of the conditions you should expect – for example, whether it is a gentle stroll on reasonably level ground, or a more challenging walk on rougher terrain. If a walk includes any particularly steep hill stretches, or other hazards such as stiles, we have indicated this. Where possible we have also listed nearby facilities for refreshments, and the nearest public access toilets. Listing in this guide does not imply AA inspection of recognition, although establishments may have an AA classification.

The National Grid reference for the start of each walk is given below the walk number. These numbers relate to the grid squares on the larger scale Ordnance Survey maps (1:50,000 and 1:25,000), which walkers may like to use in addition to the maps in this book. The paths and tracks used are all marked on such maps, and, if you should have the misfortune to miss your way, or need to make a detour for any reason, you will need such a map to reorientate yourself.

Places are suggested where you may be able to park. These have all been checked by our researchers and were found to be practicable – many are in fact official car parks. However, these suggestions are not a guarantee of any right to leave a vehicle parked, and if no distinct car park exists, walkers should park carefully and considerately where they can. Please remember that it is the responsibility of the individual to ensure that their vehicle is safely and not illegally parked, and that it does not obstruct other traffic or access – and remember that, whatever the time of day or year, farm vehicles must always have clear access to field entrances and tracks.

Keep dogs under control and if necessary on a lead. Dogs can be a serious threat to farm livestock, to deer and to other wild animals, as well as ground-nesting and ground-feeding birds – and farm animals, especially cows with young calves, can take violent exception to dogs they do not know.

Please keep to the designated paths, and if you come to a field with crops, walk round the edge, not across the middle. If you find that a public right of way has been blocked, for whatever reason, it is better to inform the Rights of Way Officer in the Highways and Traffic Department of the County Council than to attempt to argue or force a way through. If you open a gate, please remember to close it after you. Be particularly careful not to discard cans, bottles or food because these are a hazard to wildlife as well as being an eyesore. Do not discard lighted cigarettes, matches or anything else that could cause a fire.

The walks are organised according to six regions of Britain – the West Country, South and South-east England, Central England and East Anglia, Wales and the Marches, Northern England, and Scotland

SCOTLAND

NORTHERN ENGLAND

WALES AND THE MARCHES

CENTRAL ENGLAND AND EAST ANGLIA

SOUTH AND SOUTH-EAST ENGLAND

WEST COUNTRY

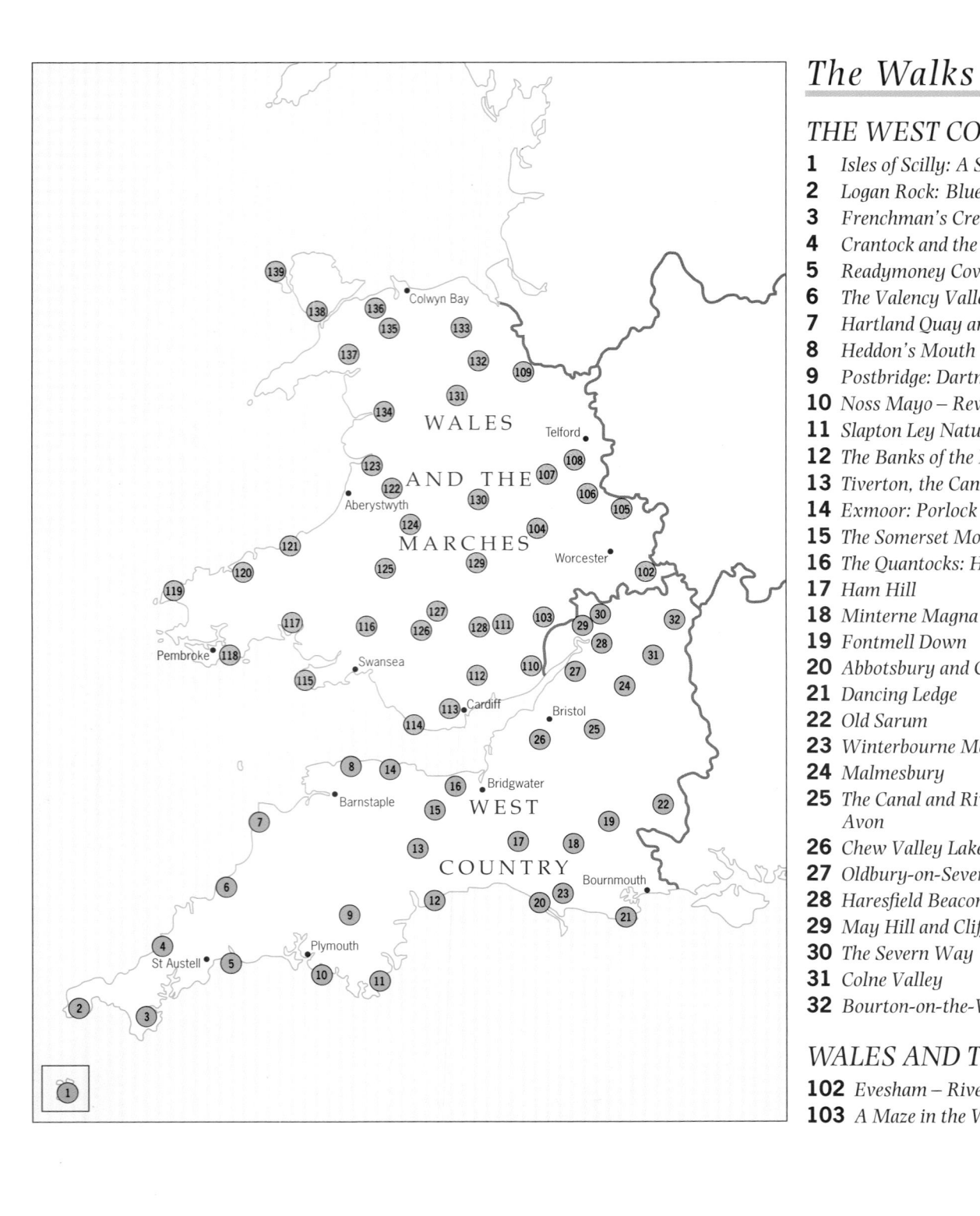

The Walks

THE WEST COUNTRY

WALES AND THE MARCHES

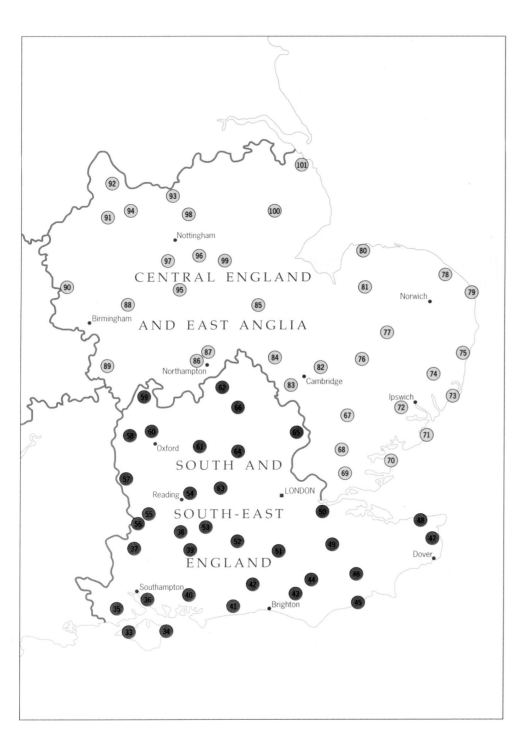

The Walks

The Walks

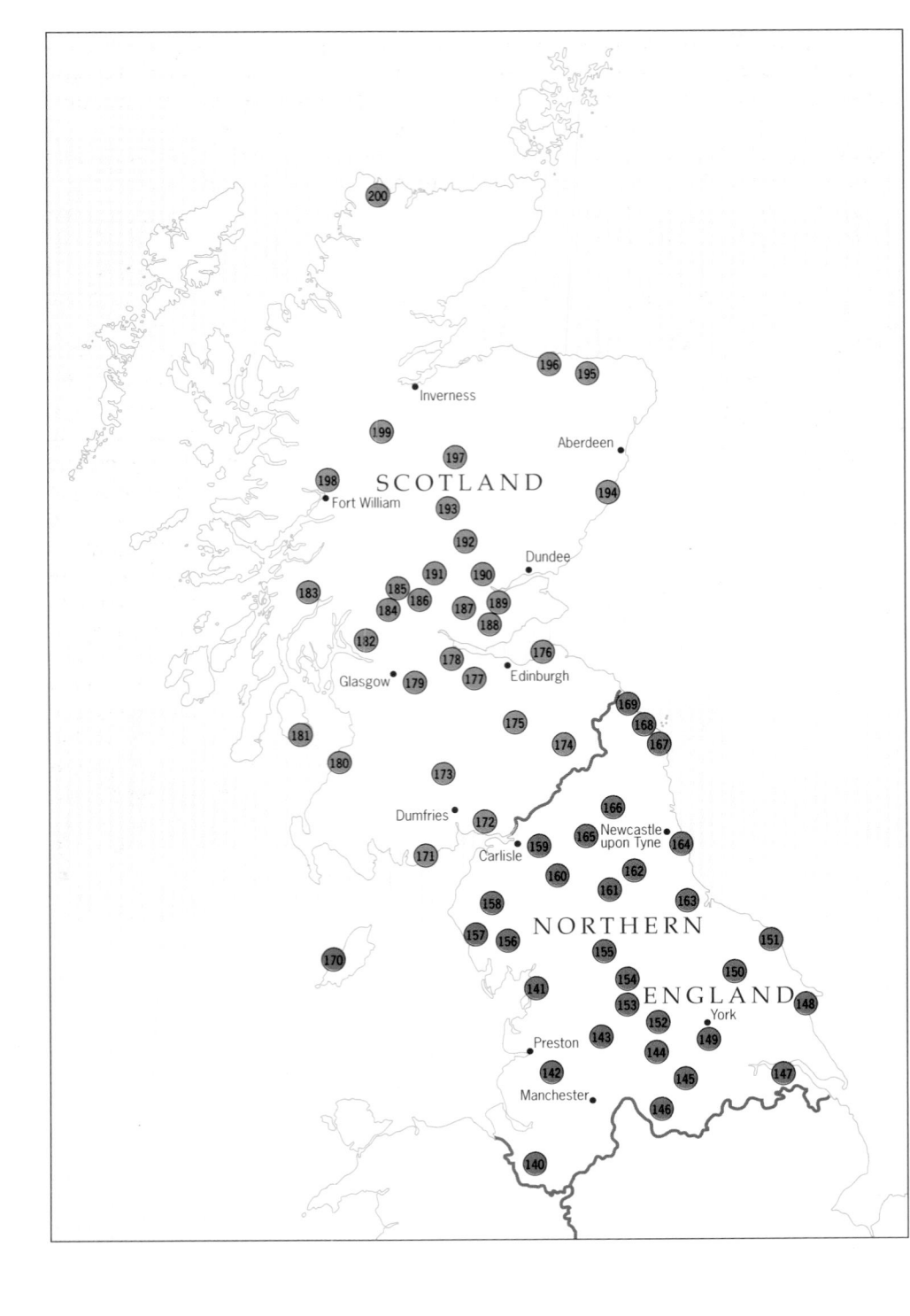

Introduction

by Paul Sterry

One of the great pleasures of walking in the countryside is discovering a new landscape and the wildlife that goes with it. Yet it is possible to walk for several miles and apparently see very little. It is only when somebody points out a clue that you realise you may have been missing all sorts of interesting things. This introduction is designed to give you a few of those clues, to help you really enjoy and make the most of your walks.

While many of the walks in this book pass through nature reserves and national parks – areas where plants and animals are particularly encouraged to flourish – others simply take you through attractive scenery, but all the walks unashamedly celebrate the traditional landscape and wildlife of Britain.

The wildlife heritage of Britain is extraordinarily rich and diverse, and a naturalist's interest in plants and animals can be satisfied almost anywhere in these islands. All you need is a keen eye, a sense of curiosity and an ability to interpret the landscape and wildlife around you.

This introduction sets the scene for the walks, and provides background information for the habitats and wildlife you are likely to encounter. Because some plants and animals are habitat-specific – that is, they occur only when certain conditions of landscape, climate and food source are met – the distinctions between these wildlife communities are highlighted in the text. Information is also provided on how to get the most from your observations, so that you can become your own nature detective. If you were not already interested in natural history, the walks will whet your appetite for wildlife watching. Using the book as a guide, weekend walkers will soon discover that an interest in natural history can really enhance your day out in the country.

Keeping Your Eyes Open
Follow the routes in this book and nature will be all around you –but there are ways to increase the range of things you see and improve your chances of seeing them. All you need to know is how, where and when to look, and the following guidelines will make your task easier.

Animals have their different methods of opening conifer cones to reach the seeds within. Diagonally left from top right, these are pinecones nibbled by mice, woodpeckers, crossbills and a squirrel. The four spruce cones below (clockwise from bottom right) show the undamaged state, and evidence of squirrels, woodpeckers and crossbills.

Choosing Your Equipment

Before you set out on a walk, consider the sort of equipment you might need. The items should be appropriate both to your particular interests and the character of the walk, of course, and above all, they should be portable. There is nothing worse than being burdened by a rucksack full of overweight and unnecessary equipment!

For the birdwatcher and anyone who wants to observe shy creatures such as deer over a distance, the most obvious piece of equipment is a pair of binoculars which should be both of a reasonable magnification and lightweight for carrying. When purchasing a pair for the first time you should bear in mind the set of two figures that accompany all binoculars – typical examples might be 8x30 or 10x40. The first number in the couplet refers to the magnification (that is, eight and ten times respectively), and the second indicates the light-gathering capacity of the lenses: the higher the figure, the brighter the image you will see.

At first, it might seem that a high magnification and bright image are obvious specifications to aim for. However, the larger the magnification and the brighter the image, the heavier and more unwieldy the binoculars become. Try a few pairs out in the shop, and aim at compromise with a lightweight pair and a specification of around 8x30. Dedicated birdwatchers invariably include a telescope and tripod among their armoury of equipment but for the purposes of the more casual observer they are unnecessary.

For a closer look at plant life, the choice of equipment is even simpler. A small hand lens is all you need to view floral details in close-up, and also comes in useful when observing insects and other invertebrates. If a pair of binoculars is all you have with you at the time, and you need to scrutinise a flower or leaf, try turning the binoculars the wrong way round to look at the fine detail. You will be surprised at how effective this can be.

The ability to identify and name the plants and animals that you encounter is part of the fun, and a good set of field guides can help here. There are excellent books available covering almost every aspect of British natural history, and there is a particularly wide – indeed, bewildering – choice relating to birds, wild flowers and trees. Some are illustrated with photographs, others with artwork. Whichever you prefer, try to select a guide which does not go into more detail than you actually want – this will only complicate matters. Included in this proviso must be a consideration of the geographical area that the book covers – so do not buy a guide that covers the whole of Europe if you are only interested in British wildlife.

Using your field guide, try to identify the plant or animal in question on the spot. Failing that, why not take a photograph for subsequent scrutiny? Most modern 35mm SLR cameras are suitable and you will need a close-up lens for flowers or a telephoto lens for birds and mammals. This also removes the temptation to pick or collect from the wild, an activity that should be avoided at all costs.

Fieldcraft Skills

Although you will have no difficulty in seeing wildlife along the walks in this book, a knowledge of the techniques and fieldcraft employed by experienced observers can be useful. A lot of this is just common-sense although some of the following tips may be less immediately obvious to the less experienced naturalist.

The approach to birdwatching depends on factors such as the habitat in question, the season, and the type of birds you are likely to encounter. Take, for example, birwatching in a deciduous, or broad-leaved, woodland. In the spring, the different bird songs give the best clues as to the species present. Singing male birds, while initially difficult to locate among the emerging leaves, can be tracked down by following the source of the sounds. From dawn until about eight o'clock in the morning is the best time of day for most species, after which they often cease singing and concentrate on feeding.

Nightingales, which may be heard on several of the walks in this book, will sing at almost any time of day and often at night as well. On a stroll in the late evening through woods, you may also hear the familiar sounds of tawny owls and the strange, grunting calls of the woodcock.

Go birdwatching in a winter woodland, however, and you will need a different approach. Many of the small songbirds gather together in mixed feeding flocks that roam nomadically through the trees. For long periods of time you will not see a single bird but do not get disheartened. All of a sudden, a noisy flock will come into range. Birds from the flock can sometimes be lured closer by

making a 'pssshh' sound with clenched teeth and pursed lips. Make sure your walking companions know your intentions beforehand, however!

Around the coast, you need to employ different techniques again. Some of the walks visit seabird colonies, which are at their busiest from May to July. Generally speaking, the birds nest on inaccessible ledges and are confident of their invulnerability. Consequently, the birds often appear almost indifferent to human onlookers; all you need is the common-sense not to approach the cliff edge too closely for your own safety.

On saltmarshes and estuaries, at their best in terms of numbers and variety of birds in the winter months, a different strategy is needed. The birds are often rather wary of human figures in this otherwise rather featureless landscape. Use the cover of bushes and hedges adjacent to the mudflats and keep low down. If you can interpret a tide-timetable with confidence, this can also be useful. Find a comfortable spot near the high-tide line and sit there on a rising tide. The water will gradually push the birds towards you and if you remain still, you will get excellent views.

When viewing mammals, remember that they have keen sense of smell. Approach deer, for example, from a down-wind position and try to keep below the skyline if possible. With both mammals and birds, however, it is often just as much fun to look for their tracks, trails and signs. With some nocturnal animals, this may offer the only likelihood of detecting their presence in an area.

Tracking

Some of our larger mammals leave conspicuous tracks which can be readily identified when found along muddy paths. Roe deer, for example, leave neat slots made by their hooves. These are smaller but more regularly encountered than those of fallow deer; and red deer prints may be encountered as well. Beware of confusion with the tracks of domestic sheep.

Other commonly encountered tracks are those of rabbits, grey squirrels and foxes. The latter are superficially similar to those of dogs, so beware of possible confusion between the two. Badgers too leave broad prints in muddy soil. Follow their trails and you may find a badger latrine or tufts of hair caught in the lowest strand of a barbed wire fence. If you come across a badger sett, however, leave it well alone. Badgers desert their homes if disturbed by human scent.

Food remnants and other signs of feeding can also provide valuable clues to the inhabitants of the countryside, particularly those that are shy or unobtrusive. Mice, voles and squirrels all have distinctive ways of eating hazelnuts and acorns – the shape of the nibbled hole and the size of the teeth marks can tell you a great deal. Pine cones too are eaten in a variety of ways according to the species carrying out the nibbling.

Don't forget to keep an eye open for droppings and pellets, which are excellent clues to the other users of your path. The droppings of rabbits and deer are easily identified. Equally so are those of foxes, which are deposited in conspicuous places on paths and rides in order to advertise the boundaries of a territory.

Using Your Senses

While we identify things around us by sight, using our other senses – particularly smell and hearing – can provide vital information about certain species. Bird calls are obvious examples where sounds can be diagnostic: with practise, most people can identify a reasonable number of our native birds by sound alone. Some insects, particularly grasshoppers and bush crickets, are also notable songsters.

The use of smell is normally associated with the identification of plants, both from the flowers and from scents derived from crushed leaves. It becomes particularly important in the identification of fungi – and the sickening aroma of the stinkhorn fungus in hedgerows and woodlands between May and October is not easily forgotten. The pungent, musky smell of foxes, used to mark territories, is another distinctive aroma of the country.

Adults tend to take most notice of plants and animals at eye level, but as anyone who has taken a country walk with children will tell you, by paying less attention to other levels in the terrain, we miss all sorts of interesting things. Children are invariably better than adults at spotting interesting plants and animals at ground level, and it is worth training

yourself to scan the ground at your feet as well as the tree canopy above. Ground level searching can be particularly fruitful on an autumn walk in woodland. Try lying on the ground and looking around for fungi – you will be amazed at how many more species and specimens you see at this level.

A few creatures leave clues which tell us about their homes. Lucky observers may find the round nests of harvest mice, woven out of shredded grasses and sited among meadow plants. Along the hedges, look for bramble leaves marked with white scribble marks: these are the homes of leaf miner caterpillars which actually live between the leaf surfaces. Logs and fallen branches on woodland floors are also good hunting places. Turn them over to find slugs, snails, woodlice and centipedes but remember to turn them back again when you have finished.

Reading the landscape

Any walk in the countryside can be enhanced by some knowledge of the landscape through which you are travelling. Seasonal changes affect every aspect of the landscape, and the time of year can have a crucial influence on what will be seen on your walk. To observe the changes, try visiting a few of your favourite walks during each of the four seasons for comparison. Whatever the time of year, you can be sure that there will be something of interest to see.

Although some plants and animals are found in a wide range of habitats, others have more specialised needs and may only occur in one particular type of habitat. Some obvious examples are aquatic plants, which are only found in freshwater habitats, and birds such as

nuthatches and tree-creepers, which are more or less restricted to woodland areas.

The walks in this book explore just about every sort of habitat found in Britain, and the notes below will help you know what to look out for in each type of landscape, at different times of the year.

Freshwater

Spring is an excellent time of year to visit freshwater habitats. From as early as February, frogs and toads return to ponds, lakes and canals to spawn, invariably returning to the area of water in which they themselves were spawned. When spawning is in full swing, seething masses of frogs or toads and their spawn may be found. If you wait patiently in a suitable location, you should hear the males' quiet, croaking calls.

During April and May many of our water birds start to nest among the vegetation that is just beginning to emerge around the margins of the water. Slow-flowing rivers and streams sometimes harbour little grebes, rather secretive birds which build floating nests of vegetation attached to water plants. Their larger relative, the great crested grebe, prefers sizeable lakes and

Droppings vary greatly from species to species and are one of the most significant clues to animal activity. Clockwise from top right, look out for the distinctive droppings of hedgehogs, rats, fallow deer, badgers, hares, stoats, rabbits, pine martens, red deer and foxes.

gravel pits but builds the same sort of floating nest. It can sometimes be found in the vicinity of nesting coots and moorhens.

Insects begin to make their annual appearance in the spring as well. Having spent the previous nine months or so as nymphal stages in the water, dragonflies and damselflies emerge as adults. There are different species associated with the variety of freshwater habitats but low-lying ponds and lakes are usually the most productive. A good way to see them is to visit the pond early one spring morning. Search carefully among the vegetation at the margin and you have a good chance of finding newly emerged dragonflies and damselflies. In this stage they are usually rather docile but remember they are also extremely delicate and should not be handled. Other springtime insects include mayflies. To see them, visit a low-lying river at dusk in May – you may be lucky enough to see a swarm of males dancing over the water.

By the summer, the dragonflies and damselflies can be seen mating and egg-laying over the water. If you sit and watch carefully, you may see pairs flying in tandem or females forcing their abdomens underwater to lay the eggs. Many of these active insects fall victim to hungry broods of waterside birds. Reed warblers and reed buntings take their toll and even young moorhens are not averse to a tasty water insect.

It is at this time of year that waterside flowers are at their most colourful. Although species such as marsh marigold have already flowered and set seed by late spring, a much wider variety of flowering plants can be found from June to September. Yellow flag, great willowherb

A good field guide will tell you all about the stonechat

and purple loosestrife are among the more striking species to be encountered.

On balmy summer evenings, there are few things more pleasant than to take a stroll along a river bank or beside a lake. The air is refreshing, and as the dusk falls you may be lucky enough to see bats hunting for insects over the water – several species hunt in this manner in southern England. If you have mixed feelings about having close encounters with bats remember that every time they catch an insect there is one less mosquito or midge to bite you! One of the walks in the book takes you near the famous bat roost in the Greywell Tunnel on the Basingstoke Canal. Although this is most important as winter refuge to these flying mammals, bats can always be seen in the summer months too.

As autumn approaches, the insect-eating activities of the bats are adopted by swallows and martins which gather over water to feed, particularly at dusk. They congregate around freshwater habitats prior to migrating south to Africa in September. Autumn is a good season for admiring and photographing the reflection of trees in the water. Keep a look out for attractive patterns of floating seeds and leaves.

At first glance, freshwater habitats in winter might appear dead and lifeless. This is far from true, however, and birdwatchers in particular are often in their element. The numbers and variety of ducks build up on lakes and reservoirs,

the birds having moved south from more northerly parts of Europe. Among the common species such as tufted duck, pochard and gadwall, look for unusual ones such as smew, goosander and scaup.

Because much of the emergent vegetation has died back, winter is often a surprisingly good time of year to take a net with you and go pond dipping. The larval and nymphal stages of freshwater insects will be numerous and you should also find water snails. Beside rivers and streams in upland areas, the lack of leaf

Several mammals and birds eat hazelnuts, and the husks can tell you whose dinner it was. Clockwise from top right, these nuts have been opened by a dormouse, a water vole, a nuthatch, a squirrel, a bank vole and a wood mouse.

cover on the trees can make the observation of resident grey wagtails and dippers easier than at other times of year.

Woodland
Many of the walks in this book pass through areas of woodland. These vary in character from deciduous forests of native species such as beech and oak, to the rather monotonous ranks of conifer plantations, comprising introduced species of trees. Although conifers in plantations have a limited wildlife appeal, in a few areas of highland Scotland remnant pockets of native Caledonian pine forest can be found, harbouring a unique and varied combination of plants and animals.

Although woodlands are fascinating places at any time of year, many people find that spring is the most rewarding season. From late March until June, the ground layer of many deciduous woodlands hosts a colourful carpet of flowers. Bluebells, ramsons, wood anemones and wood sorrel often cover large areas and keen-eyed observers may find early purple orchids in small clumps here and there.

An early morning walk in the woods can reward you with a rich dawn chorus of birdsong, and this is the time of year when fox cubs first

emerge from their dens to play. Look up into the leaf canopy of the trees and shrubs you encounter and you may see the nibbled holes caused by the myriad caterpillars in the woods. If you want to investigate further, take an umbrella with you. If you hold the open but inverted umbrella under a spray of leaves and give the branch a sharp knock, a shower of insects will fall into the umbrella. These can then be easily observed, but remember to put them back on the leaves when you have finished.

By the time summer has arrived in the woods, you will encounter family parties of birds such as blue tits, wrens and robins. The birds time their nesting so that the young birds fledge just as the woodland insects are at their most abundant. Most noticeable among these are the butterflies that fly along sunny glades and visit the flowers of brambles. Speckled woods and ringlets are widespread, and in a few places you might be lucky enough to see one of several species of fritillary. As you pass by

the trunks of the trees, keep a lookout for camouflaged moths resting on the bark.

Autumn is the season for colour in our native deciduous woodlands. The leaves of maple and ash contrast with those of oak and beech and change almost on a daily basis through September and early October. Nuts and berries are produced in abundance and woodland birds and mammals such as squirrels search the leaf litter for this fallen feast. Among the colourful leaves, there will be a wide range of fungi. If these are your particular

interest, time your woodland walk so that it occurs a few days after heavy autumn rain; this will have encouraged a sudden flush of fungi. Conifer plantations are surprisingly rich in fungi as well although the species will, of course, be different from those in deciduous woods.

Winter brings both plusses and minuses for the woodland naturalist. Gone are the woodland flowers and summer migrant birds. The leaves have also long since fallen, but this can prove to be an advantage. Deer can be much easier to see at this time of year, as can the mixed flocks of resident birds such as tits and nuthatches which feed among the branches. Resident tawny owls are often very noisy at this time of year, mostly after dark. During the day, they roost among the branches and are often quite conspicuous. Small birds also spot them more easily, and the agitated alarm calls of blackbirds and tits may show you where an owl is roosting.

Heath and Moorland

People have exploited woodland resources for centuries, and in areas of southern Britain where woods were cleared on impoverished, acid soils, a new type of habitat – heathland – gradually developed. Characterised by ling, bell heather and gorse, this is a fragile and vulnerable habitat.

In spring, the flowers of common gorse burst into life and fill the air with a heady fragrance of coconuts. Heathland birds such as stonechats and yellowhammers perch on tall sprays and sing loudly to advertise their territories. It is at this time of year that the heathland reptiles are easiest to see. On sunny days in March and April, adders and common lizards, recently emerged from hibernation, bask in the warming rays.

By July and August, the flowers of ling and dwarf gorse predominate and sometimes turn whole slopes into a blaze of purple and yellow flowers. Butterflies such as graylings and silver-studded blues occur in these habitats and are easiest to see early in the morning when they are less active. As the season progresses, spider's webs and their silken strands become more and more obvious. They are brought into stark relief when the first

misty autumn mornings arrive, the webs becoming laden with water droplets. As autumn moves into winter, hoar frosts etch beautiful patterns on the heathland vegetation and webs.

Similar patterns of woodland clearance on acid soils in upland Britain have resulted in the creation of moorland habitats. Again, the characteristic species are members of the heather family but the birdlife is rather different. In areas from the Peak District northwards, red grouse are year-round residents. During the summer months, a variety of waders breed on the moors alongside meadow pipits and merlins.

Grass and Meadowland

With grassland, the species of plants present depends on the underlying soil type: in this way, meadows on chalk-rich soils are generally much more colourful and herb-rich than those on acid soils.

Skylarks, an ever-present feature of grassland throughout Britain, can be heard singing overhead at almost any time of day and almost all year round. For wildlife observers, meadows are at their best in the summer months. Butterflies such as meadow browns, small coppers and common blues, are often abundant and visit the flowers that bloom along the hedgerows and field boundaries and roadside verges. Grasses, which are flowering plants too, also flower in the summer months – as sufferers from hay fever know only too well.

For an interesting variation on grassland wildlife, take a walk on a summer's evening. Armed with a torch, explore the grass leaves for the caterpillars of marbled whites and skipper butterflies. You might even be lucky enough to see a glow-worm.

As the autumn approaches, grassy areas often produce a rich harvest of fungi unique to this habitat. Some are closely related to cultivated mushrooms and are delicious to eat; this is also true of ink-caps, parasol mushrooms and giant puffballs. Others species may be poisonous, so make sure you are certain of your identification skills. Damp autumn mornings are also good for watching slugs and snails – because snails in particular need calcium for their shells, the species range is greatest on chalky soils.

Coastline

The coast exercises a special lure for people who enjoy country walks. There is something bracing and inspiring about a cliff-top walk or indeed a walk along almost any part of the coast where the sea is visible.

Visit the coast in the spring and cliff-top flowers will be at their peak of flowering. In some places, thrift can turn whole slopes pink, while sea campion and scurvygrass flourish around rocky outcrops. This is the best time of year to tackle one of the walks that visits a seabird colony – the sight, sound and smell of thousands of birds such as guillemots, kittiwakes and razorbills

Several different species of animal gnaw the bark off trees and shrubs, causing considerable damage in the process. The closer end of the log above shows loosened bark and toothmarks characteristic of squirrels. At the far end the bark has not been loosened, and the fine, clear toothmarks suggest the work of a bank vole.

Deer will not just nibble away at the bark, but will tear the stems off with their sharp teeth as well.

nesting shoulder-to-shoulder will stay with you for a long time. If you are interested in the rich life along the seashore, then consult a tide timetable and visit a rocky shore around the spring equinox in March – together with the autumn equinox in September, the lowest low tides occur at this time of year, and the most interesting variety of animals and plants can be found.

Saltmarsh flowers are at their best in the summer months with sea lavender

Deer shed their antlers at different times of the year. Fallow deer retain theirs through the winter, shedding around May – they may be recognised from their size (below), and from the distinctive broad, flattened form. Roe deer, however, the smallest native British deer, shed their antlers at the beginning of winter – these are much shorter, and not more than three points.

and golden samphire putting on colourful displays alongside the more subdued greens of saltwort and sea purslane.

As autumn approaches, the saltmarshes and estuaries come alive with migrant waders and wildfowl returning from the nesting grounds in northern Europe. Some of these migrants pause for a few days before continuing their journey southwards while others remain on British estuaries throughout the winter. This time of year can be extremely productive for the beachcomber, especially on an exposed stretch of sand. Winter gales often dump huge amounts of flotsam on the high tide line, along with an array of strange and colourful shells.

Wildlife in Man's World

For thousands of years, humankind has had a profound influence on the environment. So much so that there is almost no part of the British landscape that can be said to be entirely untouched, with the possible exception of some of our estuaries, coastal cliffs and highest mountain tops. Although to describe the landscape of Britain as man-made is perhaps overstating the case, almost all the habitats we find around us are at the very least man-influenced. For example, native deciduous woodlands have been felled or selectively managed for centuries, chalk downlands were created by woodland clearance and intensive grazing, and heathlands came about after woodland clearance on acid soils.

In recent decades, with the advancement of technology and consequently of our ability to alter or destroy landscapes, the pace of change has accelerated considerably. While many of these changes have had an adverse effect upon our wildlife, it has to be said that some of our native plants and animals are extremely adaptable and have coped admirably with the change.

One of the most significant human influences in modern Britain is that of farming. The varied practices employed around the land have helped shape the regional landscape in often distinctive ways as land is drained to take livestock, for example, or fields are enlarged to make the best of mechanised farming. Intensification of farming methods has, however, taken its toll on wildlife diversity. Hay meadows now often lack the herb-rich qualities of half a century ago thanks to seeding and herbicide application, and many former arable 'weeds' are now botanical rarities.

Despite these adverse changes, arable land and grazing pastures sometimes support flocks of birds in winter such as lapwings, golden plovers and rooks. Lapwings formerly bred in far greater numbers than today, the growth of winter wheat effectively excluding them because they like wide open vistas when breeding. New approaches such as set-aside schemes, where land is taken out of intensive production, and the provision of unsprayed headlands, while flawed in many people's view, may be the start of a trend to a more enlightened approach to integrating wildlife and farming.

There has also been a tendency over the last few decades to remove hedgerows, resulting in 'prairie' landscapes in many regions of intense arable farming. Where they do survive, hedgerows provide important sanctuaries for wildlife. Birds that would otherwise nest along woodland edges find them ideal habitats and berry- and nut-bearing plants grow in profusion. The informed wildlife detective can even tell the age of a hedge by its species composition. Walk along a 30 metre stretch and count the number of different woody species - each species corresponds roughly to a century of age.

From the naturalist's point of view pine plantations are relatively poor habitats, partly because the plantation species is often alien to Britain, and also because of the uniform age, single species and dense planting regime of the trees. However, recent interest in recreating woodlands of native species, some for recreational purposes and some a short-term coppice for fuel, may help redress the balance.

The road network in Britain has had a major impact on the landscape, not only in terms of the direct effects of road construction, but also in terms of the end result – far more people than ever before can visit the countryside. Partly because of their inaccessibility to humans, motorway and dual carriageway verges often serve as havens for wildlife – in a sense unofficial nature reserves. However, many of the walks in this book also encounter rural roadside verges. Here, a microcosm of the wildlife of the surrounding countryside may be found. In a way, it is fitting that roadside verges have a role to play in natural history terms since it is by road that most of us travel the countryside in the first place.

Walking for Pleasure

Walking in the countryside can be enjoyable at a variety of levels. A casual stroll through pleasant terrain can be restorative and relaxing – the ideal way to unwind after a busy working week. However, taking a more focused interest in the plants, animals and scenery along your route can add another dimension to your outdoor pursuits. Whichever walks you follow and whatever your interests, with an eye for natural history you will never get bored!

THE WEST COUNTRY

Isles of Scilly: A Scillonian Stroll

A delightful walk on St Mary's, the largest of the Scilly Isles, through quiet water meadows and on to a safe beach, then out to Peninnis Head with its fantastically shaped boulders. The walk can easily be included as part of a day-trip from the mainland.

Porth Cressa and Hugh Town from Peninnis Head

START

Hugh Town is the main settlement on St Mary's. Start the walk from the top end of High Street by the Bishop and Wolf pub.

DIRECTIONS

Where the road forks in front of the pub, take left fork and keep left at the next fork by the telephone boxes. Walk along The Strand, past the Customs House on the left, and continue uphill past the school and on down the left-hand pavement of Telegraph Road. At the end of the houses after 250yds, at a junction with a side road to the left, cross the road and go over a broken stone stile onto a signed path through the Lower Moors Nature Reserve. Where the path leaves the Reserve (after about ½ mile) continue along a road between bungalows to Old Town. Cross the road to the beach.

From the far left (east) end of the beach go down slipway steps and follow the sandy track along the beach to pass the church. Climb rocks at end of beach onto the open cliff and follow the path. Explore the rocks of Carn Leh before continuing along the coast path, taking the lower left fork after about 500yds to reach Peninnis Lighthouse. The surrounding rocks include the large protruding flat rock known as Pulpit Rock. Continue along the coast path from the lighthouse for about ½ mile to Porthcressa Beach. The start point is reached by walking down the road that passes behind the information office and toilets on the beach front and then along Silver Street to High Street.

Birds Galore

Small islands are often a paradise for birds, but the Scilly Isles are very special. They are particularly famous as staging posts for migrating birds during spring and autumn, when rare species can sometimes be spotted. At all times of the year there are numerous seabirds including herring gulls, shags and oystercatchers with their distinctive black and white plumage and orange beaks. In Lower Moors there are snipe, moorhens and mallards. A notable feature of Scillonian birdlife is the remarkable tameness of resident songbirds such as the song thrush and robin.

Peninnis Rocks

The fantastically shaped granite rocks and headlands at Peninnis have been sculpted by wind and water. Though the hollows in the rocks are caused by rain water, which has slowly worn out the basin shapes over many centuries, local legends suggest they may have been created by Druids for blood sacrifices! Individual rocks in the area have wonderful names like Kettle and Pans, and Tooth Rock, while caves and inlets include Big and Little Jolly, Sleep's Abode and Izzicumpucca. Watch out for seabirds, such as gannets, flying past the headland.

What to look out for

There is a variety of birds to be seen in the Lower Moors reed beds, with a bird hide just off the path. The marine life of these islands is among the best in Britain, and at Old Town Beach there are a number of fascinating rock pools containing small fish like blennies as well as sea anemones, starfish, porcellain crabs and lots more.

Logan Rock: Blue Sea and Golden Sand

WALK 2
CORNWALL
SW395229

This walk along west Cornwall's granite coast above golden sands includes a visit to the spectacular site of a natural cliff castle, inhabited over 2,000 years ago. At the halfway point there is a magnificent beach, though you will need to be reasonably fit and very sure-footed for the descent.

START

The village of Treen can be reached from Penzance via St Buryan or from Land's End. Start the walk from Treen's car park, which is beyond the pub and close to the shop and post office.

DIRECTIONS

Turn left on leaving the car park, then immediately left again, signposted Logan Rock, to cross a stile alongside a house. Follow a track for 50yds and go through a gate to follow a good path through fields and over three stiles to where the coast path is reached. Cross the coast path and go through a gap in the defensive earthworks of Treryn Dinas fort to reach Logan Rock.
From Logan Rock return to the coast path and turn left. At a junction take the path to the right. Continue to a junction of several paths at Treen Cliff signpost. Go straight ahead along the track, signposted 'Coast Path'. Pass between two old pill-boxes and reach a gate by some boulders and a side path to the left. Go through the gate and follow the main path downhill, steep and rocky for a while, to reach a T-junction with a broad track leading down from the car park to the beach.

On leaving the beach, retrace your steps up the path and back through the gate and boulders. Continue directly along the coast path and between the old pill boxes. After about 60yds take a right fork and follow the path along the cliff past a white-painted obelisk. Continue along the path to where it rejoins the main coast path at the Treen Cliff sign. Cross the main path and go up a track leading inland between high hedges. Follow the track where it bears round to the right to return to the car park.

Treryn Dinas and Logan Rock

The name of this spectacular headland is Cornish for 'fort on the high place'. Treen Castle, as it is known locally, is an Iron Age fortification dating from around 500BC. Perched on top of the inner pinnacle of the castle is the Logan Stone, said to weigh over 60 tons, which could be rocked by the push of a finger. When the stone was toppled from its perch in 1824 by a young naval lieutenant and his crew, there was great outrage locally and the Admiralty ordered the young officer to reinstate the stone – a remarkable feat of engineering, but the great stone no longer rocks with the ease it once did.

Undersea Cables

The white-painted obelisk on the coastal path marks the landfall of a submarine radio cable laid from France in 1880. A modern communications cable providing a worldwide link also runs out under the sea from Porthcurno.

Logan Rock is the spectacular highlight of this walk

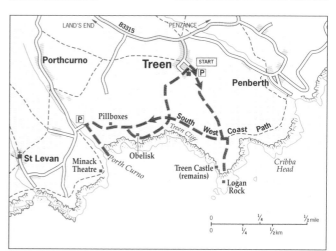

WALK 3
CORNWALL SW759261

Frenchman's Creek at Helford

A woodland walk to the quiet banks of the notorious Frenchman's Creek, immortalised by Daphne du Maurier in 1941, in her famous novel of that name.

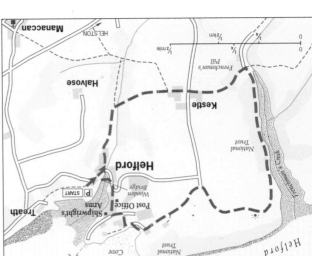

START
Helford is about seven miles east of Helston, following signs for The Lizard and St Keverne, then Manaccan and Helford, along a narrow, winding single-track road (congested in the height of summer). There is a car park just outside Helford – only residents are allowed to drive into the village.

DIRECTIONS
Leave the car park and turn right down the lane to the ford and bridge. Do not cross the bridge, but continue up the lane in front of cottages and bear steeply left to follow a path behind a thatched cottage. Follow path through the woods.

Moorings on the Helford Estuary

At a fork go right across a small stream and through an opening. Continue up a short incline and cross a stile into a field. Keep to the field edge and at Kestle go through the farmyard (can be very muddy), then through a gate between barns and Kestle Cottage. Cross road and continue down a broad track, signposted 'Frenchman's Pill'. At end of farmhouse wall, turn into field through gate and bear left, proceeding down a steep, woody incline. Turn right at the fork at bottom of hill to reach the head of Frenchman's Creek. Bear right and follow path along the creekside – beware of 10ft drop to the water! Turn right at a gnarled oak tree just beyond a plank bridge. Go up wooden steps, continue upwards and the path levels out to give magnificent views. Continue along and past field, cross a wooden stile amidst bamboo and turn sharp right up a track. Turn right at a T-junction. Follow field edge and just beyond a cattle grid go immediately left down a lane, signposted Penarvon Cove. Keep straight on at the fork, passing through a gate to reach the cove. Cross top of beach, then follow a track leading up through trees. Cross a road-end on your left and proceed through a gate to follow a short path behind some houses. Turn left at end of cottages down a track. Bear right to pass Shipwright's Arms. Follow lane through village. Cross wooden footbridge and turn left to return to the car park.

Frenchman's Creek
Daphne du Maurier used the creek for a meeting between a local beauty and a French pirate, bestowing an air of romance on what is undoubtedly a perfect venue for such an assignation. The narrow inlet may be less endearing to romantics at low tide, but the wading birds which come to feed on the mud flats would not agree.

Helford
This lovely riverside village has retained its subtle beauty and some of the best of its surrounding countryside is in the care of the National Trust. There has been a ferry to Helford Passage across the river since ancient times, and this makes a pleasant trip.

Pintail

The path through Pengwedhen Woods

Information

The walk is two and a half miles long

Level most of the way with some short, very steep sections which require care

A few stiles and cattle grids to cross

No road walking other than through Helford Village

Picnic places in woods and at Penarvon Cove

Toilets at car park and at Helford

Pub at Helford

What to look out for

There are many water birds in the muddy creek bed at low water. These include redshank, grey heron, cormorant and several types of duck in winter months. The woods are full of smaller birds as well as the larger green and great spotted woodpeckers, while buzzards may be seen wheeling above the open fields. Springtime visitors can enjoy the colourful daffodil fields at the top of Penarvon Cove.

Crantock and The Rushy Green

This walk includes the wide open spaces of Crantock beach and its undulating dunes. The village of Crantock, with its many fine features, is also visited.

Piper's Pool and Crantock Beach

Information

The walk is three miles long
Level most of the way
but with one or two short
inclines and one flight
of steps
No road walking other than
in Crantock and West
Pentire villages
A few stiles to cross
Picnic on beach
Pubs and refreshments
at Crantock and West Pentire
Seasonal toilets at Crantock
beach; all year toilets at
Crantock

START
West Pentire is reached by turning off the A3075 just over a mile south of Newquay. There is a large car park.

DIRECTIONS
Down the road from the car park entrance turn left at the junction, signposted 'Vugga Cove'. Go through a gate just past some houses and follow the broad track. Bear sharp right and go through gate. At fork, go right and down over a stile. After about 50yds, descend a short flight of stone steps. Continue along the coast path and at a slight incline turn left and cross below a putting green. After 100yds cross a granite stile and turn left at a fork to reach Pusey's Steps. The main path crosses a plank bridge then climbs the flight of steps (good views). Continue along the cliff-top path and round the impressive Piper's Pool. Continue along cliff path and over a stile. At the far bottom corner of a field, the adventurous can drop 20ft down a sand dune onto the beach; otherwise continue round to the right to reach the beach by a gentler slope. At the far end of the beach go up a wide break by a metal sign ('no river bathing') and down into the car park. Near the entrance on the right, by a National Trust marker, go up a path onto The Rushy Green. Follow a direct line across dunes aiming for a pink house with glass roof domes. To pass behind the house, follow a sandy path to a junction marked by two small fins of granite, then turn left through the zig-zag gate. At Boskenna House continue along the track (Green Lane). At road junction turn right into Crantock.
Retrace your steps to the pink house. Turn left at the junction by the zig-zag gate.

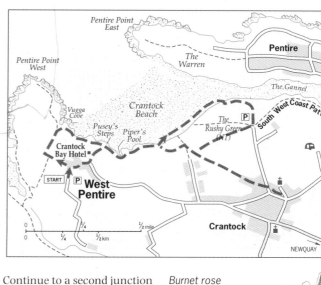

Continue to a second junction and turn right then immediately left. At the field edge turn right and follow the path round the field back past Piper's Pool. Turn left at a junction after Pusey's Steps and follow a surfaced path to the road by the Crantock Bay Hotel. Cross the road and turn right for the car park.

Pusey's Steps
This rocky access to the beach was reputedly used by a priest, Dr Pusey, who lived in the old Manor House at West Pentire, and who may well have been involved in the prolific smuggling which

What to look out for

The Rushy Green has a mass of flowering plants typically found in sand dunes, including marram grass, sea stock and sea sandwort. In the centre of Crantock are a holy well and the charming Round Garden; behind the church find the old village stocks and learn about the resourceful wickedness of an 18th-century smuggler!

Burnet rose

went on hereabouts. His ghost, said to be fairly active around dusk, is considered to be friendly!

Crantock
This delightful old village was a major commercial centre and port long before Newquay developed. Schooners off-loaded just across the river, and barges would then transport the cargo for several miles up river. The Gannel is a lovely river but a dangerous one – warning notices against swimming should be heeded.

Readymoney Cove and Combe Haven

WALK 5
CORNWALL
SX110512

A short walk, but one with some steep sections, unavoidable in this beautiful and complex area of coast.

What to look out for

Fowey is a busy yachting and boating centre and there are always vessels coming in and out of the estuary, including fishing boats. They make a fine sight through the woods at St Catherine's Point. The plant and bird life of the area is prolific. There are strong contrasts between the reedy foreshore at Coombe Haven and the salt-resistant plants like thrift, scurvygrass and sea campion of the open cliff, with woodland flowers and the ash, beech and sycamore of Covington Wood.

START

The National Trust car park at Coombe Farm is reached by turning down Lankelly Lane, signed Lankelly and Coombe, off the A3082 just outside Fowey.

DIRECTIONS

Leave the car park entrance and turn down the second track on the right, signed 'Coombe Haven ⅜m'. Fifty yards before a metal gate, at signpost, go over a stone stile on the right, signed 'Coombe Haven', and follow the steep path down through the trees to reach the beach at Coombe Haven.
From the beach go left along the coast path up a short, very steep section at first, over a stile then out along the edge of Alldays Fields. Look behind for a view of the lighthouse. Where the fields end by a small memorial stone (dedicated to G James Allday, who gave fields to Fowey in 1951), go through a metal kissing-gate.
Follow the main path to a junction with several paths. Just short of the junction, to the right, a short steep path curves up to the Rashleigh Mausoleum. The next path on the right leads out to St Catherine's Point and Castle (open to visitors).
Follow the main path in Covington Woods where it curves down to the left (this can be muddy and slippery). Bear round to the right and go down to Readymoney Cove. Facing seaward, turn right and go to far end of the beach, where steep steps and a steep path lead back up to the junction by the mausoleum. Alternatively retrace your steps up the less steeply sloping track.
At the junction of paths below the mausoleum turn right up three steps and across the flat remains of a building. Follow the path through the trees of Covington Woods, ignoring side paths, to reach a fork after 250yds. Bear left at another fork in another 250yds. At the edge of the woods, turn left, go through a kissing-gate, then follow a grassy track across cliff-top fields directly ahead. The track curves gently right to a stile and metal gate. Cross the stile and go down the lane to turn left into the car park.

Readymoney Cove

This little beach was a busy harbour in the past. There is a stony lane (called Love Lane) leading down to it through Covington Woods, its surface worn into ruts from the days when carts plied to and from the cove collecting landed goods, sand and seaweed, and delivering lime from the old kiln, which is now a shelter.

The Rashleigh Mausoleum

The Rashleigh family have been closely associated with Fowey and its environs for hundreds of years. The mausoleum was erected in the 1870s and members of the Rashleigh family are buried beneath the flagstone memorials. Family pets are said to be buried nearby.

The rocky foreshore at Combe Haven

The Valency Valley

A woodland walk along the banks of the Valency River to the enchanting Minster Church, with quiet lanes and field paths on the return.

START
There is a large car park at Boscastle. The walk starts from its far end where a gate leads on to a grassy play and picnic area.

DIRECTIONS
Cross the play and picnic area to its far left-hand corner. Go through the kissing-gate, then follow the path alongside the river, passing through another two kissing-gates on the way. After ⅜ mile go right, over a footbridge. A fairly steep path leads up to a welcome seat. Continue uphill, then bear right at a fork to reach Minster Church. After visiting the church go through a gate a the far side of the churchyard to the lane and turn right. Continue along the lane past a charming house on the left at Trecarne Gate. Halfway down the hill where the lane bends left, cross a stile into a field (signed 'Public Footpath'). Keep straight ahead into a second field. At its bottom left-hand corner go through a kissing-gate, then turn right to pass a duck pond beside a cottage.

Follow the track, bearing left at a fork, to where it comes out between houses onto High Street. (The Napoleon Inn is a short distance up to the left.) Turn right and go down High Street and the linking Fore Street, Dunn Street and Old Road and so back to the harbour and car park.

The Valency Valley
The Valency Valley is a wonderfully romantic place, made more so by its connections with Thomas Hardy, the novelist and poet. Hardy came as a young architect to assist in restoration work on St Juliot Church at the head of the valley in 1872. He fell in love with the vicar's young sister-in-law, Emma Gifford. They walked up and down the Valency Valley to Boscastle on numerous occasions and later married. Sadly the marriage proved unhappy, yet after his wife's death Hardy wrote many intense and bitter-sweet love poems about their idyllic days in the Boscastle area. Even the smallest incident was dwelt upon – the couple once lost a picnic tumbler in the stream and Hardy included this in a poem called *Under the Waterfall.*

Boscastle's Minster Church

Minster Church
The handsome old church of St Merteriana, locked into its hillside amidst ash trees and sycamores, is splendidly isolated from any traditional settlement. It sits amidst a mosaic of daffodils and bluebells in spring. The site once housed a pre-Norman chapel, and then a 12th-century monastic priory. Minster has many fascinating details. Look for the famous scissors in the tower wall. There is no explanation for them, other than that they may have come from a more ancient building.

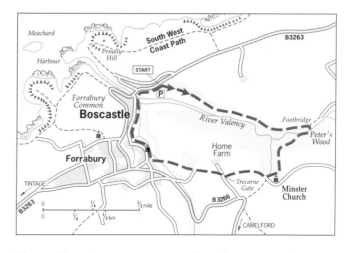

This duck pond is towards the end of the walk

Sedge warbler

What to look out for

There are many woodland birds, including willow warblers and blackcaps during the summer. Grey wagtail and dippers are also present along the course of the river, and look out for butterflies. Peter's Wood, through which the path climbs to Minster Church, is predominently oak, with an abundance of woodland flowers such as dog mercury and lesser celendine.

Hartland Quay and Coast

A visually exciting walk from the dramatic headland of Hartland Quay to the quiet cove at Dyer's Lookout. The route then turns inland through woods and fields to Stoke village before returning to Hartland Quay.

Information

The walk is two and a half miles long

Mainly easy walking. There is a slight incline between Dyers Lookout and Stoke

Several stiles

Dogs should be on leads at start of walk

Good picnic area at Dyer's Lookout

Cream teas at Stoke during the season

Toilets at Stoke

Hartland Quay Hotel serves bar meals; children welcome

Small museum at Hartland Quay

START

From the A39 turn onto the B3248, signed Hartland. Pass through the villages of Hartland and Stoke, following signs for Hartland Quay. There is a car park just inside the toll-gate and this is where to start (other car parks lower down give easy access to the pub and museum).

DIRECTIONS

From the toll booth turn left, crossing a stile beside the Old Rocket House. Follow the coast path (keeping well in from the cliff edge) across open ground to pass a ruined building, keeping to the main footpath for approximately ¾ mile. Where the path descends to Dyer's Lookout bear inland.

Go through a gate. Turn left, cross over a stile and cross the Abbey River to gain the track that curves round to the left above an isolated cottage. Go through a kissing-gate to reach a flat grassy area above the beach (short stony descent to right of an old bench looking seaward).

Retrace your steps to cross the Abbey River. Turn inland along the public footpath and follow the tree-shaded path (can be muddy). Continue uphill alongside open fields. Just before the road turn sharp left over a stile and down a narrow path between hedges. Go through a gate and cross a stile, then go over another stile into the churchyard.

From the churchyard return to the field where the path from Dyer's Lookout joins the path from the north. Continue straight ahead along the left edge of the field to reach the car park.

Old Rocket House and the Pleasure House

The Old Rocket House was built in 1892 to house the wagon and rocket equipment of the newly formed Hartland Life Saving Apparatus Company. The team gave outstanding service during many shipwrecks on this notorious coast.

The roofless building just beyond the Rocket House is called the Pleasure House, believed to have been built as a summer house in the 18th century. The large archway is said to have been incorporated so that a coach could be backed inside. The cliff top between the Rocket House and Dyer's Lookout was a rabbit warren in the 19th century.

Church of St Nectan

The 128ft tower of this 14th-century church is one of the highest in Devon. St Nectan was a 5th-century Welsh saint and legend has it that one day, when he was out looking for his cattle, robbers attacked him and cut off his head. Undaunted, St Nectan tucked his head under his arm and walked the mile or so back to his holy well at Stoke, where he finally expired. The church and churchyard of St Nectan have many memorials to shipwrecked sailors. The western end of the graveyard is called Stranger's Hill and it is here that unidentified victims of shipwrecks lie buried.

What to look out for

There are many seabirds such as gannets, guillemots and fulmars, to be seen offshore. Kestrels may often be seen hovering just above the cliff edge, and peregrines are not uncommon. Dyer's Lookout is a good place to look out for grey seals. In clear weather you should be able to see the island of Lundy which lies about ten miles north-north-west.

The view from Dyer's Lookout, with Lundy on the horizon

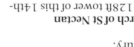

Dusk at Dyer's Lookout

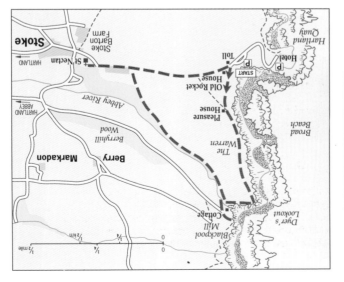

Stoke

Markadon

Berry

Berryhill Wood

Abbey River

The Warren

Broad Beach

Blackpool Mill Cottage

Dyer's Lookout

START

Pleasure House

Old Rocket House

Toll

Hotel

St Nectan

Hartland Quay

Stoke Barton Farm

HARTLAND

HARTLAND ABBEY

½ mile   ¼   0   ½ km

Heddon's Mouth

WALK 8
DEVON
SS665482

A woodland and riverside walk to the lovely beach at Heddon's Mouth, with wildlife interest well maintained between the contrasting environments of oak woodland and seashore.

START

All the roads to Hunter's Inn are single track with passing places, and include a 1 in 4 (25%) hill; great care needs to be taken. From Combe Martin, turn off to the north along a side road just before leaving the village; from Lynton turn north off the A39 at Martinhoe Cross.

DIRECTIONS

Follow the track to the right of the Hunter's Inn. Go through a gate and follow the path bearing left at a fork. At the next fork, just past a wooden seat, either path can be taken: the left branch leads above the river while the path to the right climbs slightly on its way through the woods before the two link up again at a footbridge. Cross the footbridge and turn right to follow the river downstream before passing through a gate; at the junction with another path turn right. The path again follows the river downstream to reach a grassy open space just before another footbridge. Continue along the left bank above the river to the old lime kiln. The beach is easily reached from here, but be aware of the tide and don't wander far. Return to the nearest bridge. Cross over and follow the path upstream over a stony section, to reach the higher bridge. Cross this second bridge, then pass through the gate. Turn left at the junction and follow the path. On reaching the road turn left

The valley of the River Heddon

Information

The walk is two miles long
A straightforward and generally level walk along wide paths with some short inclines
Very short road section; care needed on corners
Good picnic area on river bank
Pub and café at Hunter's Inn
Toilets at Hunter's Inn Shop
Dogs must be kept on leads

and walk back towards Hunter's Inn.

Heddon's Mouth

There are few beaches along the wild North Devon coast and places like Heddon's Mouth have provided access to and from the sea for hundreds of years. The main trade was in coal and limestone, brought by ship from Wales for the kiln. Heddon's Mouth was also used by smugglers. The name Heddon comes from 'etin', the ancient name for giant.

Heddon's Mouth is in the joint ownership of the National Trust, Devon County Council and the Exmoor Society. The Exmoor Society was formed in 1958 after a successful campaign by lovers of the moor to prevent an area of the high moor called The Chains from becoming a conifer plantation.

Lime Kilns

The well-preserved lime kiln above Heddon's Mouth beach is typical of many round the Devon coast, many of them sited at coves and beaches where coal could be easily landed. Limestone was also brought in if there was no convenient local supply. The coal and limestone were burnt in layers utilising a simple draught system and the resulting lime was used by farmers to sweeten the acidic soil.

The old lime kiln at Heddon's Mouth

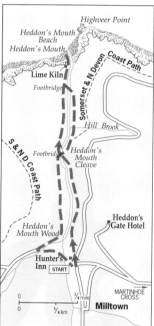

What to look out for

You cannot miss the handsome peacocks at Hunter's Inn and the woods are full of less exotic but still fascinating bird life.
Fast-moving dippers, with their distinctive white breasts, frequent the River Heddon.
Butterflies, such as pearl-bordered fritillaries, inhabit the woodlands, and look out along the coast for the stiff-winged fulmar, a rather gull-like seabird.

Postbridge: Dartmoor's Ancient Stones

A walk at the heart of Dartmoor through woods and moorland, visiting prehistoric sites on the way.

START

The Forestry Commission car park at Bellever is reached from the B3212 (Two Bridges road) in Postbridge by turning south down a narrow lane by the main Postbridge car park.

DIRECTIONS

From the entrance to the car park turn left and walk up the road keeping straight ahead at the junction. Pass the Youth Hostel on the right and continue past some farm

The woods near Postbridge

buildings to follow a short, but awkward rocky path up to a gate. Go through the gate and continue up the path. At the next gate, labelled 'Lichway', turn right, and follow the broad track, also signed 'Lichway', and after about 100yds, bear left to reach a crossing and follow a muddy track for about 100yds. Turn right along the forestry track. About 150yds up the track look out for the remains of a burial chamber just off to the right. Continue for about 200yds (a

WALK 9
DEVON
SX656772

Information

The walk is three miles long
There is a slope up into the woods and two short but very steep rocky sections.
The ground can be muddy
Short sections of linking road between paths
Take-away café and pub at Postbridge; cream teas at hotel
Picnic places in Bellever Forest and on banks of the East Dart River at Postbridge

track on the left leads into the trees to a well-preserved burial cist). The main track continues for 100yds, then follow a path leading left through the trees and into the open for 400yds to a stone circle.

Return to the main track. Continue until the mature trees end, and where the area has been recently cleared and replanted, divert to the left along an almost indistinguishable path which leads in about 500yds to the large open area of Kraps Ring settlement. Return to the main track and continue downhill to go through a

Postbridge's famous clapper bridge

wooden gate. Bear right to a minor road. Turn left and immediately right to reach the main road for Postbridge (toilets in car park opposite). Go into Postbridge to view the famous clapper bridge. Twenty yards back up the road from the clapper bridge, go left through a gate with stone stile. Follow the path signed 'Bellever' and after 50yds go through another gate and uphill to the right on a short, steep rocky section. Where the path reaches open ground at the top veer off towards the right along a faint but straight wide path. This runs alongside the approach road to Bellever. Continue on the path in company with the road to Bellever and in about 600yds cross a track and continue along the road back to the car park.

In misty conditions avoid the path from the clapper bridge across the open moor; return

instead along the verge of the minor Bellever road, reached on leaving the forest before Postbridge.

Ancient Sites

The many ancient sites on the first section of the walk date from the Neolithic and Bronze Ages. The stone cists contained burial remains and were once covered with earth and stone mounds known as 'barrows'. The substantial settlement at Kraps Ring would date from roughly the same period, though may also have been used in the Iron Age.

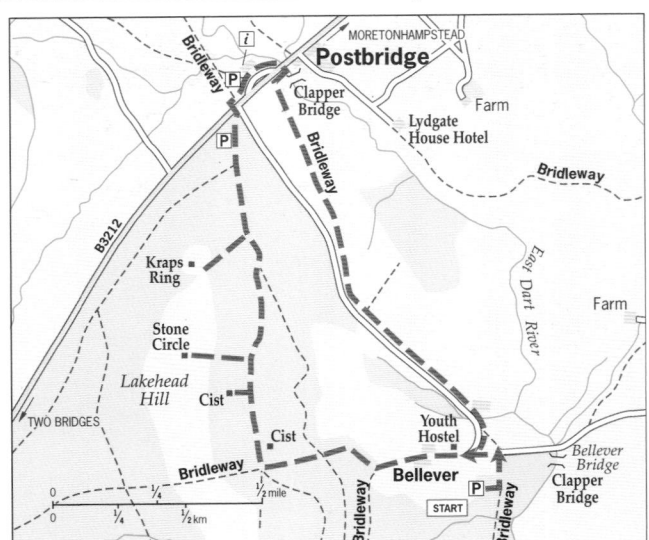

What to look out for

Conifer woods encourage birds like crossbills, siskins and redpolls, while the open moors are home to meadow pipits, merlins and ring ouzels, best looked for in springtime. The sturdy little Dartmoor ponies can be seen on the open moorland.

Noss Mayo - Revelstoke Drive

A good, mostly level walk round the southern headland of the mouth of the River Yealm, passing through the charming creekside village of Noss Mayo. Most of the walk is along the broad and amenable Revelstoke Drive.

START

The National Trust car park is reached from Noss Mayo via Netton Farm. The way is signposted from Noss Mayo but not generously – and Devon lanes can be confusing, particularly on the way back. Navigators should be on their toes!

DIRECTIONS

Leave the car park through a gate in the far left-hand corner. Go down the lane and cross a stile to turn right onto the coast path (superb views). At the entrance to the prominent Warren Cottage, go left through a gate and along a short section of path, then through another gate to rejoin the broad drive. Follow the coast path over a few stiles, continuing round Gara Point and enter Brakehill Plantation. Go through a gate by a National Trust sign indicating the end of The Warren property and continue past some old coastguard houses. Just past here a path leads down quite steeply to the left to Cellar Beach, which is worth visiting.
Continue on the main path

Information

The walk is about four miles long
Level, easy walking with a long upward incline at the finish
Short section of quiet road walking
Several stiles
Pubs in Noss Mayo
Good picnic spots along the first part of Revelstoke Drive and at Cellar Beach

Cellar Beach, just a short detour from the walk

What to look out for

Watch for boats and ships out to sea, and for yachts coming in and out of the River Yealm. Seabirds such as gulls, terns and gannets also pass along the coastal section. This area was a managed rabbit warren in the 19th century and rabbits can still sometimes be seen on the grassy open spaces. The woods on the second section of the walk are full of bird and plant life.

past the distinctive Battery Cottage. The way leads on, with lovely views of the river, through Passage Wood and Ferry Wood to reach the surfaced lane which is followed for about ½ mile into Noss Mayo.
Continue to the head of Noss Creek. Bear left up the road, then go right to reach a large car park with an adjoining children's play area. Beyond the car park entrance follow the rough track uphill, past hillside cottages on the right, and continue for about ½ mile, passing a farmhouse on the right. At a T-junction turn left to reach the car park almost immediately on your right.

The Revelstoke Drive

Revelstoke Drive is a remarkable Victorian feature – the inspiration of Edward Charles Baring, Lord Revelstoke, who owned the surrounding Membland Estate. The Drive is part of a nine-mile circular carriageway round the estate, built near the end of the last century by local fishermen during slack winters. Lord Revelstoke would drive his house guests by carriage round the drive to view his domain.

The Great Mew Stone

This rocky island lying to the east of Gara Point takes its name from the 'mewing' of the seabirds that have colonised it for centuries. The Mew Stone was occupied from 1774 when a convicted criminal was banished there with his family for a seven-year term. When the family eventually left one daughter remained, married and raised a family there. The last known inhabitant kept a rabbit warren on the island during the early 19th century. Not surprisingly, he was also a smuggler!

Noss Mayo

This lovely riverside village dates from medieval times. Its sheltered position and good anchorage on the River Yealm probably guaranteed close connections with smuggling, which was rife along the South Devon coast during the 17th and 18th centuries.

The head of Noss Creek at Noss Mayo

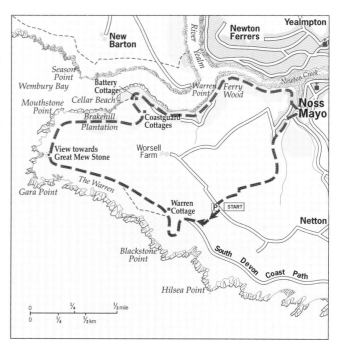

Slapton Ley Nature Ramble

This is a good wildlife walk through part of the Slapton Ley Nature Reserve, offering the opportunity to observe many interesting birds. Slapton Village has a quiet charm.

START

There is a large car park at the northern end of Slapton Ley on the A379, halfway along the shingle ridge.

DIRECTIONS

Cross the busy road at the northern entrance of the car park and turn right to join the path alongside the Ley. Turn

left at the road leading inland to cross Slapton Bridge. Turn left through a gate into the Nature Reserve and take the path by the stone fishing hut. Follow the path alongside the Ley over stiles and pass an old pillbox, later crossing over a 'tree' bridge. Keep on the path to a fork. Keep left and after about 100yds go

A family of swans at Slapton Ley

What to look out for

Slapton Ley is host to thousands of birds, including huge flocks of gulls that often roost in the inner bay of the Ley. Buzzards may be seen circling above the woods and fields, and the grey heron is a regular feeder. Many smaller birds frequent the area: reed and sedge warblers sing from the reedbeds during summer, and kingfishers are year-round waterside residents. Wildfowl are abundant in winter. The waters of the marshy borders are ideal for insects like water boatmen and pond skaters, and several species of damselfly and dragonfly are present.

along a short boardwalk. Go over a stone stile. At a junction in an open area, bear right and follow the path through woods, turning left just before a gate and stile. Walk along a boardwalk through the reed beds and at the end turn right, signed 'Slapton Village', to go through fields, passing the Kimberley Nurseries before reaching a road. Turn right into Slapton Village, then turn left up a narrow lane leading to the church. Leave the churchyard by its top gate (pubs to left and right), go right, then left and up past the post office. Continue past the Slapton Ley Field Centre on your left, then turn right down a lane signed 'Southgrounds Farm'. Cross a stile on the right and follow a public footpath sign. After about 100yds go down past a fenced-in duck pond below the farmhouse with a lovely old dovecote on its far bank.

Peaceful Slapton village was once a military training ground

Turn right beyond the duck pond to reach a stile and the junction with the boardwalk section of the path. Continue directly ahead and retrace your steps alongside Slapton Ley to the car park.

Slapton Ley

This impressive lake, originally a bay of the sea, is now penned in by a huge shingle ridge which built up at the end of the last Ice Age between what are now Strete Gate and Torcross. Streams feed the Ley and its rich waters, reed beds and mud banks are valuable feeding grounds for migrating and over-wintering birds.

Slapton Village

During World War II Slapton Sands was used for training thousands of American soldiers in preparation for the Normandy Landings. Because of these exercises the village was evacuated until after the war, and many of the houses in the village now have rendered walls, hiding damage from the shelling. A simple obelisk on the edge of Slapton Sands commemorates the US troops who trained so hard here.

The Banks of the River Otter

A pleasant and easy walk, waymarked with Heritage Coast Service signs, leading along the east bank of the River Otter from Budleigh Salterton to the lovely village of Otterton.

START
The Lime Kiln car park (pay and display, but free in winter) lies at the eastern end of Budleigh Salterton and is easily reached from Newton Poppleford on the A376.

DIRECTIONS
Leave the car park at its far right inland corner by the cricket pitch. Follow signpost to a wooden gate and follow the path alongside the river. After about ¾ mile a lane by the river bridge is reached. Cross the road through kissing-gates, then continue along the riverside path, passing through three more kissing-gates, to a small concrete aqueduct in an open area. The return route veers off to the left here (see * below), or you can continue for ¾ mile to Otterton. Follow the riverside path across meadows and past Clamour Bridge on the right, going through a metal squeeze-gate by the bridge. Where the path reaches the road turn right and carefully cross the narrow bridge to reach Otterton Mill and the village. Retrace your steps to the aqueduct.
*Follow the track alongside

the aqueduct by a line of trees on the right. Follow the track for about 150yds and look out for a signpost about

50yds before a gate. Go left between two wooden posts at the signpost. Cross a grassy area and go between two posts to continue along a broad track for about ½ mile. Cross a stile by a road, cross the road and then a stile, then go through a gate. Continue down the track through two

kissing-gates to reach a grassy area in front of some houses. Cross a lane, then go left through a gate and picnic area to the car park.

Budleigh Salterton
The town took the first part of its name from an ancient chieftain and the second part from the estuary salt pans that were exploited in medieval times. Budleigh became a popular though quiet resort for the fashionable and wealthy in the late 18th and early 19th centuries.

Otterton
This delightful village was once owned by the monks of Mont St Michel in Normandy. There was a monastery here but the site is now occupied by private dwellings. Otterton Mill is very ancient and was recorded in the Domesday Book of 1086 as a working watermill. It has been restored to working order and is now at the heart of an interesting craft centre.

The Otter estuary near Budleigh Salterton

Sir Walter Raleigh
The famous Elizabethan author and sailor was born at Hayes Barton just under two miles to the west of Otterton. The young Raleigh spent his boyhood in and around East Budleigh just across the river from Otterton. East Budleigh and Otterton were busy ports during the Elizabethan period when the River Otter was much wider and deeper than it is today.

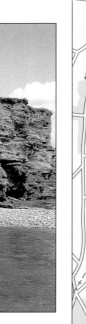

Otter

Tiverton: the Canal and Railway

Information

The walk is about
two miles long
Level, easy footpaths along
canal and old railway line
One short flight of steps and
one longer flight
A short section of road
Convenient benches
along the canalside
for picnics
Cafés at Canal Basin

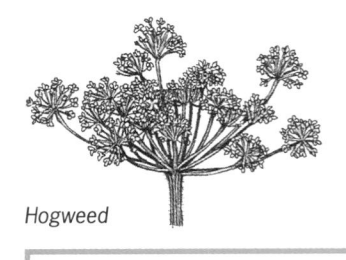

Hogweed

What to look out for

The woodland alongside the old railway line is alive with birds and rich with wildflowers. There are ducks and other water birds on the canal, while butterflies and dragonflies favour the moist verges of the canal bank. There is a chance of seeing the horse-drawn barges of the Grand Western Horseboat Company which runs trips along the canal during the season.

The remnants of two great industrial transport systems – a canal and a railway – on the outskirts of Tiverton combine to create a delightful and interesting walk, enjoyable at any time of the year.

START
The walk begins from the Old Station car park on the eastern edge of Tiverton. From the A361, turn onto the B3391 and on reaching the large roundabout at the entrance to Tiverton follow 'Town Centre' signs down Blundells Road. At a smaller roundabout turn left, then immediately left again into the car park.

DIRECTIONS
Leave the car park through an exit in its far right-hand corner. Turn left and continue along the road for about 300yds, passing a small link road (Old Road) on the left. A few yards further on turn left down a tarmac path to reach a metal gate on the

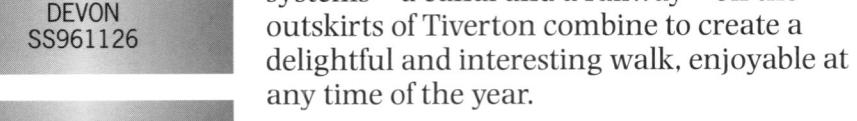

By the Grand Western Canal

right. This gives access to the old railway line which is now a cycle track and walkway. Follow the tree-lined walkway for about ½ mile to where a road bridge spans the old line. Go up the steps on the right to a road. Turn right and walk a few yards up the road to where a signposted track goes off to the right. Go along the track to cross Ford Road onto a continuation track, which leads up to a children's play area and a grassy open space. Just

Narrowboat trips are a popular attraction on the canal at Tiverton

abreast of the swings, go left down a passageway, then turn right into a cul-de-sac of houses.
From the right-hand corner of the cul-de-sac go up another passageway to a short flight of steps, which lead up and onto the canal path. Turn right and follow the canal to where it ends at The Grand Western Canal Basin, taking the steps down to the Grand Basin car park. To regain the Old Station car park from the Canal Basin car park it is necessary to cross the main road to the pavement opposite. Turn right and at the bottom of the hill recross the road to the Old Station car park.

Old Railway Line
The first section of the walk is along the route of a branch line railway built in 1848. This line took over much of the traffic of the Grand Western Canal which gradually declined. In turn

the railway was closed as road transport increased – a pattern repeated throughout the industrial transport network of Britain.

The Grand Western Canal
The 11-mile Grand Western Canal that runs east from Tiverton is the remnant of an ambitious scheme to link the Bristol Channel and the English Channel by building a network of canals and rivers. The Tiverton branch was opened in 1814 at a cost of over £220,000. It was used mainly for transporting limestone and coal to feed the limekilns at Tiverton Basin.

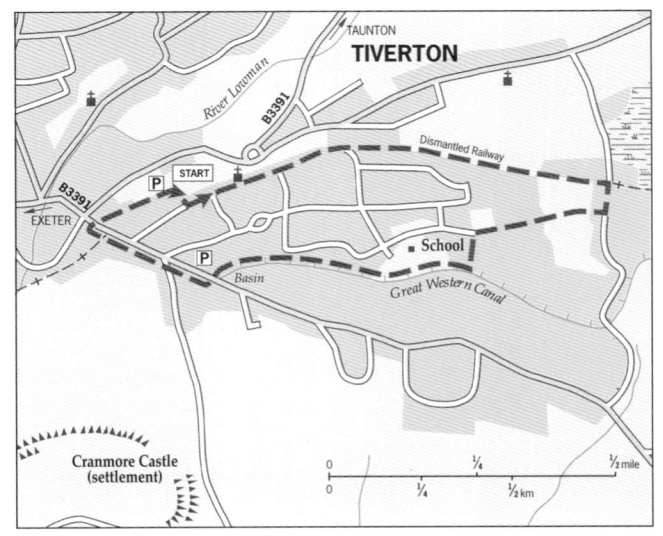

Exmoor: Porlock Bay

This is a varied walk, incorporating a village as well as seaside, marsh and woodland with lots of wildlife interest. On a clear day you can see as far as Wales.

START
Porlock Weir is two miles west of the A39 at Porlock. There is a large car park by the beach, opposite The Ship Inn.

DIRECTIONS
Take the road back towards Porlock. At the end of the railings descend the steps and turn right along the pebble beach (an alternative, easier path is soon reached behind

the ridge). After a mile pass a memorial to 11 US airmen who died when their plane crashed on the marsh in 1942. Cross a stile and continue to a gate in the fence and sign for Porlock. Turn right and cross Porlock Marsh, entering the lane at the next gate.
Follow signposts, keeping to the edge of the fields (5 gates). Continue up the lane and turn

The harbour at Porlock Weir

right along Porlock High Street. At the end of the street turn up the road marked 'Toll Road', passing the Village Hall on the right.
After the last house turn right down the footpath, following signs 'Porlock Weir'. The path leads through woods then behind some beautiful gardens at West Porlock. After 1½ miles, cross a stream, pass a hut, cross a minor road and turn left at the main road. Take the next left turn into Porlock Weir's back street; a right turn leads back to the car park.

Porlock Weir
The harbour was built along a natural creek and was mainly used by herring fishermen until the early 19th century, when it was enlarged and lock gates

added. These held water in the harbour for cargo boats to be loaded at low tide. The gates are now mainly used to let water out at low tide to scour the channel through the pebble ridge. The harbour was intended for use as an ore port, but mainly exported livestock and tan bark from the surrounding woods. Coal and limestone were imported from South Wales for burning in the kiln, now converted into a house.

Porlock Marsh
In medieval times the bay extended inland as far as Porlock. As the pebble ridge built up and streams silted up behind it, the marsh was formed, though it has since been artificially drained. There was once a duck decoy here and wildfowling continues, as does reed

cutting for thatch.

Porlock
This interesting village, with

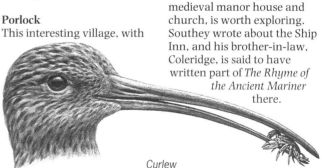

Curlew

its thatched cottages, medieval manor house and church, is worth exploring. Southey wrote about the Ship Inn, and his brother-in-law, Coleridge, is said to have written part of *The Rhyme of the Ancient Mariner* there.

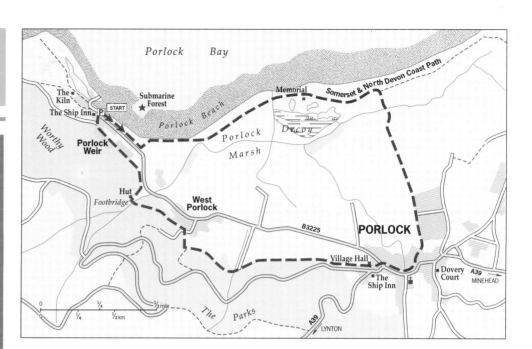

What to look out for

Beachcombing is rewarding here, and the peat, clay and tree stumps of a submerged forest can be found just beyond the pebble ridge at low tide. The marsh usually has curlew, grey heron, shelduck and many other water birds in winter. It is a route for migrant birds such as swallows, wheatears, warblers, sandpipers and finches, which stop off to rest along the coast. The mixed woodland is home to a small herd of wild red deer.

The Somerset Moors: North Curry

This walk follows the banks of the River Tone through Somerset's willow growing area. It includes the picturesque village of North Curry and part of the waymarked Curry Moor Trail.

START

The walk starts at New Bridge car park, one mile north of North Curry and seven miles east of Taunton. From Taunton take the A361 towards Street and turn right one and a half miles beyond Durston. The car park is half a mile further, on the far side of the bridge.

DIRECTIONS

From the car park take the gateway marked 'TDBC Trail'. Walk across the field to the gate on the river bank and repeat with the next field. Keep to the bank through another five gates or stiles, passing an osier bed on the left. Beyond are some old orchards. At the end of the first orchard turn left through a gateway and into the field between the orchards. Turn right over the stile (waymarked) and keep to the left of the field beyond. Go through the gate and up the road past the cottages. Before the next buildings turn left over the stile and follow the waymarks over the fields. After eight more stiles and a gate, cross a bridge with a stile, and walk straight ahead up the field to a stile in a corner of the hedge at the top. Heading

for the church, there are two more stiles before the road. Turn right into the village as far as the Bird in Hand pub. Turn back past Queen Victoria's memorial to Queen Square. Keep right down Church Road then left through the lych-gate into the churchyard. Keep to the right of the church and

What to look out for

Unimproved meadows have up to 50 species of plants and flowers in the rhynes include flag irises, marsh marigolds, lady's smock, meadow rue, ragged robin and arrowhead. Breeding birds include lapwing, curlew, snipe and kingfisher and there are many wintering wildfowl and waders.

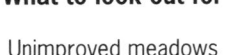

A watery channel, part of the Somerset Levels

through the kissing-gate beyond.

Walk round the pond, along the side of the field and up stone steps to the stile at the end. Keep straight ahead up the next field and between the pheasant pens. Cross a stile and turn left down the lane and right around the lodge at the end. Descend the grassy track and continue onto the moor until the track (Moredon Drove) comes to a junction. Take the gateway ahead and cross the field to the river bank. Turn left along the bank, through two gates and over two stiles back to New Bridge.

Somerset Moors and Levels

The Levels were built up on clay deposited by the sea, creating the marsh, fen and bog land which is known as the moors. Flooded in winter, they became summer pasture (the meaning of 'Somerset'). For centuries they have been

Information

The walk is about four miles long
A lot of stiles
Dogs must be on leads
The Bird in Hand pub has a covered patio and beer garden
Seats and picnic area in Queen Square

improved for hay meadows by cutting ditches known as rhynes. Haymoor Old Rhyne was built by the monks of Athelney in 1316.

Osier Beds

Willows have been cultivated here for more than two centuries for basket and furniture making and artist's charcoal. The willows are cut three years after planting, boiled, stripped of bark and soaked prior to weaving. The Willows and Wetlands Visitor Centre, two miles east of North Curry, explains the process.

Kingfisher

The Quantocks: Holford Combe

Holford Combe was described by Dorothy Wordsworth, who lived here in 1797: 'Wherever we turn we have woods, smooth downs and valleys with small brooks running down them . . . The hills that cradle these villages are either covered with fern or bilberries or oak woods – walks extend for miles over the hilltops, the great beauty of which is their wild simplicity.'

START

Holford is ten miles west of Bridgwater on the A39. Turn off between the filling station and pub, pass the church and take the second turn on the right for the village green and adjacent car park.

DIRECTIONS

From the car park, turn back towards the village, then cross the stream and bear right to follow the track around the thatched cottages. Turn right up the road, which becomes a track. Further on the track crosses and recrosses the stream in the combe, but it is possible to keep to the left-hand bank most of the way. After a mile the stream has to be crossed and there is a meeting of streams and paths. Follow the track rising up the valley to the left of the left-hand stream.
At the top turn left. Keep straight on up the hill, ignoring the two paths to the left (views to Bridgwater and the Somerset Levels). At the top of this rise, where four paths meet, take the left-hand path. The path passes through and alongside the rampart of Dowsborough hill fort, hidden under stunted oaks. (A break in the trees to the right reveals views down

The leafy path at Holford Combe

to Holford, left to Exmoor and right to Hinkley Point power station and Weston super Mare beyond. On a clear they extend to the islands of Steepholm and Flatholm and the Welsh coast beyond.) Turn right through the break in the rampart and follow the track down the ridge towards Holford. Keep along the crest of the ridge, then straight down through trees to the minor road at the bottom. Turn left along the road, which leads back to Holford Combe. Retrace your steps to the car park or fork right to circuit the village, keeping right to the main road, then left round the pub and right again to return to the car park.

Alfoxton

A mile along the road beyond the village green is the Alfoxton Park Hotel, once home of the Wordsworths. William rented the house to be near his friend Coleridge, who lived at Nether Stowey. Both wrote several poems here, although Wordsworth only stayed for a year, the owner of the house refusing to renew the tenancy because of Wordsworth's sympathy with the French Revolution.
Along the way is an old dog pound. A huntsman at the former kennels at Alfoxton was killed by his hounds whilst trying to silence them for barking at stray dogs. The Breretons, owners of Alfoxton, then erected the pound to keep stray dogs away from the kennels.

Dowsborough

This is a large prehistoric hill fort with an oval-shaped double rampart. It may be Iron Age, but there has been no excavation and it could have been occupied at any time from the Bronze Age to the Dark Ages. Roman coins have been found nearby.

What to look out for

The area is renowned for its wild red deer, and you may see deer wallows in muddy patches near the stream. Bilberries, called whortleberries around here, grow amongst the heather and under the coppiced oaks and are ripe for picking in July and August.

Ham Hill

This walk is partly within a country park, with superb views over the surrounding countryside, and has the added attraction of a ruined priory.

START

Ham Hill is five miles west of Yeovil off the A3088, or eight miles east of Ilminster off the A303. Approaching from the Yeovil and Montacute direction, turn left along the High Street in Stoke sub Hamdon as signposted. At the top of the hill turn left again for the car park next to the Prince of Wales pub and Ranger's Office.

DIRECTIONS

Take the path on the far side of the pub, towards East Stoke and Montacute. Keep straight ahead, ignoring the waymarked left turn. Keep along the edge of the old quarry pits, veering left through scrub. Keep ahead where other paths join from the left and between overgrown quarries, following the kiln waymarks. Cross the road and take the path immediately opposite.

Pass above an old lime kiln and turn left into the car park, then take the next path left, signposted 'Ham Hill Road'. Keep right after the masonry works. By the road turn right through the gateway signposted 'Norton Covert' and left along the edge of the overgrown field.

Meadow buttercup

What to look out for

The overgrown quarries provide a wonderful habitat for wild flowers and butterflies.
Elsewhere on the walk are meadows full of flowers, and the woods include many trees and shrubs, such as dogwood and the wayfaring tree.

WALK 17
SOMERSET
ST479168

Information

The walk is just over three miles long
Mostly level and dry, with a gradual climb at the end
A few stiles
Dogs should be kept on leads except on the hill
Pub with garden at start of walk; others in Stoke sub Hamdon
Ice cream van sometimes at top of Ham Hill Road
Picnic places on Ham Hill
Toilets near start of walk

Cross the stile at the end (down to the left is the site of a deserted medieval village). Descend a few yards and take the next path up to the right, following the ditch between the hill fort embankments. Keep ahead for about ¼ mile, with a fence on the right for the last part. At the end of the fence there is a junction of paths. Turn left down a steep path through the trees. Turn right up the road, then left along the bridleway. Keep ahead through the gateway and through the field to the gate at the far end. Turn left down the pavement.
At High Street detour left then right down North Street for the Priory, 100yds on the left. Return to the High Street, turn left and continue for ½ mile, then turn right, signposted 'Ham Hill'. At the

end of the lane, cross the stile and follow the combe upwards. Take the stile ahead at the top, continuing ahead and taking the second right turn to return to the car park.

Ham Hill

Archaeological finds indicate that Ham Hill was settled from Neolithic times, and on its summit is the largest (200 acres) hill fort in Somerset, dating from the Bronze Age. The fort was occupied in the Iron Age, then the Romans took it over. The quarries date back to the Roman era, continuing in importance through Saxon and medieval times, only ceasing production during the present century.

Stoke sub Hamdon Priory

Now a National Trust property, the Priory was part of the manor of Stoke – five priests were retained here to pray for the lords of the manor and their friends. After the Dissolution it was plundered for building materials. Today the remains of several farm buildings and part of a hall can be visited.

Overgrown quarry pits at Ham Hill (above), and Hamdon Priory (left)

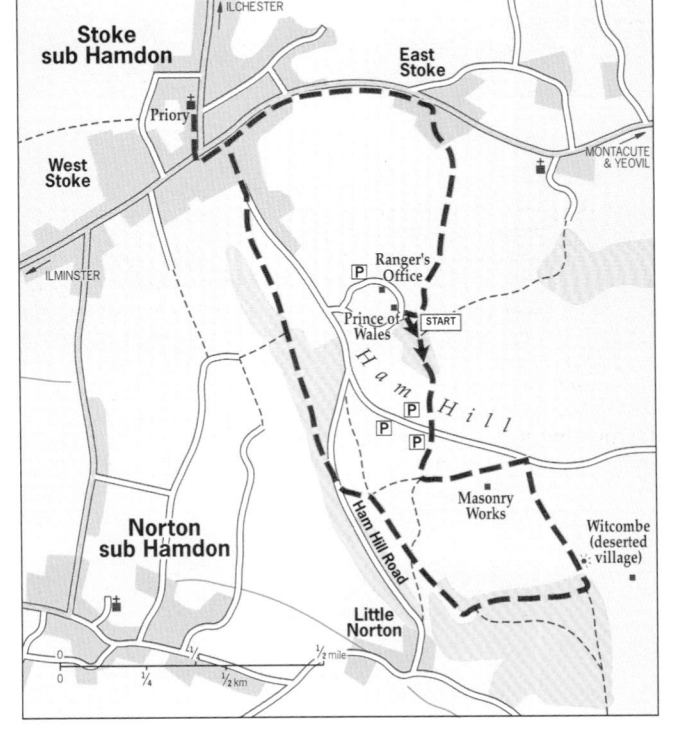

Minterne Magna and Dogbury Hill

The walk makes a gentle ascent of Dogbury Hill, with its woodland and earthwork remains, offering fine views of Blackmoor Vale and of Minterne House.

WALK 18
DORSET
ST 659043

START
Minterne Magna is on the A352, about nine miles north of Dorchester and ten miles south of Sherborne. There is parking opposite the church on the main road through the village.

DIRECTIONS
Cross the road and take the bridleway to the right of the church. Cross the ford by the stone bridge and follow the track round to two gateways.

Go through the right-hand gate and start to climb. Shortly, go left through the blue, waymarked gate. Walk straight ahead and soon go through another gate. Follow the track, bearing slightly left, keeping parallel to the stream in the trees on the left. Go through another gate and aim for the grey roof visible ahead. At the house, turn back right, up the hill, aiming for the stile. Cross the stile and immediately go

Information

The walk is about
two miles long
Fairly gentle ascent and
descent of Dogbury Hill,
otherwise level
No road walking
One stile
Picnic places in woods
on Dogbury Hill
Pubs and cafés in nearby
Cerne Abbas

through another gate on to a track. Cross the track and go through a gate, then walk on for a few yards to get a magnificent view of Blackmoor Vale. Retrace your steps to the track and turn left.
Follow the broad track through Dogbury Camp, whose earthworks are hidden in the trees on either side. Continue on the track for just over ½ mile (views of Minterne House to the right).
Go through the second gate on the right, directly opposite a small gate, and double back to the right through a thistley field towards another gate. Go through this gate and

head diagonally downhill to the left, to a small wooden gate and then yet another gate. The well-defined track then goes straight down through the field to another small wooden gate. Continue on down, joining the route near the start and retracing your steps to the car park.

Minterne House and Gardens
Minterne House is a splendid example of the work of Leonard Stokes, an architect of the Arts and Crafts movement, who built the mansion for the Digby family in 1904. The gardens had been landscaped with lakes, streams and cascades at the end of the 18th

century, and are a fine setting for the outstanding collection of rhododendrons and rare plants and trees brought back from various late 19th- and early 20th-century expeditions to China and Tibet. The gardens are open daily (closed in winter).

The Cerne Giant
A mile or two down the A352

is the famously well-endowed, club-bearing and aggressively all-male hill figure – 180ft tall. Cut into the turf of the hillside about 1500 years ago, he is generally considered to be connected with ancient fertility rites. There is an excellent view of him from the lay-by at the turn-off to the village of Cerne Abbas.

Minterne House and its lovely landscaped gardens

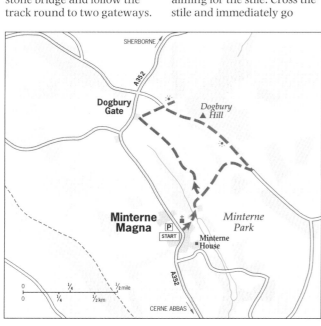

Fontmell Down

Fontmell Down, in the care of The National Trust, is one of the most superb stretches of chalk downland left to us. In summer months walkers tread the carpet of wild flowers accompanied by myriad butterflies, and the views are magnificent. About half-way, the walk passes near Compton Abbas airfield, busy with light aircraft.

Information

The walk is three miles long
There is a fairly steep climb onto and down from the Down, otherwise reasonably level. Can be muddy
Road walking through the quiet village lanes
One stile
Tearooms in Compton Abbas, on the main road. Café and toilets at the airfield (open daily, all year). Pub and tea rooms in nearby Fontmell Magna

START
Compton Abbas is on the A350, three miles south of Shaftesbury. There is parking in the large pull-in on the east side of the A350, in front of the church.

DIRECTIONS
From the parking area, go carefully as if to turn right on to the main road, but immediately go up a few steps and through a small metal gate on to the grass beside the church hall. Keep left of the hall, follow the path through some trees and down some steps. Turn immediately right down a leafy track known as Watery Lane (a mass of snowdrops in February). Turn right at the junction for a few yards. At the footpath sign 'Gore Clump 1½m', turn left down a narrow footpath. At the gate at the end, follow the blue waymark and go straight up the right-hand side of the field and then left along the top of it, under the trees.

Go through gate by National Trust sign 'Fontmell Down' and follow broad track rising slightly to the right. This eventually leads to a gate and a stile. Ignore these and continue along edge of fence until second stile. Cross it and head diagonally left towards the signpost visible across the field. At the sign keep straight on to meet the road (good view on right), down into Longcombe Bottom.
(To visit the airfield, about 200yds distant, cross the road with care and follow the sign. Retrace your steps to this point.)
To continue on the walk, use the National Trust footpath that runs along the west side of the road and emerge at a car park where there is an information board. Take the track at the far side of the car park, signed 'Not suitable for motors', and follow it steeply downhill. Eventually it becomes a road. Follow the road as it turns sharp right, with a track turning to the left. Keep on the road.
At a junction, turn left, immediately passing a farm with a dovecote on the right. Pass East Compton's old church tower in a graveyard, also on the right. Follow the road for some way, passing houses on the left, until reaching junction. Turn left, passing post box and follow the bend to the right. At the fork turn right into Watery Lane and retrace your steps to the start of the walk.

The Old Church, East Compton
The tower is all that remains of the 14th-century church. In 1906 the writer Frederick Treves described a pear tree blossoming on its summit and it was only when the tower needed restoration work in very recent years that the tree was removed to ensure the tower's safety. Nearby, among the gravestones, is the stump of an old preaching cross.

What to look out for

Around 90 different wild flowers and up to 25 species of butterfly typical of chalk grassland thrive here, including the characteristic chalkhill, common and small blues.
Field guides should certainly be taken in late spring and summer.
Birds to look out for include kestrels, buzzards, skylarks and yellowhammers.
Outside the gate to East Compton old church, look out for the stone mounting block once used by less agile horseriders.

Fontmell Down overlooks the beautiful Blackmoor Vale

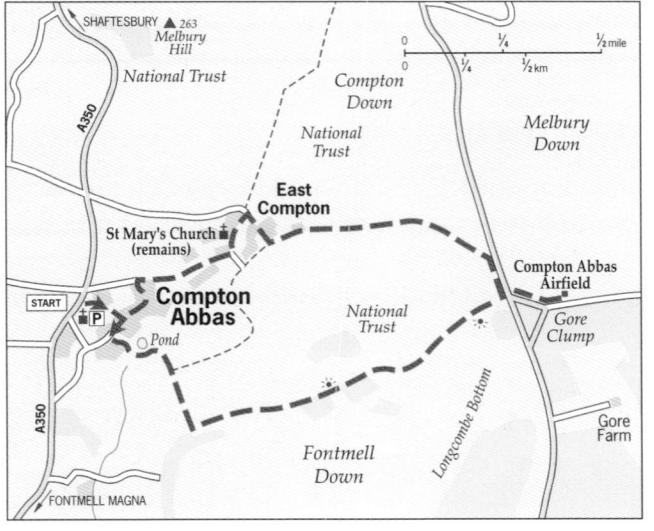

Abbotsbury and Chesil Beach

From Chesil Beach, with its huge wall of shingle, the route skirts Chapel Hill, with an optional diversion to the Swannery, and climbs to St Catherine's Chapel before visiting the village or returning directly to the beach.

START

Abbotsbury is on the B3157, eight miles north-west of Weymouth. Drive westwards through the village and follow signs to Subtropical Gardens and Chesil Beach. The car park is behind the beach.

DIRECTIONS

From the car park, cross one of the wooden bridges towards the sea. Turn left and walk along the shingle for about 200yds. At a fork, follow sign 'Coastal Footpath and Swannery' through a gate, soon gaining a view of St Catherine's Chapel. After a while the path follows a stream.

After about 250yds look out for a stile on the right with a signpost to 'Swannery'. Cross the stile and start to skirt the hill, with a good view of The Fleet, a stretch of calm water enclosed by the bank. Pass a wartime pillbox and then go through a waymarked gate. Passing another pillbox on the right, follow the track across the field to a stone marker where a choice can be made.

(To visit the Swannery take the path downhill; either retrace your steps to this stone marker to rejoin main route, or take horse-drawn carriage to Swannery car park and walk on into village. To carry on round the hill to the village, continue straight on; to rejoin walk from the village, go west along main street, turning left to follow sign 'Chapel and Beach'.) The main walk turns left and climbs very steeply up the hill, crossing a stile, to the chapel (magnificent views). Enter the chapel from the far side.

Follow the sandy track down towards the village past the farm and kissing-gate to join a lane. To visit the village, go straight on; retrace your steps to this point.

To return to the beach, turn left and left again. Pass some cottages on the right and after about 250yds go through a gate and turn left on to a track. Eventually meet the outward route by the stile and return to the car park.

Chesil Bank

This unique bank of shingle, up to 40ft high, extends for about 18 miles, from Bridport to Portland. The pebbles increase in size from west to east – so consistently that, tradition has it, a smuggler could tell exactly where he was in the dark. The bank is treacherous in stormy weather – during a particularly bad storm in 1824 one ship was carried right over the bank into the Fleet. Beachcombers have discovered parts of Spanish galleons and gold ingots.

Abbotsbury Swannery

Founded by monks in the 14th century, the swannery is a breeding ground for the only managed colony of mute swans. Several hundred can be seen at close quarters. There is a also 17th-century duck decoy. The swannery is open from April to October; for winter visiting telephone 0305 871242 or 871684.

The historic Tithe Barn at Abbotsbury

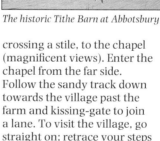

What to look out for

From Chapel Hill look out for Abbotsbury Tithe Barn – about 600 years old and one of the longest in the country, it is now used for storing locally-grown water reed for thatching. In St Catherine's Chapel you will find the prayer used by women searching for a husband – St Catherine was the patron saint of spinsters. Terns and ringed plovers nest on the shingle, and the Fleet is home to brent geese, gulls and waders in winter.

Dancing Ledge

On one of Dorset's most beautiful stretches of coastline, the highlight of this walk is a very special place which is accessible only on foot – a broad, flat shelf of rock, left by quarrying and lapped by the sea.

Information

The walk is one and a half miles long
No road walking
A few stiles
About half the walk is on level ground, but the slope down to Dancing Ledge is fairly steep. Small children and the less agile may need help
Low tide is the best time to visit Dancing Ledge. For tide times telephone Swanage Tourist Information Centre – 0929 422885
The Ledge is ideal for picnicking
Coffee shop and pub in Langton Matravers

What to look out for

The limestone grassland is excellent in summer for flowers, butterflies and other insects, especially grasshoppers and bush crickets. Butterflies may include the Lulworth skipper, found only in this area. Guillemots and razorbills are among the sea birds which frequent the coast here and nest on the cliff ledges during the summer months. At Dancing Ledge the rock pools are full of life, and there are a number of huge ammonites embedded in the limestone. Sometimes abseilers can be seen descending the cliff and on the upper ledge there is a cave left by quarrying. The drystone walls and old quarries along the route make good fossil-hunting grounds. Dinosaur footprints may not be two-a-penny, but fish bones and sharks' teeth are within the bounds of possibility.

START
Langton Matravers is about one and a half miles west of Swanage. Turn down Durnford Drove, off the B3069 through the village, and go up the hill through the gate at the end, passing a large house, then through another gate and along a very rough, stony track to Spyway Barn car park (small charge), the start point for the walk.

Dancing Ledge from the Dorset coast path

DIRECTIONS
Study the map of the Dorset Heritage Coast, then go through the waymarked gate and head across the field to the gate and stone stile in the middle of the drystone wall. Cross the next field, go through the stone gateposts and down the slope towards the sea. In late spring and summer listen for the song of skylarks. On a clear day there are especially fine views westwards of one of the very best stretches of Dorset coast, towards the strip lynchets, or terraces, of St Aldhelm's Head.

Follow the track steeply downhill to meet the Dorset Coast Path at a group of three stiles. Cross either of the two stiles facing the sea and climb down to Dancing Ledge. Once you have exhausted its delights, climb back up to the stiles. Follow the sign 'Langton 1¼', heading up the hill to a stile visible in the gorse. At the top, at the waymarked sign 'Langton 1', follow the track with a wall on the right, Sea Spray House on the left and evidence of old quarries on either side.

At a gate and stile, turn right on to the Priest's Way, a medieval trackway supposedly used by the priest from Worth Matravers on his way to take mass at the church in Swanage. Keep straight on, through a gate and stile by the National Trust 'Eastington' sign. At the junction with the track from the village to Spyway Barn, signed 'Langton' to the left and 'Dancing Ledge' to the right, turn right and return to the car park.

Just one way of getting down to Dancing Ledge

Quarrying at Dancing Ledge
The Isle of Purbeck has been extensively quarried over the centuries for its limestone, much in demand by architects for the construction of such grand buildings as St Paul's Cathedral in London and the closer Corfe Castle. Reminders of this industry remain all around the area, including a number of caves in the cliffs along this stretch of coast, such as Tilly Whim and Winspit. At Dancing Ledge, quarrying cut back the cliffs, leaving broad shelves or 'ledges'; the 'dancing' part of the name comes not from any human recreation here, but from the dancing action of the waves over the lower ledges at high tide.

Old Sarum

From the huge earthworks of Old Sarum, forerunner of the city of Salisbury two miles away, the walk crosses the watermeadows of the River Avon, skirts the village of Stratford sub Castle then makes its way back up to the ramparts.

WALK 22
WILTSHIRE
SU139326

Watercress

START
Old Sarum is two miles north of Salisbury on the A345. Either park in Old Sarum's car park (NB this closes at 4pm) or in the layby on the main road opposite the Old Castle pub and walk up to the car park.

DIRECTIONS
From Old Sarum car park cross stile and take the steps by the information board and toilets to reach the inner rampart. Turn left and follow the path, circling the rampart to reach the ruins of the old cathedral on the left. Just beyond the ruins, at the corner of the field, turn right into a gully and follow it down through a gap in the inner wall and across the embankment to the outer wall. Turn left and almost immediately take the path dropping steeply away to the right. Continue down the hill to a path and turn left. The path reaches a stile, but do not cross it – instead turn sharp right away from Sarum

Information

The walk is two and a half miles long
Steep climbs up and down the ramparts; otherwise level
Several stiles
Pub opposite entrance to Old Sarum; children's room and meals
Good picnic spots on Old Sarum
Toilets at Old Sarum

towards Stratford sub Castle. At the road, cross, and turn right. Take the first turning on the left, opposite a signpost to Devizes Road. The road continues over two small bridges and narrows to a tarmac path (views extend to Salisbury Cathedral). After crossing the River Avon turn right at the next path junction and continue with the river to the right (NB paths to the right are for fishermen only.) The path eventually leads behind farm buildings to a road. Turn right and follow the road round to the right towards Salisbury. Shortly take the footpath to Portway by the sign for Stratford sub Castle. Follow the path diagonally across to the churchyard and on reaching the tarmac path turn left. Just before reaching the top of the path turn sharp right along the bottom of the embankment towards Old

Sarum. Turn up the hill to the left and retrace your steps to the outer embankment. Turn right and follow the outer wall back to the car park.

Old Sarum
Originally a prehistoric hill fort, Old Sarum grew through Roman, Saxon and Norman times, eventually becoming a major medieval settlement with a castle, a cathedral and a bishop's palace. Today there is little remaining, but the foundations of the cathedral can be clearly seen, and there are ruins of the bishop's palace in the inner bailey. Most of the excavated finds can be seen in Salisbury's museum.

Stratford sub Castle
This ancient village – its name recalls the days when there *was* a castle above it – had a fulling mill in the 13th century. Its church dates from the 13th and 15th centuries, although the tower was rebuilt in 1711.

Old Sarum was once an important medieval city

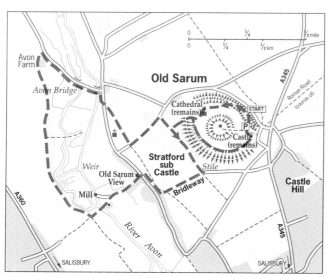

What to look out for

Gliders and light aircraft from the nearby airfield can often be seen circling ahead. The flat fields neatly divided by straight hedges to the right, after leaving Old Sarum, are the remains of a Roman settlement. Swans and geese inhabit the watermeadows of the Avon, particularly in winter, and there are pollarded willows and fine views across to the spire of Salisbury Cathedral. Watercress grows by some of the streams, and wetland flowers such as ragged robin and hemp agrimony flourish in the meadows.

Winterbourne Monkton

The steep climb up Windmill Hill can be very bracing on a windy day, but combined with a visit to Avebury, this walk will provide an interesting and rewarding day out.

START
Winterbourne Monkton is a mile north of Avebury. On entering the village look for a turning to the left marked Manor Farm and Church. Follow the road through the farm, past the church. Immediately on the left next to the church is a concrete yard where you can park.

DIRECTIONS
Turn left out of the yard and on the corner turn right down a footpath which reaches a footbridge. (To visit the village of Winterbourne Monkton cross the bridge.) Continue straight on to the left of the footbridge over rough ground to reach a stile. Follow the direction of the arrow across the field to another stile. Do not cross this stile, but turn to the left and head for a stile with a signpost on the opposite side of the field. Cross this and drop down the bank on to a farm track and turn right. Continue along the track for about ¾ mile, passing a barn on the right, to a junction of several paths, then turn left. Reach a stile leading onto

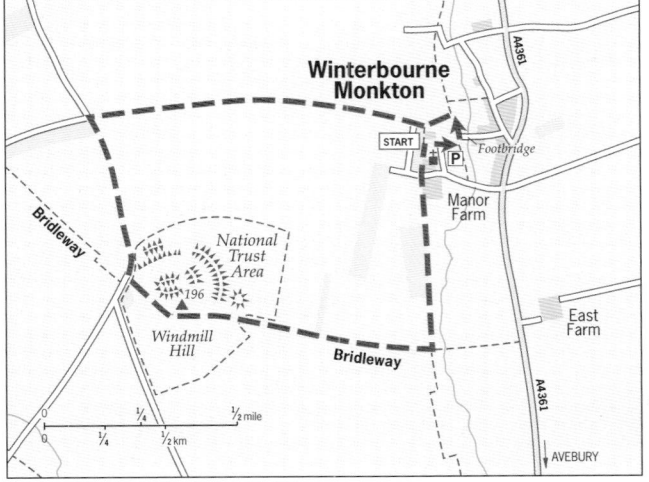

Information

The walk is about three miles long
Level ground with just one gentle hill
A lot of stiles
No road walking
New Inn in Winterbourne Monkton has a garden with play equipment; also pub, restaurant and café in Avebury
Windmill Hill suitable for picnics

Windmill Hill. Head straight up to the top where there are fenced-off mounds (good views). Proceed in the same general direction, past the mounds, to leave the area over a stile behind the last mound. Continue until the path becomes a tarmac track at the bottom of the hill. Go

Skylark

through the gate and almost immediately turn left into a field. Cross the field and continue to follow the footpath signs, crossing over a further four stiles and muddy farm tracks. Pass the farm on your right and continue ahead to the road. Turn right to reach the car park.

Windmill Hill
About 5,000 years ago Windmill Hill was occupied by a large Neolithic settlement and excavations of the site by Alexander Keiller in the 1920s yielded rich pickings. The vast amount of bones (human and animal), beads, pots, flint implements etc that were found in the ditches gave a clear picture of the community's way of life, and this is well documented in the Keiller Museum in Avebury. The 20 or so acres enclosed by three circles of ditches and banks are not in the care of the National Trust or English Heritage.

Avebury
A mile from the start of the walk lies the fascinating village of Avebury and a visit here before or after the walk provides enough of interest to fill the rest of the day easily. As well as the famous stones, there is Avebury Manor (National Trust) and the thatched Great Barn, housing a shop and the Museum of Wiltshire Folk Life. Displays here illustrate dairying and the work of the thatcher, saddler, shepherd and wheelwright. The Alexander Keiller Museum displays archaeological finds.

What to look out for

On a clear day the stone circles of Avebury can be seen from the top of Windmill Hill. Listen for skylarks and watch for kestrels on your route.

Looking back along the walk from Windmill Hill

Malmesbury

This undemanding walk starts from the historic town of Malmesbury which, with its narrow, hilly streets, ancient stone buildings and numerous craft and antique shops, is a fascinating place to explore on foot.

START

Malmesbury is west of Swindon on the A429. Start the walk from the Station Road car park.

DIRECTIONS

From the car park follow the signpost to the town centre. Cross the River Avon and go up the steps at the back of the abbey then turn right into the abbey garden. Walk across to the far right corner by the Old Bell Hotel. Cross the road and turn left. Go underneath the large mirror and follow the lane. Turn right at the bottom of the steps and continue down the lane ('Burnivale') until the path opens into a wider lane. Here turn left down the lane towards the river and go over two bridges, passing the weir on the left. After crossing a metal stile turn almost immediately to the left, away from the river bank. Cross a small flat stone bridge and follow a clear path to the right to reach a farm lane. Turn left, pass a barn on the right, and continue ahead. Pass to the right of an old stone building and through the gate. Cut diagonally across the field to the tree in the top right-hand corner opposite. Cross the improvised stile to the right of this and head towards the big Dutch barn. Follow the diagonal path across to the farmyard. Go straight through the yard and turn sharp left down the farm road.

At the bottom go through the gate on the left and follow the path round the bottom of the field. Just before the old buildings passed earlier, turn right across a stile and turn left at the bottom of the field. Go through the gap at the bottom of the wall, over the stone slab bridge, and retrace your steps back up to the abbey and the car park.

Malmesbury

Built on a hill by the River Avon in Saxon times, Malmesbury is now officially recognised in the Guinness Book of Records as the oldest borough in England. At the top of the town is the famous 12th-century abbey; only the nave remains today, but at one time it had a spire as high as St Paul's Cathedral. To learn about the history of the town, visit the Athelstan Museum in Cross Hayes. There is a tourist information centre nearby.

Malmesbury is another Wiltshire town that has retained its blind house (see Bradford-on-Avon overleaf). In fact, there are two here – one on either side of the arched gateway leading from the market place into the abbey grounds.

WALK 24
WILTSHIRE
ST933875

Information

The walk is two miles long
Level, easy walking, apart from the steps leaving the town
A few stiles
Refreshment facilities in Malmesbury
Picnic site by weir, near station car park
Toilets in Malmesbury

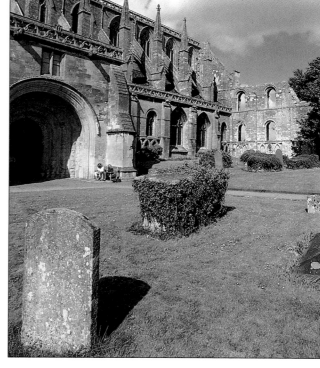

The abbey at Malmesbury

What to look out for

Evidence of prisoners' desperate and futile attempts to escape can be seen in the scratched stone by the keyholes of one of the 'blind houses'.

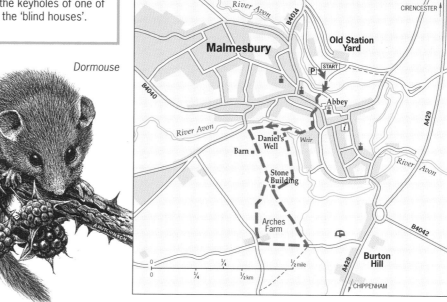

Dormouse

Fishing for tiddlers near the bridge

The Canal and River at Bradford-on-Avon

WALK 25
WILTSHIRE
ST825607

A pleasant and undemanding stroll along the well-maintained towpaths of Bradford Canal and the river, with plenty of opportunities for refreshment breaks.

Information

The walk is three miles long

Level, easy walking on good paths

One stile, if extension to walk is taken

Dogs should be kept on leads

Pub and seasonal teashop at Avoncliff; also teashop at Barton Farm; pubs, restaurants and teashops at Bradford-on-Avon

Picnic tables by the river at Barton Farm

DIRECTIONS

START

The walk starts from the railway station car park in Bradford-on-Avon.

Go through the gap at the far end of the car park, turn left along the river bank across the open area to a broad tarmac path which runs parallel with the river. Follow this path until it joins the canal opposite a swing bridge. Turn right along the canal bank, and continue to a clearly marked right turn leading down to the river. (To reach the aqueduct at Avoncliff continue along the path.) Turn right and follow the river bank back towards Bradford. After climbing the stile, keep to the right around the pumping station and up to the canal bank. Turn left at the swing bridge and follow this path until it leaves the canal bank and joins the road. (At this point you may take a detour to Bradford Lock by crossing the road. Retrace your steps and re-cross the road.) Turn left along the road for a short distance, then turn left through a small gate and head towards the tithe barn within Barton Farm Country Park, entering through the gate to the right of the beech tree. After visiting the barn, rejoin the river path, turn right and go under the railway bridge. Continue along the bank, and turn right beside the swimming pool to return to the car park.

Barton Farm Country Park

Now in the care of English Heritage, the huge Tithe Barn forms the focal point of the complex here. Built in the 14th century, it belonged to Shaftesbury Abbey and was used to store the tithes of grain elicited from the estate's tenants. Thousands of stone tiles cover the roof and immense, but exquisitely graceful timbers support the weight. The complex now houses craft shops and refreshments.

Bradford's Blind House

Originally used as a chapel, this tiny stone building on the ancient town bridge is thought to have become a prison at some time in the early 18th century. Such places were sometimes referred to as 'blind houses' because there were no windows, and conditions inside were abominable. It is possible to obtain the key from a nearby shop and go inside.

The old stone bridge in the centre of Bradford-on-Avon

What to look out for

There is always something to see on the canal and river – narrowboats, dinghies, birdlife and anglers. At a right angle to the large Tithe Barn is its much smaller predecessor.

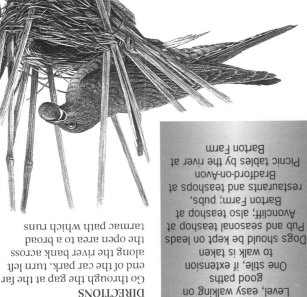

Cuckoo

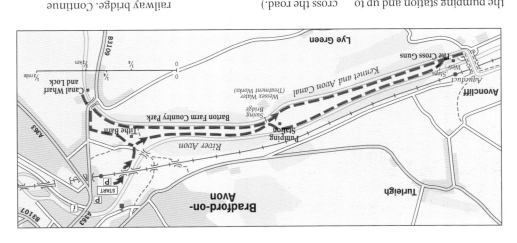

Chew Valley Lake

The lake forms a lovely focal point to this very attractive walk, with its information centre, nature trails and picnic area.

WALK 26
AVON
ST573614

START
Chew Valley Lake is bordered on the southern side by the A368 south of Bristol. Start from the car park nearest the dam at the northern end of the lake, signposted 'Picnic Area'.

DIRECTIONS
Turn left along the main road and take the first right along Denny Lane. Shortly turn left over a stile onto a signposted public footpath. Follow this tarmac lane down into the valley and, just before the bridge and a sign, 'Strictly Private Property', take the signposted footpath on the right into the woods. Continue in the same general direction for about ¾ mile, through fields and across several stiles, with the river meandering along in woodland to the left. Eventually the path reaches the edge of Chew Magna at a gate and stile in the hedge. Go through the gate and turn right to visit the village, but otherwise head back diagonally in a south-easterly direction across the brow of the field you have just walked across. Go through a gate and follow the field edge to a stile in the hedge. Cross this and the road below and take the footpath (Pitts Lane) signposted opposite. Continue past a farm, through a gate and past another farm to reach a stile. Cross this and follow the left-hand field edge to a gate, marked 'Public Footpath'. Continue along a narrow path, which can become overgrown, and go through another gate to reach an open area known as Knowle Hill. The walk continues in a southerly direction down the hill to reach a road. Turn right and immediately past

Knowle House turn right, as signposted, into the courtyard and between the two buildings and go through a gate on the left into a field. Carry on towards the lake, now in view, and follow the path to reach the main road. On the opposite side, to the right, is the entrance to the lake's lower car park. Follow the lakeside path to return to the upper car park.

Chew Valley Lake
The Bristol Water Company began construction of the lake in 1950 and six years later it was opened by HM The Queen. One of the largest artificial lakes in the south-west of England, it has a perimeter of ten miles and yields about ten million gallons of water every day. Now a Site of Special Scientific Interest, the lake is very popular with birdwatchers.

Information

The walk is three and a half miles long
Very few gradients, but some muddy sections
A lot of stiles
Pubs in Chew Magna
Café at car park
Picnic area beside the lake
Toilets at car park

Coot

What to look out for

The lake is an important inland site for wintering wildfowl, including a small but regular flock of Bewick Swans, and there are displays on wildlife at the car park.
Thousands of tufted ducks, pochards and gadwall can be seen from October to March. The members of the sailing club are often active on the lake, and anglers can be seen on the banks, fishing for brown and rainbow trout.
Pitts Lane is a fascinating example of an ancient hollow lane, with properly layered hedges containing a variety of species – the more species there are, the older the hedgerow.

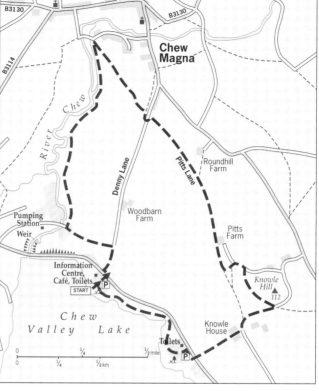

The view from Knowle Hill

Oldbury-on-Severn

An undemanding walk on absolutely level ground, with the Severn estuary providing interest for the first part – it is well worth taking binoculars.

WALK 27
AVON
ST609925

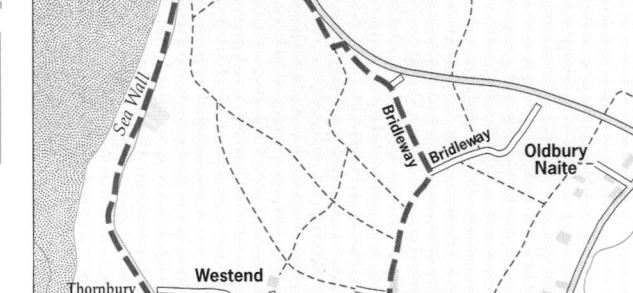

START

Oldbury lies on the south bank of the River Severn about three miles north of the Severn Bridge. Park in the car park in Church Road, by the bridge, opposite the Anchor Inn.

DIRECTIONS

On leaving the car park, go through the pedestrian gate to the right, signed 'Thornbury Sailing Club'. Follow the road to the clubhouse, passing the sluice gates to the left, and turn right along the sea wall. Continue for about ¾ mile, with the nuclear power station looming ahead. On reaching the power station, turn right along the signposted path until reaching a road.
Turn right here then shortly right again, where signposted, and climb the gate into a field (usually cattle here). Follow left-hand field edge to a stile by a ruined building and continue on to two gates. Go through the left-hand gate, then turn right along the track just before reaching the road. This bridleway can be very muddy indeed.
Where the track divides, turn right. The lane turns into a metalled road. Continue to the fork and take the public footpath signposted almost ahead, between houses. Cross two stiles before reaching The Toot. Cross the double stile in the right-hand corner and continue straight ahead to a stile hidden in the hedge. Cross this and head for the stone stile between stone walls.
Continue to steps and the road. Turn left past the Ship, then cross into Church Road.

The Toot

Oldbury Camp, otherwise known as The Toot, is an Iron Age hill fort. Covering about ten acres in all, it has a double bank and ditch on the north and east sides, and a single bank on the west. The discovery of coins here indicates that it was in use in Roman times, too. Now it

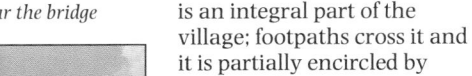

A safe mooring near the bridge

is an integral part of the village; footpaths cross it and it is partially encircled by streets and housing.

Oldbury Church

Perched on a hill in the flat plain alongside the Severn, Oldbury's church can be seen for miles around and is a useful landmark throughout the walk. It is dedicated to Arilda, a local saint in Saxon times. The only other church in the country bearing her name is at Oldbury-on-the-Hill, about 15 miles away. Views from the churchyard are superb, and it is possibly to make out the route of the walk from here.

Grey plover

Haresfield Beacon

This walk takes in two contrasting spurs of the Cotswold escarpment – the open aspect of the Shortwood spar, overlooking Standish Woods, and the narrow, steep Haresfield Beacon, almost craggy by comparison, offering far-reaching views across the Severn valley towards the Forest of Dean.

START

The Cripple Gate National Trust car park is situated two miles north of Stroud, accessible from the A4173 Gloucester road at Edge. From here travel south following the Haresfield Beacon signs.

DIRECTIONS

From the squeeze-stile, beside the National Trust information panel in the car park, follow the track south-west to the Topograph Viewpoint. Take track due north and just before reaching the wall, turn left down a woodland track parallel to the road.
At the foot of the incline cross a stile. Continue for about 20yds and fork left, following the wall/fence round and up to a stile. Keep to the wall at the foot of the steep Haresfield

Information

The walk is two miles long, three with optional extension
Firm paths, with one brief, but steep ascent on to Haresfield Beacon
A few stiles
No road walking
Dogs must be on lead
Pub (Edgemoor Inn) on Cotswold Way, a quarter of a mile south of Edge on the A4173
Picnic places on grassy Shortwood spur

Beacon bank for about ½ mile. Eventually the path turns to the right and where you see a stile on the left, take the path slanting sharply right on to the tip of the ridge. A grass path climbs the ridge steadily through the light thorn scrub, ascending quite steeply to the beacon site and trig point via rampart ditches. Follow the southern rampart of the hill fort eastward to a stile. Join the fenced path beside a field (good views). Where the principal promontory fort ditch cuts across the neck of the ridge the path encounters a hunting-gate and wall squeeze-stile, then winds down through more broken ground to the road.
(To extend the walk turn left at the collection box,

following the road as far as Ringhill Farm. At the farm turn right following 'Cotswold Way' signs. Continue along the path, passing the Siege Stone, dated 1643, commemorating the siege of Gloucester. On reaching the road and wellhead, turn right and continue along the road for about ½ mile. Turn right at the sign for Haresfield Beacon and return to the car park.)

For the main walk bear immediately right down the steps next to the National Trust collection box,

signposted 'Cotswold Way'; this path slants left and shortly rejoins the outward path, rising to the stile. Ascend the incline, maintaining course at the top and walking parallel to the wall over the Shortwood pasture to reach the car park.

Shortwood Topograph

This unusual relief plinth stands in the midst of three Cotswold escarpments of precious unimproved calcareous grassland and beech woodland. The view extends over Standish Woods, the twin towers of the de-commissioned Berkeley Nuclear Power Station, three loops of the Severn, the Forest of Dean and the Black Mountains.

Haresfield Beacon

At the 50-mile mid-point of the Cotswold Way between Chipping Campden and Bath, the Beacon is surmounted by Ring Hill camp and the old Ordnance Survey triangulation station, made obsolete now by satellite mapping. The narrow ridge bears the scars of many centuries of surface quarrying.

Haresfield Beacon is perfect for kite flying

May Hill and Clifford's Mesne

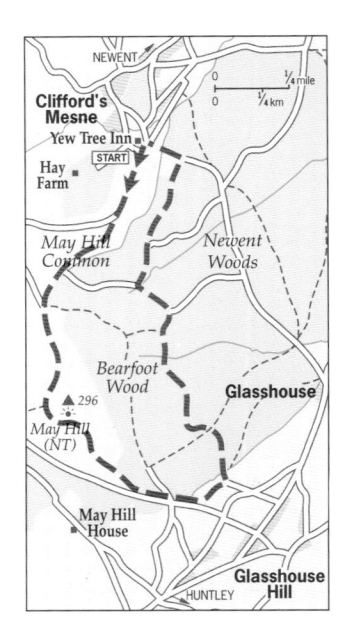

A simple climb to a viewpoint commanding panoramic views – west to the Black Mountains and east to the Cotswolds – this is a walk of constant change; a bumper package of exercise and wildlife interest.

START
Park directly above The Yew Tree Inn in Clifford's Mesne.

DIRECTIONS
Follow the tarmac lane steeply uphill to a cattle grid to enter May Hill Common. Twenty yards further on, a sign ('May Hill') directs left. Ascend to a bridle-gate and on to May Hill. Follow the broad path slightly left through the wooden posts leading up the gentle ridge to the 971ft summit. Pass round the western perimeter to the right of the pine plantation (far-ranging views). Continue to the Silver Jubilee plaque, about 30yds into the trees. Leave the hill in a southerly direction by walking from the plaque, passing to the right of the stone triangulation point and heading towards the

right-hand edge of the pine wood ahead, keeping to the meandering beaten track towards the River Severn. The path descends to a bridle-gate. Entering the lane, descend beyond a cottage and then pass to the left of a water tank, continuing to a fork. Take the left lane (a bridleway which can be muddy) leading down beside a solitary cottage with a large conservatory. Meeting a road at the bottom, go left (waymarked) to pass a gate and, ignoring paths to left and right, keep ahead on path marked '193', which winds through the predominately coniferous Newent Wood. In about 150yds, just before the track ahead rises to the left, go right, then in 20yds turn left. At the next track junction keep left uphill. At the second track junction, in 650yds, turn left uphill, then in just over 300yds turn right downhill. In another 200yds or so branch left and at the end of the track cross a stile and turn left onto the lane to return to the start point.

May Hill
The name May Hill is said to derive from the custom of neighbouring parishes contesting ownership of the hill on May Day. May Hill Common, but not the summit ring, belongs to the National Trust. The conifer plantation on the summit, which gives distinction to the pudding-shaped hill, was supplemented with new stock to celebrate Queen Elizabeth II's Silver Jubilee in 1977. The panorama ranges over the Forest of Dean, the Black Mountains in Wales (Waun Fach at 2661ft is the highest hill in view), the Malvern

Range, the broad spreading Severn vale and the Cotswold escarpment.

National Birds of Prey Centre, Newent
Just over a mile north of Clifford's Mesne on the minor road to Newent, is this fascinating centre, open from February to November, which is home to eagles, hawks, vultures, falcons and owls. Weather permitting, there are flying displays every day, demonstrating the ancient skill of falconry. The centre has breeding aviaries, a falconry museum, gift and coffee shops.

A stand of trees at the summit of May Hill

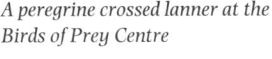

A peregrine crossed lanner at the Birds of Prey Centre

The Severn Way

A splendid riverside ramble which loops back via an old canal and the hilltop village of Apperley. A natural extension north along the Severn Way embraces Deerhurst, with its remarkably intact Saxon church and nearby chapel.

START

The walk begins five miles south of Tewkesbury, via the A38 and B4213, signposted 'Apperley' and 'Tirley'. Park carefully near the gate on the east side of Haw Bridge on the B4213.

DIRECTIONS

Cross to the wicket gate (waymarked) on the south side of the B4213, passing through the yard of Bridge House. Crossing the stile, signposted 'Severn Way Path', enter the long riverside meadow. After 500yds cross stile in left-hand hedge, then keep right and proceed along the riverside flood bank via stiles and gates. After the new floodgate the path sweeps round a pylon to a stile/gate and bridge over the old Coombe Hill Canal. Passing the old lock, keep right along the river and continue to the stile leading onto the road at Fletcher's Leap (to the right are Wainlode Cliff and the Red Lion Inn).
Turn left, following the road north to the bridge over the old canal. Beyond this turn right through the bridlegate on Warren Way path (Coombe Hill Canal Nature Reserve). Proceed along the inter-stream causeway (rough in places), through Cobney Meadows for ¾ mile then turn left over a stone and brick footbridge and along a winding lane leading up to the road by Apperley Hall Farm. Cross directly to the facing bridleway, rising steadily uphill, and on joining the minor road turn right.
At the post box cross the stile left, traversing the pasture towards the white-painted house. A stile gives access into a metalled lane. Turn right, passing the church, duck pond and green and seeking the footpath immediately after the two new houses, via a gate to the left.(To visit Deerhurst, a mile distant, continue north along the village street then take footpaths down the hill; return along the riverbank on the Severn Way.)
The main walk continues due west beside the fence to a waymarked stile, descending into a valley, crossing two further stiles en route, to the open road at The Coal House Inn. Follow the road, left to the river to join the Severn Way. Turn left (right if you are returning from Deerhurst), through the waymarked Severnside Caravan Park via a stile, with two further stiles to negotiate to complete the walk.

Odda's Chapel

This rare survival from the Saxon period was dedicated on 12 April 1056 and was built by Earl Odda in honour of his brother Aelfric. It is now in the care of English Heritage.
The priory church of St Mary is considered one of the most important monuments of Anglo-Saxon England, founded in the 7th century and becoming established over the next three centuries. Originally a Benedictine monastery with a 30,000 acre estate, it was here, in 1016, that King Canute made a treaty with Edmund Ironside. The chapel is open at any reasonable time.

The Severn Way

The Severn Way was created by Gloucestershire County

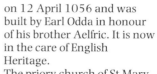

The river from Haw Bridge

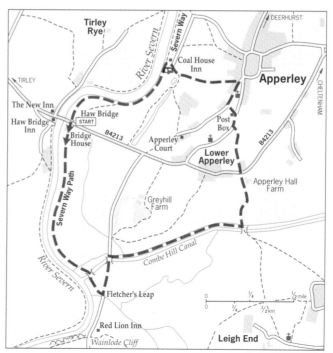

Council in 1989 and the east bank path is currently waymarked for 50 miles south of Tewkesbury with the distinctive 'Severn Trow' symbol. Eventually there will be a walkers' route along most of its 200-mile course from Plynlymon Fawr to Bristol. In this county there will be paths on both banks. In 1430 an Act of Parliament named the river the 'King's Highway of the Severn' because three-quarters of its length was navigable. It is famous for its elver (baby eel) fishing (see elver deterrent notice at the end of the Coombe Hill Canal) and its tidal 'bore', beloved of surfers and canoeists.

Colne Valley

The near perfect harmony of Cotswold villages within their landscape present a quintessentially English rural scene. Though the walk starts little more than a mile from the tourist rendezvous of Bibury, we find peace and beauty in full measure.

START

Ablington is a mile west of A433 at Bibury. Park safely and considerately in the village, then commence the walk at the old mill on the east side of the Coln bridge. Alternative parking is available at Swains Bridge at Coln Rogers.

DIRECTIONS

Follow the lane leading north-west beside attractive gardens overlooking the mill-stream, beyond a gate the track proceeds past kennels, swinging up round a walled enclosure. The track descends to a gate then runs directly across the side valley, rising to a gate. With drystone wall to the right, advance to a gate and enter Potlicker's Lane. From Lampits Farm this green track carries regular traffic. Meeting the minor road go forward finding a narrow path leading left by the grove and down into the valley. At the foot of the lane, beside the Village Hall, go right, crossing the broad Swains Bridge. At the road fork bear left, towards Lower Farm (Stratford Place Stud) and turn left, crossing the open gravel yard to the steps to the right of the barn. Pass along the bank above a drystone wall to a stile in the curve of the paddock fencing, proceed downwards via a gate and cross the low fence stile. Passing through the old hedge line, keep right upon the bank (ignore track to a gate beside Winson Mill) and continue above the mill to a gate, joining the road directly into Winson to your right. Go left at the road junction to the triangular green. Keep right, past the church, then left by the Coln Valley Fish and Game Company (the 'Smokery'), descending the narrow lane bearing left to find a white wicket gate on your right and concrete footpath marker. Cross the paddock to a second wicket gate, then cross the stile footbridge and go through the poplar grove, passing up through the larch plantation to a gate. Do not go through the gate, but bear right between conifers and fence to reach a gate/stile. Ascend the pasture, crossing to the far corner to a gate to rejoin the outward route at the Ablington Downs dry valley.

Cotswold Villages

Ablington has several classic Cotswold houses of which Ablington House, dating from 1650, must be pre-eminent. Its high pitched gables stand proudly behind a high drystone wall; the 19th-century stone lions came from the Houses of Parliament. Coln Rogers church, though not directly en route, is well worth a visit. It is almost unique in the Cotswolds in that it has a largely intact Saxon chancel and nave and its secluded, almost farmyard setting ensures that it retains its centuries old tranquility. Winson is a compact village centred upon a small green which is dominated by the Georgian manor and the Saxon/Norman parish church. Notice the table tombs and old school house in the churchyard.

Information

The walk is three and three quarter miles long
Gently undulating, but with muddy patches in wet conditions and one section overgrown with nettles in summer
Road walking only in villages
Dogs must be kept on leads
Several stiles and gates
Pubs and café at Bibury, ice cream at the Trout Farm, refreshment van regularly at Arlington Mill
Picnics in dry valley below Ablington Downs

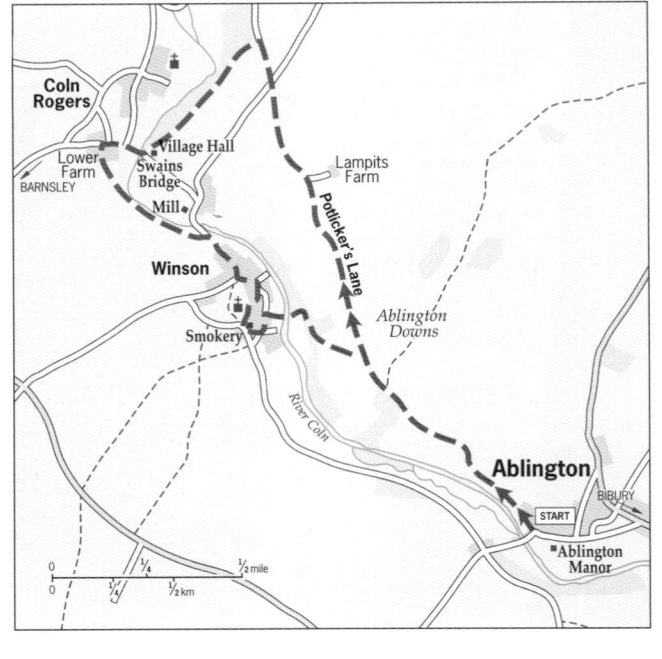

What to look out for

In the intriguingly named Potlicker's Lane you can judge the age of the hedgerow by the variety of woody species of tree, thorn and shrub that flourish within it. During the drive from Bibury notice the quaint signpost at the first junction in Ablington 'Bibury 4/3'.

Winson church, Saxon in parts, has some fine table tombs in its churchyard

Bourton-on-the-Water

WALK 32
GLOUCESTERSHIRE
SP170208

A quiet country stroll incorporating a delightful village, pastureland, streams and tranquil lakes. Bourton-on-the-Water, known as the 'Venice of the Cotswolds', has a splendid array of visitor attractions, and no shortage of teas and ice cream.

Wyck Rissington church

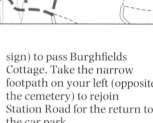

Information

The walk is three and three quarter miles long
Easy route and level walking, can be muddy after rain
Very little road walking
Excellent for dogs on leads
A large number of stiles and gates
A range of pubs and cafés in Bourton-on-the-Water
Plenty of picnic places

Common vole

What to look out for

In Wyck Rissington church see the carvings of Jester Irland in the porch and the discreet reference to composer Gustav Holst on the organ. Holst lived in the village for a short while in 1892–3, residing at Mace's Cottage (the first cottage on the right on the walk into the village).

START
Bourton-on-the-Water lies adjacent to the Fosse Way, five miles north of Northleach, three miles south of Stow-on-the-Wold. Start the walk from the large car park off Station Road.

DIRECTIONS
Follow Station Road north, branching right along Roman Way. Find the stone steps beside Woodlands House at the entrance to Moor Lane. Cross the stile into a pasture field, follow the hedge to a second stile then angle half-right across the marshy ground, crossing a wooden bridge to another stile. Follow the left-hand hedge to the stile and cross a farm track via a kissing-gate. Maintain company with the left-hand hedge via a stile and footbridges over branches of the River Dikler. Crossing a large pasture, pass through two gates and bear left via gates on to the road and turn right into Wyck Rissington. Follow the street, passing the pond and church. Directly after the last building on your right, where the tarmac road bends left, branch right to follow the track, bending right then left through two gates, for a distance of ⅛ mile to reach a short pasture lane with an old hedge on the left. At the end go right through the gate, along the bridleway beside the left-hand hedge and along the field edges for ¼ mile. Shortly after a bend, pass through field gate on left, crossing pasture to a second gate, following the right-hand hedge to a metal gate into a field. Continue to a bridle-gate into the lane, going right towards Rissington Mill. Where the shingle track bears right, cross the stile on the left and after the subsequent kissing-gate pass between the garden wall and tennis court to a pair of footbridges across the Dikler. Bear right, initially beside the river, to cross the pasture half left to the stile, then cross the long pasture to a wicket gate. A confined path sweeps round beside the lake, and on reaching the lane junction go left to the gate and use the squeeze-gap beside the entrance to Bury Barn. Follow the lane, bearing right (ignore footpath sign) to pass Burghfields Cottage. Take the narrow footpath on your left (opposite the cemetery) to rejoin Station Road for the return to the car park.

Bourton-on-the-Water
This is a pretty village of Cotswold stone buildings and lawns sloping down to the River Windrush. Its many tourist attractions include a one-ninth size model of the village itself, an eight-acre bird garden, a motor museum and village life exhibition.

Wyck Rissington
This charming village has neat cottages picturesquely lining a tapering green. The duck pond has an old cart slipway where, as in Constable's *The Haywain*, wagons were drawn into the water to expand the wooden wheels to fit their metal rims more snugly.

The River Windrush at Bourton-on-the-Water

SOUTH &
SOUTH EAST
ENGLAND

The River Yar

A walk round the estuary of the River Yar, rich in bird and plant life, also taking in fields, woodland and the route of the old railway line.

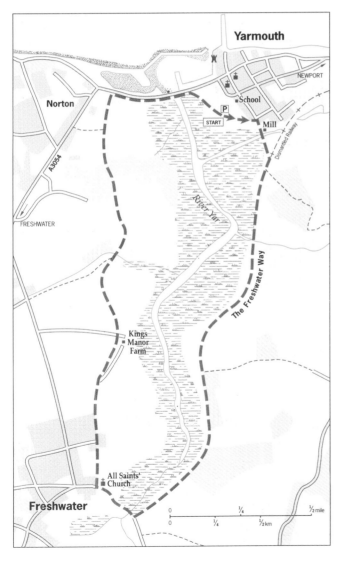

WALK 33
ISLE OF WIGHT
SZ353895

Information

The walk is four miles long
Mostly level ground, but parts can be muddy
A lot of stiles
Pub near the church in Old Freshwater; morning coffee and bar food
Seats along the old railway line and at All Saints' church
Picnic area at the end of the walk, with tables and benches

START
Yarmouth is in West Wight, on the A3054. Start from the large car park just south of the harbour, next to Yarmouth School.

DIRECTIONS
Take the gravelled path from the corner of the car park diagonally opposite the entrance. Walk past the old water mill to join the old railway line, turning right and walking down the side of the estuary for 1½ miles. At the causeway, turn right and walk along the road to All Saints' Church. Take the path between the churchyard and The White Cottage, and follow this path, crossing two stiles. Just before the farmyard, turn left over a double stile and cross the field to another stile and a kissing-gate, with the farm on your right. Walk past the entrance to Kings Manor, over a stile, and along a farm track. This track rises gently and then falls: look for the path on the right signposted 'Yarmouth', and follow this through a field to a stile in the left-hand corner. Walk straight ahead to a narrow path which goes down through woodland to join a roadway.
Turn left and walk to the main road (A3054). Turn right across the Yar Bridge. Immediately after the bridge take the path to the right which leads you back to the car park.

An Ancient Mill
The mill at Yarmouth was built to harness the power of the sea as the tide flowed in and out of the estuary. There has probably been a mill on this site since the time of the Domesday Book. The present mill was built in 1793 and the old sluice gates which controlled the water flowing in from Thorley Brook can still be seen.

A Poet's Family Grave
Alfred Lord Tennyson lived at Freshwater and his wife, Emily, is buried in the churchyard of All Saints' Church, together with other members of their family. The graves are at the eastern edge of this beautiful churchyard.

What to look out for

The estuary is a rich feeding ground for wild birds. Look out for teal, wigeon, grey herons and waders during the winter; terns can be seen during the summer. As well as the birds, there is an abundance of plant life by the water and in the oak woodland. There are wild roses and honeysuckle in the summer, blackberries in the autumn. As you walk over the Yar Bridge, there is a fine view of the harbour and of Yarmouth Castle.

The old tide mill at Yarmouth Harbour

The Duver at St Helens

'Duver' is a local word, meaning a narrow sandy spit, and this walk begins and ends close to the beach. A fairly short walk, it has the added attraction of walking right across a harbour on the broad top of an old mill wall.

Yarrow

Information

The walk is one and a half miles long

One short section of the footpath is narrow and can be muddy – otherwise an easy route

No stiles

Café on the beach, a few yards from the end of the walk

The sand dunes of the Duver are ideal for picnics

START

St Helens is four miles south-east of Ryde. The Duver lies at the eastern end of the village, off the B3330. The walk starts from the National Trust car park.

DIRECTIONS

Leave the car park and turn left along the roadway. On reaching the boatyard walk to the right across the grass and follow the raised gravel path along the edge of the harbour. Turn left across the old mill wall, continue round St Helens Mill and up Mill Road to the right, which climbs between caravans and houses to the village green. Turn right at the Green and follow the road to branch right and enter St Helens Common. The footpath back to The Duver is signposted right. Follow it down between the trees and across the footbridge back to the car park.

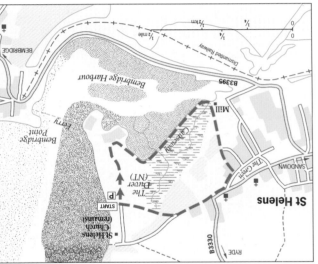

On the Beach

A path leads from the car park directly to the beach, only a few yards away. Steps lead down to the sand-and-pebble beach. Here there is a café for drinks and ices and an enchanting row of beach huts made from converted railway carriages. At the northern end of the beach is all that remains of the old church of St Helens. The tower appears intact from the land, but if you scramble round to the seaward side you will find only a flat brick wall, painted white to be a landmark for ships.

What to look out for

The Duver is a paradise for botanists, and is said to contain nearly one third of the plant species of the whole of the Isle of Wight. In June pink thrift is in bloom, while later in the year, the autumn squill raises slender purple spires. There are many butterflies – look out for the marbled white, the brown argus and the green hairstreak. The short, springy turf is kept neat by the large rabbit population, and benefits low-growing plants such as thyme.

Walking Over the Water

The causeway across the old tide mill. As you walk over it, you can see the mill pools, and the dam, used to control the flow of water for the old tide mill. The harbour here was once a gaps where the tide once flooded in to power the mill.

The harbour at Bembridge borders the early part of the walk

Wilverley Inclosure, The New Forest

This walk follows one of the Forest's lesser-known woodland paths, ending up on an open plain, and is excellent for the whole family.

WALK 35
HAMPSHIRE
SU253006

START
Wilverley Inclosure lies immediately to the east of the A35, six miles south-west of Lyndhurst. The car park is on the eastern edge of the Inclosure, just off the Sway–Burley road.

DIRECTIONS
Go through the Inclosure gates and after about 20yds take the gravel 'drive' to the left, passing a marker post on the right. Shortly reach some recent birch/conifer planting on the left and notice ahead another green and yellow marker post. Fifteen yards before this post, turn right, going up at right angles, then veering slightly left alongside one of the fallen tree trunks. The way may not be very clear at first, but continue uphill, veering slightly right again and out into a glade of beech trees, with larches ahead. Head on through the left side of the glade and turn right onto a track that comes up from the left.
Negotiate two fallen tree trunks before reaching the bottom of the hill. Follow the

The path through Wilverley Inclosure

Information

The walk is two miles long, but can be shortened to one and a half miles or extended to three
Level walking except for one gentle hill
No road walking
No stiles, but there may be fallen tree trunks to cross
From the car park is a short trail for the physically disabled with seats *en route*
Plenty of picnic places
Toilets near Wilverley Plain car park

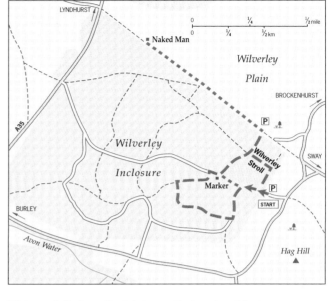

path up again and where it appears to divide at a beech tree, stick to the most obvious path, bearing right through another glade. At a junction, turn right and at the gravel drive turn right again. An information panel here describes the Forestry Commission's conservation practices. Shortly, where another drive joins from the left, note the Victorian Wilverley Inclosure marker. To take the shortest option, continue straight on from here to reach the car park in about 300yds.
To continue to Wilverley

Plain, go left along the joining drive to the edge of the Inclosure and out through the gate.
(To see the 'Naked Man' described below, turn left here and follow the edge of the Inclosure for just over ½ mile. Retrace your steps to the gate.)
To return to the car park go back through the gate and take the first track to the left. Turn right at the T-junction for the few yards back to the car park.

The Ancient Forest
Wilverley's 500 acres were

first enclosed for tree planting in 1775, when naval shipbuilders needed the oak from 60 acres of trees to construct one large warship. Nowadays, the production of timber remains the Forestry Commission's main concern, but some local residents still have ancient 'Commoners' rights'. These include the grazing of animals and the collection of firewood – you may well see stacks of this 'Assignment Fuelwood'.

The Naked Man
The New Forest provided first-rate cover for smugglers bringing their illicit cargo in from the sea, but sometimes they were caught and punishment was harsh. The Naked Man is a tree stump, all that now survives of a tree from which many a smuggler and highwayman was hanged.

What to look out for

This is one of the best places in the New Forest for fungi in the autumn. Keep an eye open too for wood ants' nests, which may be several feet across. There are often wild ponies around the edges of the Inclosure, and buzzards wheel overhead.

The River Hamble

A boat trip is always appealing, and this walk begins with a short ferry ride across the River Hamble. The route then goes round peaceful saltmarshes to the shingle beach on Southampton Water and returns across the common.

START
Approach Warsash from the A27 at Sarisbury, turning down Barnes Lane. On reaching Warsash, turn right into Shore Road at Barclays Bank, following the sign to the Foreshore and Public Hard. Follow the road round, passing a car park, to reach Passage Lane car park.

DIRECTIONS
From the car park take the path beside the toilet block to the river's edge to wait for the ferry (there has been a ferry crossing here for 500 years; exact landing point may vary according to the tide). Note the time of the last return crossing.

At Hamble walk along the foreshore with the river on your right. At the ice cream hut go left across the dinghy park to the road. Carefully follow the one-way system uphill for 50yds to the Green and turn left to walk across the parking area to a path leading into a copse.

Cross a plank bridge and follow the path through the trees to a field. Cut across the corner of the field and go through the trees on another plank bridge to the river's edge.

Continue along the edge of the river and at a junction of paths, go straight on, then round to the right and all the way round the marshy creek to a marina. At the barbed wire fence follow the path to its right, going

WALK 36
HAMPSHIRE
SU489062

Information

The walk is just under two miles from the ferry landing
Very limited road walking
Mostly level and easy going, good in any season, though it can be very muddy in places
Picnic on or near the beach
Pubs and cafés with gardens in Hamble
Toilets in Warsash car park and on Hamble foreshore

through a kissing-gate and straight on. Walk alongside a ditch until the path meets the road.

Cross the road and turn right along the shingle to the anti-aircraft gun. Continue either on or just behind the beach. Before the jetty, look out for a wide gravel track to the right at a small wooden waymarker post. Take this track across the Common to emerge back on the road at a metal, waymarked gate.

Turn left and walk with care on the road. In a few yards a diversion can be made over a boardwalk on the left to a tranquil pond where moorhens scuttle about

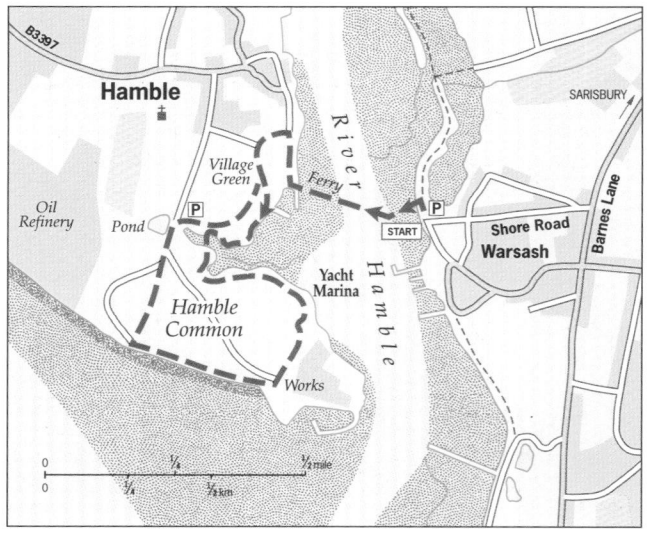

The marina on The Hamble

among the reedmace and water lilies. Back on the road, cross over to a car park. Go through the gate and take the sometimes slightly overgrown path to the right of a BOC liquid oxygen tank.

Just before the river's edge, go left through bushes over a plank bridge and into the field. Keep straight on along its edge and retrace your steps through the trees to the Green and the fore-shore. To explore the village, turn left for about 150yds.

Hamble Common in History
The Common's strategic position at the confluence of the Hamble River and Southampton Water has been exploited over the centuries. An Iron Age earthwork is visible, and in 1544 Henry VIII ordered a fort to be built here, one year before his *Mary Rose* sank in the Solent. The anti-aircraft gun, repositioned on the beach, dates from World War II.

Chilbolton

WALK 37
HAMPSHIRE
SU383389

A lovely walk of a good length that takes in the watermeadows of the Rivers Test and Anton.

DIRECTIONS

START
Chilbolton is east of the A3057, five miles south of Andover. Start from West Down car park at the southern end of the village, just off the A3057.

DIRECTIONS
Cross the road and follow the 'Test Way' ('TW') sign to Totton, along the trackbed of former railway. On reaching the road turn left – take care as this road can be very busy. (For a shorter walk turn right and almost immediately right again. Follow the road to the bridleway signposted right and continue with the route directions at * below.) Having crossed the bridge, turn right along the road to Longstock. Keep on this road (not turning off to Longstock) and continue up the hill. Opposite the drive to Fullerton Manor, turn right and follow the field edge. Continue in a straight line across the field as signposted. On reaching the old railway line trackbed, turn left to a cross-track. Here turn right through a gate. Cross the river and at the end of the path through woodland turn right through a gate. Cross the main road and turn right into the corner of the field. Follow the fence uphill and continue on the bridleway to emerge on to a road. Turn left and after a few yards turn right along the signposted bridleway.

*Continue across two bridges to Chilbolton Common. At the far side of the common turn right, pass the white thatched cottage, go across the playing fields and follow the path to meet the road. Turn left, cross the road and take the path leading across West Down to return to the car park.

Chilbolton Common
This lovely open area, between the villages of Wherwell and Chilbolton, is typical of the watermeadows that used to be a feature of all Hampshire's chalk rivers, and the common is designated a Site of Special Scientific Interest. For centuries the common has been grazed by cattle, and it still is.

Wherwell
A number of legends are attached to the nearby village of Wherwell, but the most famous is that of the cockatrice. The story tells of a duck's egg which hatched into a cockatrice – a sort of cockerel with a serpent's tail. The creature grew to be enormous and devoured villagers, until a reward was offered to anyone who could kill it. A man named Green lowered a shining piece of metal into the monster's den and, thinking its reflection to be an enemy, the creature fought until exhausted. Green was then able to stab the beast to death.

Information

The walk is four miles long, with a shorter alternative

Easy, mainly level walking

No stiles

Dogs must be kept under control, particularly on Chilbolton Common

The Mayfly pub, near the car park, offers food and a pleasant riverside garden

What to look out for

You can see swans and snipe in winter – on Chilbolton Common, where there is a rich variety of wild flowers. Watercress grows at the water's edge. There is evidence of the old railway line on the first part of the walk, which follows the trackbed of the former Andover-Romsey line, known as the 'Sprat and Winkle'.

Crossing the second bridge

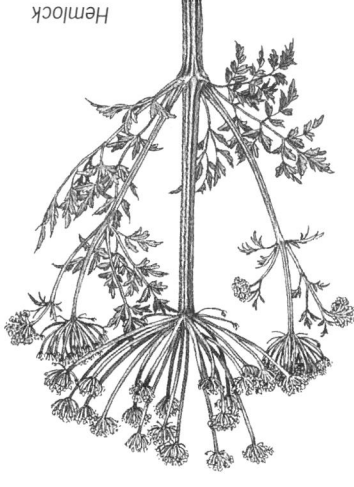
Hemlock

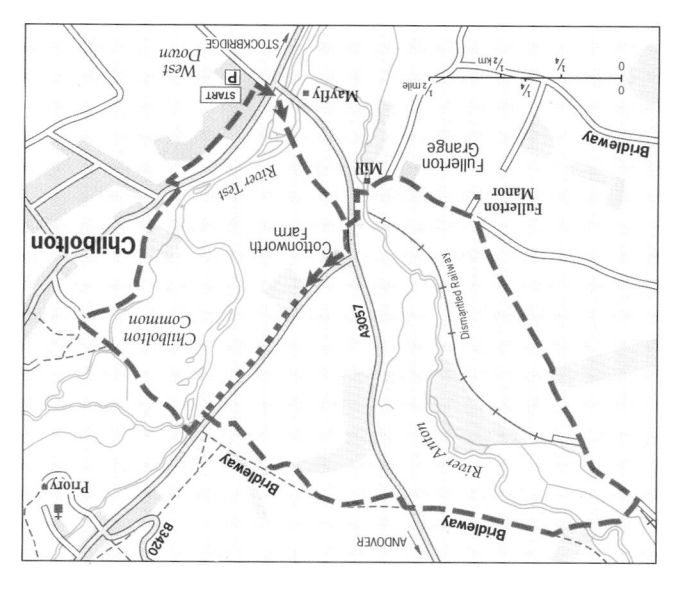

Greywell

WALK 38
HAMPSHIRE
SU722512

This is a very appealing walk with the attractions of water and bridges, castle ruins and a spooky sealed off tunnel which is home to hundreds of bats.

START
Greywell is five miles east of Basingstoke, just south of the A30. Start the walk from Greywell Pumping Station which lies to the east of the village along a minor road leading to North Warnborough and Odiham. There is parking for several cars on the approach road to the Pumping Station, but take care not to obstruct the gates.

DIRECTIONS
Turn left on to the road and take the first track, signed 'Footpath' on the left. Cross the rickety stile by a gate at the end of the path, turn right and keep close to the hedge. The ruins of King John's Castle can be seen over to the left. Cross the stile on to the canal towpath and continue right, to the swing-bridge. Turn left over the canal and

Information

The walk is just under two miles long
Level, easy ground
Virtually no road walking
Several stiles to cross
Pub in Greywell village for bar meals and morning coffee
Grassy area around castle suitable for picnics

continue towards the ford. Immediately before the ford take the footpath to the left, over a stile.

Cross the field and turn right on to the canal path over another stile, passing the ruins of King John's Castle and the remains of a lock before reaching the tunnel. Steps on the right lead down to the tunnel entrance, but take care as they can be slippery and end abruptly at the water. Turn left over the tunnel and follow the path to the road. Cross the stile and turn right on to the road, then turn left, opposite the Fox and Goose public house. Continue through the village and, immediately before the first house on the left, take the footpath (not signposted) across the field. Go over the footbridge, signposted 'Wallace Memorial Reserve, Greywell Moors' then cross another stile. Turn left out of the woodland and continue through the field to the gate opposite the Pumping Station. Be sure to fasten this gate securely.

King John's Castle
A brief history of the castle is displayed on a board by the ruins – all that is left of the triple-storey keep forming part of a small fortress built in about 1207 by King John as a stopping place between Windsor and Winchester.

A Tunnel Full of Bats
Bats are always sure to capture the imagination, and although there is no access to the tunnel and its inhabitants cannot be seen, the very presence of these creatures provides an excellent source of interest on this walk. Just under ½ mile long, the tunnel is the biggest, and one of the

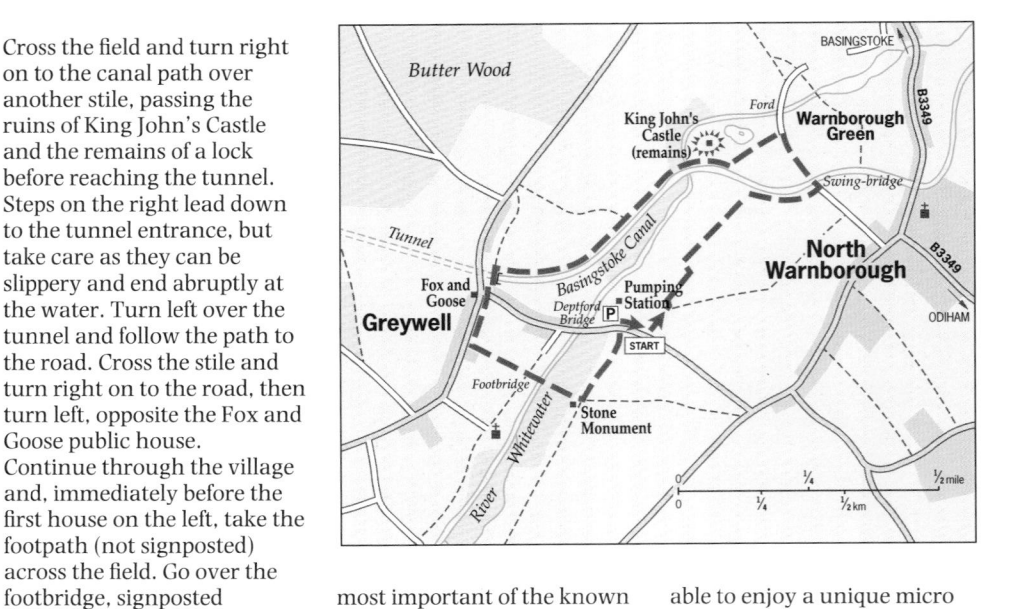

most important of the known bat hibernation sites in Britain, thought to contain up to 2,000 bats of five species during the winter. Due to a spring here which keeps the temperature constant, and the collapse of the tunnel ensuring the colony is undisturbed, the bats are

able to enjoy a unique micro climate. Plans to reopen the tunnel to canal traffic are causing much concern to conservationists.

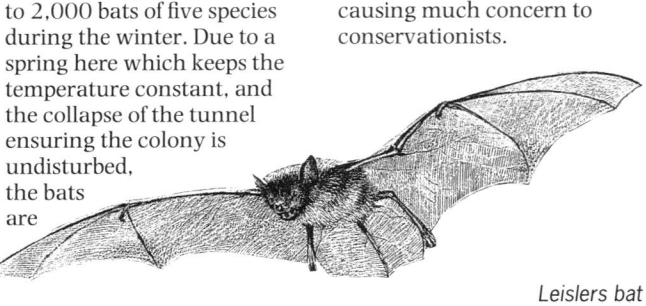

Leislers bat

What to look out for

For over a century the Basingstoke Canal has been famed for its rich plant and animal life and whatever the time of year the most casual observer is sure to spot something of interest here. Among the most easily recognisable creatures are dragonflies: more than a dozen species are found on the canal. Kingfishers, moorhens, dabchicks, coots, swans, water voles, sticklebacks and perch can also be seen.
The profusion and variety of water plants is exceptional.
Along the hedgerows blackberries, sloes and hazelnuts can be found in autumn.

The swing bridge on the River Whitewater at Odiham

Selborne Common and Romany Workshop

WALK 39
HAMPSHIRE
SU742335

The Zig-Zag path up the steep side of Selborne Hill makes an adventurous start and finish to the walk and up on the Common are the trees, flowers, birds and butterflies that Gilbert White wrote about in his *Natural History of Selborne*.

Information

The walk is about two and a quarter miles long
The Zig-Zag is fairly demanding
200 yards of pavement walking
No stiles
Picnic places en route
Pub with children's play area, tea rooms and restaurant in village
Toilets in car park

START
Selborne is about three miles south-east of Alton on the B3006. There is a car park behind the Selborne Arms on the main road through the village.

DIRECTIONS
Follow the path near the entrance to the car park signposted 'Footpath to Zig-Zag and The Hanger'. Go through a kissing-gate and left to start the climb up the Zig-Zag. Pause now and then to admire the view of the village and the surrounding countryside that opens up as you climb; there is a bench between the 18th and 19th bends, and at the top turn left to find another one.

Turn right around the back of the bench on to a track and keep straight on, ignoring another track off to the left. After a while the woods open out and the grassy Common lies to the right of the path. Diagonally opposite there is a pond once used by grazing cattle – to see it, keep on the main path until it veers to the left and is joined by a track from the right. Take this track, heading for a silver birch, behind which lies the pond.

Retrace your steps to the original path and turn right. The trees close in here. At a four-way crossing of paths with a signpost, go left for a few yards to another four-way signpost. Go left again on a wide track, following the sign 'Selborne via Church Path'. Down in the woody area to the right are badger setts.

Eventually the wide track comes to an end beside a beech tree. Take the path to the left of the tree, and turn right shortly afterwards to retrace your steps to the top of the Zig-Zag.
Go back down the Zig-Zag and return to the car park entrance, then cross the lane and meet the main road through the village.
Turn right to walk along the pavement for 100yds to see the unique Romany Folklore Museum and Workshop. Retrace your steps to return to the village centre and the car park.

The view over Selborne village from The Hanger

Romany Folklore Museum and Workshop
Peter Ingram has been restoring and decorating gypsy caravans for over 30 years, and there are always living-wagons in various stages of repair to see. The little museum illustrates traditional Romany life, and the shop sells gypsy crafts as well as lucky charms. The museum is open most days, but to check, tel: 042050 486.

What to look out for

At the top of the Zig-Zag there is a Sarsen or Wishing Stone, placed there by Gilbert White who, with his brother, cut the path in 1753. The flora and fauna of Selborne Hill and Common are especially rich, and it is worth taking field guides with you. The beechwoods harbour wood warblers in spring, and boast a harvest of fungi in autumn.

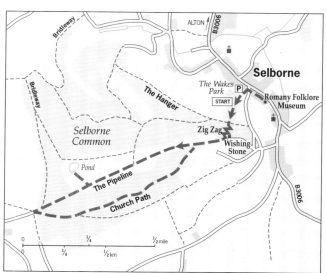

Kingley Vale

Information

The main walk is four and a half miles long
One long, well graded climb on to Bow Hill
All on clear tracks, except half a mile along a quiet country lane
Muddy in places, but generally well drained chalk
Pub with garden in Stoughton village

From a downland vale this walk climbs gently through woodland to one of the finest viewpoints on the Sussex Downs, then down through the ancient yew forest of Kingley Vale.

START

Park at the Forestry Commission car park and picnic area beside a sharp bend in the unclassified road linking Walderton and East Marden, about a mile north-east of Stoughton. Easiest access by car is from the B2146, Chichester-to-South Harting road, about two miles north of Funtington.

DIRECTIONS

Start the walk from the car park through a double gate and along a roughly metalled Forestry Commission track, heading north-east, with woodland to your right. After ¼ mile keep on main track and go round to the right. After another ¼ mile, at a fork where the main track bears left, go straight ahead, still on a roughly metalled track which soon narrows and begins to climb through thick woodland.

At the point where the track comes out into the open, go straight ahead, now with woods to your left and a wide view along the valley towards Stoughton on your right. In about 100yds fork left on a narrower path through mixed woodland and scrub.

After ¼ mile turn right along a gently descending path through scrub. At a T-junction with a wider track, turn left, still through woodland, mainly mixed beech and yew. After a further ½ mile emerge onto Bow Hill, crowned by four prominent Bronze Age barrows.

(To extend the walk down into Kingley Vale, you can pick up the nature trail, marked by green posts, on the other side of the barrows.) The main walk follows the track, passing to the right of the barrows. Go forward between mixed yew and scrub, soon on a broad woodland ride (can be muddy). Where the wood ends, turn right at a T-junction and follow a clear track for almost a mile down to the lane at Stoughton. Turn right through the

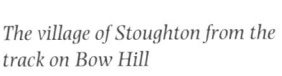
The village of Stoughton from the track on Bow Hill

village, passing the church and the Hare and Hounds pub, both on the left. The car park is now a mile away up the valley. Follow the lane at first, where it bends to the right, go ahead over a stile and beside a hedge on your left. After ½ mile rejoin the lane and turn right for the car park.

Kingley Vale

Kingley Vale is a National Nature Reserve, notable for what has been described as the 'finest yew forest in Europe' with many specimens more than 500 years old. Over 50 species of bird breed within the reserve and, during the spring and summer, a wide variety of wild flowers can be seen, especially in open areas of chalk downland.

Brown hare
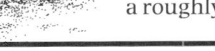

What to look out for

A viewing table on Bow Hill provides a guide to the exceptional views which can be enjoyed from this 676ft summit. To the north, various points on the Downs are clearly identifiable, including Butser Hill and Beacon Hill. To the south there is a wideprospect across Chichester Harbour to the Isle of Wight, with the spire of Chichester cathedral prominent in the foreground. Open areas of ground in the brooding yew forest are rich in downland flowers and butterflies.

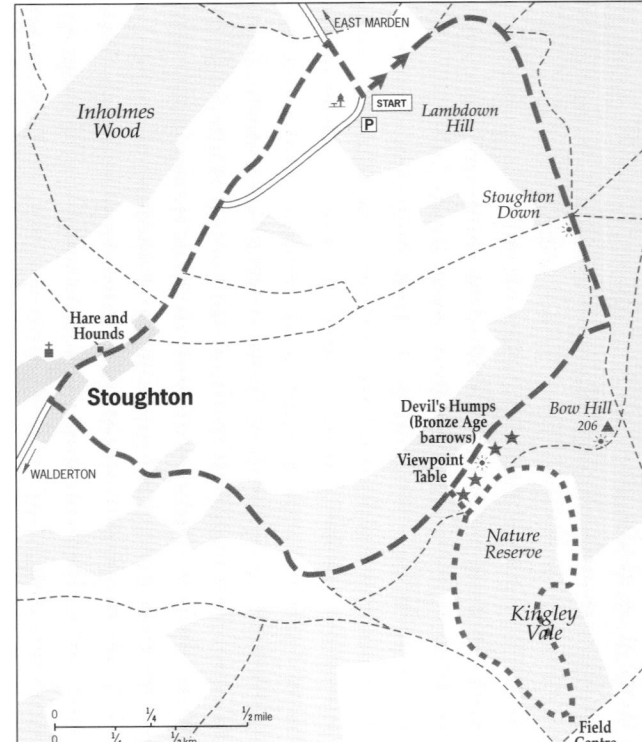

Arundel Park and the River Arun

WALK 41
SUSSEX
TQ018073

This easy walk links several of Arundel's main attractions. Without deviating far from the route you can feed the fish in a trout feeding pond, hire a rowing boat on Swanbourne lake, wander round the wildfowl reserve and round off the day with a visit to the famous castle.

Information

The walk is about three miles long
Level, easy walking
Half a mile of road walking, mostly on good verge
One stile
Dogs are not allowed around lake
Cafés along route; also Black Rabbit pub with garden
Picnic areas in Arundel Park

Arundel Castle stands high above the River Arun

START
Arundel is on the A27 between Worthing and Chichester. Park at the Mill Road car park (charge) if you can't find free parking along the east side of Mill Road between the town and Swanbourne Lake.

DIRECTIONS
From the right side of Mill Road, where there is a wide path beneath an avenue of lime trees, go over a footbridge to the right of the stone road bridge. Stay in Mill Road for just a few yards before forking left onto a signposted path, passing to the right of the castle trout feeding pond. The path continues along the left-hand edge of Swanbourne Lake (from the far end it is possible to extend the walk up into Arundel Park, returning the same way) before doubling back to the right along the other side of the lake. Rejoin Mill Road and turn left, passing the entrance to the Wildfowl and Wetlands Trust reserve on the right. In just under ½ mile, about

60yds before the Black Rabbit pub, turn right over a stile and double back along the river bank, with the perimeter fence of the wildfowl reserve on your right.
Where the river bends away to the left, turn right on a narrower path which brings you back to Mill Road. Turn

left over the footbridge crossed at the beginning of the walk and retrace

your steps to the start point.

Arundel Castle
The castle, seat of the Duke of Norfolk, Earl Marshal of England, occupies a superb situation, set high up amidst spacious parkland overlooking the River Arun. The first castle on the site was built in 1086, probably incorporating an even earlier Saxon fortress. It was dismantled by

Parliamentarian troops in 1651 and what exists today is the result of a series of major restorations carried out over the following 200 years. The final work on the building was completed in 1903, using a style in keeping with the 13th-century original.

Arundel Town
The market town of Arundel occupies a steep slope overlooking the River Arun.

It was once a busy port with a large trade in timber, but the river is now only navigable for small boats. Although the history of the town is closely linked with that of the castle, it has enjoyed an independent existence, being created a borough before the Normal Conquest. As well as its castle and wildfowl reserve, Arundel has an interesting Toy and Military Museum.

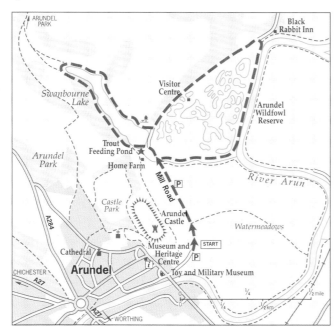

What to look out for

More than a thousand ducks, geese and swans from all over the world live in the 55 acres of pens, lakes and paddocks of the Wildfowl and Wetlands Trust, which is also a sanctuary for many wild birds. Wild diving duck are attracted by the clear pools, while waders come to feed in the watermeadows and man-made 'wader scrape'. Rarities include the shy water rail, which nests among the reed beds – listen for its grunting, squealing call. There are hides overlooking the different habitats as well as a large viewing gallery.

Billingshurst

WALK 42
SUSSEX
TQ086260

This walk follows field paths to visit a restored lock on the Wey and Arun Canal. It is a generally easy walk on level ground, but the paths can become overgrown, and route finding requires some concentration.

Information

The walk is three miles long
Almost all on level ground, though there is some rough ground; also one awkward plank bridge
Lots of stiles
Pubs and cafés at Billingshurst

START

Billingshurst is on the A29, London–Bognor Regis road. A free library car park opposite the National Westminster Bank is signposted to the west of the A29 in the centre of the village.

DIRECTIONS

From the library car park, go along the road to the left of the library. At crossroads go forward into Mill Way, later Arun Road. Between house numbers 46 and 48 turn right, up driveway, bearing left in front of a row of garages. Beyond the last garage, turn left (before stile) and follow path into copse. After about 100yds, where main path continues right into copse, bear left into the field by the signpost. Follow the right-hand field edge, turning left at a four-arm signpost; keep the hedge on your right. After 200yds follow signposts right, and after another 50yds follow sign left along an enclosed field for ½ mile. Turn right beside an overgrown pond and follow the path up between fenced fields. Cross over metalled track and continue forward, then after about 100yds go through a broken gate, bear left and down across rough pasture.

Rowner Lock

After 100yds, cross over a small stream (between two stiles). Turn left over a stile and climb across a meadow heading towards right-hand cottage, go through gate and cross over road. Cross stile ahead and proceed forward along fenced field edge. After about 250yds cross the stile by a shed and continue right, downhill along a bridleway to cross the river Arun over a sluice. Bear left and cross the water meadow to reach the Wey and Arun Canal at Rowner Lock. Retrace your steps from Rowner Lock, over the Arun, back up the bridleway to the shed. Return along field edge to the road.

Turn left and, after 100yds, go right along a track through farm buildings. Continue along the track for about ½ mile, ignore gate into field, continue left around field edge with copse on your left. Turn right on to a signposted footpath with a hedge on your right, and walk up through the buildings at Tedfold, turning left where signposted. Continue forward along public footpath through fields for about ¼ mile towards Billingshurst. At the houses, bear right along a paved alleyway and continue forward crossing over two cul-de-sacs. On reaching a small children's playground bear

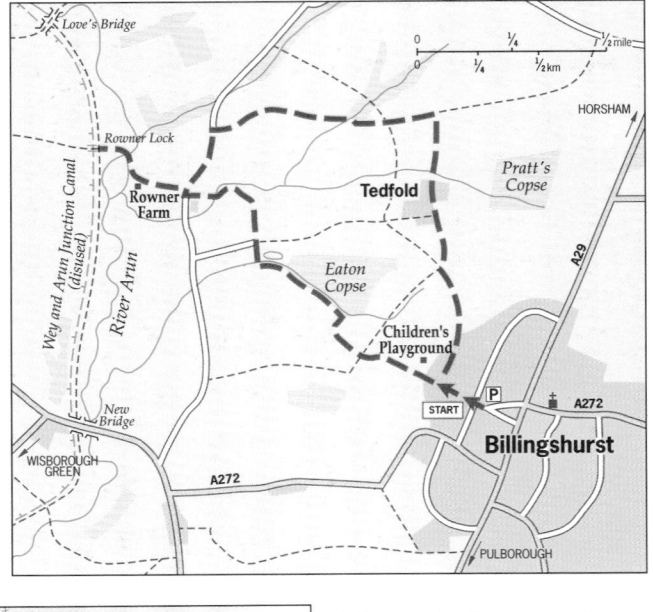

left to rejoin the outward route beside the garages. Retrace your steps to the library car park.

The Wey and Arun Canal

The canal was opened in 1816, but was never a commercial success, struggling on against growing competition from the railways until 1871. A hundred years later, the restoration of Rowner Lock was one of the first major projects undertaken by the Wey and Arun Canal Society, formed with the ultimate aim of re-opening 'London's lost route to the sea' over its entire 23-mile length. This goal is still a long way off, but much work has been completed – within walking distance of Rowner Lock are the reconstructed Northland lift bridge to the south and Love's Bridge to the north.

The pretty village of Billingshurst

What to look out for

The walk passes former paddocks where grass and wild flowers have, at the time of writing, been allowed to grow unchecked, attracting lots of butterflies in summer, including meadow browns, gatekeepers and large skippers. The canal provides a haven for many water plants and insects, with a variety of dragonflies. You should see fish in the shallow water of Rowner Lock.

Barcombe Mills and the River Ouse

WALK 43
SUSSEX
TQ434147

This is an easy stroll along the banks of the Sussex Ouse, with an opportunity to extend the journey further upstream, either on foot or by hiring a rowing boat at the Anchor Inn.

START
Barcombe Mills can be reached along a lane from the A26 about three miles north of Lewes. There is a large signposted grass car park (may not always be open).

DIRECTIONS
From the entrance to the car park, turn right. In a few yards fork right along a drive at 'No entry for vehicles' sign. In 25yds, just before Pikes Bridge, turn right through a squeeze-stile. After 180yds go left over a stile/footbridge and continue forwards along the right bank of the Ouse. After another 300yds go forward over a stile and across a concrete outflow platform by a pumping station, then walk on with the river on your left and the reservoir bank on your right.

After 300yds turn left over the next bridge and bear left along the river bank for 350yds. Cross a stile by a farm gate and go over bridge. Squeeze past gate and turn right into a farm track. In about 50yds turn right between houses, following a footpath sign along a narrow path through trees. After about 100yds go over stile by a pillbox to rejoin the Ouse, now on your right, and keep to the river bank for ¼ mile. Cross over stile by weir and proceed towards the Anchor Inn.

(From here it is possible to extend the walk along the Ouse, either on foot or by rowing boat, to Isfield and beyond.)

Retrace your steps from the Anchor Inn to bridge by which you crossed the river. Do not re-cross the bridge but continue along the farm track with the Ouse on your left at first. The track leads back to Barcombe Mills. At Mill Farm, a few yards beyond a green gate, turn left down a track in between houses.

(At the next junction, a right turn leads to the Angler's Rest pub and the tea room, restaurant and shop at the old Barcombe Mills railway station. Return by the same pathway.)

To complete the walk, keep

Goldeneye

straight ahead past another 'No vehicles' sign. At the gateway to Barcombe House the track crosses, in quick succession, a side stream, the main river, passing the site of the mill, then another stream next to a large trout pool and a weir, before crossing Pikes Bridge to rejoin the outgoing route.

Barcombe Mills
The Domesday Book records a flour mill at Barcombe Mills, but the most recent mill, built in 1870, was burned down just before World War II. Today a grassy mound and two millstones mark the spot. The road past the mill was owned by the miller, who charged one shilling for a carriage and horse, sixpence for two wheels and one horse, one shilling for motor cars and two shillings for steam engines. The sign detailing these charges can still be seen.

What to look out for

The station buildings at Barcombe Mills, although extensively converted, still retain several old railway notices.
On either side of Pikes Bridge, the brick bridge over the old canal, two former locks have been converted to fish ladders to allow sea trout to pass upstream.

Information

The walk is about three miles long
Completely level, easy walking
No road walking
Several stiles and one gate, which may be padlocked
Pub (Anchor Inn) half way round the walk; another at Barcombe Mills Station, where there is also a tea room and restaurant
Picnics discouraged along the river bank

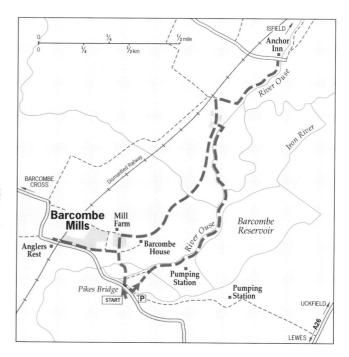

The Anchor Inn on the River Ouse

Ashdown Forest

Through the landscape described by A A Milne in the Winnie-the-Pooh books for children, this walk visits the 'Enchanted Place' described in *The House at Pooh Corner*, climbs gently through Five Hundred Acre Wood, and goes on to 'Pooh Sticks Bridge'.

WALK 44

SUSSEX
TQ471325

Information

The walk is three and a half miles long, with a half-mile optional extension to Pooh Sticks Bridge

Most of the walk crosses Ashdown Forest, much of it on open heathland

Several stiles and a couple of gates

No refreshments but plenty of picnic spots

DIRECTIONS

START

Park in the Wren's Warren forest car park to the west of the B2026 about two and a half miles south of Hartfield.

After about 500yds fork left past some houses to join a lane. Turn left, and shortly, at a road junction, go right. In front of the gateway to Andbell House turn right between staggered rails and along a woodland track.

(To visit Pooh Sticks Bridge, continue along lane past Andbell House turn right and cross a low wooden barrier in the far left corner of the car park, go forward for a few feet and turn right along a wide forest track.

After about 500yds fork left

Cross a low wooden barrier in the far left corner of the car park, go forward for a few feet and turn right along a wide

(To visit Pooh Sticks Bridge, continue along lane past

Andbell House and in a few yards turn right along the public bridleway [very muddy] to the bridge. Return the same way.)

After 200yds along the woodland track, turn left along a small unmarked path. Shortly leave the wood via a wooden gate, and cross a meadow to re-enter woodland in the bottom left corner of the field. Walk through the wood, cross a stile then go ahead along the side of the field to the far corner. Cross stile and go through gate, then walk up a drive with woodland on the left. At junction, go ahead along drive and through farmyard to gate by the B2026. Turn right and after about 100yds cross road by The Tile Barn Cottage. Follow footpath to descend between banks to a stream. Cross over narrow earth bridge and after another 500yds turn sharply right on the

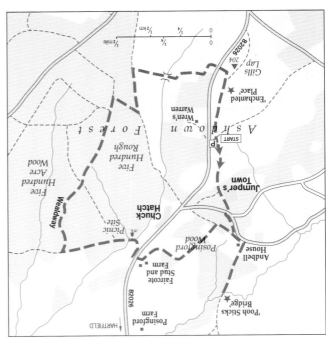

Wealdway, marked by yellow arrows and then wooden posts as it climbs through Five Hundred Acre Wood. Make sure you go through the gateway past a stile. After about ¼ mile, in a grove of beech trees, turn sharply back to the right on a well-worn, descending path. At a T-junction with a forest ride, with buildings of Wren's Warren across the valley ahead, turn left on a ride across open forest.

After another 300yds or so, turn right on a ride which crosses a valley and climbs towards Gill's Lap. Towards the top, bear left with the ride and, after 100yds, turn right along a narrow path out to the road.

Go through the 'Quarry' car park, almost opposite. Leave the car park over a plank bridge in the right corner. Go forward beside the quarry to join another ride. Turn right and descend (to the left of the track is the site of A A Milne's 'Enchanted Place'). Continue downhill to return to the car park.

Ashdown Forest

This is the largest area of unimproved heath and woodland in south-east England, covering over 6,000 acres.

Much of the ancient woodland was felled to provide charcoal for the iron industry in the 16th and 17th centuries, leaving extensive

open areas of gorse and heather with scattered clumps of trees. Timid fallow deer, foxes and badgers thrive here, but are rarely seen by day.

The original Pooh Sticks Bridge in Ashdown Forest

What to look out for

Gorse, heather and bracken predominate on the open heath, with thinly scattered Scots pine and silver birch. Beside the stream in Wren's Warren Bottom you will find mosses, ferns and liverwort. Look out for hovering kestrels, stonechats perched on the gorse, and butterflies, including the silver studded blue, amongst the heather.

White clover

Hastings

WALK 45
SUSSEX
TQ860117

This walk, fairly strenuous but full of variety and interest, lies entirely within the Hastings Country Park, an attractive 580-acre area of undeveloped coastline.

START
The Hastings Country Park lies to the south of the unclassified road linking Ore, east of Hastings, with Fairlight and Fairlight Cove. Park in one of the two main car parks, signposted from the road, near Fairlight church.

DIRECTIONS
From the car park, head for the sea, passing to the left of a row of coastguard cottages.

On nearing the cliff edge, turn right at bollard 14. The path soon descends into Warren Glen, veering inland, with a fine panorama of the low cliffs spread out ahead.
Towards the bottom of the hill, turn left down a flight of steps, and head towards the sea along the floor of the glen. Cross a stream and climb steeply.
At the top of the hill reach bollard 13. For the shorter

Gorse in full flower on the cliffs above Fairlight Cove

Information

The full walk is just over three miles; the shorter version is one and a quarter miles
Several steep climbs and descents, aided by steps; the shorter route eliminates the toughest section
No road walking
A few stiles and a gate
Café behind main car park near Fairlight church
Large grassy picnic area adjacent to seaward car park
Visitor Centre open on weekend afternoons

walk omitting Fairlight Glen, turn right here, along the edge of a wood (directions continue at * below).
For the full walk, go half right, up a flight of steps. At the top, cross an open area, past bollard 12, keeping a fence on your right, and descend more steps. At bollard 11, turn left and walk seawards. (At the bottom of the hill, a path to the left provides a detour, descending steeply through an area of bare, crumbling cliff to a pebbly beach. Return the same way.)
Continue along the coastal path, going straight on at bollard 10. About two thirds of the way up the hill, turn

right at bollard 8, signed to Fairlight Upper Glen. A path winds through woodland, along the side of the glen. At a T-junction with a wide grassy path, turn left and climb steadily. At the head of the glen, just beyond bollard 9, double back to the right, keeping to high ground on the other side of the glen. Back at bollard 11, retrace your earlier route across high ground and down the steps to bollard 13. Here, turn sharp left along the wood edge.
*After almost $\frac{1}{2}$ mile, cross a stile and turn right across pasture at the head of Warren Glen to a second stile near a house. Now cross open, undulating ground, aiming for a wireless mast. On

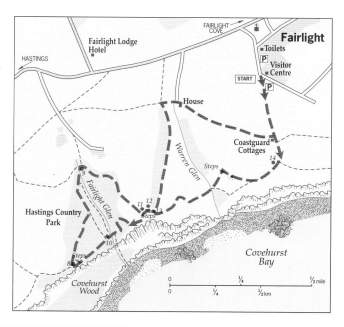

woodland which extends right to the edge of the eroded clay and sandstone cliffs. In the sheltered depths of the glen, the cool and humid atmosphere helps to support a wide variety of ferns and mosses.
The more open slopes of nearby Warren Glen are a mass of bluebells in the spring, and wide tracts of bright yellow gorse are a striking feature in most seasons.

A grassy path on the clifftop

nearing the coastguard cottages passed earlier on the walk, go through a bridle-gate and cross a field to join your outgoing route. Turn left, back to the start.

The Glens
At Fairlight Glen a tiny stream tumbles down the valley through dense, ancient

What to look out for

The Hastings Country Park embraces areas of heath, grassland, seashore and woodland, and provides habitats for a wide variety of wildlife. Butterflies observed here include brimstone, peacock, small tortoiseshell and common blue, and a variety of migrant birds pass through the area in spring and autumn; skylarks and corn buntings are resident.

Rolvenden's Secret Garden

From one of The Weald's prettiest villages, this walk goes through the churchyard to a wood where there is a glimpse of the original walled garden which featured in Frances Hodgson Burnett's *The Secret Garden*.

START

Rolvenden is two miles south-west of Tenterden on the A28. Start the walk from Rolvenden church at the south end of the main street. There is some parking by the lych gate. Avoid the narrow lane by the war memorial.

DIRECTIONS

At the main church door go right along the grass path at the side of the tower and, keeping to the right-hand side of the churchyard, follow a track to a kissing-gate (leave on the latch or sheep may get through). Bear half-left down the line of oaks and climb up to a redundant stile. Keep ahead past three sycamore trees and head towards the stile on the edge of the wood – known as The Wilderness – following a path through the trees. On crossing the old Great Maytham driveway (gate on the left) there is the first glimpse of the walled 'secret garden' on the left. After another view the path runs gently downhill to a stile.

Turn sharp left to cross another stile and proceed along the side of a field. At the far end go over a stile (which has a dog gate) and follow an enclosed path. Beyond another stile, by a pond, continue in the same direction and go through two farm gates to the road at Rolvenden Layne.

Turn left, taking the pavement on the far side, to reach Great Maytham's main entrance. Continue on the road for a few yards to find a stile (with a dog flap) set back in the trees on the left.

Once in the field, pass two holly bushes and touch the field corner on the left. Keep ahead to pass between two tree clumps and join the outward path back to Rolvenden church.

Rolvenden

Rolvenden has a wide main street lined with weather-boarded cottages. Its church was built by monks from Canterbury in around 1220 and has remained largely unchanged since 1480. The village, which has more than once been declared 'the best kept' in Kent, is known for its locally produced Korker sausages, invented in the butcher's shop opposite The Bull. Rolvenden has a small motor museum housing cars which take part in the annual London-to-Brighton Run.

Rolvenden Layne

When fire swept through Rolvenden in 1665 the population moved here to start a second village. Already here was the Tudor house where John Wesley preached in the late 18th century.

Great Maytham

Frances Hodgson Burnett rented this house in 1898 and it was a blocked-up door in the old walled garden that inspired her to write *The Secret Garden*. After her departure in 1907 the mansion was virtually rebuilt to a design by Edwin Lutyens. The garden and its door may be viewed on summer Wednesday and Thursday afternoons.

The church at Rolvenden

The Pond at Worth

With the Garden of England's best soil and some of its warmest weather, the market garden village of Worth remains a peaceful haven. At the entrance to the village is the famous 'Ham Sandwich' signpost.

START
Worth is a mile south of Sandwich off the A258. Start the walk by the pond opposite the church. There is parking in The Street between the Blue Pigeons and the post office.

DIRECTIONS
From the pond walk past the church lych-gate and The Blue Pigeons. Keep on the pavement to pass the post office and reach the 'Ham Sandwich' signpost. Cross the main road at this point and go up the narrow footpath at the side of the driveway opposite. The hedged path runs for 400yds to a junction.
Turn left here, pass Felder Cottage and continue on the track which runs alongside a blackcurrant field. As the blackcurrants give way to apple trees do not swing right into the field with the main track, but keep straight ahead to pass through a gap. The path runs gently downhill to the corner of the orchard.
Turn left onto an enclosed footpath. On reaching a road go directly over and turn left at the side of a driveway on a path marked 'link 6'. The path rises gently and runs between two fields. Continue over the main road on the path by the Upton House lodge.
The footpath follows the side of a field before becoming enclosed and after a double bend enters the churchyard at a kissing-gate. Carry straight on and at a second gate turn left to return to Worth church.

WALK 47
KENT
TR332567

Information

The walk is just under two miles long
Mainly level easy ground
No stiles
Both pubs in Worth have nice gardens, offer bar meals and welcome children
Picnic by village pond

Worth
This is a village of Flemish-style brick cottages. The wood shingle tower on the church has acted for years as a landmark for shipping avoiding the Goodwin Sands. The oldest parts of the church are the Norman pillars on the south side and a Norman archway which can be found through the door on the left in the nave.
The Old Blue Pigeons opposite the church was the original pub; the present day hostelry of the same name now occupies the former rectory next door.
The St Crispin pub dates from 1450 and is said to have been named by veteran soldiers from the Battle of Agincourt, fought on St Crispin's Day in 1415. The village pond

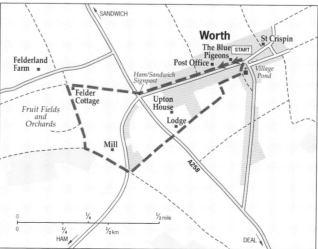

Flemish-style houses at Worth

may be the remains of a sea creek used by Thomas Becket during his escape to France.

Ham & Sandwich
The two places from the famous signpost are Ham, a hamlet dating from at least the 13th century, and Sandwich, a port whose name means 'settlement on sand'. It was necessary for Sandwich to obtain its water from Worth, and the Delf Stream, dug from springs to the north, runs beside the main footpath.

Reculver's Sea Bed Paths

WALK 48
KENT
TQ697224

Information

The walk is three and a half miles long
Level, easy ground
No road walking
No stiles
Pub at Reculver serves bar meals; children are welcome
Grassy area within ruins and by paths suitable for picnics
One café
Interpretation Centre for information

Goat's-beard

What to look out for

The marsh is a resting place for hundreds of migratory birds. Kestrels may be seen, and there are reed and sedge warblers in the reedbeds in summer. Along the shore, terns fish in summer and brent geese arrive from Siberia in autumn. The grazing marshes and fields inland are renowned for sightings of birds of prey in winter, including hen harrier, merlin and rough-legged buzzard. Along the sea wall clovers and other wild flowers attract butterflies, and common lizards bask in the sun.

This is an unusual walk around part of the old sea bed which separated Kent from the Isle of Thanet. The paths, built high above the silted channel, offer very easy walking and afford fine views in all directions – perfect for birdwatching.

START
Reculver is a mile east of Herne Bay, just off the A299 Thanet Way. Start the walk from the King Ethelbert pub. There is parking near the end of the road, opposite the pub.

DIRECTIONS
Turn towards the sea and walk up the path leading to the ruins of Reculver's church. The path runs between the south side of the church and the grassed site of a Roman fort. Where the path runs down into the old shoreline go left towards the present seashore. Follow the sea wall and between crossing a stream and reaching a gate turn right to walk on to a high bank. The bank, known as the Rushborne Sea Wall, turns left round the back of Lobster Farm and runs in a south-easterly direction deep into the old channel. Continue, ignoring any turnings back to the sea. Look out for occasional waymark posts, and later follow the bank as it turns sharply south to reach the railway. Do not cross the tracks, but turn left along the high path running parallel to the line. Stay by the railway until crossing the River Wantsum then immediately turn left down the slope to follow a sea-level track alongside the water flowing towards the sea. The path rises to meet the sea wall at Coldharbour Salt Lagoon. Turn left and follow the wide path back to the ruins of St Mary's Church which can be seen 1½ miles away.

Reculver
Once this was Kent's most north-easterly point – when the Romans built a fort here in AD43 the sea was nearly a mile away, but by the Elizabethan era the headland had been so badly eroded that the sea was only a quarter of a mile from the buildings. By 1809 the cliff was so close that the villagers panicked and moved over a mile inland, building a new church there. The two 12th-century towers at Reculver are the remains of the original church, built as part of a monastery during the 7th century. Constant raids by the Danes eventually forced the monks to flee to Canterbury, but they gave their church to the community. When the villagers too were forced to leave by the encroaching sea, they left the two towers as landmarks for shipping. An annual service is held in the ruins in July.

Wantsum Channel
The Isle of Thanet was once separated from Reculver on the mainland by a tidal channel a third of a mile wide. For centuries most crossings were made to the south where the Roman road ran to the sea opposite Sarre. By 1500 a programme of deliberate drainage, together with natural silting, had prevented shipping from using the channel, which has now shrunk to the River Wantsum drainage dyke.

The twin towers of Reculver's ruined church

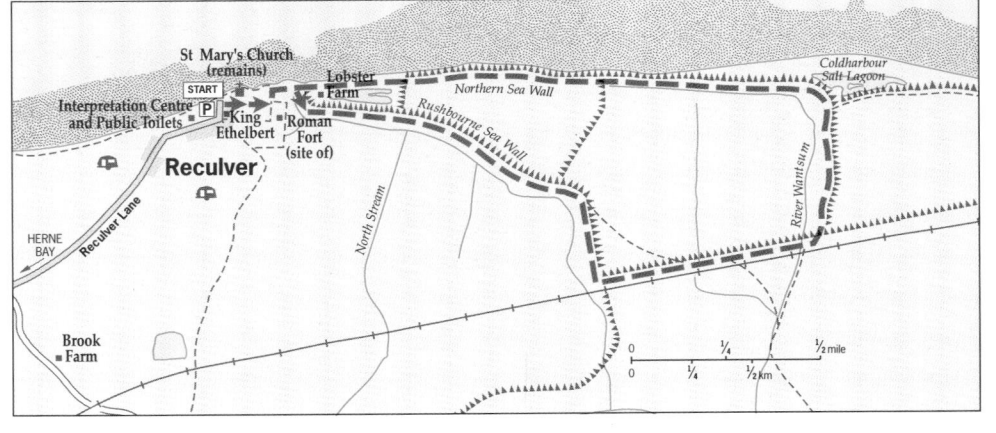

The Medway at East Peckham

WALK 49
KENT
TQ487667

This is a short, pleasant waterside walk that is packed with attractions, including a canal lock, a nature reserve, an island and a unique view of oast houses.

Information

The walk is around two and a half miles long
Level, easy ground
Several stiles
Pubs in East Peckham: The Merryboys does not allow children inside but there is a garden: bar meals and morning coffee served; The Queen Tavern allows children in at Sunday lunch time and has a garden
Grassy area at lock suitable for picnics

START

East Peckham is four miles east of Tonbridge, off the A26. Start the walk from The Merryboys pub in the village centre. There is a car park in the road opposite the pub and behind the Methodist church.

DIRECTIONS

Walk south past the fish and chip shop to the next crossroads by the Queen Tavern. Turn right to follow a farm track leading to a footbridge. Bear half right to reach Sluice Weir Lock on the River Medway. Cross the lock gates and go left to walk over the weir stream on the high concrete bridge.

Turn right along a woodland

footpath which follows a fence. At a stile the path enters the Beltring Hop Farm nature reserve. After a footbridge, the path passes between a lake and a stream before entering a large field. Turn half right to walk parallel to the stream to find a three-arm signpost by a footbridge. Cross the stream and turn immediately right across a second bridge. Follow the path ahead, which turns left past a wood to a point near the far corner of the field. A wooden waymark post indicates the approach to a bridge flanked by stiles leading on to Bullen Island in the Medway. Keep to the right on the island to cross the next bridge, which spans the main navigation channel.

On the mainland the path follows the River Bourne to a stile. Turn left over a footbridge and go immediately right to follow the Bourne upstream. Cross the water again on reaching another footbridge by

In Beltring Hop Farm's nature reserve

Millstream Cottages. Turn right on to a footpath which follows a fence. After a double bend the path, known as the King's Highway, widens to run below two banks. Cross a stile to enter Snoll Hatch and turn right to follow the main street past the former post office and round the corner. A pavement follows the road into the centre of East Peckham.

East Peckham

There is no old church in this village because the community has drifted south to the river, leaving its 14th-century church isolated two miles away. On its present site the village has three pubs surviving from the days when hop pickers from London thronged the area every autumn.

Whitbread Hop Farm

The hop farm, where hops were handpicked until as recently as 1969, has the largest group of Victorian oast houses and galleried barns in the world, now housing two award-winning museums. Of the many events and attractions here, the greatest must be the magnificent shire horses that pull the Lord Mayor of London's golden coach, making the two hour journey to the City each November in their specially built horse box.

King's Highway

The east-west footpath linking Little Mill with Snoll Hatch was part of the original Tonbridge-to-Maidstone main road until replaced by a 'new' road in 1763.

Common rockrose

What to look out for

Kingfishers frequent the River Medway and cuckoos can be heard in spring. On Bullen Island purple loosestrife, thistles and cow parsley grow among the many meadow plants. Along the River Bourne, several species of dragonfly can be found resting among the reeds.

Lullingstone Castle

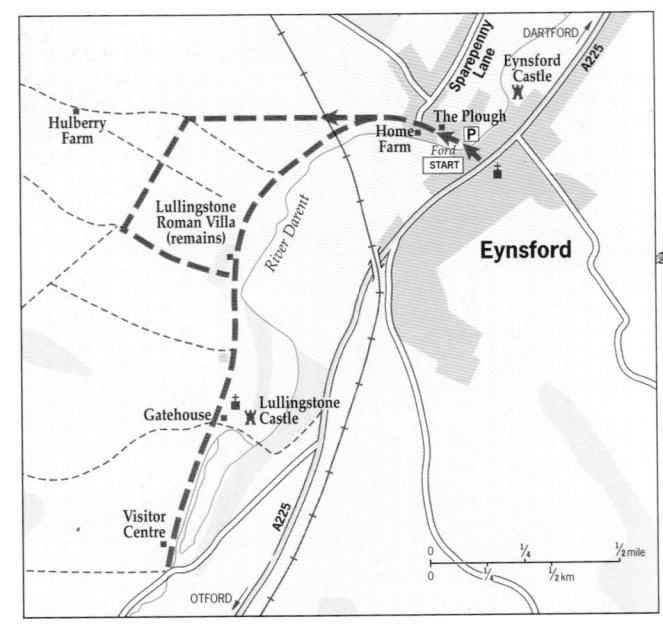

Short-tailed field vole

Artist Samuel Palmer called this area 'the veil of heaven', and historian Arthur Mee described the view down the Darent Valley as 'unique on the map of rural England'.

START
Eynsford is five miles south of Dartford on the A225. Start the walk from the ford, just off the main road, opposite the church. There is a car park at the side of The Plough public house.

DIRECTIONS
From the ford walk past The Plough and Sparepenny Lane, with Home Farm on the left. After the road bends, bear half-right up a slope and go through a gap by a gate. Follow the footpath which rises half-right up the sloping field to cross the railway line.

The path continues in the same direction to a stile near the end of a row of trees marking the line of a metalled farm drive.
Cross over to a second stile and continue half-right to a stile by a grass farm track. Cross the stile opposite, which is slightly higher up, and keep by the fence on the left.
At the far end of the field cross another stile and turn left on to a narrow path which runs down the hill. In the wood there is a stile, then some steps before meeting a metalled lane. Turn right to visit Lullingstone Castle. Beyond the castle gateway a 700yd riverside footpath leads to a visitor centre. Retrace your steps back to Lullingstone Roman Villa and follow the lane, waymarked with a 'D' for the Darent Valley Path, passing under the railway viaduct to return to Eynsford.

Eynsford
The partly Norman church figured in the dispute between Henry II and Thomas à Becket when the archbishop appointed a new priest against the wishes of Sir William de Eynsford. His

Information

The walk is just over two miles long
Several stiles
One unmanned level-crossing
The Plough at Eynsford serves special children's meals in the restaurant; children are also welcome in the bar, and there is a patio
Tea shop in post office
Café and picnic tables at the visitor centre

What to look out for

Home Farm breeds Highland cattle, which until recently were rarely seen outside Scotland, and from the top of the hill there may be the odd sighting of deer. Among the creatures along the river are water voles and damselflies. Birds include swans, kingfishers and herons.

ruined castle (English Heritage), which incorporates Roman materials, can be visited. John Wesley used the narrow 16th-century bridge by the ford as an open-air pulpit.

Lullingstone
Altered extensively in Queen Anne's time, Lullingstone Castle has fine state rooms and beautiful grounds. The 15th-century gate tower was one of the first gatehouses in England to be made entirely of brick. Catherine of Aragon's pomegranate symbol can be found carved on the rood screen inside the little St Botolph's Church, known as 'the church on the lawn'. Visitors may go through the arch and over the lawn to visit the church even when the castle is closed. It was on this grass that the rules of lawn tennis were devised in 1873. The Roman villa dates from the first and second centuries and includes an extensive bath complex. The mosaic floors are exceptionally well preserved. The site is roofed for protection, with additional exhibits in a lighted gallery.

Eynsford from Hulberry Farm

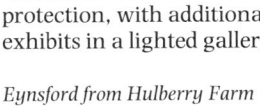

Outwood Mill

Following a pleasant walk through woodland and across Outwood Common, this is a walk that can be muddy underfoot.

START

Outwood is best approached from the A23 south of Reigate, crossing the M23 on a minor road. There is parking on Outwood Common, opposite the windmill, for about ten cars.

DIRECTIONS

Take the path through gate into the woods, passing the cricket ground on the right. At the back of the pavilion, take the path leading diagonally into woods on the left.

In about 250yds, just before the stream at the bottom, bear right, and keep on the right bank of the stream. At junction turn right and almost immediately cross a stream over a plank. Follow the path up to the left for about 100yds to a more substantial bridge and cross the stream again. At the top of the bank turn right. Follow the path for about ⅛ mile, keeping to the left where it forks at the edge of the woods. At the next junction, after about ⅛ mile,

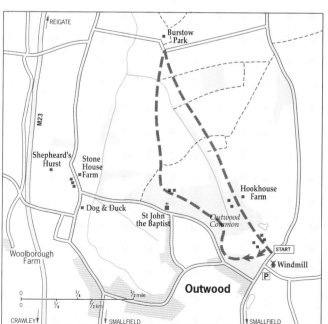

WALK 51
SURREY
TQ327456

Information

The walk is three miles long
Level walking, can be
very muddy
Several stiles – one very high
Pub with a garden just
beyond Outwood Common
No refreshment *en route*

turn right through the wooden barrier. Keep forward, past the cottages on the right. (To visit the parish church of St John the Baptist, turn left by the cottages.)
Continue along track past cottages, maintaining the same direction for approximately ½ mile between field edges, heading towards farm buildings, to a lane. Turn immediately right over a stile on to a public footpath. From now on keep forward in a straight line through fields, over four stiles and across tracks for about a mile, until eventually returning to the common.

Outwood Windmill

This is claimed as England's oldest working post mill. Built in 1665, it originally had a companion which has long since disappeared. The mill is open to visitors on Sunday afternoons (closed in winter); there is also a small museum, a collection of old coaches, a shop and a picnic area on the site.

Outwood Common

Part of the scenic Harewood Estate which belongs to the National Trust, the common is freely available to the public.

Visiting Outwood's 17th-century wooden windmill

What to look out for

Jays inhabit the woods and there are lots of blackberry bushes, providing an autumn feast for many bird species. Listen out for the tapping of the great spotted woodpecker.

Shere

This walk starts from the pretty village of Shere and, combined with a visit to The Old Farm, makes a lovely day out.

DIRECTIONS

There is parking along the lane leading to the church.

START

Shere is just off the A25 east of Guildford. Start the walk from the village church.

Walk to the end of the lane and take the footpath signposted to the right of the church. After 300yds at the gate continue straight ahead across the field to a small gate at the top. Continue along path beside trees, then cross the railway line and keep forward along path, through through bracken and, on

Keep on this path, taking the left along the signposted footpath called 'High Fields', turn left at the end of the path. After a few yards, by a house opposite Burrows Lea Farm. Continue to the road and turn right along a narrow path by a high brick wall. Continue to the road and turn right at the waymark post turn right the next field. At the zig-zag gateway and across

divides at the end of the houses. Continue to a road and carefully cross over onto a narrow path leading into the woods. Keep on this path through the woods, and on

START

the unfenced railway line. Turn right and carefully cross the tracks, take the path ahead. Keep straight on

to a lane, by a row of cottages, bear round to the left notice, emerging by a track by a Thames Water borehole

On reaching a fork, bear left down the path running through a hollow, down to the ford and passing under a fallen tree. Just before the ford and footbridge turn right through a gate, alongside the stream – the Tilling Bourne.

Turn left out of the gate at the end of the field and keep straight ahead to the lane a few yards ahead. Turn right

until reaching a triangle of roads, cross the road ahead and turn right onto the signposted bridleway, keeping on the main path through the woods (ignore paths to right).

and continue right, past another ford, back into the village.

The Old Farm

This working farm behind the church offers demonstrations every weekend in April, May and August. Sheep shearing, spinning, weaving, rope-making, threshing and corn grinding are some of the country crafts on display.

Shere

This is a delightful village well worth exploring. In the Malt House in Shere Lane there is a museum of local bygones dating mainly from Victorian times. The museum is open on five afternoons a week from Easter to September, other times by appointment.

Information

The walk is two and a half miles long

No road walking, but woods are popular with mountain bikers

No stiles

Seating by the church

Pubs and teashops in Shere

No dogs allowed at the Old Farm

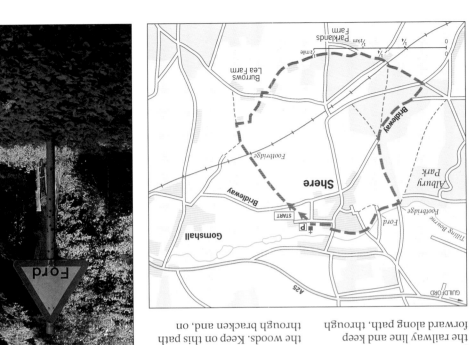

Ford and bridge at Shere

Frimley Green

WALK 53
SURREY
SU891563

From Frimley Lodge Park the walk goes along the canal then through woodland of pine and silver birch on sandy paths.

START

Frimley Green is three and a half miles south of Camberley on the A321. The walk starts from Frimley Lodge Park, next to the church. For the parking area, drive into the park, bear right and follow the signs 'Canal South & Trim Trail'; the parking area is by a miniature railway.

DIRECTIONS

From car park walk a few yards up the track to the canal. Turn right onto towpath and continue for about ⅜ mile to the road bridge. Go up the steps and turn left across the bridge. Opposite Potters pub, turn left along a track and bear right along the signposted bridleway. Almost

Information

The walk is one and a half miles long
Level, easy walking, with one short flight of fairly steep wooden steps
No stiles
Seats along the canal
Dogs prohibited on the play areas in the park
The King's Head pub has a garden and play area
Frimley Lodge Park, at the start of the walk, provides lots of attractions and facilities

The Basingstoke Canal at Frimley Lodge Park

immediately bear left off the main path along a narrow footpath.

Continue through the pine woods at the back of a school, keeping to the left wherever there is a choice. On reaching the marked bridleway turn left and keep left at the next signpost. Remain on this path for about ⅜ mile and eventually emerge onto Windmill Lane.

Continue ahead to the road, turn left and after a few yards cross the narrow bridge over the canal (with care – there is no pavement). A few yards ahead is the King's Head pub. Take the path to the left, immediately after the bridge, leading back down to the canal towpath. Turn right and return along the canal to the car park.

areas, picnic sites with barbecue facilities, a trim trail, a miniature railway (which operates on selected Sunday afternoons), a pitch and putt course and a pavilion with a cafeteria.

The Canal

Built between 1789 and 1794, the Basingstoke Canal was once busy with barges carrying timber for ship- and house-building, grain, malt and other produce from north Hampshire to London, returning with cargoes of coal and manufactured goods. It was formally re-opened in 1991 by HRH The Duke of Kent after a long programme of restoration begun in 1974.

The canal is stocked with fish, and day fishing tickets can be purchased at all local tackle shops. They must be obtained in advance.

Grey squirrel

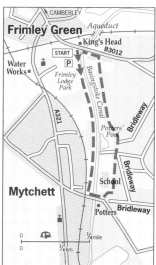

Frimley Lodge Park

Covering nearly 70 acres of meadowland and mature woodland, Frimley Lodge Park includes formal play

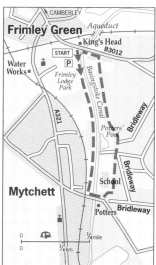

The miniature railway at Frimley Lodge Park

What to look out for

Grey squirrels and woodland birds can be seen among the pine trees throughout the year; fungi, such as the colourful but poisonous fly agaric, abound in autumn. There are pike in the canal, where moorhens can usually be seen.

The River Thames and Hurley

This leisurely riverside walk along the Thames, here replete with a number of islands, is particularly attractive and interesting throughout the year. The great river is alive with river craft and ducks.

Information

The walk is just under two and a half miles long
Level, easy ground
A few stiles
Pub and hotel offering bar food in Hurley
Grassy areas to picnic beside the river

START
Hurley is on the southern bank of the River Thames just west of Cookham, off the A4130. Start from the village car park next to Tithecote Manor, opposite the church.

DIRECTIONS
Turn left out of the car park along footpath past Tithecote Manor heading towards the River Thames, with a red brick wall on your right.

After about 150yds go up and over the bridge over a branch of the River Thames to one of the many islands in this reach, and then turn right to follow the footpath to Hurley Lock.

Pass through both sets of lock gates and forward to bridge. Go over the bridge across the river and left to follow the riverside path beneath the horse chestnut trees along the edge of the meadows for about ¼ mile.

Go through the gate so that the private woodland is on your right and the river on your left. After 50yds, just before bridge, turn right down the path into the wood by the sign 'Private fishing only'. Cross the stile (or squeeze through the gap) and turn right along the track. After about ¼ mile, pass a caravan site on your right, crossing cattle-grids at each end of the site.

At the far end of the caravan site, the track turns sharply to the right. At this point take the footpath on the left, overlooking the backs of houses, to the road into Hurley. Cross the road and go along Shepherds Lane past the cricket ground on the right.

After about ½ mile, at Field House, turn right down the right of way and cross the stile.

Go along the edge of the field to the track. Turn right over the stile along the track, with another caravan park to the left, and continue to road. Cross road and take the footpath opposite, by the old flint and brick wall of Tithecote Manor. Go over a stile and proceed to the car park.

What to look out for

You'll find yourself watching the river traffic at Hurley Lock because of the sheer number and variety of pleasure cruisers on this reach.
There are large horse chestnut trees along the riverside meadows and in the private woodland.
There's plenty of wildlife, including jays in the woodland, and along the river there are Canada geese, mallards, coots and moorhens.
The medieval dovecot in the grounds of Tithecote Manor can be seen from the car park.

Hurley Lock
The locks and weirs of the River Thames work together to make the river safe for navigation, and at the same time help to conserve water by regulating the flow. Hurley Lock is one of the 48 or so to be found on the Thames between Lechlade and Teddington.

Hurley Priory
Edward the Confessor's sister, Editha, is said to have been buried here in a Saxon church. This was rebuilt by the Normans before 1087 when a Benedictine Monastery was founded here. The monastery was suppressed by Henry VIII, the buildings passing to the Lovelace family, and all that remains is part of the cloisters, a fillet of the refectory, two barns and the dovecot.

A quiet stretch of the River Thames at Hurley

The Castle at Donnington

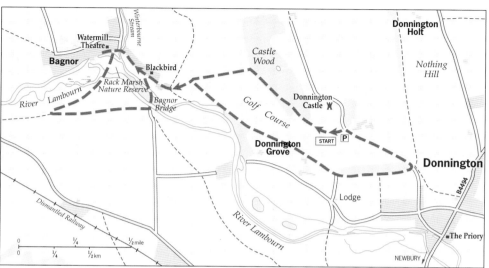

The combination of castle ruins and nature reserve with a clear chalkland river, make this walk interesting and enjoyable for all ages.

START

Donnington is on the outskirts of Newbury just north of the A4. Start the walk at Donnington Castle which is west of the village on a minor road off the B4494 (signposted 'Donnington Castle'). There is a free car park.

DIRECTIONS

Facing the castle on the car park side, turn left and take the path down a slope into Castle Wood. (If you don't wish to visit the castle first, you can leave the car park by the path in the top left-hand corner.)
The path from the castle joins the path from the car park at a wooden gate. Continue through the wood with the golf course to your left until

you reach a stile and gap in the fence. Go through the gap and turn left, watching out for motorised golf carts crossing, and proceed down the path between a hedge and a fence, signed 'Footpath'.
Continue over the meadow, following sign 'Lambourn Valley Way' to the gate. Go through the gate and turn right along a gravel drive into Bagnor.
Continue through Bagnor past the Blackbird pub, ignoring a signed footpath to the right. Turn left along the road signed to the Watermill Theatre. Turn left again along the signposted by-way across the Winterbourne stream into Rack Marsh Nature Reserve. Cross the River Lambourn, go over the stile (it can be really boggy just here) and bear half

Information

The walk is three and a half miles long
Gentle, even ground. The nature reserve can be very boggy
Very little road walking
A few stiles
Pub in Bagnor; Watermill Theatre restaurant in Bagnor serves lunches on weekdays and matinée Saturdays
Grassy area for picnics around the castle
Dogs will need to be on leads through golf course

right away from the river. Cross the stile and follow the path with a new fence on your right.
Where you see two five-bar gates on opposite sides of the path, go through the gate on the left and keep left along the edge of the field. Cross the stile into the next field – this stile is fenced at the bottom and dogs might need lifting over. Continue to the road at Bagnor Bridge.
Turn left back to the 'Blackbird' and retrace your steps along the gravel lane, past the houses, through the gate and across the meadow to the 'Lambourn Valley Way' sign. Turn right, continuing along the edge of the golf course, passing Donnington Grove, a

castellated house, on the right. Continue past a large farm complex on the right and at the end of its walled garden, just before the tarmac drive turns sharp right, turn half left along a path through the trees and proceed to the road. Turn left up the approach road to Donnington Castle to return to the car park.

Donnington Castle

An information board at this ruined castle gives a brief history. During the Civil War Sir John Boys, Governor of the Castle, held it for the Royalists through two sieges. In 1643, after the first battle of Newbury the parliamentary General declared that he would leave no stone of the castle standing unless Sir John surrendered, but Boys continued to stand fast, even when much of the castle was in ruins, and at last the enemy withdrew.

The remains of Donnington Castle

Walbury Hill

Catching the thermals from Gallows Hill

This is an exciting, fairly strenuous walk with plenty of interest – and the views are magnificent! The gibbet on Gallows Hill holds a macabre fascination, while at 974ft Walbury Hill, crowned by its huge hillfort, is the highest chalk hill in Britain.

Information

The walk is three and a half miles long
Generally level ground but with one steep hill to go down and another very steep hill to climb
Very little road walking
No stiles
Plenty of grassy places for picnics
Dogs will need to be on leads

Red-legged partridge

What to look out for

The downs are rich with wildlife, including foxes and deer, partridges and pheasants, and there are usually skylarks winging overhead in great bursts of song. This is chalk downland, and plenty of lime-loving plants grow amongst the short grasses, including wild thyme, marjoram, mignonette, small scabious and harebell. Birds of prey often ride the updraughts on Inkpen Beacon, but the only hanging you will see on Gallows Hill these days is from hang gliders; model aircraft enthusiasts congregate here too. From the top of the ridge (on a clear day) you can look into five counties: Berkshire, Hampshire, Wiltshire, Oxfordshire and Buckinghamshire.

START
Walbury Hill is about five miles south-east of Hungerford, south of the A4 and east of the A338. Start at the car parking area between Walbury Hill and Gallows Down.

DIRECTIONS
Go along the wide flinty track across the top of Walbury Hill, crowned by its large hillfort. Continue along the track until you reach the road then turn right through the gate and go downhill along the bridleway to the left of the field with woodland down on your right. Go through the gate at the bottom of the bridleway and turn right onto the byway between tall bushes. Continue along this track past Lower Farm and the Keeper's Bungalow and onto the metalled road at Combe.

At the T-junction turn right and continue along the road for 500yds before turning left along the track to Wright's Farm. Carry on past the farm buildings, through the gates. Keep to the right-hand edge of the field going up the steep hill, ignoring the stile on the right by the tree.

At the top of the hill stop to admire the view and recover from the climb! Go through the gate and turn right along the edge of the woodland, ignoring the track immediately on your right. Turn right again when you reach the track on the top of Gallows Down. Continue along the track past the gibbet to the starting point.

Combe Gibbet
The siting of the gibbet on the top of Inkpen Beacon – known also as Gallows Down – was to expose those executed there to the gaze of as many as possible, to let them be a mute and awful reminder of justice. It is a grim structure, a very high frame with a crossbar from which two felons could be hung side by side, as in 1678, when a man and woman were hung for a notorious murder. The present frame is not the original, but the latest in a number of replacements over the years, a grim landmark.

Walbury Hillfort
This is the largest Iron Age hillfort in Berkshire, the single bank and ditch which surround it enclosing an area of 82 acres. The main entrance was in the north-west corner, but there was another small one on the south-east side. The fort has not been excavated, but it is thought that the circular depressions inside it may be the relics of hut circles. An obvious choice for defensive purposes, the hill now offers magnificent views.

WALK 57
OXFORDSHIRE
SP293866

The White Horse at Uffington

Information

The walk is about one and three quarter miles long
Easy ground with very gentle hills
One stile to cross
Grassy areas for picnics

This walk has something to interest everyone – the chalk-cut figure of the White Horse, the ramparts of Uffington Castle and the ancient Ridgeway footpath along the hills.

START
The White Horse is just off the B4507, six miles west of Wantage. Start from the large car park on Woolstone Hill.

DIRECTIONS
Go through the gate in the corner of the car park and take the path which bears right and uphill across the field.
Cross over Dragonhill Road to the chalky path opposite, bear left to see the White Horse and look down into the dry valley (the 'Manger') below.
Continue for a few yards before bearing right to the white trig point and Uffington Castle hillfort.
Turn left past the trig point and cross the stile onto the Ridgeway, a long distance footpath. Turn right along the Ridgeway to the point where another track crosses it. Turn right here for the return to the starting point (or continue ahead for about ¾ mile to visit Wayland's Smithy, a Neolithic long barrow; retrace your steps to this point and turn left for the car park).

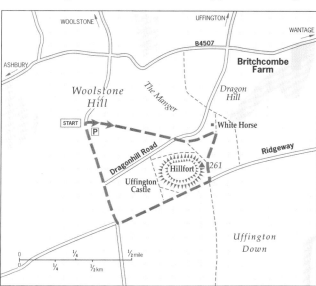

The White Horse
Some say that the White Horse was set up by King Alfred in AD871 to commemorate his victory over the Danes at the Battle of Ashdown, but most scholars believe it to be an emblem of the Iron Age tribe who occupied Uffington Castle. There are many legends connected with the horse. In particular, it was thought lucky to make a wish while standing on its eye, though to protect the figure this practice is no longer allowed.
The horse measures 355ft from nose to tail and 120ft from ear to hoof, and its outline is cut two or three feet into the chalk, the trenches being some 10ft across. In the past the villagers of Uffington came up here every seven

The chalky White Horse is seen most clearly from above

years to 'scour' the horse, ie to weed the trenches. This was done with great festivities, with games and dancing, and the villagers would sing:

> 'The owld White Horse
> wants zettin to rights
> And the squire hev promised
> good cheer
> Zo we'll gee un a scrape to kip
> un in zhape
> And a'll last for many a
> year ...'

The 'Manger' of the White Horse
This is a classic chalkland 'dry' valley (with no river), created during the Ice Age when the subsoil was frozen and the summer melt flowed down the valley as a stream.

The grooves on the left are probably avalanche tracks.

Uffington Castle
Uffington Castle, an Iron Age hillfort crowning Uffington Hill, consists of two banks and an intervening ditch encircling a level grassy expanse of about 8 acres. From the ramparts there is an enchanting view over the Vale of the White Horse, with

its scattered villages and patchwork of fields.

The Ridgeway
The Ridgeway was a trunk route in Prehistoric Britain, running along the dry top of the Downs rather than the marshy and forested vale. It is now a long-distance footpath which stretches from Avebury in Wiltshire to Ivinghoe Beacon in Buckinghamshire.

What to look out for

Chalk-loving downland plants such as wild thyme, marjoram and kidney vetch occur in profusion, and the site is good for butterflies from May onwards. The downland once swarmed with sheep, but their presence is less today.

The River Windrush at Minster Lovell

This walk is in the lovely valley of the River Windrush, with meadows, bridges, the ruins of an old mansion and abundant wildlife.

WALK 58
OXFORDSHIRE
SP324115

Information

The walk is three miles long
Mostly level, even ground, but can be rather muddy
Virtually no roadwalking
A lot of stiles to cross
Pub in Crawley with a children's play area; restaurant in Minster Lovell serves afternoon tea
Picnic places in the meadows
Dogs will need to be on leads

START

Minster Lovell is about two miles west of Witney just off the B4047 between Witney and Burford.
Start from the parking area at the top of the lane to the Hall and church.

DIRECTIONS

Turn right out of the parking area and proceed for about 100yds along the road. Turn right over the stile just past Manor Farm and go across the meadow, bearing left towards the chimney of Crawley Mill. The River Windrush and the ruins of Minster Lovell Hall are on your right.

After 1½ miles, cross the stile and go along the edge of the fields, crossing two more stiles to reach a track. Walk up the tree-lined track for about 600yds, turn right at junction by a house and descend into Crawley. Turn right with care (Lamb Inn on left) and continue along the pavement to cross the River Windrush. Beyond the bridge ignore the first farm gate, cross the road and take the path on your left through the narrow gate opposite the mill complex. Follow the track round to the right for about ¼ mile. Go through the gate and turn right at another gate a few feet ahead, then go up the edge of the field to the road. Cross the road and go over the waymarked stile. Cross the narrow field to the stile and go downhill through the woodland, over stile and through a meadow. Continue forward, crossing two waymarked stiles. After second stile bear right to cross another stile (by a gate) into a meadow. Continue along meadows, with river on right, and eventually cross stile and follow path through pine woods. At end of trees turn right over plank bridge. Cross another stile and head for Minster Lovell Hall, going through the gate to the

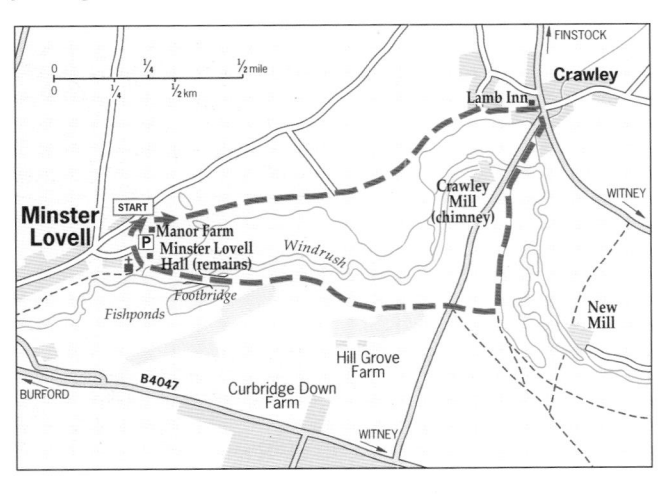

stately ruins. Walk through the grounds, past the church and back to the starting point.

Minster Lovell Hall

This romantic ruin is now managed by English Heritage. It was built in the 15th century by William Lovell on the site of a Priory which had been in his family since the time of King John. William's grandson, Francis, cuts something of a sinister figure in history as confidante and favourite of Richard III. When Richard lost his throne to Henry VII at Bosworth Field, Lovell fled the country, but returned and was last seen at the Battle of Stoke. It is said that he returned to his home and hid in a secret vault, tended by one faithful servant, who alone knew of his whereabouts. She died, taking her secret to the grave and leaving the last of the Lovells walled up alive. In 1708 workmen discovered an underground vault containing the skeleton of a man, sitting at a table. Even as they looked the whole crumbled to dust!

The ruins of the great house of Minster Lovell

Rabbit

What to look out for

Hazelnuts, sloes, elderberries and blackberries growing in the hedge in autumn prove a great attraction for birds and small mammals.
Wet meadow flowers grow in profusion and colourful damselflies can be seen in May and June.

Information

The walk is just over two and a half miles long
Level, easy ground
Very little road walking
Several stiles to cross
Pub in North Newington with children's play area
Grassy areas for picnics along the walk
Dogs will need to be kept on leads

Fox

What to look out for

Wildlife is abundant in this area; brown hares are often seen in the open, while spotted flycatchers prefer the woods. Along the hedgerow listen out for songbirds such as yellowhammers and lesser whitethroats. In the meadow by Park Farm at the start of the walk are defensive earthworks dating from the Civil War. There is also a fine 17th century dovecot.

The Moated Castle at Broughton

This is a gentle walk across parkland, meadow and field, in an area that is richly steeped in Civil War history.

START

Broughton is about two miles south-west of Banbury on the B4035. The start is in North Newington, a short distance north of Broughton. There is plenty of parking in the main street.

DIRECTIONS

Go down Park Lane at the east end of North Newington. Turn along a grassy path with a wall on the right and a fence on the left. Cross the stile and traverse the meadow, then go through the gate, over the road and cross the stile opposite. Head across the middle of the field towards the church spire. Cross the road and turn slightly right to go over the stile. Bear right to head diagonally across the

Broughton Castle's sturdy gatehouse

field, still keeping the spire ahead. Enter the next field via two stiles on either side of a track, proceeding diagonally across this field, heading slightly to the right of the spire. On your left is the Sor Brook lined with pollarded willows.
Go over stile and cross the road to the gatehouse of Broughton Castle. Turn right past the gatehouse and then left over the stone stile into the park, with the moated

castle and church on the left. Walk straight up the hill, past the woodland and cross stile to leave the park. Cross the field to the barn and turn right onto the fieldside track to the road.
Go through the gate and cross the road to the waymarked route. Cross the stile and continue along the edge of the field with the hedge on your right. Go through the wooden gate in the corner of the field and along the edge of the next field. Turn right over the stile and go diagonally downhill, continuing on the track to return to North Newington.

Broughton Castle

For the last 600 years Broughton Castle has been

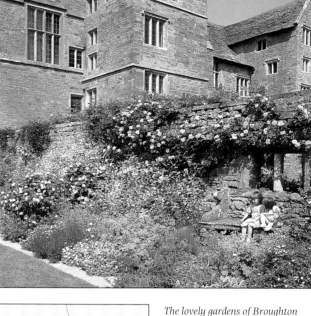

The lovely gardens of Broughton Castle

the home of the Fiennes family. Here, in the tense weeks before the outbreak of the Civil War, eminent Parliamentarians like Hampden and Pym met with William Fiennes, Lord Saye and Sele ('Old Subtlety' to his contemporaries). During that war the castle suffered little damage, and at the Restoration 'Old Subtlety' tactfully installed a painting of Charles II embarking for England, placing above it the inscription (in Latin) 'There is no pleasure in the memory of the past'.
The Castle is open to the public on the afternoons of Bank Holiday Sundays and Mondays (including Easter), on summer Wednesdays and Sundays; Thursdays too in July and August.

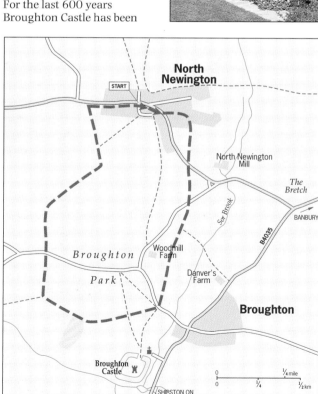

The Railway at Tackley

This is an easy walk with the attraction of three forms of transport – the railway, the canal and the route of a Roman road.

START
Tackley is east of the A4260 to the north of Kidlington. Start from the station – there is room to park along the road here.

DIRECTIONS
Carefully go over the level crossing, then follow the bridleway signed 'Kirtlington' which bears right as it runs parallel to the railway, close by on your right, for about ½ mile to a junction.
(You can make a worthwhile detour to view the River Cherwell and the Oxford Canal. To do this, turn left and then right and follow the path over the river and the weir to Pigeon's Lock. Retrace your steps to rejoin

Information

The walk is two and a quarter miles long
Level, easy walking
One stile to cross
Very little road walking
Pub in Tackley
Grassy areas for picnics

the main walk).
The main route turns right, with a glimpse of the River Cherwell through the trees on your left. Continue under the railway bridge and then turn right over the stile signed 'Oxfordshire Way Footpath'. Cross the field with the railway now on your right, then bear left and cross the stile by the little footbridge under the willows. This is on the line of Roman Akeman Street.
Turn left over the footbridge and then right through the meadow, following the path to the left round the edge of the field.
Turn right through the gap and follow the path along the field edge. At the boundary go through the gates and across the track into a meadow with the mellow stone buildings of Court Farm on your left. Go through the gate onto the road and turn right into Tackley. Bear right at the green and continue

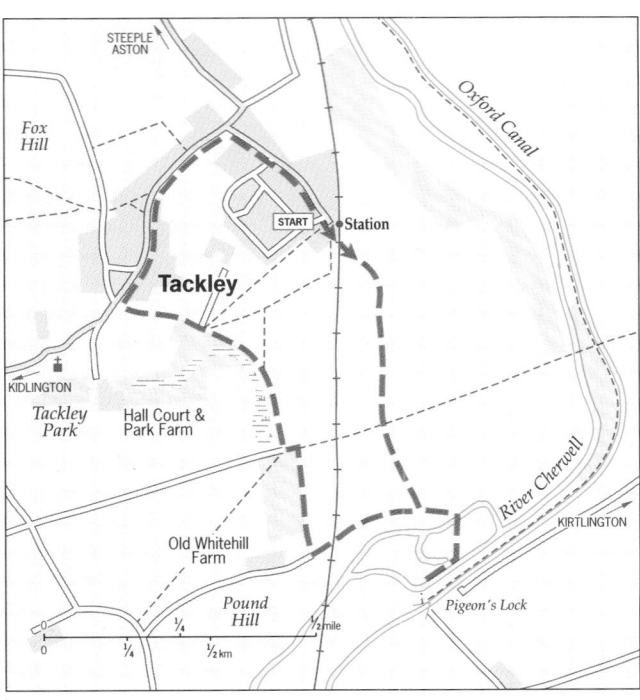

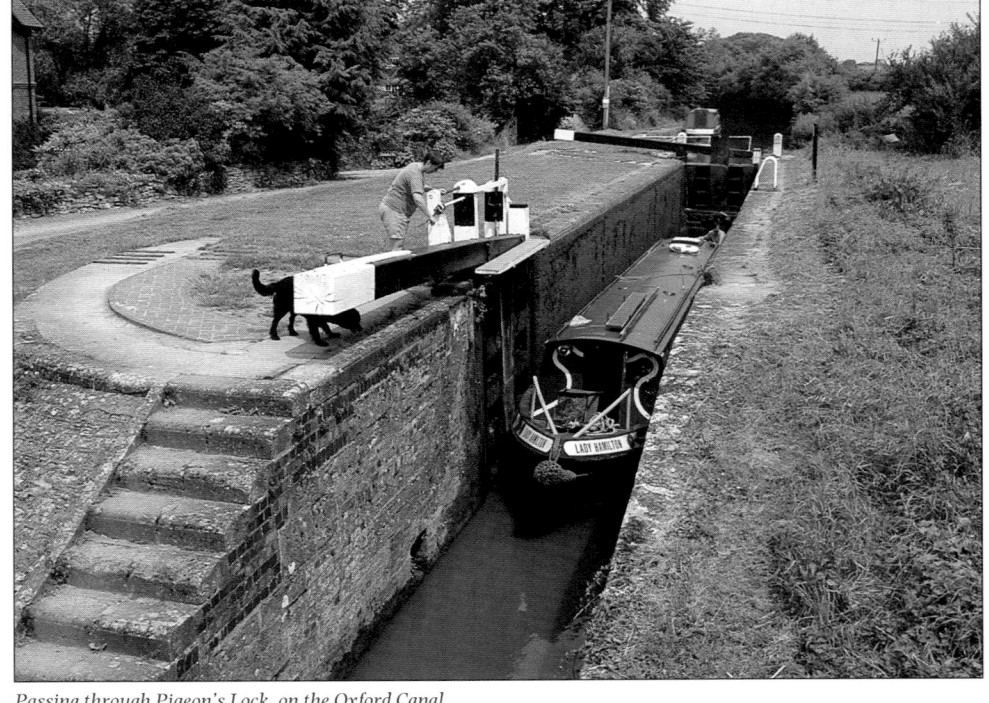

Passing through Pigeon's Lock, on the Oxford Canal

through the village to Nethercote Road (signed 'Station'). Turn right here to return to the starting point.

The Railway
The Oxford to Birmingham line was built by the Great Western Railway Company in 1850 to the 7ft broad gauge, later converted to the standard 4ft 8½ins. You can still see how far apart the two lines are, and how, over 140 years later, the line is still very busy.

Roman Akeman Street
Akeman Street is the name given to the Roman road which runs from east to west through the south Midlands to Cirencester and Bath. This road crossed the River Cherwell from Kidlington, and the walk directions locate the line of it. When you reach this point, look west and you will clearly see the raised bank on which the road ran.

The Oxford Canal
Opened on New Year's Day 1790, the Oxford Canal was built on a parallel line with the River Cherwell and the two waterways still share this pleasant valley.

What to look out for

The old gateway near Court Farm is dated 1620 and is ornamented with shields. A similar gateway, dated 1615, faces the road. This used to stand at the entrance to the demolished manor house. There is also a large 17th-century dovecot.
The River Cherwell and the Oxford Canal, with their rich vegetation of reeds and rushes, are a haven for wildlife, including ducks, herons and other waterbirds.

The Thame Valley at Cuddington

With bridges over the River Thame, abundant wildlife and historical interest, this pleasant walk has universal appeal.

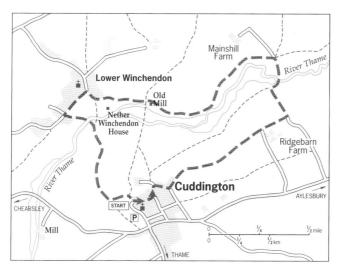

WALK 61
BUCKINGHAMSHIRE
SP737112

Information

The walk is three and a half miles long
Level, easy ground
Several stiles to cross
Very little roadwalking
Pub in Cuddington
Grassy meadows suitable for picnics

START
Cuddington is just off the A418 between Thame and Aylesbury. The start is near the church, where there is room to park.

DIRECTIONS
Turn right behind the church and walk down the street past Tibby's Lane and turn right into Frog Lane. Turn left down the bridleway at the junction of Frog Lane and Spicketts Lane. Follow this green lane for ½ mile, passing Ridgebarn Farm on the right. Where the lane turns right, cross the waymarked stile on the left. Follow the side of the meadow and turn right in the corner of the field to the old pollarded aspen (don't cross the stile). Turn left here to cross over the River Thame. Continue straight ahead with a line of pollarded willows on your right. Cross over the stile and turn left over the next stile. Continue along the edge of the meadow and at the second stile head diagonally across the meadow to a track with an overgrown enclosure on the left.
Bear left with the track and cross the stile. Turn right to follow the waymarked route across the water meadow to the Old Mill at Nether (or Lower) Winchendon. Bear round to the right and cross the stile by the barn. Turn left along the track into the village passing, on your left, a wild boar enclosure and Nether Winchendon House. At the junction by the church turn left, and in 300yds, opposite the telephone box, turn left again onto the footpath past 'Langlands'. Cross the wooden slat bridge over the River Thame and continue up the causeway. Turn left along the grassy path with bungalows and a duck pond on your right. Turn right to go up Tibby's Lane into Cuddington.

Lettice Knollys and Nether Winchendon House
The 16th-century manor house in Nether Winchendon, with its glorious twisted brick chimneys and great gateway, was the birthplace of Lettice Knollys, friend of Elizabeth I. She was married three times, first to the Earl of Essex, then to Elizabeth's favourite, the Earl of Leicester, and lastly to Sir Christopher Blount. Lettice lived to the enormous age of 95, and at 92 could 'yet walk a mile in the morning'.

Wild Boar
Wild boar are bred at Nether Winchendon. These animals became extinct in England during the 17th century, the last record of them in the wild being in 1683. Boars are larger than domestic pigs and are brownish-black in colour. The young are brownish yellow with dark stripes. They are forest animals and in olden times the hunting of them was deemed a lordly sport.

What to look out for

There are large numbers of pollarded willows in the meadows by the river, and this ancient form of woodcraft still provides local farmers with stakes and posts. In the hedges are hazelnuts, blackberries, sloes and elderberries, while reeds, rushes and marsh marigolds line the fast-flowing river. There is a small area of wilderness where such plants as brambles and hogweed grow amid hawthorn, ash and horse chestnut trees, providing varied habitats for the rich wildlife. Look out for lesser spotted woodpeckers, willow warblers, moorhens and herons as well as rabbits and kestrels. There is an early (1772) single-handed clock in the tower of Nether Winchendon church. Inside the church its loud ticking and the swinging of the 14ft pendulum and 60lb bob give an eerie sense of the passing of time.

The lovely old 13th-century church at Cuddington

The Ouse Meadows at Olney

WALK 62
BUCKINGHAMSHIRE
SP886504

Information

The walk is three and a half
miles long
Level ground with one
small slope
Several stiles to cross
Very little roadwalking
Pubs in Clifton Reynes
and Olney
Grassy areas for picnics
beside the River Great Ouse

A combination of riverside stroll and pastoral ramble, this lovely walk has lots of interesting features along the way.

START
Olney is on the A509 eleven miles north of Milton Keynes. Start from the layby on the A509 south of Olney, with Emberton Country Park on your left.

DIRECTIONS
Cross the A509 and go over a stile to the footpath. Turn right over a white stile and plank bridge and turn left along the edge of the field. Cross stile and follow the path straight across the next field, aiming to the right of the large willow. Go through the gap in the hedge and cross this field, which has a plank bridge in the middle. At the waymarked stile/bridge, cross into the meadow beside the River Great Ouse.
Bear slightly to your left aiming for the clump of trees on the river bend. Leave the trees on your left and go up the slope to the track. Turn left and continue, going through a gate and past a line of bushes. Bear right beneath the horse chestnut trees and cross the stile. Go straight over the field and cross the next stile, then cross two more fields to reach the road. Turn left into Clifton Reynes.
Turn left through the village and bear left at the church, where the road becomes a track. Turn right through the gate and go diagonally across the field. Cross the stile and bear right down the grassy slope to the river, crossing by the footbridge. Cross the meadow and another footbridge, heading straight for Olney church, with the river on the left. Go through the gate past the former mill house and bear round to the right, then through the gate to the church. Turn left through the churchyard to the main street in Olney.
Cross the road and turn left.

Water rail

Either return directly to your car or turn right for a detour through Emberton Country Park.

William Cowper
The town of Olney is inextricably linked with the 18th-century poet, William Cowper, who lived here for 19 years – the happiest in his sadly troubled life. His home is now a museum (open from Tuesday to Saturday and Bank Holiday Mondays). Cowper knew and loved this Buckinghamshire landscape well, and it featurs often in his writing.
Cowper frequently walked from Olney to Clifton Reynes to visit Lady Austen – who inspired him to write much of his best poetry – and stayed in Clifton Reynes with the rector and his wife.

The lofty spire of Olney church is a landmark for miles around

What to look out for

There is a rich wildlife in the watermeadows beside the Great Ouse and within the Emberton Country Park. Attractively landscaped from old gravel workings, the park consists of a series of lakes, frequented by migratory waders and wildfowl.
Olney Church has a large and impressive medieval tower with a 180ft spire, unusually lofty for Buckinghamshire.
On Shrove Tuesday the famous Olney Pancake Race is run, and has been every year since 1445 (except for a break during World War II), when a local woman apparently hurried to church still clutching her frying pan. The race starts at The Bull on the Market Square, pancakes being cooked at 11.30am with the tossing starting at 11.45am.
Participation in the race is limited to Olney residents, but of course anyone can go and watch.

Burnham's Magnificent Beeches

Here is a woodland walk with a difference – and one that cannot fail to impress. Woodland, dells, clearings, ponds and pathways seem designed to entrance and captivate.

WALK 63
BUCKINGHAMSHIRE
SU957851

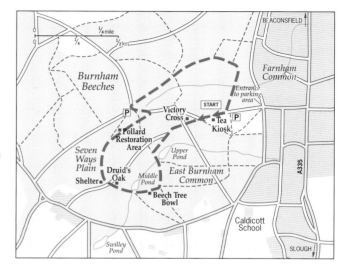

Autumn in Burnham Beeches

On reaching the road, turn left for about 250yds then right, opposite a parking area, along the path marked by a barrier in the bottom of the hollow.

Where five paths meet go half right ahead. Follow the path till it forks at the summit of a short, steep incline, then bear left. The main path bears to the right where another path crosses diagonally. Keep to the main path and after about 100yds turn right and descend to the stream 100yds ahead. Cross the stream and carry on back up to the road 50yds ahead and East Burnham Common.

Burnham Beeches

This lovely area of mixed beech wood was purchased by the Corporation of the City of London in 1880. Still owned and managed by that body, it is a permanent public open space, and an official guide can be bought at The Glade café.

Pollarded Beech and Oak Trees

The ancient craft of pollarding involves periodically lopping trees at between eight and 12ft above the ground so that they provide successive crops of new wood on an established trunk. It also increases the lifespan of the tree by slowing down the rate of growth, and the average age of the ancient pollards of Burnham is 350 years. With about 700 of them, this is the largest stand of such trees in the world.

Sadly, since pollarding ceased in the 1820s the trees are now ageing rapidly, but Burnham Beeches has several 'Ancient Pollard Restoration' sites, where old trees have been pollarded anew in an effort to save them.

Information

The walk is two miles long
Level, easy walking with a few gentle slopes and just one short section that is a bit steeper
No stiles
Ice cream on sale at East Burnham Common
Café at East Burnham Common
Plenty of places to picnic

What to look out for

The 450-year-old Druid's Oak is the largest oak tree growing here, with a circumference of 30ft!
Upper Pond and Middle Pond were created artificially in 1800. Now naturalised with reeds and water lilies, they offer a home to wildlife including dragonflies, moorhens and mallards.
Seven Ways Plain is the site of an Iron-Age fort, possibly associated with the 7th-century British chieftain, Caedwalla. Today its banks and ditches are not easily distinguished.
Among the birds that frequent the beeches look out for nuthatches, great spotted woodpeckers and treecreepers – and in summer you might be lucky enough to hear a nightingale.

START

Burnham Beeches is just north of Slough by Farnham Common, off the A355. Start at East Burnham Common car park. There is plenty of room to park. Note: East Burnham Common is not near East Burnham village.

DIRECTIONS

Turn left from the car park and walk up the road to the crossroads signed 'Victory Cross'. Continue straight on.

After 150yds turn down the first path on your left to Upper Pond.
Go over the dam to the right of the pond and carry on up the path beneath the pine trees. After 50yds turn right along a small path into the pine trees (just before a fork in the main path) and right again at the next well-defined crossroads of paths. After about 150yds pass an enormous old beech bowl and reach Middle Pond.

Cross the dam with the pond on your right and bear left. After 150yds reach a clearing and keep on the main path. The 'Druid's Oak' is on your right.
Cross the road by the shelter and in 20yds, where the paths join, bear right to cross 'Seven Ways Plain'. After 200yds bear right at a junction of three paths, and continue for about ½ mile through an Ancient Pollard Restoration Area.

Berkhamsted Common

A varied and interesting walk, with the attractions of thickly wooded Berkhamsted Common, and the grassy earthworks of an ancient castle to explore.

START

Berkhamsted is on the A41, four miles north-west of Hemel Hempstead. Start from Berkhamsted Castle. There is room to park beside the railway or in the station car park.

Information

The walk is three and a quarter miles long
There are a couple of gentle hills
Some road walking on pavements
Several stiles to cross
Grassy places for picnics
Dogs should be kept on leads

DIRECTIONS

Walk up Brownlow Road with the castle on your right. Cross the road where it curves to the right and go up Castle Hill. Follow the public footpath by Berkhamsted Cricket Club. Continue along the grassy path between the fields in the bottom of the valley, crossing over four stiles. At the fifth stile cross a muddy track with Well Farm on your right, and continue up the valley towards the woods of Berkhamsted Common. Cross the stile by the gate and go straight up the path to the woods.

Go into the woods over the stile, following the path uphill between the trees and the belt of bracken and silver birch, to the top of the slope. Turn left onto the wide path

The verdant countryside of Berkhamsted Common

which crosses the path you are on, and immediately turn left again where the main path veers round to the right.

After about 50yds take the left-hand fork in the path and continue for about ¼ mile to a large oak tree. Brickkiln Cottage will be visible on your right. At the oak turn left to the stile at the wood's edge. Cross this stile and go down the edge of the field, over the next stile and up the side of the next field.

At the boundary cross another stile and continue along the field's edge past a small pond guarded by a stag-headed oak. Go through the gap and along the edge of the field, cross the stile by the gate and turn left into the hummocky meadow.

Go round the edge of the meadow, following footpath signs, to Castle Hill Farm and turn left down the track through the gate. Cross the road and bear left along the grassy footpath downhill. Continue along the pavement to the road junction. Turn left here and then right, back to the starting point.

Berkhamsted Castle

Not much remains to be seen of this Norman fortress which William the Conqueror gave to his half-brother. It has been

The ruined foundation walls of Berkhamsted Castle

a ruin since Elizabethan times, when its stones were taken away up the hill to build Berkhamsted Place – now, too, demolished. Yet it was here that William received the submission of the Saxon nobles, following his famous victory at Hastings.

The castle's most illustrious owner was undoubtedly the Black Prince, eldest son of Edward III.

In 1838 a large section of the outer defences had to be demolished to make way for the railway.

Berkhamsted Common

During the Middle Ages this was a common wood used for grazing, and most of it was included in the great park of Berkhamsted Castle. Today much of the area is National Trust property.

What to look out for

Berkhamsted Common is a refuge for wildlife. Look out, in particular, for grey squirrels, and fallow and muntjac deer. The edible dormouse is found here, one of only a very few sites in Britain. In autumn you can find a lot of interesting fungi, both the bracket types such as oyster mushrooms growing on the trees, and species which grow on the woodland floor.

The River Rib at Standon

This is a gentle, enjoyable walk, with plenty to see and do.

Information

The walk is two and a
quarter miles long
The ground is mostly level
and even
Virtually no roadwalking
One stile to cross
Pubs in Standon
Grassy areas for picnics
by the river and on
the village green

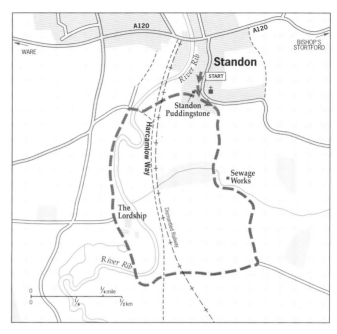

START

Standon is on the A120 about a mile to the east of the A10, six miles north of Ware and six miles west of Bishop's Stortford. Park in, and start from the High Street, which is south of the A120.

DIRECTIONS

Walk south down the High Street passing the church on your left, then bear left with the 'Standon Puddingstone' on your right. Keep forward and shortly turn right along the concrete road. When this turns to the left, go straight on along the grass track over the stream and through the belt of oak and ash trees.
On reaching the field turn left and continue around it, turning right at the corner, with the hedge always on your left. At the end of the field go through the gap onto the grassy track and turn right along it. At the next field boundary cross the old railway line. Continue, crossing the Harcamlow Way (not signed), to bear right and reach a stone bridge over the River Rib. Cross the river and go through the gate. Carry straight on along the little causeway over the meadow to join the track. Go through the gate, passing a large house, 'The Lordship', on your right and cross the track to a stile. Go over the stile and keep

straight on through the meadows, with the river on your right. Go through the gate to the road and turn right to cross the river by the footbridge beside the ford. Continue past the old paper mill and straight on back to Standon.

'The Lordship'

This house in the peaceful river valley was the home of Sir Ralph Sadleir, gaoler of Mary, Queen of Scots, at Wingfield and Tutbury. The present house is but a fillet of the splendid mansion

The former paper mill at Standon

What to look out for

The old railway line, now almost unrecognisable, used to run north to Buntingford. The line opened in 1863 and closed in 1965.
The former paper mill, by the ford, was steam powered and worked turning rags into paper between 1713 and 1855.
The Standon Puddingstone, formerly in the church wall, is a lump of natural stone formed of many tiny flint pebbles from a river of long ago, cemented together with a natural cement.
Wildlife is abundant. Look out for grey herons by the river, as well as goldfinches, rabbits, water voles and kestrels.

of Sir Ralph's day, which was said to rival Hatfield House itself, both in splendour and in hospitality. Queen Elizabeth I stayed here on two of her famous 'Progresses' and James I, on his way to London and his new throne, stayed here with Sir Thomas, Sir Ralph's son, in 1603.

The First 'Flying Man'

In 1784 an Italian, Vincenze Lunardi, arrived in Standon by balloon, completing the first successful balloon flight in England. Setting out from Moorlands, some 30 miles away, Lunardi had completed this remarkable journey in just two hours.

Ampthill Park and Woodlands

This is a scenic walk with spectacular views over open countryside. It includes wide open grassland, water and woodland areas and is adjacent to the attractive small town of Ampthill which has an interesting Georgian centre and lots of antique shops.

START

Ampthill is seven miles south of Bedford and just north of junction 12 of the M1. Start from St Andrew's Church on the road to Maulden. There is ample parking in the town.

DIRECTIONS

Follow the clearly marked footpath to the left of the church down Rectory Lane into Holly Walk. Keep left along the edge of the graveyard and follow the yellow signposts for the Greensands Ridge Walk, through the holly tunnel and over Church Hill until you meet the road (can sometimes be busy). Cross over and go through the kissing-gate to the right. Follow the path into the woods and take the right-hand path down a sunken tree-lined avenue to Ampthill Park House. The path here can be muddy. Keep to the track by the western edge of the house, and at the far corner go over a stile onto the footpath running south-west past Park Farm and up the hill. Cross the stile into the park and keep forward past the reservoir (on the left) and up on to the ridge. At the top, turn left. On the right-hand side of this path is Katherine's Cross. Keep following the central path, going eastwards towards the lodge, skirting the left-hand side of the lodge. Continue through the kissing-gate and alongside some allotments before coming out on to Park Hill. Go down Chapel Lane to return to the town.

Ampthill Castle and Katherine's Cross

Ampthill Park is the site of old Ampthill Castle, where Henry VIII imprisoned Katherine of

Blackberry

Aragon for some years during and after the trial and subsequent divorce. This site is now marked by Katherine's Cross, carved with rather sad verses. It also offers panoramic views over the Bedfordshire countryside, and well-placed seats and picnic tables enjoy the same views. The parkland is the remnants of an ancient deer park which once surrounded the castle and was landscaped by 'Capability' Brown in the 18th-century.

What to look out for

The walk starts along the appropriately named Holly Path, its trees covered in berries during the winter – food for mistle thrushes. Blackberries too abound during late summer and early autumn. Look out for pochards and tufted ducks on the reservoir, especially in winter, and the many types of dragonfly and damselfly that hover over the water on sunny summer's days.

The view across Ampthill Park

Holly Walk

This sunken track, bounded on both sides by a thick holly hedge, forms a natural tunnel of trees. It once formed part of the area known as the Warrens which, as the name suggests, were used to breed rabbits for the supper tables of the medieval inhabitants of Ampthill. In 1800 the Ampthill Enclosure Award meant that the Warrens largely disappeared and the land was given over to agricultural or forestry use.

Houghton House

Lying just half a mile north of Holly Walk, the ruins of Houghton House perhaps deserve a detour. This Jacobean country house is thought to have been John Bunyan's 'House Beautiful' and the hill outside Ampthill his 'Hill Difficulty' from *The Pilgrims' Progress*. Houghton House is now in the care of English Heritage.

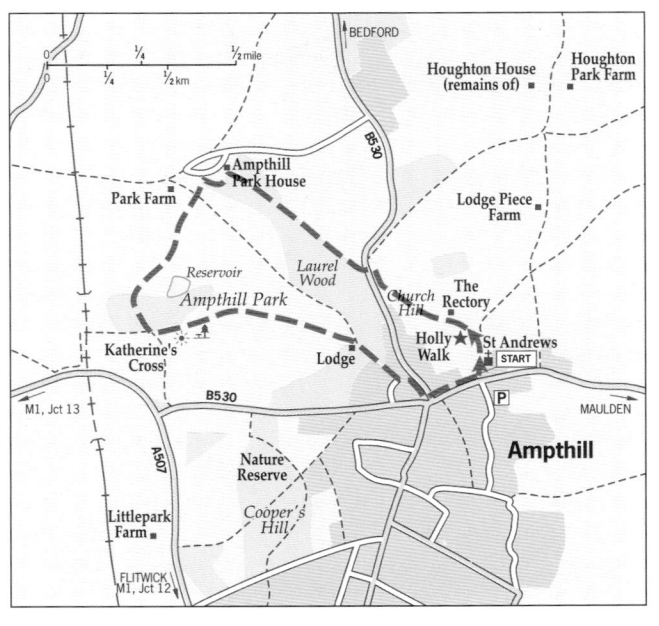

CENTRAL ENGLAND &
EAST ANGLIA

Idyllic Finchingfield

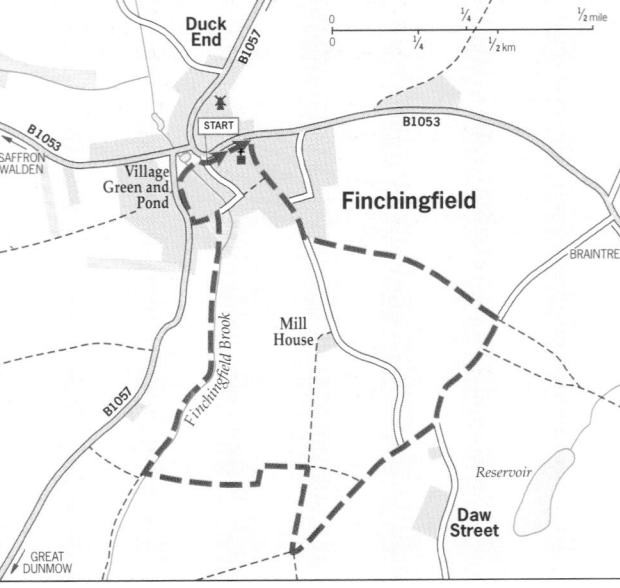

This walk is centred on what is perhaps the loveliest village in Essex, with a stream-fed duck pond inhabited by a wide variety of ducks and geese, an old windmill and the little Finchingfield Brook, teeming with wildlife.

START

Finchingfield is at the crossroads of the B1057 from Great Dunmow (nine and a half miles) and the B1053 from Braintree (eight and a half miles). Start in the centre of the village near the duck pond.

DIRECTIONS

From the village green follow the main road up the hill past the parish church and turn right into Vicarage Road. Continue for about 400yds and then turn left onto the footpath over the fields with the hedge on your left. Go through the gap at the field boundary and carry straight on to the road.

Turn right along the minor road for about ½ mile, passing a trackway and another minor road forking on your left. Where the road turns sharply to the right carry straight on along the concrete track until it turns sharply to the left. Carry straight on across edge of field for 150yds, then turn right up gentle slope along hedge on your right. Finchingfield Church tower comes into view directly ahead as you walk up the slope. At the corner of the field, turn left and carry on down the gentle slope, with the hedge on your right.

Turn left at the boundary and then right over Finchingfield Brook and right again following the right of way across the bottom of a garden with the brook on your right. Go through the gap and continue alongside the stream and then over a tributary brook and past some sheds. Continue with the brook on your right past some very large old willow trees. Carry on into the woodland over a ditch. When the path forks take the left-hand branch and continue between the fences to the tall aspen trees. Turn left (there's a footbridge over the brook on your right) and follow the path to the road. Turn right at the road and go into Finchingfield, bearing round to the right and back to the village green.

Finchingfield

The village green and the wide pond encircled by old houses must be the most photographed scene in Essex, and justifiably so, for it is the archetypal English village. The white-painted windmill, a post mill, overlooks the village from the north. Set across the entrance to the churchyard at the bottom of the hill is a long timber-framed building which, until the Reformation, was the hall of the Guild of the Holy Trinity, a religious and charitable body.

The name of Finchingfield originated as 'Feld of Finc' in Saxon times when it meant a clearance in the forest belonging to the people of 'Finc'.

Information

The walk is three miles long
Level easy walking
Very little road walking
One stile
Pubs in Finchingfield
Village green in Finchingfield
perfect for picnics

The heart of the village

Newt

What to look out for

Finchingfield Brook, which runs to the River Pant, is a haven for wildlife – look out for dragonflies, pond skaters, newts, tadpoles and sticklebacks. It is lined with reeds, rushes and sedges, and is typical of those Essex streams which flow over the great masses of ground up rock left behind by the glaciers of the Ice Age.

The Castle at Pleshey

This is an easy and very interesting walk, with fascinating ancient earthworks, a water-filled moat inhabited by ducks and other wildfowl, and some lovely wide green lanes.

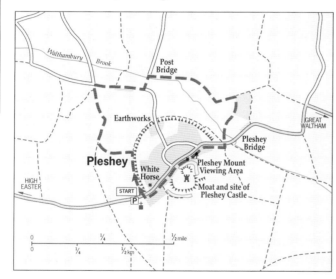

START

Pleshey is just north of Chelmsford, west of the A130, near Great Waltham. Start the walk outside the White Horse pub at the western end of the village, opposite the church. Be sure to park carefully and considerately by the church.

DIRECTIONS

Take the public footpath to the left of the White Horse pub. On the right, between the path and the pub, is part of a deep, defensive ditch, a mile in circumference, which is probably pre-Roman.
At the field boundary turn left and, keeping the hedge on your right, walk along the edge of the field. Go through the gap in the hedge at the corner of the field and turn right onto a very pleasant and open green lane.
At the road turn right, past some houses, to the T-

What to look out for

The defensive ditch seen on the first part of the walk is part of the evidence that Pleshey was inhabited before the Romans came.
Bushes of sloe, hawthorn and elder line the green lanes, while the stream is overhung by willows, and growing with sedges and reeds. Both harbour a rich wildlife: look out for willow warblers, lesser whitethroats and yellowhammers.

junction. Turn left across the bridge over Walthambury Brook and right along the bridleway beside the stream

(can get rather muddy). The bridleway soon becomes a green lane, along which you continue as it bears

The delightful village of Pleshey

round to the left. Turn right opposite the electricity transmission pole along the footpath (signed) past some newly-planted trees.
At the field boundary cross the wooden bridge over Walthambury Brook, and bear left along the footpath to cross a field of young willow trees and reach the road.
Turn right onto the pavement to Pleshey Mount viewing area, which is off the road on your left, opposite the

telephone box. Complete the walk along the main street through Pleshey.

Pleshey Castle

Ancient Britons, Romans and Saxons were all here, but it was the Normans who built a sturdy castle on the Saxon mount, and Richard II who caused its demise.
In September 1397 Richard came to Pleshey to visit his uncle Thomas, Duke of Gloucester, and invited him to ride to London, apparently to 'discuss matters of state'. His

real purpose was to have his uncle kidnapped and murdered.
Pleshey Castle was subsequently allowed to fall down, and all that remains today is a brick arch. It is privately owned, but arrangements to visit can be made via Strutt and Parker, Chelmsford (tel: 258201; an admission charge is made). There is an information board at Pleshey Mount Viewing Area, which has well-kept grass and seats overlooking the moat.

Hanningfield Reservoir

The central theme of this pleasant walk is water. It passes a large modern reservoir, now a haven for wildlife, and a small holy well, frequented by the devout in ancient times.

WALK 69
ESSEX
TQ737976

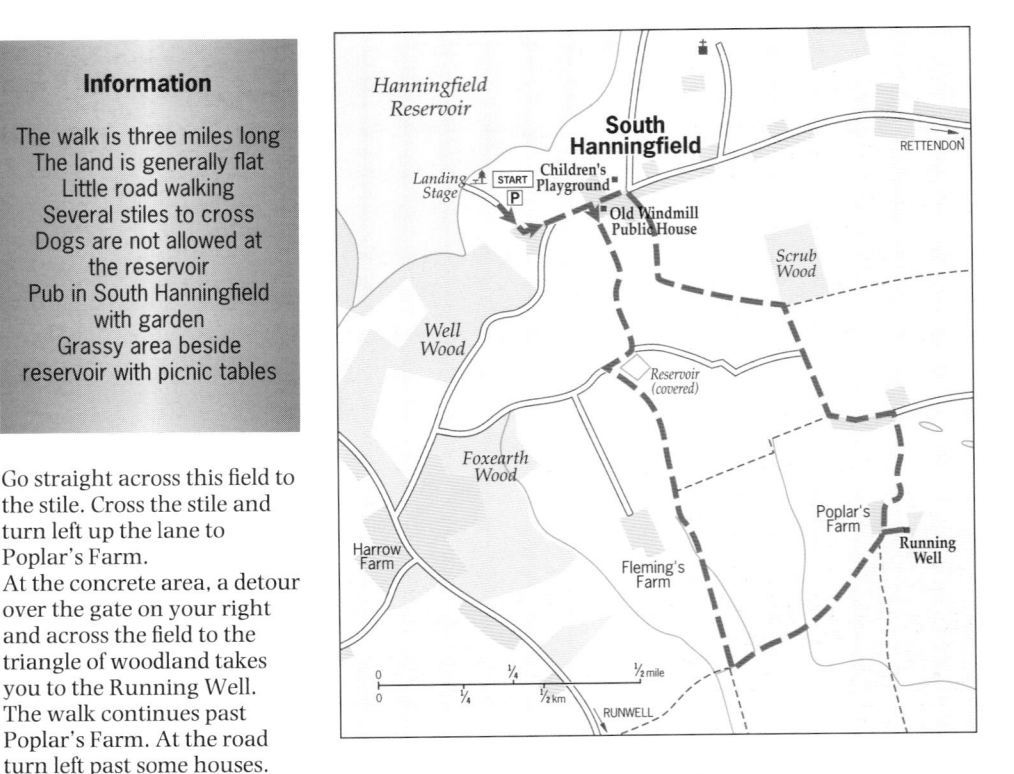

START

South Hanningfield is just west of the A130, three miles north of Runwell. Start from the grassy pay-and-display car park (closed November to March) near the landing stage overlooking the Hanningfield reservoir.

DIRECTIONS

Turn left out of the car park up the road to South Hanningfield. At the junction bear left into the village. Turn right to the footpath at the Old Windmill pub. Go over the stile behind the pub and turn left. Bear right across the field following the 'public footpath' sign.
Turn right and then left on the far side of the field, following the waymarks. Go over the stile onto the road. Turn right and then left over the stile beside the covered reservoir. Cross the field to the ash tree.
Go through the gap to the right of the ash tree and straight downhill past Fleming's Farm, seen to your right. Turn right over the stile and bridge and then left across the field, keeping the hedge on your left. At the field corner turn left and cross the stile. Go straight ahead across the field and through the gap into the large field.

Go straight across this field to the stile. Cross the stile and turn left up the lane to Poplar's Farm.
At the concrete area, a detour over the gate on your right and across the field to the triangle of woodland takes you to the Running Well. The walk continues past Poplar's Farm. At the road turn left past some houses. Where the road bears left take the stile straight ahead and go along the edge of the field towards the woodland. Turn left over the stile and head straight across the field, bearing to the right of the

Hanningfield Reservoir

trig point.
At the corner of the field turn right along the boundary, keeping the hedge on your right. Go through the gap into the next field and head diagonally across to the stile, which brings you out opposite the playground. Turn left onto the road back to the reservoir.

Hanningfield Reservoir

This important reservoir was created by the flooding of thousands of acres of farmland. The man-made lake, which cannot be seen easily from the road, has become an important nature reserve and over-winter site for waders and wildfowl.

The Running Well

This holy well has recently been cleaned and restored, and the annual Boxing Day walk along footpaths to the well has been revived. A book about the history of the well, *The Running Well Mystery*, was published in 1983 by The Supernaturalist of Wickford.

The Roman Fort at Bradwell-on-Sea

This is an interesting and exciting walk, with views across the wide Blackwater estuary and over the North Sea, dotted with skimming sails. It includes a beach, a nature reserve, and a Saxon chapel, which was founded on the walls of a Roman fort.

START
Bradwell-on-Sea is about nine and a half miles east of Maldon, on the estuary of the River Blackwater. Start at Eastlands, just over two miles east of Bradwell-on-Sea along the East End road. There is space here for parking, but use it carefully and considerately.

DIRECTIONS
Set out along the causeway towards St Peter's Chapel, following what was the old Roman road and later the pilgrim's route. At the chapel bear left past the modern bird look-out tower which stands on or near the site of the northern wall of the Roman fort. Go through the gap into scrub land on your left, and follow the path onto the sea wall towards the headland (Sales Point) and the beach.
At Sales Point, where the sea wall turns left, there is a magnificent panorama of the Blackwater estuary and the North Sea.
You can descend to the beach here, where the sandy ridge on the seaward side has locked itself firmly onto the sea wall. Retrace your steps to return to the starting point.

WALK 70
ESSEX
TM023078

Information

The walk is two and a quarter miles long
Flat, easy walking
No road walking
No stiles
Dogs should be kept on leads
Grassy area for picnics within the Roman fort

Othona Roman Fort and St Peter's Chapel
The Roman fort was built on a little island at the mouth of the Blackwater in the 3rd century AD. From these walls the Roman legionaries, auxiliaries from North Africa, scanned the North Sea for German pirates.
Later, in AD653, Bishop Cedd built his chapel across the Roman wall, utilising the wall's firm foundations, as well as taking bricks and tiles from the fortress itself.

Thames Sailing Barges
These beautiful flat-bottomed cargo vessels, many of them built nearby at Maldon, at the head of the Blackwater estuary, were formerly used

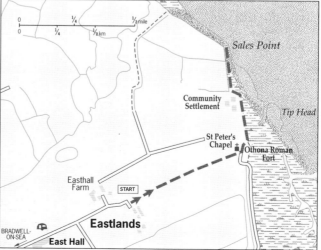

Sales Point, the destination of this walk, overlooks the Blackwater estuary and the North Sea

to ferry cargo up river and round the coast and were specially designed to sit securely on the mud at low tide. They are powered by a great mainsail and prevented from drifting with the wind by the use of lee-boards.
There was always an annual race downriver – a great event in which these vessels competed against each other – and in recent years there has been a revival of interest in the craft.

The Coast at Walton on the Naze

This highly enjoyable walk around the Naze peninsula is of interest to all ages, with wildlife, lots of shipping and an excellent beach.

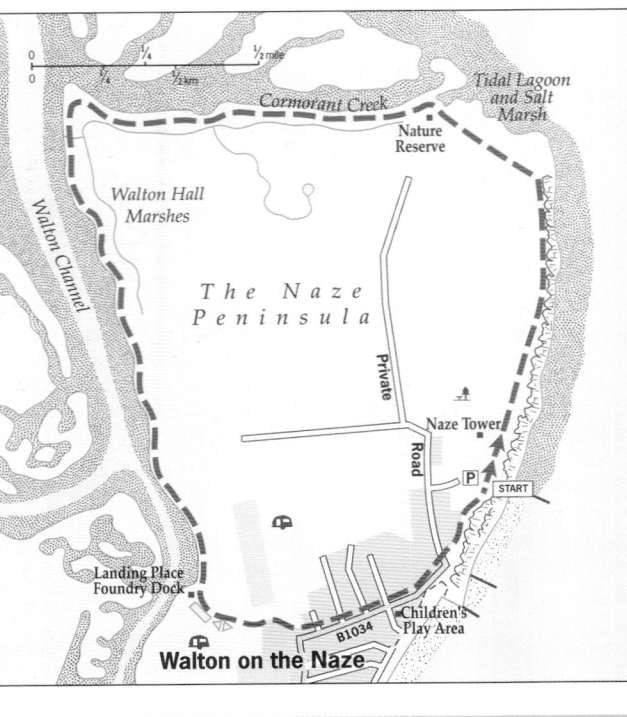

Walton on the Naze

WALK 71
ESSEX
TM265235

Information

The walk is three and three quarter miles long
Level, easy ground; rather exposed to winter winds
No stiles
Road walking on pavement only
Grassy areas for picnics on the cliff-top

START
Walton on the Naze is northeast of Clacton on the B1034. Go through Walton and start from the large grassy car park (charge) at the Naze Tower.

DIRECTIONS
Turn left out of the car park past the café and follow the cliff-top footpath, with the sea on your right and Harwich and Felixstowe ahead across broad Hamford Water (the cliff down to the beach is crumbling into the sea so keep clear of the edge!) Keep straight on to where the cliff merges with the beach and then turn left along the top of the dyke. A tidal lagoon and salt marsh stretch away on the right and the John Weston Reserve, run by the Essex Naturalist Trust, is on the left. Follow the dyke round to the left, following the ever-widening creek, and left again at the next corner. Continue along the dyke, with the open water of

The Naze – a crumbling coastline

Walton Channel to the right and the expanse of Walton Hall Marshes to the left, to reach the landing place at Foundry Dock. Turn left along the footpath.
Proceed along the edge of the field, with the hedge on your right, as far as Naze Park Road. Turn left past the shops and telephone box to the children's play area. Just beyond the play area turn right towards the beach and then left to follow the cliff walk above the tearoom and beach huts back to the car park.

Walton – Threat from the Sea
Walton used to be 'Walton-le-Soken', but for many years now it has been Walton on the Naze. 'Naze', or 'nose', refers to the shape of the headland – and certainly old maps suggest that 300 years ago it was shaped like a snub nose. But this coast is falling into the sea; a print of Walton in

Colourful beach huts at Walton on the Naze

1787 shows the now vanished All Saints parish church towerless and about to succumb to the waves. The last great flood here was during the notorious storm surge of 1953, following which a new sea wall had to be built across the top of the 'nose', some way inland from the original. Land reclaimed by the sea is not a new problem here, indeed the whole of the little archipelago around Hamford Water (the 'Secret Water' of Arthur Ransome's tale) was formed in the past by the drowning of a low-lying stretch of coast.

Black-tailed godwit

What to look out for

The Naze is renowned for the waders which visit its extensive mudflats.
Among the easiest to recognise are curlews, bar-tailed godwits, oystercatchers and redshanks.
Other wildlife includes the Essex skipper butterfly, found on grassy banks.
The dyke isa good spot for watching the shipping – ferries, commercial vessels, pleasure craft, and the occasional Thames sailing barge. Fossils just fall out of the cliffs as they crumble into the sea, and while most are shells, shark's teeth are also being washed out of the clay.

The Stour at Flatford

WALK 72
SUFFOLK
TM075335

This walk gives a taste of the countryside which so inspired the artist John Constable. Anyone familiar with his paintings will experience a feeling almost of *déja vu* when they see Flatford Mill, Willy Lott's House, the River Stour, and the view of Dedham Vale from Fen Lane.

Information

The walk is just under two miles long

A few stiles

National Trust tea room at Bridge Cottage

DIRECTIONS

START

Flatford is just off the A12 between Ipswich and Colchester. Take the B1070, avoiding the centre of East Bergholt, and follow the signs for Flatford. Start the walk from Flatford Mill car park (charge).

DIRECTIONS

Turn left from the car park onto the road (one way — traffic coming from behind). Towards the bottom of the hill, take the footpath behind the hedge, marked with a yellow arrow, which follows the right-hand side of the road (if it is very wet and muddy, you may prefer to stay on the road). The path, well worn and with overhanging branches from the trees to the left, goes across open fields with

Gorse

The River Stour at Flatford

uphill, emerging briefly onto the road from time to time. Continue straight on beside the field to reach a seat beside the road and a view of the Old Hall to the right. Take the wide gravel track (Fen Lane) going left from the road, signed 'Private Road, Public Footpath to Dedham and Stratford' (somewhere along here Constable found the view for *The Cornfield*). Continue downhill, keeping to the main track, ignoring the footpath and stile off to the right at the bottom of the hill. The track bends left, and just beyond a junction with another footpath to the left, bear right and go over a bridge. Keep on the main track, which comes to a dead end with metal gates, then take footpath leading to the footbridge over the River Stour. After crossing the bridge via two stiles, go left on to the path following the river bank. This is a well defined path across open fields with

occasional lines of trees (where the path splits there is an option of following the river bank). Cross the stile. (The track off to the right leads to a river lock and a pretty view of Flatford Mill with the Stour in front: over the bridge,

the lane to the right takes you to the other side of Flatford Mill, with the famous millpond and Willy Lott's House.) From the bridge, take the road to the left, and then go left up some steps, following the path back into the car park.

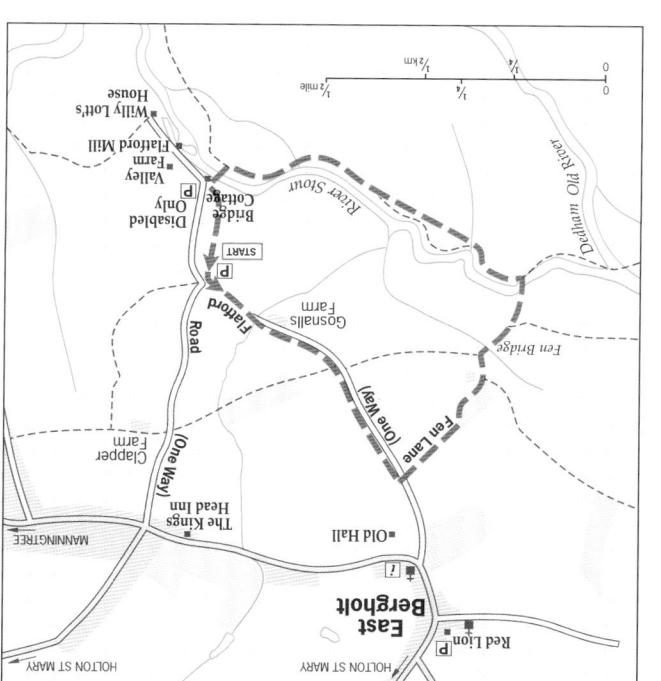

East Bergholt · MANNINGTREE · HOLTON ST MARY · Red Lion · Old Hall · The Kings Head Inn · Clapper Farm · Fen Lane (One Way) · Flatford Road · Gosnalls Farm · Fen Bridge · START · Bridge Cottage · Disabled Only · Valley Farm · Flatford Mill · Willy Lott's House · River Stour · Dedham Old River

0 1/4 1/2 mile

0 1/4 1/2 km

Flatford Mill

Flatford Mill, built in 1733 and now a field study centre owned by the National Trust, provided the inspiration for many of his fine paintings. Along the southern bank of the Stour is a view of the side of the mill, with its sluice gate and trees overhanging the river bank. On the other side of the mill is the quiet millpond, and Willy Lott's House beyond – a scene instantly recognisable from *The Hay Wain*.

The Granary Collection

This is a fascinating museum, displaying tools used by thatchers, blacksmiths, boat builders and wheelwrights, and a collection of cycles dating from the 1830s.

What to look out for

The hedge on the first section of walk dates back to medieval times. You can easily check its age by multiplying the number of woody species you can find in a 30yd section of hedge by one hundred years. This hedge contains field maple, elm, oak, hawthorn, holly and blackthorn.

Marsh and Forest at Orford

This is a delightful walk, taking in a stretch of the River Ore, a section of woodland and the charming village of Orford, with its imposing castle close to the start and finish. The birdlife on this part of the Suffolk coast is outstanding.

WALK 73
SUFFOLK
TM424496

Information

The walk is just under four miles long
Mainly level
Little road walking
A few stiles and a gate to cross
Pub opposite car park, and pub and hotel in main village
Grassy area around castle suitable for picnics

START
Orford lies at the end of the B1084, ten miles east of Woodbridge. Start from the pay-and-display public car park at Orford Quay, opposite the Jolly Sailor public house.

DIRECTIONS
Follow the road down to the quay, and turn right signed 'Public Footpath'. Follow the path round to a gate, go through, and climb the steps, turning left onto the path along the riverside embankment. In the distance, to the left, are the multiple radio masts on Orford Ness, and further south, a hangar and structures that resemble pagodas – part of a World War I airfield.
After ½ mile, go over two stiles (about 80ft apart), and continue along the river bank around Chantry Point. Where the river turns to follow the west side of Havergate Island, turn right (public footpath sign 'Richmond and Orford'), and cross the stile.
Follow a wide track with fields on either side, and turn right where the track emerges on to

a road. Just before the farm on the right ahead, take a sandy track to the left, signed 'Public Footpath'. Continue past a barn and a footpath sign to the right, keeping to the track which bends round to the

A pretty corner of Orford

right at the trees. Follow the edge of the plantation, past the trees, and on past a small group of cottages on the left and a track leading to a farm on the left. Keep to the main track for the time being, ignoring the public footpath off to the right, which leads back to Orford.
The track is now gravel rather than sand. At the four-way 'Public Footpath' sign at the lodge turn right, with a forward view of the church tower and the yellow balconies of the fire tower in the distance. The track joins the road coming into Orford just past the tower, opposite the village sign.
Take the right fork down Mundays Lane to Market Hill. The castle is off to the right. Go left towards the church, and turn right down Church Street. This carries on into Quay Street, and back to the car park.

Orford Castle
Built by Henry II in the late 1160s, Orford Castle has two major claims to fame. It is the oldest castle for which there exists any documentary evidence – in this case the Pipe Rolls, which are the financial records of the King's Exchequer. Secondly, it has the first castle keep to be cylindrical inside, and polygonal outside. This 'inside out' structure, reinforced by three projecting rectangular turrets, was designed both for all-round defence and to make it less likely to collapse should its foundations be undermined during a siege. The castle (English Heritage) is open daily except Mondays.

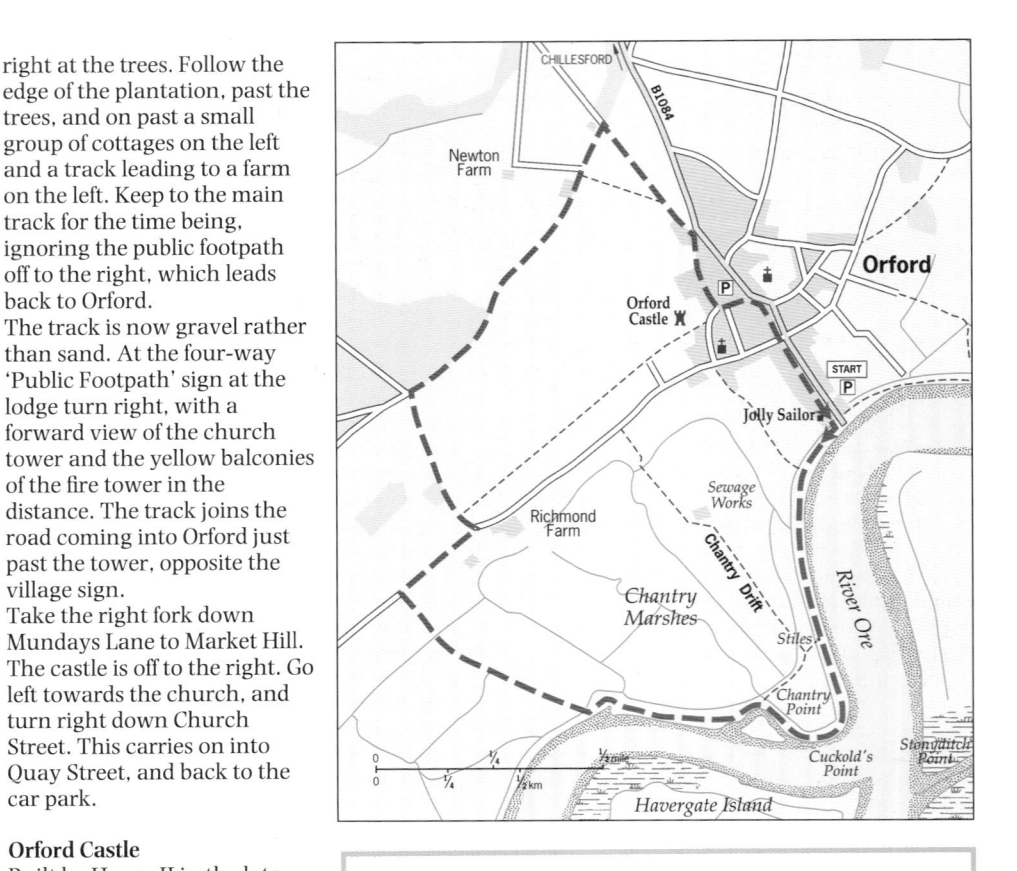

What to look out for

Havergate Island, just across the river, is an important RSPB reserve and is one of the few places in Britain where pied avocets not only breed, but spend the winter. Thousands of other coastal birds can also be seen here year-round.

Framlingham

WALK 74
SUFFOLK
TM286636

This walk starts in an interesting town which is full of character and has a splendid castle. The route then heads out into the countryside, with panoramic views across rolling farmland.

START
Framlingham is about seven miles west of Saxmundham on the B1119. Park on the corner near the church and castle, or in the car park for the castle itself if you intend to visit.

DIRECTIONS
Set off along the one-way road (with the flow) until you come to a crossroads. Go straight on down the B1119 for Saxmundham, passing the Fire Station on your right. Where the road bends left, take the track forking off to the right, signposted 'Public Bridleway North Green'. Keep straight ahead on this main track for about ¾ mile and pass through a gate.
(If following the shorter route, go right here towards New Barn and resume directions at * below.)
Head for the left hand end of a clump of trees. Here, before the trees, the path turns 90 degrees to the left along a hedge, then right at the end. Go right on to a bridleway

Information
The walk is three and three quarter miles long; the shorter option is just under three miles
Mostly easy tracks
There are several pubs in Framlingham, including The Castle Inn at the start
Framlingham Green, next to the castle, is suitable for picnics
Toilets in Framlingham

heading towards more trees. The track passes a plantation, and then turns 90 degrees left and then right at more mature trees (signpost). The track passes a wood on the left, and where the main track bends left towards Home Farm, go straight on, then after 50yds turn right at a public footpath sign. The path goes up a gentle incline to join a gravelled track.
*Pass through Edwards Farm, where the track becomes surfaced. Follow this to the road, turn right and in 50yds turn right down a signposted footpath across the field. On reaching the houses, continue straight on around the back of them on a small footpath. Where this emerges on to a small housing estate, go left and then right on to the road leading into

The church tower

Framlingham Castle

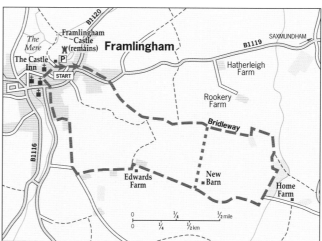

Framlingham. Go straight on at the cross roads, then join the road with the church opposite. Turn right to return to the castle and start point.

Framlingham Castle
Built in 1190 by the notorious Bigod family, Framlingham was one of the first castles not to include a keep, having instead 13 separate towers, linked by a curtain wall – a

Saracen idea brought back by returning Crusaders. While all but one of the internal buildings are now gone, the walls and towers are well preserved, and it is possible to walk right around the top, from where there are magnificent views.
It was at Framlingham in 1553 that Mary Tudor organised her army of supporters to march on Lady

Jane Grey, and here that she later proclaimed herself Queen.

Saxtead Green
Not far from Framlingham, Saxtead Green is well known for its 18th-century post mill, so called because it was built on a single pivot post which was balanced by wheels running around a circular track. The mill has two pairs of stones, and a fantail which keeps the mill into the wind, and worked until 1947.

What to look out for
The rolling farmland here offsets a magnificent Suffolk skyscape. The land is drained by many streams and ditches. Look out for birds in the hedgerows in summer and listen for skylarks above.

Heath and Coastal Marsh at Walberswick

Walberswick stands amidst marshes and heath, flanked by a broad shingle beach – a sleepy village with neat houses and beautifully trim gardens. Part of the walk goes through a National Nature Reserve.

WALK 75
SUFFOLK
TM500749

Information

The walk is four and a half miles long
Level, easy terrain
A few stiles/gates
Virtually no road walking
Pub and tea room
Ice cream van usually on car park in summer

The River Blyth

START
Walberswick lies at the end of the B1387, to the east of the A12 between Saxmundham and Lowestoft. Start the walk from the free car park opposite Southwold Harbour.

DIRECTIONS
From the car park follow the river wall inland to the footbridge. Turn left, on to the tarmac cycle track, and follow its path through bracken and gorse bushes. Where the tarmac track bends left, at sign 'BR', the walk veers right down a bridle path marked with yellow-topped posts. Continue straight on, ignoring track on left, and eventually the gorse gives way to heath. Go through a gate and after ¼ mile the track emerges on the busy B1387. Turn right here, and about 250yds down the road, take the bridleway on the left, keeping to the left of a small wood.

Shortly after the path bears left, it crosses a minor road (offering the option of returning directly to the village). After crossing the road, the signed route goes right, then left beside the gate at the entrance to conservation land. After 100yds the open marshes appear and you should head for the brick tower of a ruined windmill. To the right, in the distance, is the unmistakable bulk of the nuclear power station at Sizewell, 7 miles south. Turn left at the windmill to cross a stile on a wooden bridge, and follow the path beside the dyke. Keep to the left bank for nearly ¾ mile and, where a large footbridge crosses the dyke to the right, take a small footbridge left onto a path parallel to the dyke.

Soon after, turn left onto a boardwalk which crosses the area of marsh grasses. The path dodges through a thicket, then goes right to a field corner; close by are two World War II pill boxes, the second with a wooden seat in front. It is worth pausing here to enjoy the excellent view across marshes and coast. Turn sharp right just past here, and where the path goes over a small rise, bear left, back onto the road. There is a green with a play area here, as well as the Heritage Coast Centre and refreshments.

Heritage Coast Centre
The Suffolk Heritage Coast is an Area of Outstanding Natural Beauty and the small centre in Walberswick is one of several which provide displays to help visitors appreciate the area.

Southwold
Only a mile north, and accessible on foot either by footbridge or ferry across the

Southwold's famous lighthouse

river, Southwold is an interesting small town with lots of green open spaces – the legacy of a disastrous fire in 1659. Wherever you stand in this little town, you can see a white lighthouse looming above the houses and the roof-tops. Not far away is a Mecca for beer drinkers – Adnam's Brewery.

What to look out for

This area has always been outstanding for birds. In winter it's one of the most likely spots to see a great grey shrike, and in summer the scrubby heath is home to nightjars, stonechats, lesser whitethroats and nightingales. The reed beds hold breeding marsh harriers, bitterns and bearded tits, and sometimes a rarity such as the purple heron or a spoonbill. Adders, common lizards and slow worms are quite common.

The King's Forest at West Stow

The walk follows a marked trail, taking in a pleasant mix of wide tracks and tiny paths through the conifer plantations, broad-leaved trees and clearings of The King's Forest.

The path through The King's Forest

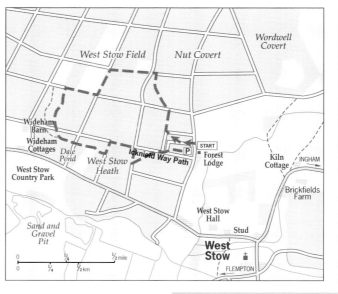

Information

The walk is two and a quarter miles long
Level, easy ground
Dogs should be kept on leads
Pubs at West Stow and Icklingham
Picnic area at car park

START

West Stow is just north of the A1101 between Bury St Edmunds and Mildenhall. Follow signs 'West Stow', turning left just before the village with signs 'Forest Lodge'. Park at the Forest Lodge car park.

DIRECTIONS

From the car park, walk along the main track just past the lodge to reach a sign on the left indicating the start of the King's Forest Trail. Go down this path, following the yellow-topped posts. In about 50yds the path turns right to go through a dense plantation of trees (yellow markers are on the tree trunks here). After crossing a narrow track, the path bears sharp right and in about 150yds crosses a wider track. The path winds for 250yds through well-spaced trees with some undergrowth. Where it comes to a junction with a track, turn left and continue, to emerge onto a clearing. Follow the path down the left-hand side of the clearing, continuing with a younger section of forest on the right, and arrive at a junction in another large clearing. Here turn left along the side of the clearing, and at the bottom turn right onto the track following the lower edge, past a short block of trees on the right, then on to another clearing on the right-hand side.

Look for a yellow-topped post where a small path goes off to the left into the wood, and follow it, weaving through conifers and deciduous trees. Continue across a bridleway which runs roughly parallel for the first 50yds or so. Continue, following yellow markers, through a plantation of mature conifers

Muntjac

with little ground cover. The path crosses a track and after 100yds enters a section of deciduous trees, then winds on, emerging at a junction with mature conifers ahead. Turn left onto the track for about 100yds and at the next junction turn right onto a bridleway. At the next crossing of paths, go right and soon take the small path going left by a yellow marker into deciduous trees,

continuing into mature, well-spaced pines. The path goes right at the next junction and after 100yds, just after a slightly wider track, bears left through a plantation of younger trees before

What to look out for

Thetford Forest, of which The King's Forest is a part, is one of the last strongholds of the red squirrel in England. It is also home to four species of deer – fallow, red, muntjac and roe. The latter are most common, and the only species not introduced here. Although they exist in large numbers, they are timid and not easy to see, keeping to small groups rather than large herds.
The muntjac are the descendants of escapees from Woburn Park in Bedfordshire at the end of the last century.

emerging briefly on the right-hand side of a very small clearing. Continue straight on, back to the car park.

West Stow Country Park
Within this area of heath and grassland is the famous reconstruction of West Stow Anglo-Saxon village, open daily during the summer, with an excellent visitor centre. The original village was preserved after being buried in a sandstorm.

Forest Rides at East Harling

This pleasant ramble through Forestry Commission rides has the added variety of a river and some open pasture land, the whole walk providing a great deal of wildlife interest.

An old bridge over the River Thet at West Harling Common

Information

The walk is about two and
a half miles long
Level, easy ground
Some road walking
No stiles
Dogs should be kept
on leads
Pub in East Harling about two
and a half miles away
Grassy picnic area
at the start

START

This walk starts about five miles east of Thetford at West Harling picnic site. From the A1066 turn onto a minor road towards East Harling, then look for signs to the picnic area. There is plenty of room for parking vehicles here.

DIRECTIONS

From the picnic site, walk away from the road along a wide ride which is bordered by a mix of beech, oak, sycamore and pine.
Keep on this track for about a mile, ignoring tracks to the right and left, then, when a rough field appears on the left, take the next sandy track to the right, with a field on the left and a beech hedge on the right.
(Alternatively it is worth continuing straight on for ¼ mile passing an old cottage on the left until reaching an old bridge with a clear flowing river. Retrace your steps back to the turning).
After a few hundred yards the sandy track bears to the right, but continue straight on along a grassy track, passing some farm buildings on the right.

Just before a gate into a pasture turn right along a path between two fences, then into a field. Continue, with the fence on your left, to re-enter the forest. Follow the forestry ride and at a junction of four tracks continue straight on. Shortly afterwards, at a second major crossing of paths, turn right – do watch out here for cars and caravans on their way to the caravan site.
Continue along this track to the road, then turn right to return to the picnic site in about ¼ mile.

BRECKLAND

For centuries Breckland was largely an open area with few trees – it largely consisted of wide, open heaths and ploughed land which, in times of low farm prices, went out of cultivation.
After World War I large parts of the Breckland were bought and planted with conifers by the newly formed Forestry Commission, whose remit was to make Britain more self-sufficient in timber.
Breckland heath is a habitat unique to this part of Britain. Many of the plants only occur here, and stone-curlews – strange, nocturnal waders – have their stronghold in this part of East Anglia. Afforestation and ploughing of the land are considered serious threats to the survival of this fragile ecosystem.

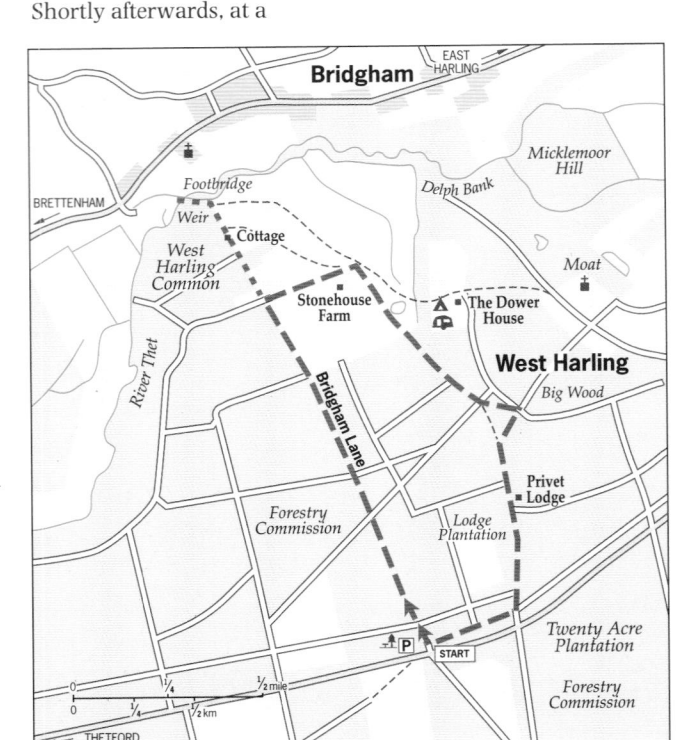

Mignonette

Information

The walk is about three
miles long
Level, easy ground,
but can be very muddy
and slippery by marshes;
care needed beside
dykes and reed beds
A little road walking
on a no through road
No stiles
Dogs should be kept
on leads
Pub offering bar snacks
in Ludham, with garden;
also a small café
in the village
Grassy area by staithe
suitable for picnics, also one
or two places along route
Toilets by staithe

Marsh thistle

Ludham Marshes

An interesting and easy walk, close to one of
the Broadland waterways and providing fine
views across traditional grazing marshes.

START

Ludham is about 14 miles
north-east of Norwich. From
Wroxham, take the A1062 to
Ludham, continue through
the village centre, then
shortly afterwards take the
turning on the right,
signposted 'Womack Staithe'.
There is parking on the
staithe near the shop and
toilets.

DIRECTIONS

From the staithe, walk on
down the lane beside the
moorings, past some
attractive houses on the right,
until you come to the 'County
Sailing Base'. Immediately on
the left-hand side of the Base
is a footpath (do not take the
track marked 'bridleway'
which is to the left of the
footpath). The footpath runs
along a low bank, with
Womack Water on the right;
to the left are extensive
grazing marshes. After about
½ mile, at a cottage, the path
turns left and then runs
alongside the River Thurne,
though separated from it by a
bank of reeds. After about ¾
mile chalets can be seen on
the far bank, and the path
soon leaves the river by a
pumphouse. Cross a dyke on

a plank bridge, taking care at
either end where it is a little
rough, then turn left along a
grassy track which is
bordered on either side by
dykes. After about ¼ mile, go
through a gate then turn left
along another grassy track
which is partly bordered by a
wood on the right-hand side.
In about ¼ mile the track
bears right by a house and
emerges to join the outward
route by the 'County Sailing

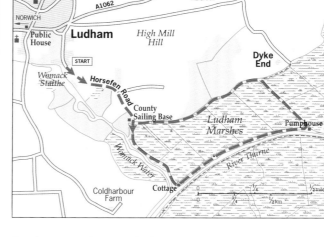

Base'. Retrace the route back
to the start point.

Grazing marshes

The grazing marshes in
Broadland have traditionally
been grazed by cattle during
the summer. The rich
pastures were particularly
good for fattening cattle, and
animals were driven down on
foot by drovers from as far

away as Scotland. The
marshes were drained by a
system of dykes, and water was
returned to the river by pumps
– originally wind-powered,
then steam driven and most
recently fuelled by diesel. The
older methods were the least
efficient and consequently the
grazing marshes would
frequently flood in winter,
providing a marvellous habitat
for wildfowl.
In the 1960s and 1970s many
of these old grazing marshes
were ploughed up to be
intensively farmed for cereals,
but farmers are now being
encouraged to return the land
to the more traditional grazing
practices. Hopefully, this will
prevent the further pollution of
the Broads and herald the
return of its rich plant and
animal life.

*A drainage channel across
the marshland*

The Dunes at Winterton

A pleasant walk through dunes and farmland that shows a flat landscape is not necessarily a dull one.

START

Winterton lies about 8 miles north of Great Yarmouth, on the B1159. Start the walk from the beach car park at the eastern end of the village – a charge is made in summer.

DIRECTIONS

Walk back towards the village and turn right before the first bungalow. Continue across the sand hills and tun left on to a track between two houses. Go striaght ahead at the crossroads and continue on this track towards East Somerton for about ¾ mile, passing Winterton church and farm buildings on the left. The track bends right past Manor Farm and a ruined church, and bear right on the concrete track beyond Burnley Hall. At the next junction bear left, and turn right just before the trees. Continue on this roadway for about ½ mile, and turn right on to a rough track.

After a short distance, turn left, keeping the hedge on your left, towards some farm buildings. Turn right here, keeping the buildings to your left, and follow the track towards the sea, reaching a gate on your right beyond some trees. (For a slightly longer walk, go straight ahead here to cross the dunes, walking back to the car park along the shoreline.) Pass through the gate, and follow the track along the back of the sandhills for just over a mile, back to Winterton. Follow the track between two houses, and at the crossroads turn left to retrace your route to the car park.

A Storm-wracked Coastline

Often appearing deceptively peaceful, this stretch of coast was notorious for its shipwrecks in stormy weather. The 18th-century writer Daniel Defoe reported that half the village of Winterton was built of timbers from wrecked vessels, and in one winter's night 200 coal ships were lost offshore. Tombstones in the church bear witness to the many lives lost at sea. The sea has also invaded this coastline, breaking through the dunes and flooding the land. Since the most recent flooding, in 1938, the dunes have been reinforced with concrete in some places.

The tall tower of Winterton Church serves as a good landmark

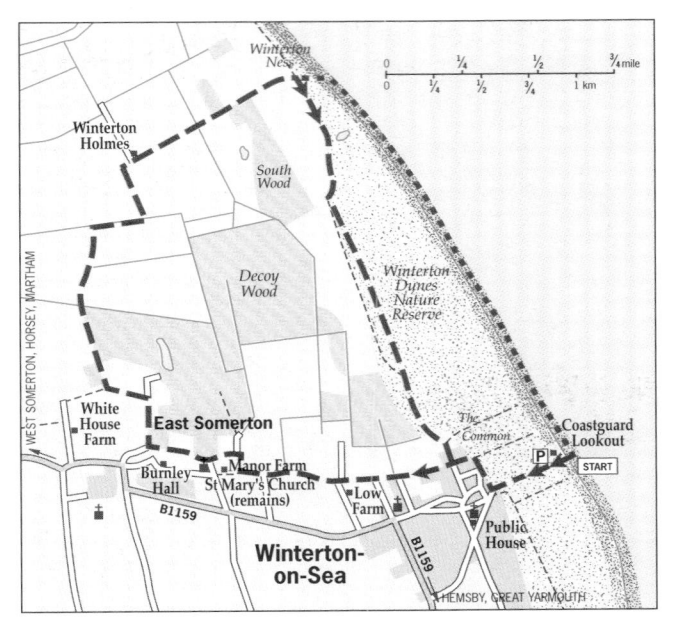

What to look out for

The dune system is a National Nature Reserve, and rich in a variety of wildlife. The drier areas of the dunes support heather, and ferns and other wetland plants grow on damper patches. Watch out for adders. Little terns nest on the beach, so keep to the main track and observe all warning signs to avoid disturbing them.

Burnham Thorpe

This pleasant walk follows in the footsteps of the young Horatio Nelson, who was born in the village, through pastures and along tracks down to the salt marshes and creeks of the North Norfolk coast.

START

Burnham Thorpe lies about four miles west of Wells-next-the-Sea and about a mile inland. Turn off the main coast road (A149) on to the B1155 then take minor road south to the village. Start the walk from Burnham Thorpe church, just to the north of the village centre. Park in front of the church's main gate.

DIRECTIONS

From the main gate of the church, walk away from the church across the grass and on to a track. Bear right and almost immediately take the signposted footpath on the left, crossing over stile and keeping hedge on the right. Go through a gateway into a large meadow with a number of ponds. Keep the hedge on the right until reaching a grove of trees, then bear left keeping trees to the right. As the trees come to an end bear right to a footpath sign and stile. Cross stile and climb the bank of a disused railway, then go left and after about 100yds turn right down the bank. Follow the path up a gentle hill with a hedge on the right, cross into next field and continue in the same direction until reaching a road by a cottage. Turn right and after about 200yds, where the houses end, turn left down a track. Keep straight on. Eventually sea, dunes and salt marsh come

What to look out for

The meadows near Burnham Thorpe church can be good for wild duck, especially in winter. Many common butterflies are found along the hedgerows during summer.
In winter look out for brent geese, especially on the coastal sections. Both churches on the walk are worth a visit.

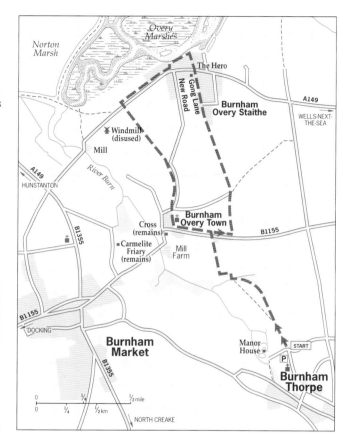

into view. Continue until the track becomes metalled and the outskirts of Burnham Overy Staithe are reached. At the main road cross over by The Hero pub and follow the narrow lane (East Harbour Way) down to the staithe. (A path to the right

Low tide at Burnham Overy Staithe

runs along the sea wall to the beach at Gun Hill.) Follow the road around to the left. The road then turns inland back to the main road. Here turn right, walking along the footpath by the main road until the coast path is signed; this runs parallel with the road but just within the field. Shortly before the tall black windmill turn left, crossing the road and proceeding up a wide track. Eventually reach a minor road and turn right. Follow this road until it bends to the right, just before Burnham Overy Town church. Go straight ahead through the churchyard then turn left along the road for about ¼ a mile. Turn right by the cottage and telephone box to meet the outward route, and retrace your steps to the start point.

Burnham Thorpe Church
Horatio Nelson's father was rector here from 1755–1802 and the great naval hero was born in Burnham Thorpe in 1758. The rectory where he was raised was later demolished. The church has a small exhibition on Nelson's life, including a cross made of timbers from HMS *Victory*.

Castle Acre

A fascinating walk through water meadows and along tracks and lanes linking the ruins of a castle and a priory.

START
Castle Acre is about four miles north of Swaffham just off the A1065. Turn off the main road at the hamlet of Newton. There is room for parking in the village, but take care not to cause inconvenience. The walk starts from the church, towards the western end of the village.

DIRECTIONS
From the main gate of the church walk away from the village, and at the end of the churchyard wall turn left down South Acre Road. Continue down to the River Nar.
Just before the river, turn left over a stile then follow a gravel path by the river towards a bridge. Climb a stile

The lovely ruins of Castle Acre Priory in a rural setting by the river

to the left of the bridge onto the road, then turn left. After about 200yds turn right down Cuckstool Lane.
At a break in the hedge on the left, enter the castle remains. Walk up the hill, keeping the boundary hedge on your right, and at the top, just before the road, turn right over a stile. Follow a path into a field keeping the houses on your left.
Cross the next stile and bear left, keeping the houses on the

Information

The shorter walk is about three miles, the longer about four and a half miles
Mostly level easy ground though there are some gentle hills
About a mile of road walking, mostly along a wide (sometimes rough) verge
Several stiles
Pubs and a café in the village
Suitable picnic sites at the castle and by the ford
Toilets at entrance to Priory

What to look out for

The castle mound has some interesting plants, native to the chalk which forms the basis of the mound. The tall yellow candelabra-like flower heads of the woolly mullein, a plant largely confined to East Anglia, can be seen in July.
There are trout in the River Nar, best spotted from the bridge by the ford.

left. Cross another stile by a horse chestnut tree and walk down a gravel path on to the road.
For the shorter walk, cross over at this point and go down North Street, opposite, continuing to St James Green; continue directions at * below.
(For a longer walk turn right and after about 300yds take a track up on the left for about

The River Nar at Castle Acre

¼ mile. Keep right and walk across the common, crossing a small ford and then, after 100yds, take the right-hand track. At the road turn left and walk back towards the village, bearing right at the second road junction to reach St James Green.)
*At the crossroads turn right. At the next junction, turn right by Rose Cottage onto a road with a wide verge. Continue along the verge until the next road junction then turn left.
After just over ½ mile, pass a manor house on the right then turn left down a track.

At the bottom of the hill bear left. Continue uphill on the track for about ½ mile to join a road, then turn right and follow the road, bearing left by the drive down to the priory. The start point is a short distance further on.

The Castle and the Priory
Castle Acre is a marvellous ruin, standing high above the River Nar. It is also on the line of a Roman road, The Peddars Way.
The castle was built in the 11th century but all that survives are the massive earthworks and the Bailey Gate, which forms an impressive entrance into the centre of the village.
The Priory, also dating from the 11th century, lies in a beautiful setting down by the river at the other end of the village. After the dissolution of the monasteries in 1537 it fell into decay, but despite the subsequent plundering of its stone, it still remains a most spectacular ruin.

Reach and the Devil's Dyke

A pleasant walk through typical flat fenland scenery, with numerous waterways and the occasional windmill. A great attraction is the Devil's Dyke, a huge and ancient earthwork which dominates the landscape.

Information

The walk is just under three miles long
Mostly level, easy walking, with one short climb; can be muddy
No stiles
Very little road walking
Pub in Reach serves bar food; no children under 14, but there is a large garden with play area
Pubs in nearby Swaffham Prior and Burwell

Marsh marigold

START
Reach is off the B1102 approximately seven miles north-east of Cambridge and five miles west of Newmarket. It is situated on a minor road between Burwell and Swaffham Prior. Parking is available by the village green.

DIRECTIONS
Walk down The Hythe at the north-west corner of Fair Green to Reach Port. Cross the bridge here, turn left and follow the farm track past the aptly named Water Hall on the left and Rose Cottage on the right, with Spring Hall further down the road. Cross the bridge on the left and turn right on to Barston Drove, a farm track which follows the foot of Church Hill.
Turn left onto a track (once part of the disused railway line), then right over the bridge and left, signed 'Burwell and Devil's Dyke', onto the disused railway track which runs through a nature reserve in a cutting. Take the sloping path up the bank and walk along the edge of the field. A series of fairly steep steps takes you up the embankment, then turn left at the top along the Devil's Dyke. Follow the dyke back from here to Fair Green.

Reach Village and Port
During Roman times, when the fens were wet marshland, Reach was a small port. It continued to thrive well into the 18th century because a navigable canal had been constructed to join it to the River Cam. The port started to decline in the 19th century when the fens were drained, leaving the village surrounded by hundreds of square miles of fertile farmland, much as it is today. The relatively high chalk hill to the south of the village provided many boatloads of 'clunch', an important building material used to construct local homes, farms and churches. University buildings in Cambridge and the cathedral in Ely were reportedly supplied with Reach clunch.
Reach Fair, started in 1201 by the citizens of Cambridge, has been held annually ever since and the Mayor of Cambridge still performs the opening ceremony. The scene of many gatherings of local farmers and agricultural labourers, it also attracted some 600 fossil diggers, who

What to look out for

In summer this area is a sea of colour, the yellow fields of oilseed rape are splashed with the bright red of poppies and the white sails of the windmills at Swaffham Prior stand out against a blue sky. A pair of binoculars would be useful.
Hedgerows provide a haven for wildlife, and in late summer and early autumn blackberries, rosehips and sloes are there for picking. Reach Lode supports a variety of water life, and the small nature reserve is home to some unusual plants.

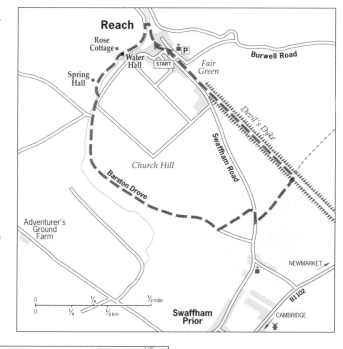

The village of Reach is at the northern end of the Devil's Dyke

worked out in the fens digging and washing fossils which, when ground up, were used as the first artificial fertiliser.

The Devil's Dyke
The Devil's Dyke, or Devil's Ditch as it is sometimes known, is a seven-mile military ditch and embankment constructed between 370–670AD to protect the farmland from invading tribes from across the North Sea. The steep sides and huge ditch, in parts up to 60ft from top to bottom, provided considerable protection.
The Reach end of the ditch was demolished towards the end of the Dark Ages when relative peace led instead to the construction of Fair Green, the village green.

Wimpole Park

This pleasant circular walk offers views over rolling countryside, unusual for Cambridgeshire, as well as a wide variety of rare livestock, a folly, a lake and the chance to visit Wimpole House and Wimpole Home Farm (National Trust properties).

START
Wimpole Park is seven miles west of Cambridge on the A603 and five miles north of Royston on the A1198 (Ermine Street). Start the walk from the large free car park by the stables.

DIRECTIONS
Walk past St Andrew's Church across the gravel drive to the front of the main hall, and follow the railings west to go through the kissing-gate on the right by the yew tree. (The walk can be extended by about ½ mile by keeping straight on here and following the path along West Avenue to the plantation, where a right turn will lead you to join the main walk at the Chinese Bridge – see * below.)

The main walk continues straight on to the ha-ha, where you turn right through another kissing-gate into the field. From here follow the red waymarker posts north to the Iron Bridge, with a view of The Folly straight ahead. Cross the stile and follow the marker posts to the lake and

What to look out for

Wimpole's landscape has changed considerably through the centuries and you may be able to see signs of the ridges and furrows which mark the sites of medieval villages. The lake and woodland areas provide a rich habitat for a variety of wildlife and waterfowl, whilst the buildings provide a haven for seven different species of bat.

Information

The walk is approximately two miles long, but can be extended by half a mile
The paths are well maintained, with only a short stretch along a quiet lane; National Trust path closes at dusk
One stile
Dogs must be kept on a lead within the parkland
Restaurant, tea room and National Trust shop at Wimpole Hall
Picnic places within the park; The Folly is particularly suitable
Toilets and baby room at the stables

The magnificent façade of Wimpole Hall

the Chinese Bridge.
*Cross the bridge and turn left round the edge of the field up to The Folly. From here follow the marker posts eastwards to Oddy Doddy Lane, then turn right down the hill past Thornbury Hill Cottages and Home Farm. Shortly after passing Home Farm take the path on the right through another kissing-gate. This will lead across the fields back to the car park.

Bat

Wimpole Hall
Wimpole Hall was built by Sir Thomas Chicheley in the mid 17th century and has been altered and extended by successive generations of owners. It only achieved something approaching its present form in the late 18th century whilst in the ownership of the Earls of Hardwicke. The house was left to the National Trust by its last owner, Mrs Elsie Bambridge, the daughter of Rudyard Kipling, on her death in 1976.

The grounds too have undergone great changes over the years, assuming their 'natural' looks in the second half of the 18th century at the hands of such famous landscape artists as Robert Greening, 'Capability' Brown and William Eames. Books and leaflets giving a more detailed history are available from the shop.

The Folly
The Folly is perhaps the most imposing feature on the landscape and provides the perfect spot for a picnic. It was designed by 'Capability' Brown to provide a romantic outlook from the main house, and also served as the head gamekeeper's house until the 1940s. Views from here are dramatic, and a quick examination of the graffiti on the walls will show that people haven't changed greatly over the centuries!

Godmanchester and its Water Meadows

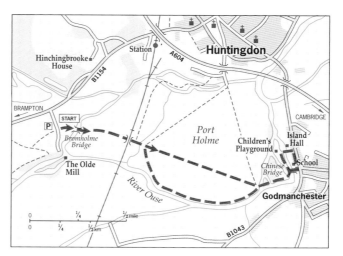

This walk combines water meadows, wooded tracks, historic buildings, river craft and locks. For those interested in botany the path passes through a Site of Special Scientific Interest.

START

Bromholme Lane is two miles south-west of Huntingdon on the A604 and a mile east of Brampton. Turn south on the road signposted to The Olde Mill public house. Park the car near the track leading to the reservoir.

DIRECTIONS

Take the marked track eastwards over the bridge, with Hinchingbrooke House in view to the north across the water meadows. Go under the railway bridge (high speed trains cross here) and through a kissing-gate on to Port Holme. Take the central path eastwards across this SSSI and through a second kissing-gate on to the banks of the River Ouse. This leads on to a good footpath which crosses four footbridges and several small islands before leading into Godmanchester.

Cross the Chinese bridge and turn left past Queen Elizabeth's Grammar School. Follow the road for a couple of hundred yards to Mill Yard car park, then turn left again and cross the bridge opposite Island Hall.

Retrace your steps as far as Port Holme, take the left-hand path after the kissing-gate and follow the river bank as far as a small beach in a large loop of the river. (Avoid going straight on towards the railway as the path can be very overgrown.)

Veer off to the north-west where you will soon meet the original track near the railway bridge. A short walk will bring you back to Bromholme Lane.

Godmanchester and Island Hall

As you approach the small and attractive town of Godmanchester the diversity of architecture to be seen across the river is striking. This is The Causeway, now designated an Outstanding Conservation Area. Originally a Roman settlement, Godmanchester continued to prosper through the ages, but still maintains a village atmosphere with a population of just 3,000. Of particular interest are the Chinese bridge, a replica of the original dated 1827, and Island Hall, a large riverside mansion built in 1730 with well-maintained riverside grounds. It is open to the public on summer Sunday afternoons.

Hinchingbrooke House

Although not quite on the route of this walk, Hinchingbrooke House can be clearly seen to the north from Bromholme Lane and Port Holme meadows. Now a school, it belonged at one time to Oliver Cromwell's grandfather and both James I and Charles I are said to have been guests here. The house has limited opening to the public during the spring and summer. Cromwell has many connections with this part of Cambridgeshire. He attended school in nearby Huntingdon and was later Member of Parliament for the town.

The Chinese Bridge at Godmanchester

What to look out for

When crossing Port Home meadows (SSSI) keep your eyes open for the rich assortment of wild flowers.
The land here has been farmed under a traditional haymaking/grazing regime which has given rise to its botanical diversity; look for yellow rattle, ragged robin and marsh orchids among the display.
Butterflies are numerous on sunny summer days, as are dragonflies and damselflies closer to the river.

Ferry Meadows

Woods and meadowland, river and lakeside are all included in this pleasant walk on well-maintained paths, and there is a great deal of wildlife interest.

START

Ferry Meadows Country Park is situated in a bend of the River Nene just west of Peterborough. It is two miles east of the A1 Alwalton exit on the A605, just north of Orton Wistow. Follow country park signs and park in the large car park (charge on Bank Holidays and summer weekends).

What to look out for

Three lakes provide roosting and feeding grounds for a wide variety of waterfowl. The sympathetic management of the land is further encouraging many species to nest in the woodland. Here, and in the protected grassland areas, primroses, cowslips and bluebells flourish in spring and you may be lucky enough to find southern marsh or common spotted orchids. Many species of butterfly and dragonfly have been identified here too.

DIRECTIONS

Start the walk at the visitor centre and follow the path skirting the bottom of Overton Lake eastwards to Ham Bridge.

Cross and turn right to reach Bluebell Bridge. Cross the river and turn first left opposite the golf course, up the wooded Riverside Walk and along the river edge (or take the higher Bluebell Walk which has a tarmac surface). Part-way along the path there are a few low steps to be climbed.

Follow the path left to Ferry Bridge where you cross back over the river into Gunwade Meadow.

Turn left and continue down Ferry Walk to Gunwade Lake; here turn right over the pontoon bridge. Proceed past the children's play area on the northern edge of Lynch Lake, turning first left along the path that will bring you back to the visitor centre.

Ferry Meadows Country Park

This country park contains over 1,200 acres of countryside, including three lakes. The presence of water is felt everywhere – the park is sited on the flood plain of the River Nene – and results in a wide variety of water and

Gunwade Lake is the largest of three at Ferry Meadows

wetland conditions. There is also archaeological interest, with the site of a 1,700 year old Roman farm, well and fishponds within the park and the site of a Roman fort within the golf course across the river. Gunwade Lake, the largest of the three, is the site of the National Watersports Centre, which organises a wide variety of courses and activities.

Originally set up by Peterborough Development

Corporation, the park is now run by the Nene Park Trust 'to provide in perpetuity enjoyment of countryside recreation for the people of Peterborough and visitors to the city'. The park has its own station on the Nene Valley Railway, a popular preserved steam line.

The Nene Valley Basket Industry

Along the river edge, shortly before reaching Ferry Bridge, is a plantation of willows, or osiers, which once formed the basis of the local basket-making industry. In order to preserve the plantation, the trees are cut back every few years – taking over the role originally fulfilled when the willow pliable wands were harvested to be woven into strong baskets.

Harlestone Heath

This walk through the woods of Harlestone Heath is beautiful at all times of year, and especially in the spring and autumn. There are any number of other paths to explore.

START
Harlestone is on the north-west edge of Northampton, just outside the suburb of New Duston on the A428. Park in the lay-by by a garden centre, opposite the main entrance to Harlestone Firs Saw Mill. Start the walk from these gates.

DIRECTIONS
Go through the gates and take the path to the left. The track eventually curves round to the right, with a sawmill straight ahead, and leads to a fenced plantation of young trees in front of the mill. A wide grass verge continues to the right, but take the smaller, sandy track to the left.

Follow this track round to the right through the woods and continue straight over at the crossways, with beech trees to the right, and continue for some distance until turning right in the dip. Just after a track joins from the left, reach a crossways and go straight on. Turn right at the next junction, distinguished by four large beech trees, and walk down the fine, wide avenue. Just past a clearing on the right by the mill, a road joins from the right, returning to the start point.

WALK 86
NORTHAMPTONSHIRE
SP711637

Information

The walk is just under two miles long
Level, easy ground
No stiles
No road walking
The Cottage Tea Rooms (at garden centre by the parking area) serve snacks and light meals
There are many picnic places throughout the woods

The entrance gate to Harlestone Heath

Great spotted woodpecker

The Spencer Family
Harlestone Heath, or Firs, is owned by Lord Spencer, as is much of the land in this area, but he is happy to allow public access to the rides. Nearby Church Brampton and Chapel Brampton are also part of Lord Spencer's estate,

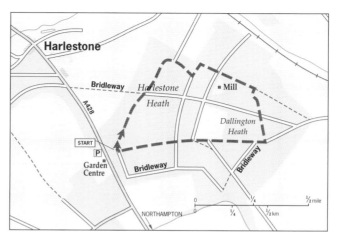

as is the village of Harlestone. The church at Lower Harlestone, built in the 14th century of orange-brown stone, is well worth a visit. The Spencer seat is at nearby Althorp House. Before 1500 the Spencers were modest farmers in Warwickshire, but then the acquisitive and shrewd Sir John Spencer began amassing lands. The family was awarded a barony in 1603 and an earldom in 1765 and has advanced its

On the edge of the wood

What to look out for

Despite the extensive planting of conifers, Harlestone still has many beautiful deciduous and broad-leaved trees – it is worth taking a field guide to identify the species. Great spotted woodpeckers may be heard in the woods.

status over the centuries with a series of beneficial marriages. Like all great families its members have dabbled at times in politics and affairs of state, but farming and the running of their estates has always been their first priority.

The Woods at Maidwell

This is a most attractive walk which is particularly lovely in the spring and autumn, though it provides a great deal of wildlife and wildflower interest at most times of the year.

START

Maidwell is some ten miles north of Northampton on the A508.

Park either in the village, or at the top of the lane leading to Hall Farm, taking care not to cause an obstruction.

DIRECTIONS

Follow the lane down past Hall Farm, where the outline of a medieval fish pond can still be discerned, then up and down past Dale Farm Conservation Area. Take the right hand fork after the stream at the bottom and go up the track to Dale Farm, branching right down a small track by the barn. (For a much shorter walk, go down the lane to the bridge at the bottom. Here take the

Creeping
speedwell

footpath to the right up through the woods and over the footbridge and stile by the yellow-tipped post and so back to the start point across the fields.)

The main track, which is waymarked, passes more farm buildings on the right. Follow the fence round to the left and keep straight on at the end of the wooden fence. Turn right at the end of the field, keeping the hedge on your left. Keep straight on through two fields,

then turn to the right towards the woods and at the corner go into the trees and descend the bank. Cross a stream and climb up through the woods to meet a track. Turn right here and walk up and along the edge of the wood for quite a long way. Shortly before the end of a field, reach a yellow-tipped post on your right which signals a stile and footbridge back through the woods. Do not follow this sign, but turn left along the footpath across the field. Climb a stile into the next field and then another. Then aim for the left of the house ahead, cross another stile and so re-enter the village at the start point.

Medieval Fish Ponds
The site of medieval fish ponds can be clearly seen in the field

What to look out for

This walk offers an excellent variety of flowers, trees, birds and animals in their natural surroundings. Maidwell Dale and Wood are untypical of much of Northamptonshire, reminiscent instead of a corner of the Peak District.

on the left of the bend in the lane, shortly after the start of the walk. Before the comparatively recent invention of refrigeration and fast transport, fish ponds were used to supply fresh fish to the tables of mansions and monasteries.

The track leads through Maidwell Dale farmland

Hartshill Hayes Country Park

WALK 88
WARWICKSHIRE
SP307941

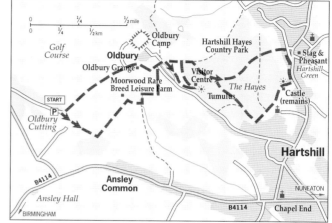

Starting with a section of the 'Centenary Way' footpath, this varied walk goes through Hartshill Hayes Country Park on the Atherstone Ridge. The scenery in this area includes farmland, open grassland and a large wood, and the route partly follows a disused railway line.

Information

The walk is three and a half miles long
Undulating ground, not generally steep, but muddy in places
A lot of stiles
Some lane walking
Dogs should be kept on leads through Moorwood Rare Breed Leisure Farm and under close control in the country park
Pub at Hartshill Green; no children's room
Grassy areas suitable for picnics at Oldbury Cutting and Hartshill Hayes Country Park
Toilets at Hartshill Hayes Country Park

START
Oldbury Cutting Picnic Area (free parking) is four miles north-west of Nuneaton, at a sharp bend in a lane north of Ansley Common.

DIRECTIONS
From the bottom of the hill in the picnic area follow the waymarked 'Centenary Way' along the green embankment. Cross a farm track via two stiles and after about 125yds (muddy), turn left over a stile. Cross fields on a well-defined path, climbing two more stiles, to reach a large field to the east of Moorwood Farm. From the top left corner of the field bear right to the bottom corner and take the stile on the left signed 'Hartshill Hayes Country Park'.
Cross a small field, climb two stiles in quick succession and bear left, passing a path junction to a fenced way beside a narrow pool. At the end, bear right uphill on an enclosed path to a stile. Go over a rise in the field beyond, heading diagonally towards a red-roofed bungalow, to reach

Oldbury Lane via a stile at the far corner, opposite an (unsigned) entrance to Hartshill Hayes Country Park. Passing through a kissing-gate into the Park, turn right and skirt a covered reservoir to join a path to the visitor centre. Return to the open hillside and descend to the right, beside a large wood, the Hayes, passing the adventure play area. The path enters the wood and skirts its lower

edge, then swings inwards. At marker post 3 descend to the left. Ignore post 4 and follow the main path to the edge of the wood, where a causeway and steps lead to a road above. Turn right to Hartshill Green where the Stag and Pheasant pub overlooks the small green and a bus shelter commemorating the poet Michael Drayton. Climb Castle Road (footpath alongside) to a waymarked path on the right, opposite Abbey Cottage, and follow it past the ruins of Hartshill

Castle. Keep within the edge of the woods to a cross-path from a kissing-gate and houses on the left. Turn right and proceed to a junction with a broader track, taking the middle track back to the open hillside.
To return to Oldbury Cutting, go out to Oldbury Lane, where you first entered the country park, and descend to the right, passing Oldbury Grange on the left and the entrance to Moorwood Rare Breed Leisure Farm.

Hartshill Hayes Country Park
The county council's 136 acres of open hilltop and woodland overlook the Anker valley, with views far across neighbouring Leicestershire

Bluebells in the country park

Common dog violet

What to look out for

From the path through Moorwood Rare Breed Leisure Farm many unusual breeds of farm animals can be seen in the fields. At Hartshill Green note the unusual dedication of a bus shelter to an Elizabethan poet – the locally-born Michael Drayton. The path back to the country park passes the rather scanty ruins of Hartshill Castle.

to the rocky tors of Charnwood Forest. Facilities include a visitor centre and café, toilets and a car park (charge).

Moorwood Rare Breed Leisure Farm
The farm (admittance charge) offers visitors the chance to see around 30 rare breeds of farm animals. Spinning demonstrations are given, and there is a tea room with a children's play area.

Stratford's Shire Horse Centre

This is a pleasant, easy walk from Stratford-upon-Avon, visiting the Shire Horse Centre and Farm Park and the lovely village of Clifford Chambers, and crossing the River Avon to the church where Shakespeare lies buried.

START

The walk starts from the centre of Stratford-upon-Avon, but can be started from Clifford Chambers (ample roadside parking), or from the Shire Horse Centre (parking free for visitors). The Centre is one and a half miles south of the town, off the B4632.

DIRECTIONS

From the Gower Memorial to Shakespeare, walk towards Clopton Bridge. Turn through gates to the Old Tramway and follow it for a mile, passing the new bypass, Severn Meadow Road (A4390) to the junction of the A3400 and the B4632. Turn right along the B4632 (footpath) for about 200yds.

Opposite Cross o' th' Hill Farm climb a stile and go diagonally right to a waymark post left of Springfield House. Bear right along the field-edge, passing the house, to the gateway ahead and follow a track across the next field to the Shire Horse Centre.

If not visiting the Centre, turn left along the byway for about 100yds to the waymarked gateway on the right and take the public footpath to a stile into a meadow. Turn left and, towards the end of the meadow, veer right to a stile. Cross the next field to a kissing-gate, and make for a railed bridge over the little River Stour. Beyond the bridge, a fenced path skirts a fish farm and passes Old Mill to the end of Clifford Chambers' main street, with the Manor House to the left. Turn along the village street, and about 100yds before the

Information

The walk is just under four miles long
Level, easy ground
Several stiles
Some road walking along a surfaced footpath
Dogs should be kept on leads at the Shire Horse Centre and through neighbouring pastures
Refreshments, including meals, at the Shire Horse Centre. Pub at Clifford Chambers for bar meals; no children's room
Grassy areas suitable for picnics at the Shire Horse Centre and by the River Avon

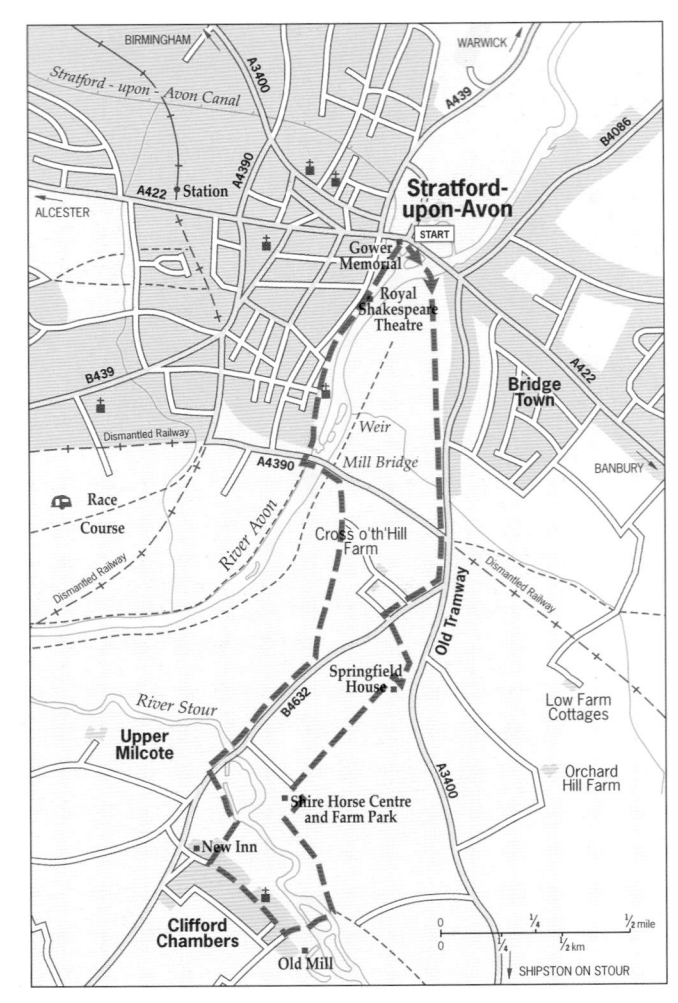

Stratford's Trinity Church across the waters of the River Avon

New Inn a public footpath, signed to the right, passes between bungalows. After it curves left, a weir on the Stour can be viewed by diverting along a short path to the right. Return to the original path and continue to a metal gate, then between railings and the river to stile. Bear right along a field-edge to the B4632.

Turning right on its footpath for nearly ½ mile, climb a stile on the left and cross a field to a fence bordering a drive. Follow the fence to a gate and descend a surfaced path to a stile below the bypass embankment. Turn left to a kissing-gate by the Avon and go under the bypass. (As an alternative to the main route, follow the riverside path into Stratford.)
Beyond the bypass, cross

Mill Bridge and turn to follow Mill Lane to Holy Trinity Church, where Shakespeare lies buried. Go through the churchyard and out by the main gate. Turn right for a few yards, enter the Avonbank Gardens and walk through them, past the theatre, back to the Gower Memorial.

What to look out for

On leaving Stratford via the Old Tramway, you will pass one of its wagons and a notice giving the history of the line. At the Shire Horse Centre there are a dozen great heavy horses and several rare breeds of farm animals. The famous swans of the River Avon can still be seen.

Clifford Chambers
Though close to busy Stratford, this charming village can be enjoyed without the distraction of through traffic. There is a gem of a half-timbered rectory and an interesting church.

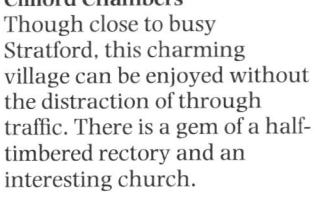

Carrion crow

The Canal at Brewood

This is a most enjoyable and easy walk with plenty of interest, the last stretch being along the Shropshire Union Canal. An atmosphere of peace and solitude prevails along most of the walk, which is ideal for lovers of wildlife.

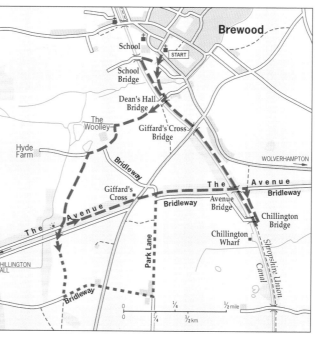

START
The village of Brewood is eight miles north of Wolverhampton just off the A5 and the A449. Start the walk from the church of St Mary and St Chad in Church Road, a short distance from the main square. There is plenty of parking in the village.

DIRECTIONS
Walk to the church along Church Road, away from the centre of the village, and turn left into Dean Street. Cross the road opposite the church and take the alley immediately at the side of Dean Cottage. After 25yds turn left onto the track and then immediately right over a stile into the field. Follow the hedge on the left and cross a stile, then a small brick footbridge, then two stiles leading up to the road bridge over the canal. Turn right to cross the bridge and follow the winding track for about ¼ mile. Turn left at the sign for the farm. After 100yds pass a handsome red brick farmhouse on your right and turn left over a stile, following 'Staffordshire Way' signpost. Follow the path through the pasture for about ½ mile, keeping to the line of trees on the left. Cross two stiles in short succession before reaching The Avenue. Turn left and continue to cross Avenue Bridge. (To extend the walk at this point, follow the 'Staffordshire Way' sign, to cross The Avenue and go over a stile to cross the lane. Go through a kissing-gate and into a long pasture, keeping to the hedge line on the left. After about 500yds, cross the stile and turn left onto the footpath. Just past cottages, cross the road ahead (Park Lane) and continue forwards up the lane, following it round to the left by a group of houses and continuing for about ½ mile. When Brewood church comes

into view, turn right down the bridlepath through a gateway just before the lane turns to the left again. Walk through woods for about 500yds and cross Avenue Bridge.)

Walking at Brewood

Bear right along a path leading to the field alongside the canal.
Follow the line of the canal along the field and at the far end turn right into the track leading over canal bridge. Proceed with great care down a steep path at the left-hand

Information

The walk is about four miles long
Level, easy ground, except for steep descent to canal towpath at Chillington Bridge
Several stiles
Dogs may be let off leads under supervision along the towpath
Various pubs in Brewood village
Parts of the towpath are suitable for picnics

side of the bridge to reach the towpath. Turn right along the towpath, passing under Avenue Bridge and two road bridges (the second was crossed at the beginning of the walk). Just before the next bridge, follow a pathway up to the right to come up onto the track by the school and walk the short distance back to the village, retracing your steps to the church.

Chillington Hall
Chillington has been the home of the Giffard family since 1178. The present house was built by Sir John Soane in 1786 and the park was designed by that most famous of landscapers, 'Capability' Brown. Both are open to the public on Thursday afternoons between May and September.

What to look out for

Avenue Bridge is a particularly handsome structure, designed to be in keeping with Chillington Hall and Park. The canal was cut particularly deep at this point so as to be kept out of the view of the Giffard family. Giffard's Cross is a short distance from Avenue Bridge. It is also named after the Sir John Giffard who, it is said, shot an escaped panther there with a crossbow in 1513. The panther had originally been sent from Africa as a gift.

Thor's Cave

A lovely walk from the village of Wetton, which rises to the spectacular entrance of Thor's Cave, named after the Norse god of thunder, before descending into the beautiful Manifold valley.

START

Wetton village is on a minor road one mile west of Alstonefield and about six miles north of Ashbourne. The National Park car park lies on the southern edge of the village.

DIRECTIONS

From the car park turn right, walking away from the village centre towards Grindon. Take the first turning right, signposted 'Wetton Mill', then in 200yds turn left at sign 'Wetton Mill/Manifold Valley'. After about 30yds, turn off the road to the left, following a walled green lane, signposted 'Concessionary path to Thor's Cave', for ¼ mile.

After crossing a stile by a gate, continue along a track for another 50yds, then turn right over a stone stile and follow the waymarked path down the field, to the right of the hill. At the end of the second field cross a fence stile and descend on a sometimes

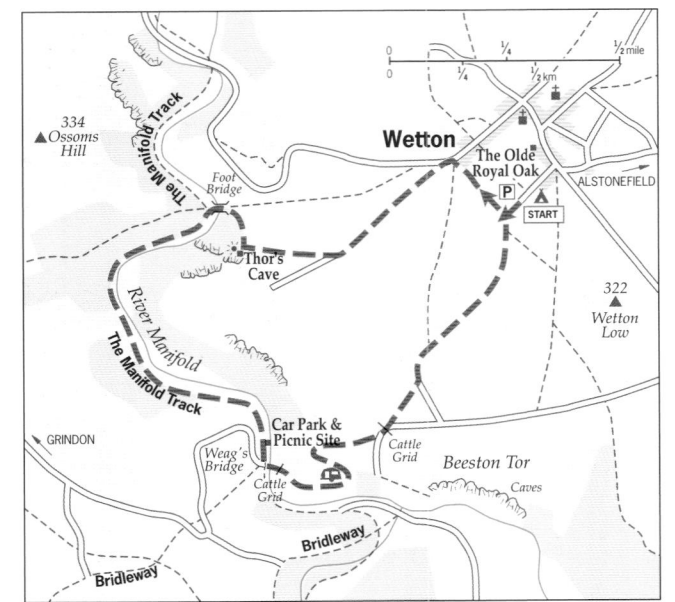

WALK 91
STAFFORDSHIRE
SK109552

Information

The walk is three miles long
Varied terrain, with one steep descent and ascent and an easy, level section on a former railway track
A few stiles
Some road walking on quiet lanes
Dogs should be kept on leads
The Olde Royal Oak in Wetton has a family room
Picnic site at Weag's Bridge
Toilets at car park

Bird's-foot trefoil

slippery path to the cave, which is prominent in the limestone crag above (take particular care with children here). After visiting the cave (superb views), descend via the steep flight of steps (slippery after rain) to the valley.

Cross the footbridge, turn left and follow the 'Manifold Track' (not signed) along the winding, wooded course of the river, which is to your left for about ¾ mile to Weag's Bridge. Turn immediately left over the bridge and follow the minor road which shortly climbs steeply uphill for about ½ mile. After crossing a cattle grid, turn left over a stone stile and ascend across a field, keeping the wall to your left.

At the top of the field turn left onto a lane, which will bring you back to the start point in about ½ mile.

Thor's Cave

Set 300ft above the Manifold Valley in a huge limestone cliff, Thor's Cave was inhabited by prehistoric man and evidence found here suggests that the cave was occupied more or less continuously until Romano-British times.

The Manifold Track

This leisure route uses the line of the former Leek and Manifold Light Railway, which ran on a narrow gauge track up the valleys of the Rivers Hamps and Manifold for 30 years from 1904. It catered mainly for local traffic, particularly taking milk from the Staffordshire hills to the Potteries, and featured delightful primrose yellow carriages and unique tank engines, originally designed for use in India.

The mouth of the spectacular Thor's Cave

What to look out for

The River Manifold disappears into underground channels during the summer months, reappearing at Ilam, several miles downstream. This is a common feature of rivers running across the limestone rock in this part of the Peak District, which is known as the White Peak because of the predominant colour of the rock. If you look carefully at the rocks in the many dry stone walls which cross-cross the landscape, you will find the fossils of sea lilies and shells, laid down in a shallow, tropical sea some 300 million years ago.

Early purple orchids and meadow cranesbill will be found in summer by the path into the valley from Wetton, and in May and June listen for blackcaps and willow warblers.

Castleton and Cave Dale

This is an easy exploration of the best of Derbyshire's limestone country, centred on the busy tourist village of Castleton, with its famous caves and castle. The walk climbs up the rocky gorge of Cave Dale, then descends steeply back to the village.

The view from Peveril Castle, high above Castleton

WALK 92
DERBYSHIRE
SK149829

Information

The walk is two miles long
Involves some steep sections
Several gates, stiles
and cattle grids
Dogs should be kept
on leads at all times
Pubs and cafés in Castleton
Picnic places in Cave Dale
Toilets at car park

START

Castleton stands at the head of the Hope Valley on the A625 Sheffield to Chapel-en-le-Frith road. Park in the large village car park (pay-and-display) in Cross Street.

DIRECTIONS

From the car park, turn left along Cross Street, passing the Town Ditch on the left. In a few yards, at The Castle pub, turn right (Castle Street). Passing the church on the left, enter the Market Place. Turn left to pass the war memorial into Bargate, then in 50yds turn right, signposted 'Limestone Way'. Cross a wooded stile where the rock walls narrow, and

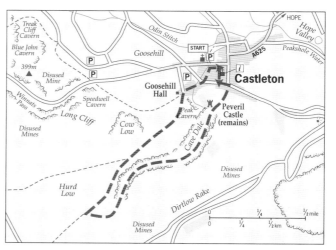

Castleton

start the climb up through the dale (Peveril Castle stands high on its precipitous crag above you to the right). Follow this path to a metal gate near the head of the dale, where the gradient eases. Now keep a dry stone wall on your right and later pass through a metal gate. At the next metal gate, turn sharp right into a walled green lane which leads over the hill. (Cave Dale is now visible to the right, and on reaching the crest of the hill, the face of the 'Shivering Mountain' of Mam Tor is on the left.)

Pass through an old metal gate and keep ahead, descending more steeply now. At the foot of the hill pass through a gate onto a walled lane, with Goosehill Hall on your left, to re-enter Castleton at Goosehill Bridge. Afterwards keep left to walk down the footpath beside Peakshole Water, which issues from the huge mouth of Peak Cavern. On reaching the main road, turn right into Cross Street, with the car park almost opposite.

What to look out for

The grassy slopes of the Derbyshire Dales are rich in flowers, including early purple orchid, cowslip, bird's-foot trefoil and common rock-rose. On some of the steeper slopes, particularly below crags, is the rare limestone polypody fern. Butterflies include orange tip, green hairstreak and common blue. The woods are home to chaffinches, willow warblers, wood warblers, spotted flycatchers, and great spotted and green woodpeckers.

Caves and crags

Castleton is at the heart of an area where streams sink suddenly beneath the porous white limestone rock into the spectacular caves which have been formed by this water erosion over the years. Many of the caves are open to the public. Peak Cavern (open Easter to October), in the village, has the largest cave entrance in Britain and once housed a community of rope makers.

Speedwell Cavern, at the foot of the Winnats Pass, is entered by boat on an underground canal cut by

lead miners; the Treak Cliff and Blue John Caverns in the hills to the west, have the best displays of the rare semi-precious stone, Blue John, which is not found anywhere else in the world. Blue John and Speedwell Caverns open all year; Peak Cavern open Easter to October.

The craggy gorges of Cave Dale and the Winnats Pass are thought to have been formed when swift currents of meltwater from Ice Age glaciers cut through the 300 million-year-old reef limestone.

Peveril Castle

Originally built by William Peveril, son of William the Conqueror, Peveril Castle (English Heritage) occupies a commanding site overlooking the village. In ruins now, the castle is reached by a steep, zig-zag path from a corner of the village square and is open all year.

Wood warbler

Creswell Crags

In the seemingly unpromising location of the Derbyshire-Nottinghamshire coalfield, this walk takes in one of the most famous British prehistoric sites, and has the added bonus of some fascinating wildlife and an excellent visitor centre.

Information

The walk is about one and a half miles long
Clear, level field paths
Little road walking
A few gates and some steps
Dogs must be kept on leads
Pubs and restaurants in Creswell village
Toilets, information and picnic area at Creswell Crags Visitor Centre

The dramatic scenery of Cresswell Crags

START
The Creswell Crags Visitor Centre is one mile east of Creswell village, on the B6042 road, between the A616 and A60 on the Derbyshire-Nottinghamshire border. The car park closes at 5pm.

DIRECTIONS
From the Visitor Centre car park, walk east past the picnic area along the track through the trees for about 100yds to a gate. Turn left here, along the waymarked bridleway and follow the well-defined farm track towards Hennymoor Farm. Just before reaching the first hedge, turn left again and follow a grassy track, keeping the hedge to your right. Shortly, a small gate leads onto Crags Road (B6042). Turn left here and in about 30yds, turn right on to another bridleway via a barred metal gate. Keep on this bridleway for about ½ mile, with a shelter belt of trees on your right, passing Bank House farm on the right.
Reach the A616 on the outskirts of Creswell village and turn left, and after 100yds turn left again back on to Crags Road (B6042), signed 'Creswell Crags Visitor Centre'. On reaching the traffic lights, turn right on to the path which runs around Crags Pond, passing in turn Church Hole Cave and Boat House Cave on the south bank, and Mother Grundy's Parlour, Robin Hood's Cave and Pin Hole Cave on the north bank by the road.
At the eastern end of the lake keep left and, just before reaching the road, go down the steps on the right, with the stream to your right, and return to the Visitor Centre and car park.

The Creswell Caves
One of the world's earliest works of art was found by archaeologists investigating the caves of Creswell. The engraved image of a horse was found on a fragment of rib bone from Robin Hood's Cave, and other examples were found in the cave known as Mother Grundy's Parlour. They are thought to have been the work of a wandering tribe, known as Creswellian man, which settled in the gorge as the Ice Age glaciers retreated about 13,000 years ago. But the occupation of the Creswell caves began long before that. The bones of Ice Age mammals such as hyena, bear, reindeer, bison and woolly rhinoceros have been found, and the first evidence of man is the crudely-fashioned stone axes and scrapers dating from about 43,000BC and used by the Neanderthal people. Occupation of the caves continued more or less continuously through Roman and medieval times.

The Welbeck Estate
The crags and pond at Creswell were part of the estate of nearby Welbeck Abbey. The pond was created by the Duke of Portland for duck shooting, and Boat House Cave was where he moored his boats. Originally founded by monks of the Order of the White Canons, the present Abbey dates from the 18th century and now occupied by Welbeck College.

What to look out for

The spectacular magnesian limestone gorge of Creswell Crags is a Site of Special Scientific Interest (SSSI) because of its geologic importance and natural history. The series of caves which mark its sides are the home of long-eared and other bats, and the valley floor is rich in wild flowers such as great willowherb, yellow archangel and common comfrey. Introduced species such as the bright yellow monkeyflower have made their home here.
Crags Lake was created in the mid-19th century by damming the stream, but soon became colonised with moorhen, little grebe and water vole. The stream supports water crowfoot, water starwort with water figwort. Look out for the jackdaws, spotted flycatchers and pied wagtails which nest in the rock crevices.

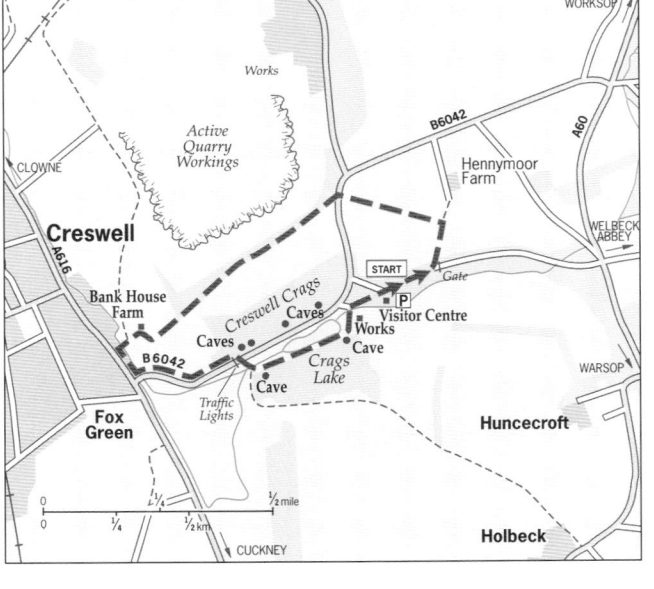

Cromford Canal

WALK 94
DERBYSHIRE
SK302569

Explore Derbyshire's industrial heritage, from the site of Richard Arkwright's first cotton mill, along a beautifully-restored canal, and back through delightful woodland.

START
Cromford Wharf and Meadows are just off the A6, 18 miles north of Derby and three miles south of Matlock Bath. There is plentiful parking on Cromford Meadows and at the High Peak Junction.

DIRECTIONS
From Cromford Wharf, set out south along the towpath, signed 'High Peak Junction', with the canal on your right. Follow the towpath for just over a mile to reach High Peak Junction. There is a choice of routes here. (The shorter alternative is to cross the Derwent at High Peak Junction by the footbridge, signed 'Holloway', and walk up the lane towards Lea Bridge, where you meet the longer route at * below.) The main walk continues for about ⅛ mile to the Leawood Pump House, crossing the Derwent by an aqueduct and

What to look out for

The Cromford Canal is a haven for wildlife, with a profusion of wild flowers including blue water-speedwell, water mint, forget-me-nots and marsh marigolds. Birds include mallard, coot, moorhen and, if you are lucky, the occasional kingfisher, while small mammals which may be seen include water shrews and water voles.

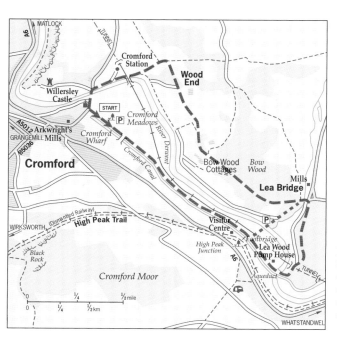

Arkwright's Cromford Mill, built in 1771

then turning left over the railway tunnel entrance on the path through Lea Wood to reach Lea Bridge*. At the road turn left and cross bridge, then branch right through squeeze-stile into a wood. Follow the main path, bearing left through this pleasant mixed woodland. Eventually emerge onto a green lane and at fork, keep right on a well-defined path. Continue across four fields and through wood. At the far end continue to a crossways and turn left to descend to the road, joining it under the railway bridge. Pass Cromford Station and the entrance to Willersley Castle (private). Carefully cross Cromford Bridge to return to the car park.

Cromford Canal
Built to serve Richard Arkwright's Cromford Mill (the first water-powered cotton mill in the world), the Cromford Canal was opened in 1793. It was heavily used for the transportation of cotton and other goods until the coming of the railway in the 1860s. The five and a half mile stretch between Cromford and Ambergate has been restored.

Lea Wood Pump House
This distinctive building, with its classically-shaped chimney, was built in 1840 to pump water from the nearby River Derwent into the canal. The original steam-powered beam engine is still inside, and is currently under restoration by enthusiasts. It is occasionally open to the public at summer weekends.

Sir Richard Arkwright and Cromford
Richard Arkwright transformed textile manufacturing from a cottage industry to a factory operation, and his first mill, the fortress-like Upper Mill near the start of the walk, was built in 1771. It now includes a visitor centre. At the height of its production the mill employed 500 workers, many of whom lived in Arkwright's model village of Cromford, and many of his cottages still survive. He amassed a great personal fortune, but he died in 1792, just before the completion of his stately country house, Willersley Castle (private), near the end of the walk.

Shrew

Information

The walk is about three and a half miles long
The first part, along the canal towpath, is easy; the return is more strenuous
Several squeeze-stiles
Dogs should be kept on leads, except in Cromford Meadows
Picnic area in Cromford Meadows, near the start; also at High Peak Junction
Pubs and cafés in Cromford
Toilets at Cromford Meadows

Three Leicestershire Villages

This is an adventurous and exacting walk. It visits three villages in a particularly attractive corner of Leicestershire and takes in a wide variety of countryside, from pasture to plough, and from green lane to cricket pitch.

START
The village of Gaddesby is just north-east of Leicester on the B674 (off the A607 from Leicester to Melton Mowbray). Park in the village and start the walk from its centre, by the church.

DIRECTIONS
Walk away from the church down Church Lane, turn right onto the road at the bottom and left down a tree-lined avenue, following the footpath sign, just past the Cheney Arms pub. Cross the river by the wooden bridge and cross the field to a gate ahead in the wire fence. Ignore the yellow arrow pointing left to the field corner and instead turn half-left and

aim for half-way along the field boundary, where a little bridge crosses a brook. Turn half-right in the next field and aim for the far corner, just down from which is a stile. Cross the next field to the clump of trees in the opposite left-hand corner. Climb both stiles and cross the next field to a stile a little way up the opposite hedge, then walk straight across the next field to a stile half-way up the opposite hedge. Cross the next (bumpy) field to a stile by a gate, a few yards to the left of the modern twin barns. This gives on to an often very muddy track leading to the village of Barsby, coming out by the King William Inn. Walk

WALK 95
LEICESTERSHIRE
SK690130

Information

The walk is about four miles long
Easy walking
Virtually no road walking
A lot of stiles; possibly some electric fences to roll under
Dogs should be kept on leads
Pubs in all three villages, all serving food and welcoming children
Various picnic spots along the walk

down Main Street towards the church, and cross the road into Baggrave End and then Church Lane. Take the path to the left and pass through the kissing-gate. Cross the field, past the pond, to a stile in the right-hand corner, then cross the next field to a double stile in the opposite corner. Walk down the field to a stile by a solitary tree and some gating, and on to an iron kissing-gate under a chestnut tree. Cross the drive, go through another kissing-gate, cross a field and then two bridges by the cricket ground. Turn left at the road. This is the village of Ashby Folville. Turn right at the Carington Arms and go up Highfield End. Ascend the flight of steps by the footpath sign, climb the stile, go straight across the field to the gate and turn left down the

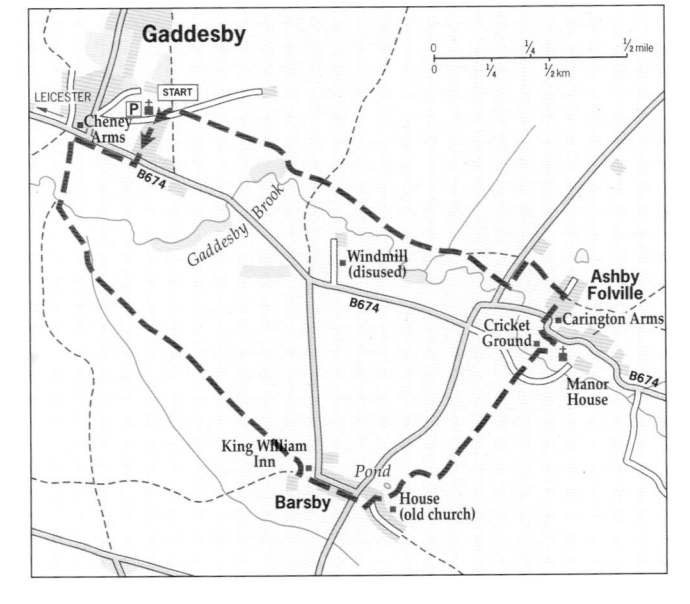

The church at Gaddesby (left)

lane. Go through the gate on the right before the bridge and follow the path through the meadow. Gaddesby church spire is clearly visible ahead. Cross a footbridge and stile, go straight across the next field to a stile, and then cross the next two fields and one more stile. Cross another field and a stile marked by a red-tipped post, make for the right-hand corner and cross into the field. Follow the southern boundary beside the stream. Turn right at the farthest corner up the hedge line to the hill top, where a yellow marker shows the way across a stile, then walk through another field and cross a stream. Walk up to a gate near a brick building and climb the nearby stile. Turn left along the track back to Gaddesby church.

The villages
Though time has not stood here, their character has remained largely unspoilt. Gaddesby has a particularly interesting church with fine medieval workmanship. In Barsby a house called Godson's Folly was originally built as a mortuary chapel.

The Canal near Hose

An easy, enjoyable and interesting walk from the village of Hose, through farmland and along the Grantham Canal, a delight for lovers of wild flowers.

START
Hose village is about six miles north of Melton Mowbray in the Vale of Belvoir, accessible from the A606 and A607. Park carefully and considerately in the village and start the walk from the village green.

DIRECTIONS
From the village green, take the path to the right of the church (Church Walk), turn right onto the road and keep straight on down the track ahead as the road bends to the right. Continue straight on down the bridleway, waymarked with a horseshoe sign, and, with the industrial building on your right, walk through an open gate and follow the path along the course of a stream. Carefully negotiating a gate into a field – there is a 10ft drop into the stream immediately on the left – continue for about 250yds. Cross the stream by the stone bridge and cross the field to a gate leading onto a green lane. Go through the gate at the end of the lane, turn right and go through a gate into the next field. Follow the hedge on your right and keep left of the farm buildings. Go through the

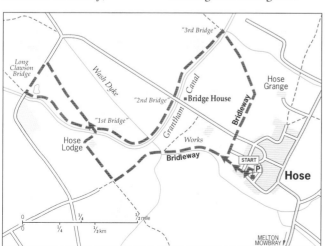

gateway ahead and turn right, heading for the gate by the canal. Cross the bridge and follow the farm track to the road at the end. Turn left here and after 250yds turn left again through the small gate of the cottage garden, and then through another gate onto the canal towpath just before Long Clawson Bridge. Keep on the towpath past the first bridge, along a beautiful willowed stretch, across a stile, and over a second bridge. Cross the canal at the third bridge and go through the gate ahead. Though the designated footpath cuts diagonally across the next field, fencing has made it easier to begin by walking left-handed round the posted electric fence, to reach the hand-gate in the far side. Then cross the rest of the field diagonally in the direction of the village to the right hand of two gates.

Now follow the hedge for two

The Grantham Canal at Hose

WALK 96
LEICESTERSHIRE
SK736293

Information

The walk is three and a half miles long
Level, easy ground
Very little road walking
No stiles, but a fence may have to be climbed if the gate won't open
Pub (Rose and Crown) in Hose village, very welcoming to children and walkers
Canal towpath perfect for picnics

fields, passing through a gate, and turn left onto the road for the short distance back into the village.

The Grantham Canal
The Grantham Canal curls its way from Grantham through the Vale of Belvoir to the River Trent at West Bridgford, just south of Nottingham. Opened in 1797, it enjoyed 50 years of success before beginning to decline in the middle of the 19th century. The last commercial boats used it in 1917, and it was closed altogether in 1936 when its owners refused to renew the lock gates. As can be seen on this walk, weirs were constructed at some locks in the 1950s, but there is still hope of reopening the canal for pleasure boats.

What to look out for

Though disused for many years, the Grantham Canal still has an important role – that of a huge refuge for nature, 33 miles long and 50ft wide, or 50 square miles. Eighty-two different species of wild flowers have been observed along its length, and the very attractive stretch included in our walk is home to some of them.

The West Leake Hills

This delightful walk goes up into the hills above West Leake village, where there are panoramic views over Nottingham and its surrounding countryside, returning through a landscape of woods and pastures.

START
West Leake is some ten miles south of Nottingham City Centre and is easily accessible from the A453, the A6006 or from the junction of the A6 and M1 (junction 24) at Kegworth. Park in the village and start the walk from the eastern end of West Leake.

DIRECTIONS
Where the road turns right out of the village there is a large field entrance with a bridleway marker. Enter the field and follow the track up the hill (Fox Hill). Almost immediately there are good views, initially of the huge power station to the left, then into Leicestershire to the right and behind. Fine woodland soon takes the place of the power station on the left. Keep straight on when the track meets a farm lane, and straight on again past another little road coming in from the left. When the lane eventually bends to the right, turn left, following the public bridleway sign along the ridge of Crow Wood Hill. Rushcliffe Golf Course is to the right. Follow the path onto and along the edge of the golf course and continue, with the trees on your left, past an old red-brick barn on your right. As the golf course comes to an end, continue along the path, following the bridleway sign, through some trees to reach a gate. Go through the gate and, following the blue arrows, keep along the edge of the field, with the wood on the left (remarkable views right of Nottingham in the distance).

At the corner of the field turn left through a gate, follow the path along the left of the hedge and pass through a gate into the wood. Turn right along the track which almost immediately bends to the left, later descending between two arms of woodland. At the bottom turn left along the track to the barn, then right along the farm lane. Just before the line of trees ahead, turn left along a track which, after a while, becomes a path that leads along the edges of the fields and so back to your starting point at West Leake.

What to look out for

The view of the city of Nottingham from the hill on this walk is particularly impressive – it is not often that you see such a large city set in its surrounding countryside. The woods have a rich variety of flora, including masses of bluebells, particularly in the recently felled areas; lesser celandine and greater stitchwort add contrasting colour.

Information

The walk is about four miles long
Ascent and descent of hill are fairly gentle
No stiles
Pub (Star Inn) just to the south of the village at the crossroads; also pubs in nearby East Leake
The woodland section is among several good picnic places along the walk

Nottingham
Nottingham is a city which has grown extensively in recent times and yet, at its heart, still manages to retain a little of the flavour of the days when it was a bustling county town famous for its Goose Fair and Castle. In fact it has a very long history and it was an important fortress from pre-Roman days until the late Middle Ages. Its many excellent museums and other attractions include the award-winning Brewhouse Yard Museum, the Lace Hall, a fascinating reminder of the Nottingham lace industry, and the hi-tech 'Tales of Robin Hood' in which visitors are transported back to Sherwood Forest in 'time cars'.

Fields of rape above West Leake

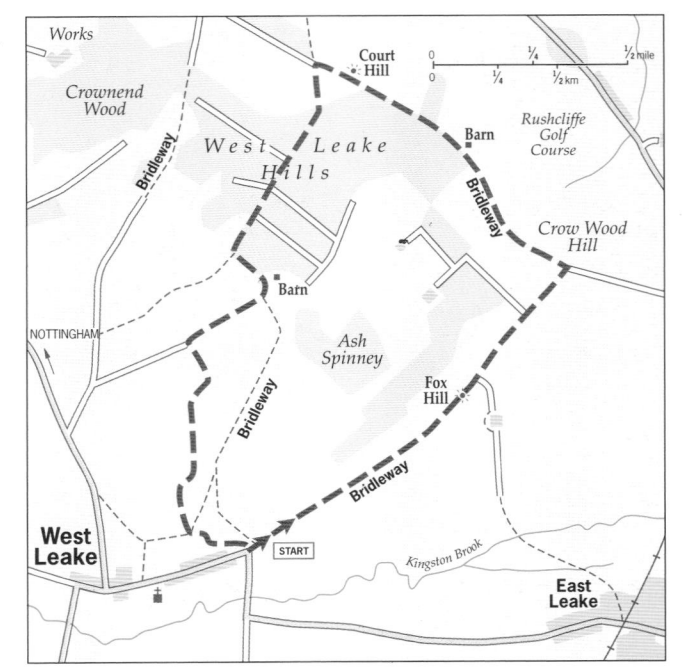

Rufford Country Park and Abbey

Information

The walk is about one and a half miles long
Level and easy going
No road walking
No stiles
Dogs should be kept on leads
Refreshments available at the Mill (north end of the lake) and the Stable Block (at the south)
Various excellent picnic sites in the Park, near the car parks at the southern and northern end, and near the lake
Toilets at the Mill and the Craft Centre

This is a pleasant and easy walk around the lake at Rufford Country Park, on the edge of Sherwood Forest, and includes a visit to Rufford Abbey and Craft Centre.

START

Rufford Country Park is three miles south of Ollerton and 16 miles north of Nottingham on the A614. It is well signposted. It can also be reached with ease from Mansfield via the A6075 or B6030. Start the walk from the main car park (there may be a charge). There is also a car park near the Mill at the north end of the Park.

DIRECTIONS

From the north-west corner of the main car park, head north following signs 'Ice House'. Here there is a choice of routes. Either continue straight on, looping right-handed after a while to arrive at the side of the lake, or turn right at the Ice House, signed 'Rufford Lake', walk across the Broad Ride and turn left along the edge of the lake. There are picnic sites adjacent to both routes.

Whichever route you choose, continue round the lake past the Mill, cross the footbridge and then turn right to continue through the very attractive woodland. Later bear right to cross three footbridges and then turn left to visit the Abbey and craft centre before returning to the car park.

Rufford Abbey

Rufford has a history which goes back to well before the Norman Conquest when it was the property of Ulf the Saxon, but after the invasion it was given by the new King William to his nephew Gilbert le Gaunt. It was his grandson, the Earl of Lincoln, who founded a religious order here with Cistercian monks from Rievaulx Abbey in Yorkshire.

Rufford Abbey, at the heart of the country park

The Abbey of Rufford itself dates from 1147.
The estate passed into the Savile family at the Dissolution, and remained in their hands until 1938 – it now belongs to the county council – and there are still the remains of the Elizabethan house.

What to look out for

Rufford Lake is a nature reserve, and there is a special bird sanctuary at its southern end. Many different sorts of waterfowl can be seen on and around the lake, including Canada goose, mute swan, mallard, pochard and tufted duck. Great crested grebe, moorhen, coot and grey heron are among the other types of waterbird to be seen here.
The park has a flock of rare Mouflon sheep, which look almost like a small breed of deer, especially when, in the autumn, the rams charge each other and lock horns.

The Craft Centre

The Craft Centre includes a shop selling pottery, jewellery, textiles, glass, woodwork, leatherwork and metalwork, while the Gallery holds regular exhibitions. There are also lectures and craft demonstrations. Nearby are an arboretum, formal gardens, sculpture exhibition orangery, restaurants and bookshop.

Mallard

The Reservoir at Denton

This is a very enjoyable and interesting walk from the village of Denton, which goes across an old railway track, round the reservoir and back across the fields via the Grantham Canal.

WALK 99
LINCOLNSHIRE
SK869324

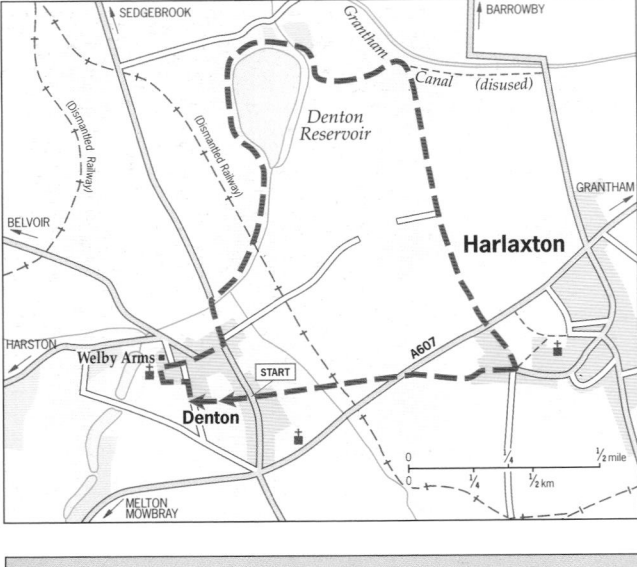

START
Denton is three miles south-west of Grantham, just off the A607. Park carefully and considerately in the village. The walk starts at the telephone box, behind a tree in Main Street.

DIRECTIONS
Take the signed footpath opposite the telephone box. Go through a gate and follow the path under horse chestnut trees and through a kissing-gate. Turn right along the road for a few yards, then turn left at the footpath sign. Go through two kissing-gates to reach the road in front of the church. Turn right and follow the road round past the Welby Arms. Keep straight on at the junction with the main road and go left at the next junction. Walk down to the bridge over the stream and turn right through a gate along the signed footpath. Cross two stiles, then the old

railway line, then another stile and carry on alongside the stream. Do not cross the stile and bridge on your right, but continue over the stile by the white gate, leading to Denton Reservoir. Walk about three quarters of the way round the reservoir, then look out for a footpath sign on the left, directing you down some wooden steps and across a footbridge.

This path leads through the fields and over two stiles. At the end of the second large field, where you meet the Grantham Canal, pass through the gap in the hedge, turn right over a stile by a five-barred gate, going away from the canal. Follow the path

Teal

Information

The walk is about three and a half miles long
Easy walking, with a few gentle inclines
A lot of stiles
Pubs in Denton and Harlaxton serve food; children welcome
Reservoir banks ideal for picnics

which leads along the edge of two fields and then comes out through a nine-barred gate on a track leading away from a farm to the road.

Cross over the road and walk down Rectory Lane, turning right at the bend into West End, on the edge of the village of Harlaxton. Continue down the track ahead and keep straight on to cross a stile. The footpath now bears half-right over the field, aiming to the right of the trees where a stile is set into the hedge bordering the road. Go over this stile, cross the road and take the footpath through a gate opposite, leading across the field back towards Denton. There are two stiles to cross on either side of the old railway line, then a footbridge.

Walk up to a stile in the far right-hand corner of the next field and return to the start.

Denton Reservoir and the Grantham Canal
Originally built as a feeder for the Grantham Canal, the Denton Reservoir can hold up to 61 million gallons of water. The canal dates from the 1790s and runs from Grantham to West Bridgford, where it links with the River Trent. It fell into a decline in the middle of the 19th century, losing the battle with the railways, and finally closed in 1936.

The village of Denton

What to look out for

The reservoir is popular with anglers who come to fish for roach, perch, bream and pike. It is also a favourite spot for birds, including mallard, teal, grey heron, great crested grebe, moorhen and coot, especially in winter.

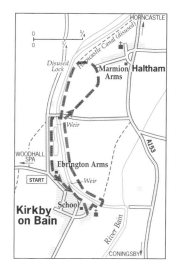

Kingfisher

What to look out for

The River Bain attracts a good deal of wildlife, and it is fairly common to see grey herons in the vicinity. There is also a chance of seeing the sudden blue flash of the shy and elusive kingfisher as it flies low over the water.

Kirkby on Bain and Haltham

A delightful walk between the villages of Kirkby on Bain and Haltham, taking in pastureland, views of an attractive water mill and a stretch of the River Bain.

START

Kirkby on Bain is six miles south of Horncastle, just off the A153. Park carefully and considerately in the village and start the walk from the Ebrington Arms.

DIRECTIONS

Turn left along the pavement opposite the Ebrington Arms and follow the road round until turning left through a kissing-gate, opposite the village shop.
Follow the path until it emerges at the end of a road joining from the right. Turn left then right here, down a path past the primary school, then left at the end to go through a churchyard. Do not cross the stile at the end of the path. Instead, cross the bridge over the river and turn left over a stile.
Follow the river bank, crossing another stile, and soon after the schoolyard on the opposite side of the river, branch right, away from the river, following the yellow arrow. Cross another stile and go along the edge of the field, with the mill on your left, and up onto the bank alongside the river. Climb the stile by the ridge at the end of the

bank, and cross the road and the stile opposite.
Walk right-handed across the field towards the farm in the distance. Cross the dyke and follow the field round to the left, then proceed to cross a stile to the

WALK 100
LINCOLNSHIRE
TF240627

Information

The walk is about two miles long
Level, easy ground
A lot of stiles
Pubs in Kirkby on Bain and Haltham, both welcome walkers and children and serve food
Various picnic places along the walk

left of the red-brick house. Walk up the road to the bend. Turn right here for the short distance to the village of Haltham.
Past the Marmion Arms, continue straight on at the bend in the road, following the footpath sign. The path swings round to the left and crosses a bridge and stile. Continue to the river. Do not cross the bridge, but turn left along the bank to proceed across a series of three stiles. Turn right at the road, over the bridge, left at the junction and so back to the start point.

The Horncastle Canal

At the point where the walk returns to the river for the

final time, the route turns left along the bank at a disused lock. The River Bain was canalised, opening in 1802 to provide a link from Horncastle to the River Witham, south of Tattershall, which in turn linked with the North Sea at the Humber Estuary to the north and the Wash to the south.
The canal owners fought a prolonged battle in the 1850s in an attempt to prevent the railway coming to Horncastle, but they lost and the canal's business began to decline. It carried its last cargo in 1878.

The Horncastle Canal and bridge near Kirkby on Bain

The Mill and Two Churches

This is a pleasant and interesting walk, with a working mill, a canal, two churches in one churchyard and the site of a medieval priory.

START

Alvingham is three miles north-east of Louth. Start the walk at the west end of the village, from a parking area signed 'Two Churches', which is to be found near the mill in Church Lane.

two of three bridges leading over the canal. Turn left and walk along the towpath, crossing a stile after ½ mile. After about ¼ mile the canal curves to the left. Cross the stile and turn right onto the lane by the bridge, then after

Information

The walk is three miles long
Level, easy ground
A few stiles
No pub in village,
but plenty in Louth nearby
The towpath of
the canal is suitable for
picnics

What to look out for

Alvingham is a delightful village with much to see, including a pottery, a working blacksmith's forge and even village stocks. Along Grange Lane, extensive vistas open out across the desolate marshland, where lapwings display in spring.

on along the edge of a lawn, over a stile and across the field, keeping the fence to your left. Climb another stile, go down the path and turn right at the junction of paths. Go straight across the road, following the footpath sign, and so return to the start point.

Alvingham Mill

There has been a watermill in Alvingham since the time of the Domesday Book. The present mill, which may well be on the site of the original, was built in the 17th century and its machinery installed in 1782. The mill is open on Bank Holidays and some summer afternoons.

The open track near Alvingham (left) and Alvingham Mill (right)

It then follows the line of a dyke, round a couple of bends, until it comes to a lane. Turn right here past Grange Farm, and proceed along Grange Lane for about ¾ mile. At a junction go straight on then after a right-hand bend turn left up a track, following a footpath sign. Keep straight

DIRECTIONS

Walk over the road bridge past the mill, through the farmyard and through the gate into the churchyard. Turning right, follow the hedgeline and cross the first

the bend turn right over another bridge, passing through a gateway, signed 'bridleway'. This track passes to the left of a cottage and windpump and then crosses the dry bed of the River Lud.

WALES AND THE
MARCHES

Evesham – River and Town

This is an easy walk in the Avon valley, linking Twyford Country Centre, with its many attractions, and Evesham, a lovely town with lots of historic buildings and attractive riverside parkland.

START

Twyford Country Centre is nearly two miles north of Evesham and 200 yards beyond the bypass. Admittance and parking are free. At the car park, a map of the centre and surrounding country includes walks marked by the county council's Countryside Service.

DIRECTIONS

From the car park follow the track past the children's play area. Go through a gate and descend. Keep straight on past orchards on the right (Please do not pick fruit or collect windfalls) and down the steps to the river bank.

Turn right along the river. Downstream, The Bridge Inn stands on the far bank and a ferry sometimes crosses to it. Opposite the inn, climb a stile to a meadow and continue under the bypass, through or over three fences and a footbridge to the next field. (Here you can shorten the walk by climbing a stile by the metal gate at the far right corner, and turning right along the track. Continue at * below.)

The main walk continues to reach Evesham by skirting around the marshy area to leave the field by a metal kissing-gate hidden in the hedgerow ahead, then follows the path under the Worcester–Oxford railway line to join an unmetalled track. Where the track swings right at the end of the chain-link fence, take a path into bushes and go through a metal gate. Continue over a slipway and past moorings (with care – narrow unfenced path by the side of the river) to an old mill at the edge of the town.

At the road, turn left and proceed along it to a junction. Keep ahead to Bridge Street and turn right to the half-timbered Round House, or Booth Hall, at the top. Bear left into the Market Place and pass through the Norman Gate to the Abbey Precinct. To return to Twyford, go back to the mill by the river and follow the road to a junction. Keep ahead along Common Road and under a railway arch.

*Continue past the stile mentioned on the short-cut above and walk left of a hedge to Oxstalls Farm. Skirt the buildings to the right and, on the far side, turn right along a field margin beyond a hedge. At the field corner bear left to the farm gate. Carefully cross

The banks of the Avon

the bypass to the former railway, signed 'Footpath', and cross the stile. Continue until the track from Twyford is reached and return to the Centre.

Twyford Country Centre

The site includes a garden centre, farm shop, wildlife and falconry centre, crafts centre, cane centre, natural health and beauty shop, conservatory centre, country café and children's play area.

Evesham

In the Abbey precinct, occupying a beautiful site above the Avon, two parish churches stand almost side by side. Nearby is the 110ft-high Bell Tower, added to the Abbey only a few years before the Dissolution of the Monasteries.

What to look out for

In summer the River Avon is lively and active, with fishermen lining the bank and holiday cruisers and narrowboats going to and fro. There are wildfowl on the water, and thistles in the riverside meadows attract goldfinches in the autumn.

A Maze in the Wye Valley

This walk is in the beautiful Lower Wye Valley. Following the river bank downstream, it crosses the Wye via two ferries and returns from the foot of Symonds Yat Rock along a quiet lane, rising gently to give fine views.

START

Whitchurch is on the B4164, five miles south-west of Ross-on-Wye, just off the A40. Park at the Jubilee Park beside the B4164 (parking free at time of going to press, but a charge may be introduced in the near future), or in the car park (charge) of the neighbouring Wye Valley Leisure Park.

DIRECTIONS

Cross the bridge leading to the Maze in the Jubilee Park and turn left along a tarmac track to the Church of St Dubricius. The riverside path can be reached by going through the churchyard, or alternatively by following the footpath to the right at the end of the wall through the

The River Wye below Symond's Yat Rock

kissing-gate, from which a narrow flagged path leads to the river.

Turn right, to go downstream past the Wye Valley Leisure Park, then pass through a kissing-gate to a large riverside meadow. Beyond the meadow the path ends at Ye Olde Ferrie Inne. A chain ferry is operated by the inn (but not in adverse weather conditions, nor when the river is in flood. If the ferry is not operating, or if you wish to shorten the walk, continue the route at * below).

Take the ferry to the far bank, where there is a pleasant walk downstream to the Ancient Hand ferry at the Saracen's Head Hotel. Re-cross the river there and turn right along the

track, which runs past the rear of Ye Olde Ferrie Inne * to the B4164.

Follow the road ahead, past a telephone box, and fork left up a lane.

Shortly, at a junction, keep straight ahead between two white cottages, then pass to the left of another white cottage ('Crossways'), to where the track bends left, below a United Reformed Church. Continue straight ahead through a kissing-gate to a field and follow the right-hand hedge down to a second kissing-gate on the

B4164. Turn right here for the Jubilee Park, and to return to the starting point.

The Jubilee Park

The Park's attractions include the Jubilee Maze – a hedge maze constructed in 1977 to commemorate the Queen's Silver Jubilee – with lovely gardens and countryside walks, the Museum of Mazes, the Amazing Puzzle Shop, the World of Butterflies, a garden centre and a restaurant. There is also a Tourist Information Centre here. The park is closed from Christmas to the end of January.

The Parish Church of St Dubricius

Dubricius was a 6th-century bishop, teacher and founder of churches.

According to legend, when Peipiau, the King of Erging, discovered that his daughter was pregnant, he ordered her to be put in a sack and drowned in the Wye, but the girl was washed ashore alive. The king then tried to burn her to death, but next morning she was found nursing her child, Dubricius, whose Welsh name, Dyfrig, means water baby.

The church, on a site dating from Saxon times, is mainly 12th century.

Croft Castle and Croft Ambrey

This an easy figure-of-eight hill walk on National Trust land, linking the late-medieval Croft Castle with the even older fortification of Croft Ambrey, a mile away and 400ft higher.

START
Croft Castle is seven miles south-west of Ludlow, off the B4362. Start from the free car park (small charge if you are not visiting the castle). There is a map of the estate, which is always open to the public without charge.

DIRECTIONS
From the car park, walk back along the drive and cross a cattle-grid. Turn immediately left, down a path through woods to the Fishpool Valley. Ascend the valley track to the left, passing a stone-built Gothic pumphouse and a pool. At the track junction on the left, just before the next pool, turn left by the remains of a lime kiln, go along the side-track for about 10yds, then leave it for a path on the right. Fork right and climb to Ambrey Cottage, there meeting a broader path, and turn left through a gate. (To shorten the route, avoiding the climb to Croft Ambrey, continue the walk at * below). Bear right to a gate leading into Croft Wood, climb the path and cross a track to reach the top of a rise

(splendid view). Go through a gate and bear to the left of a wire fence to a path (another magnificent view). From a stile on the right climb a path bearing left. It swings through the ramparts of the hillfort and over the high ground in the centre. Beyond the hillfort descend a path through ferns, and fork left. There is a view east to the distant Malvern Hills, before the path bears left and drops to a stile. Turn right along the path beyond and right again through a small wooden gate. Descend between trees and go right along the track at the bottom. Ignore a major track (after about 70yds) bearing left and continue to a fork,

Mole

where a lesser track descending to the left leads back to Ambrey Cottage. *Pass through the gate used before and bear left of a covered reservoir to descend open grassland. Follow the path through a line of old, twisted chestnut trees, down a meadow and under more trees to a gate, from which a track leads back to the car park.

The church in the grounds of Croft Castle

What to look out for

A wide variety of trees can be seen, including many unusual non-native species. Look under the overhangs of the Castle towers for house martins' nests and watch for buzzards soaring over the hillfort. Fallow deer, badgers and polecats are among the creatures who inhabit the area. The chain of five pools in the Fishpool Valley is a lovely example of late 18th-century 'picturesque' landscaping; the remains of a lime kiln can be seen near the Gothic pumphouse.

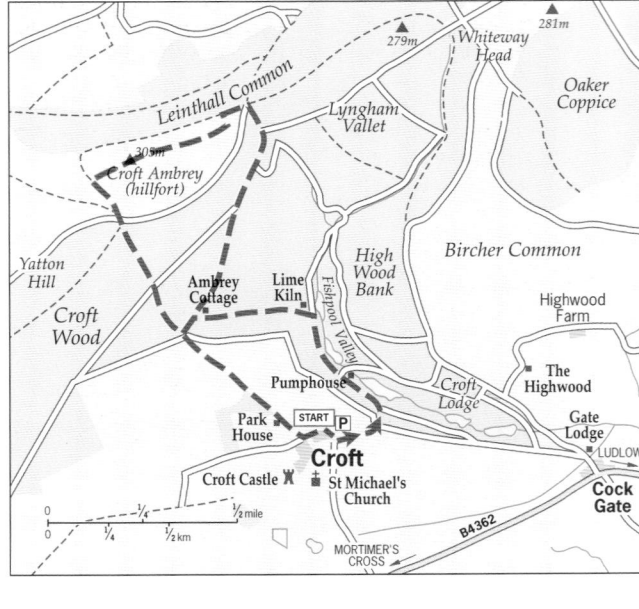

Croft Castle
The stone walls of the castle date from the 14th and 15th centuries, but the interior was thoroughly 'modernised' in the 18th. The Croft family lived here until 1746, and returned after buying back the castle in 1923. Although it remains the family home, it now belongs to the National Trust and is open at weekends and on selected days from Easter to October.

Croft Ambrey
The 1,000ft-high hillfort, covering 38 acres, was occupied from the 4th century BC until the Roman invasion of Britain. Today it provides some of the loveliest views of the Welsh Border country.

The Lickey Hills

This walk explores part of the lovely 524-acre Lickey Hills Country Park, with its varied scenery of pools, woods, open grassland and a golf course – and there are magnificent views from Beacon Hill.

START
The Lickey Hills rise at Rednal, on the south-western outskirts of Birmingham. Leave the M42 at junction 1 and take the B4096. This leads directly to the free public car park behind the Old Rose & Crown, off Rose Hill.

DIRECTIONS
From the car park pass left of the café to a large pool and skirt it to the right. Follow a chain of small ornamental pools uphill and pass between two of them to join a broad track. Opposite a green bank with picnic tables branch right, climbing very steeply and soon forking left. At the top of the track turn left, climbing again and forking right by a seat. Cross a diagonal path and continue through blackberry bushes, then bear left along a path beside Scots pines. At the cross-path turn right through the pines and veer left, between toilet blocks, to the open plateau of Beacon Hill. Cross to the battlemented toposcope (sadly vandalised)

at 987ft above sea level and enjoy the views, before descending right towards Birmingham. Walk along well worn grass paths, passing a North Worcester Path marker post, and on your right an Ordnance Survey Trig point, then descend through woods. After 200yds descend log steps and at the bottom turn left, soon crossing (carefully) the municipal golf course. In 300yds, on the far side of the course, the path runs right beside a line of trees and reaches a cross-path. Turn right along a heavily wooded bridleway for about 200yds, then bear right along the edge of the golf course. Finally turn right through an attractive beech avenue to return to the car park.

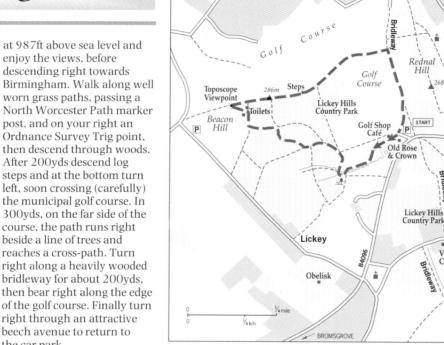

George V in 1935. It once bore a plaque recording the gift of 34 acres of hillside to the citizens of Birmingham by the Cadbury family in 1907.

The Lickey Hills Visitor Centre
Information about the country park can be obtained at the visitor centre, which stands half a mile south of the B4096, along a path starting from a footbridge east of the Old Rose & Crown. Cars can reach it by turning right from the car park and left along Warren Lane, just before the church.

The North Worcestershire Path
During the walk you will see waymark posts with the initials 'NWP'. These indicate the route of the North Worcestershire Path, a 21-mile walking route from Forhill Picnic Site, on the Roman Ryknid Street, to Kinver Edge.

What to look out for

The pool at the start of the walk is home to a variety of wildfowl, and in summer there are yellow flag irises at its edge and an array of wild flowers on the bank beside the path. In the woods you may hear the drumming of a great spotted woodpecker; look out for the wood warbler and redstart, both summer visitors to the area. You may see squirrels, but the little muntjac deer are much more timid.

Kite-flying on Beacon Hill

Beacon Hill
As its name suggests, the hilltop provided a link in the chain of burning beacons that once covered the country to warn the population of

danger, such as the Spanish Armada in 1588, or to celebrate victories and anniversaries, as it did at the Queen's Silver Jubilee in 1977. The stone fountain below the toposcope dates from the Silver Jubilee of

Information

The walk is one and a half miles long
Hilly ground; well-defined paths
No road walking
Dogs should be kept on leads when crossing golf course
No stiles
Light refreshments at café near start of walk and at Lickey Hills Visitor Centre
The plateau of Beacon Hill and the grassy area by the car park are suitable for picnics
Toilets at Beacon Hill

Upper Arley - River, Woods and Reservoirs

From the delightful little Severnside village of Upper Arley, the walk follows a lovely path downstream, before climbing to circle Trimpley reservoir and lagoon, high above the river, and returning through woods and farmland.

WALK 106
HEREFORD & WORCESTER
SO766802

START
Upper Arley lies beside the River Severn, three and a half miles north of Bewdley. It is accessible via a lane from Shatterford on the A442 Kidderminster–Bridgnorth road.

Alternatively, cars can be parked free at Kidderminster, Bewdley or Bridgnorth stations and the village reached by steam train on the Severn Valley Railway. At Upper Arley there are public pay car parks on each side of the river. Start from the pedestrian-only river bridge across the Severn.

DIRECTIONS
From the eastern end of the long metal footbridge head south (downstream). At a large house ('Worrall's Grove'), leave the waymarked Worcestershire Way, keeping to the riverside path. Pass under Victoria Bridge, beneath which there is a stile to cross. After about 200yds, another stile leads into a sheep pasture. A notice board gives information about Trimpley Reservoir.
Skirt the trees bordering the river, cross a railed footbridge and climb to the left to reach the reservoir. Bear right along

Information
The walk is three and a half miles long
Clear paths and bridleways; some hills
Virtually no road walking
Dogs should be kept on leads in the sheep pasture beside Trimpley Reservoir
A few stiles
Pub on each side of the river at Upper Arley, with gardens but no children's rooms; bar meals served; tearoom in village
Plenty of open grassland at Trimpley Reservoir, suitable for picnic

What to look out for

At Upper Arley note the jetties used by the former chain ferry. Early in the walk there are signs indicating the Worcestershire Way, an official 36-mile walking route from Kinver to the Malvern Hills. The riverside path goes under the splendid Victoria Bridge of 1861. The Trimpley Reservoir, built in the 1960s to supplement Birmingham's Elan Valley water supply, gives fine views west across the vast Wyre Forest. From the farmland towards the end of the walk look left for the Shropshire Giants, Titterstone Clee Hill and Brown Clee Hill. Much of the walk is within sight – and sound – of the steam trains on the Severn Valley Railway.

its bank and left at the end, before dropping down to the smaller lagoon and walking anti-clockwise round it to the stile and gate leading into woodland on the far side. Cross the Severn Valley Railway (with care!) and ignore a left-turn, but higher up fork left, and soon bear left along a broader track to the end of a surfaced lane by the waterworks' entrance. Enter the Arley Estate opposite and follow the bridleway through

Ground Ivy

Eymore Wood. It descends, crosses the Worcestershire Way, and climbs steadily through mature forest to a hilltop crossways. Take the track ahead, descending through tall, straight pines to a bridge over a stream.
The way soon rises out of the

woods and crosses high farmland to a lane. Turn left and descend to Upper Arley.

Upper Arley
The little village is beautifully set beside the broad River Severn. The Valencia Arms, in Frenchman's Street, took its name from the courtesy title of the eldest son of Lord Mountnorris, Lord of the Manor. Next door, protruding into the road, stands the battlemented Arley Tower, built in 1842 by the then Lord Mountnorris. Its purpose was to block the view from the house of Mr Sam Willcox, who had refused to sell his home to his lordship. No planning permission was required in those days!
The street climbs to St Peter's Church, which houses the tomb of a crusader, believed to be the unfortunate Sir Walter de Balun. He joined the Eighth Crusade in 1270, but never reached the Holy Land, dying of injuries received in a tournament on his wedding day.

The River Severn at Upper Arley

A Traditional Working Farm

This walk begins at the Acton Scott Working Farm Museum and passes through the gentle hills and pastures of Ape Dale, in the Shropshire Hills Area of Outstanding Natural Beauty.

START

Acton Scott Working Farm Museum is two and a half miles south of Church Stretton and three quarters of a mile east of the A49 Shrewsbury–Hereford road at Marshbrook. Parking is free for farm visitors, who are welcome to leave their cars while walking local footpaths.

DIRECTIONS

From the waymarked stile in the corner of the car park cross to a stile at the far corner of the field. Enter woodland and descend along its edge to a stile on the left. Turn right through a field to a corner stile with two waymarks. Follow the right-hand arrow over a large field and continue for about ½ mile to a stile at the bottom right, with a fine view ahead to Wenlock Edge.
Descend the next field, cross a double stile and continue to the bottom left corner. Turn right for a few yards, then left on to a track. The way swings right along a dismantled railway for about 75yds to a right-hand gate. Bear right here and join an old bridleway bordered by trees. Swing left at the top of the field and continue along the upper field-edge and through a gateway, heading towards a stone barn.
Just before the barn turn right through a gate and follow a hedge over a rise and down the other side, to where a track continues to a cottage on Henley Lane. Turn right and climb to the church.
From a gate at the far right corner of the churchyard follow the right-hand hedge, then veer down to a waymark post under an oak. Descend to a stile by a gate, climb the field beyond to a solitary oak and bear right to a gate on a lane. The museum is to the right, beyond crossroads.

Acton Scott Working Farm Museum

The museum is managed by Shropshire County Council on 23 acres of land belonging to the neighbouring Hall. Work as it would have been done in the pre-tractor age goes on daily in the fields and outbuildings. Various crafts are demonstrated, including those of dairymaid, wheelwright, blacksmith and farrier. The farm is open from April to November; closed Mondays except Bank Holidays.

Parish Church of St Margaret

Though the date 1722 can just be made out over the south porch, there has been a church here since 1291 and the building was restored in the early 19th century. A brass plate to Elizabeth Mytton (died 1571) shows her with her husband and eleven children. From the footpath leaving the north-west corner of the churchyard there is a magnificent panorama of the Long Mynd and Ragleth Hill.

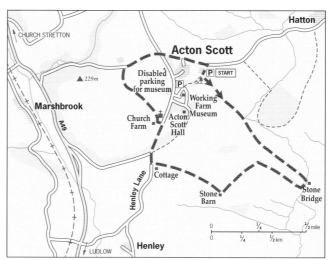

The wheelwright's workshop

Horse-power at Acton Scott Farm

On Wenlock Edge

This is mainly a woodland walk on National Trust land at the northern end of the 15-mile long Wenlock Edge. Beginning with Blakeway Hollow, now a rough, sunken lane but once the main road from Much Wenlock to Shrewsbury, it passes the viewpoint of Major's Leap.

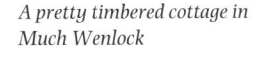

The path to Blakeway Hollow

START

The A458 Shrewsbury–Bridgnorth road crosses the northern end of Wenlock Edge at Much Wenlock. Start the walk from the National Trust's free car park, which is signed a quarter of a mile along the B4371. There are also car parks in Much Wenlock, including one for visitors to the Priory.

DIRECTIONS

At the car park, cross the grass to a gate, climb steps and turn left into a hedged, unmetalled lane (Blakeway Hollow), following sign 'Blakeway Coppice' for about ½ mile to reach a signpost at the edge of the wood. (Two miles can be cut from the walk by following the Harley Bank arrow to the right and continuing the route at * below.)

Follow the 'Blakeway Coppice' sign and fork left to a gate. After about 50yds take a stepped path on the left, signed 'Major's Leap'. The narrow path follows the wooded crest of the ridge for about ½ mile until a short path to the right leads to the Major's Leap viewpoint. Return to the edge of the escarpment, where a path outside the trees, high above a limestone quarry, is followed to the right (Shropshire's highest point,

1,792ft Brown Clee Hill, to the left).

After about ½ mile, before the end of the quarry and above the quarry buildings, an old track angles back and steeply down to the right. Descend it to join the main track bearing right through the woods. After about 250yds bear right to return to the entrance gate. Follow the signposted Harley Bank path to the left, * soon descending steeply through Harley Wood. After about 300yds, take a path forking

up to the right and after another 300yds bear right again up a stepped path at a signpost. At the top turn left and continue for about 150yds to a horse barrier and an old milestone.

Turn right through a gate and keep ahead to the stone buildings at Stokes Barn. Go through a gate and bear right by the barn entrance and signpost 'Much Wenlock'. Another signpost points the way down to a small wooden gate, from which the path descends through fields to a stile on Blakeway Hollow, with the car park to the left.

Much Wenlock

This lovely and interesting little town lies below the northern tip of Wenlock Edge. The ruins of its Cluniac Priory (English Heritage) date from the 12th and 13th centuries. Features of the town include the half-timbered Guildhall of 1540, a local museum, a magnificent church and many other fine buildings.

A pretty timbered cottage in Much Wenlock

Major's Leap

The Royalist Major Smallman of Wilderhope Manor is said to have survived a leap on horseback from the limestone crag when escaping from Roundhead troops during the Civil War.
From the Leap there is a fine outlook across Ape Dale, with a distant view of the Berwyns in North Wales.

Honeysuckle

What to look out for

Fossils can be found in the pale limestone of Wenlock Edge, which also nurtures many flowering plants, including orchids, not found in other soils. It is possible to look down into one of the limestone quarries, and in Harley Wood there is an old milestone.

A Traditional Working Farm

This walk begins at the Acton Scott Working Farm Museum and passes through the gentle hills and pastures of Ape Dale, in the Shropshire Hills Area of Outstanding Natural Beauty.

START
Acton Scott Working Farm Museum is two and a half miles south of Church Stretton and three quarters of a mile east of the A49 Shrewsbury–Hereford road at Marshbrook. Parking is free for farm visitors, who are welcome to leave their cars while walking local footpaths.

DIRECTIONS
From the waymarked stile in the corner of the car park cross to a stile at the far corner of the field. Enter woodland and descend along its edge to a stile on the left. Turn right through a field to a corner stile with two waymarks. Follow the right-hand arrow over a large field

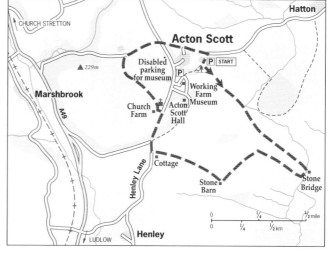

Horse-power at Acton Scott Farm

and continue for about ½ mile to a stile at the bottom right, with a fine view ahead to Wenlock Edge.

Descend the next field, cross a double stile and continue to the bottom left corner. Turn right for a few yards, then left on to a track. The way swings right along a dismantled railway for about 75yds to a right-hand gate. Bear right here and join an old bridleway bordered by trees. Swing left at the top of the field and continue along the upper field-edge and through a gateway, heading towards a stone barn.

Just before the barn turn right through a gate and follow a hedge over a rise and down the other side, to where a track continues to a cottage on Henley Lane. Turn right and climb to the church.

From a gate at the far right corner of the churchyard follow the right-hand hedge,

then veer down to a waymark post under an oak. Descend to a stile by a gate, climb the field beyond to a solitary oak and bear right to a gate on a lane. The museum is to the right, beyond crossroads.

Acton Scott Working Farm Museum
The museum is managed by Shropshire County Council on 23 acres of land belonging to the neighbouring Hall. Work as it would have been done in the pre-tractor age goes on daily in the fields and outbuildings. Various crafts are demonstrated, including those of dairymaid, wheelwright, blacksmith and farrier. The farm is open from April to November; closed Mondays except Bank Holidays.

Parish Church of St Margaret
Though the date 1722 can just be made out over the

south porch, there has been a church here since 1291 and the building was restored in the early 19th century. A brass plate to Elizabeth Mytton (died 1571) shows her with her husband and eleven children. From the footpath leaving the north-west corner of the churchyard there is a magnificent panorama of the Long Mynd and Ragleth Hill.

The wheelwright's workshop

On Wenlock Edge

WALK 108
SHROPSHIRE
SO613997

This is mainly a woodland walk on National Trust land at the northern end of the 15-mile long Wenlock Edge. Beginning with Blakeway Hollow, now a rough, sunken lane but once the main road from Much Wenlock to Shrewsbury, it passes the viewpoint of Major's Leap.

The path to Blakeway Hollow

Information

The walk is three and a half miles long
Mainly gentle hills, but some steep descents in woods
No road walking
Dogs should be on leads through fields at end of walk
One stile
Refreshments (seasonal) *en route* at Stokes Barn; pubs and cafés at Much Wenlock
Grassy area suitable for picnics at car park

START

The A458 Shrewsbury–Bridgnorth road crosses the northern end of Wenlock Edge at Much Wenlock. Start the walk from the National Trust's free car park, which is signed a quarter of a mile along the B4371. There are also car parks in Much Wenlock, including one for visitors to the Priory.

DIRECTIONS

At the car park, cross the grass to a gate, climb steps and turn left into a hedged, unmetalled lane (Blakeway Hollow), following sign 'Blakeway Coppice' for about ½ mile to reach a signpost at the edge of the wood. (Two miles can be cut from the walk by following the Harley Bank arrow to the right and continuing the route at * below.)

Follow the 'Blakeway Coppice' sign and fork left to a gate. After about 50yds take a stepped path on the left, signed 'Major's Leap'. The narrow path follows the wooded crest of the ridge for about ½ mile until a short path to the right leads to the Major's Leap viewpoint. Return to the edge of the escarpment, where a path outside the trees, high above a limestone quarry, is followed to the right (Shropshire's highest point,

1,792ft Brown Clee Hill, to the left).
After about ½ mile, before the end of the quarry and above the quarry buildings, an old track angles back and steeply down to the right. Descend it to join the main track bearing right through the woods. After about 250yds bear right to return to the entrance gate. Follow the signposted Harley Bank path to the left, * soon descending steeply through Harley Wood. After about 300yds, take a path forking

up to the right and after another 300yds bear right again up a stepped path at a signpost. At the top turn left and continue for about 150yds to a horse barrier and an old milestone.
Turn right through a gate and keep ahead to the stone buildings at Stokes Barn. Go through a gate and bear right by the barn entrance and signpost 'Much Wenlock'. Another signpost points the way down to a small wooden gate, from which the path descends through fields to a stile on Blakeway Hollow, with the car park to the left.

Much Wenlock

This lovely and interesting little town lies below the northern tip of Wenlock Edge. The ruins of its Cluniac Priory (English Heritage) date from the 12th and 13th centuries. Features of the town include the half-timbered Guildhall of 1540, a local museum, a magnificent church and many other fine buildings.

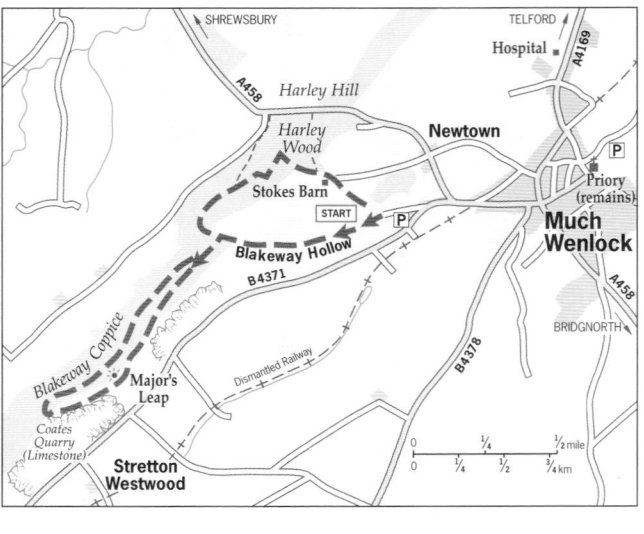

A pretty timbered cottage in Much Wenlock

Major's Leap

The Royalist Major Smallman of Wilderhope Manor is said to have survived a leap on horseback from the limestone crag when escaping from Roundhead troops during the Civil War.
From the Leap there is a fine outlook across Ape Dale, with a distant view of the Berwyns in North Wales.

Honeysuckle

What to look out for

Fossils can be found in the pale limestone of Wenlock Edge, which also nurtures many flowering plants, including orchids, not found in other soils. It is possible to look down into one of the limestone quarries, and in Harley Wood there is an old milestone.

Shropshire's Lake District

This is an easy, level walk round Cole Mere and along the Shropshire Union Canal to Blake Mere, thus visiting two of the nine meres, or lakes, in this geologically unique area known as 'the Shropshire Lake District'.

Beautiful 'lakeland' scenery

WALK 109
SHROPSHIRE
SJ435328

Information

The walk is about three and a half miles long
Level, easy ground
No road walking
Dogs should be kept on leads
No stiles
Nearest pubs and cafés are at Ellesmere
Grassy area beside car park suitable for picnics
No bathing or paddling in meres
Toilets at Cole Mere

START

Colemere Country Park is two and a half miles south-east of Ellesmere, between the A528 and the B5063, and immediately north of the hamlet of Colemere. Start the walk from the free car park beside the lake.

DIRECTIONS

From the car park set off clockwise round Cole Mere by joining the path along its western shore. At the far end of the mere, ignore a right fork and continue to a lane. Turn right, past a lovely thatched, black and white cottage, to the Shropshire Union Canal, and follow its towpath to the left until another large lake (Blake Mere) appears on your right. (The walk can be extended by 2 miles here by following the canal past Blake Mere and through a short tunnel. After about ¾ mile cross a bridge over a spur of the canal and turn right into the small town of Ellesmere. Walk through the town and return along the A528 (footpath), passing the Mere, the Cremorne Gardens and the Boat House Restaurant. Regain the canal at the road junction with the A495.)

The main route, after viewing Blake Mere, returns along the towpath and passes under the lane to the next bridge, about 700yds farther on. Cross the bridge, then follow the path to the left through Yell Wood. Bearing right, the path goes down the east side of Cole Mere and returns to the open grassy area near the car park.

The Meres

The nine meres in the Ellesmere area are relics of the Ice Age glaciers that covered Britain 25,000 years ago, extending south of Shrewsbury. The withdrawal of the ice left a thick coating of glacier debris, or moraine, but pockets of ice survived in hollows and when they melted, meres were formed. They could be described simply as enormous puddles, mostly without streams flowing in or out, which are sustained by rainfall or the water table. The largest of the lakes, The Mere at Ellesmere, covers 116 acres and has a visitors' centre.

What to look out for

Cole Mere is a lake of great interest for its bird life and the activities of its sailing club. Great crested grebes are common in winter, woodpeckers drum on old trees, and bats fly over the water at dawn and dusk. It is the only place in England where the rare least yellow water-lily can be found. Beyond Blake Mere is a short canal tunnel, and many holiday narrow boats pass along the Shropshire Union Canal in summer.

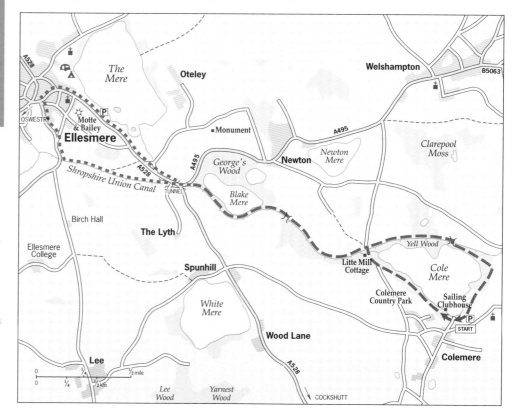

The Windcliff Walk and 'The 365 Steps'

WALK 110
GWENT
ST524973

This is a fascinating walk with outstanding views, but take care descending the 365 steps, for they are steep in places and you need to be steady on your feet.

Information

The walk is one and a half miles long
The gradient up to the Eagle's Nest viewpoint is fairly gentle, but the descent by the 365 Steps is steep and should be undertaken with care; if in doubt, return along the outward route
No road walking
No stiles
Pub in St Arvans village, bar meals and morning coffee served

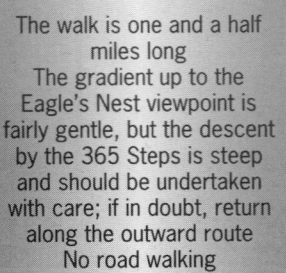

Wood mouse

START
Leave the A466 (Chepstow to Monmouth road) just north of St Arvans and follow a narrow lane signposted 'Wyndcliff' to reach a small car park on the right.

DIRECTIONS
Follow the signposted path from the car park up through the trees to shortly reach a seat on the right (fine view across to the Severn Bridge). Continue along the track, well shaded by the overhanging trees, to a clearing with another seat. (Through a gap in the hedge on the left is a view of the Iron Age hillfort known as Gaer.) Keep following the main track which now levels out, and by a 'viewpoint' sign go down some steps to the Eagle's Nest viewpoint. After taking in the splendid view return to the clearing mentioned above

and follow a path down to the left, signposted '365 Steps'. The first flight of steps is soon reached. On reaching a platform, pause to admire the view and then continue down an old ship's ladder with the open sides protected by iron rails. Below the ladder the steps continue in helter-skelter fashion down through a break in the cliffs. The path then crosses the hillside, threading its way between moss-covered boulders, past gnarled yew trees and weather-sculpted rocks. Then continue on between two rock outcrops.
Descend the final steps and continue through the trees to emerge on to a more open track leading to an old quarry, now used as a car park. Continue up a wide track and after about 200yds turn right up a narrow path which leads up through the

trees via a few steps to reach your starting point.

The Eagle's Nest
Perched on the edge of the cliff, 700ft above the River Wye, this magnificent viewpoint has upper and lower decks. As well as the

sweeping river, Chepstow race course and castle can be seen. In the distance gleams the Severn estuary, with the county of Avon on the far side, reached via the elegant Severn Bridge.
On the other side of the Wye are the cliffs known as

The River Wye from Eagle's Nest (above) and some of the 365 steps (right)

Wintour's Leap, named after a Royalist colonel who was chased by Cromwell's forces during the Civil War. He reputedly escaped by jumping off the cliff (with his horse) to land safely in the river.

The 365 Steps
In 1828 Osmond Wyatt, the Duke of Beaufort's steward, laid down the steps as an attraction for early tourists who came to admire the scenic beauty of the Wye Valley.

What to look out for

There is every chance of seeing squirrels, woodpeckers, nuthatches and great tits along this walk, possibly even the tiny goldcrest. This is also a good area for butterflies, which may include holly blue and the large silver-washed fritillary.

White Castle

This is an enjoyable walk through unspoilt countryside to the east of Abergavenny in Gwent. It passes an interesting church, before proceeding through fields and up to a fairy-tale hill-top castle.

START
Follow the B4521 from Abergavenny (Skenfrith Road) to Llanvetherine and park in a small lay-by opposite the church.

DIRECTIONS
Cross the road and proceed to the church, crossing a stone stile opposite the porch, then a wooden footbridge spanning a stream. Go up a green lane between tall hedges for a short distance and then cross over a stile on the left. Cross field, passing a long barn on the left. Follow the hedge on the left to reach a gate and continue, looking out for a footbridge by which to cross a brook. Bear right across the next field to reach another footbridge. You are now on Offa's Dyke Long Distance Path.
Cross the next field, then a stile and another field, gaining height as you go. Continue, to cross a stile in the hedge on the right. Later, just before a barn, cross a stile then turn right to pass the end of the barn and go over

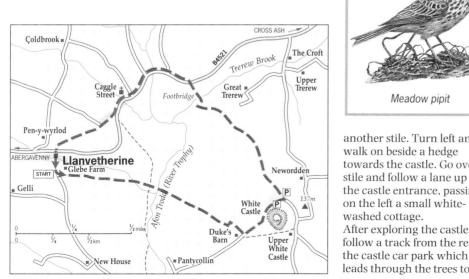

Skirrid Fawr (above) and the gatehouse tower of White Castle (right)

another stile. Turn left and walk on beside a hedge towards the castle. Go over a stile and follow a lane up to the castle entrance, passing on the left a small white-washed cottage.
After exploring the castle, follow a track from the rear of the castle car park which leads through the trees to a stile. Beyond the stile follow a fence on the right.
Pass through a gate at the end of the first field and follow the fence down to another stile, then continue through the next field and go over a stile beside a gate. Now look out for a stile on the right, cross it and soon afterwards cross a footbridge over a stream. Go straight across the next field to a stile in the left hand corner.
Cross the road and turn left. Follow the road over a bridge, past a chapel, then take the lane on the right. After about 50yds up hill go over a stile by a gate and go straight ahead, keeping to the left of a line of trees to reach a stile in a hedge. Walk straight across the next field to reach another stile and then head diagonally down through another field to reach the final stile just above the starting point.

White Castle
The castle's ancient name, Castell Gwyn, means White Castle, and if you look closely

WALK 111
GWENT
SO363172

Information

This walk is three miles long
One ascent up to the castle
A lot of stiles
No dogs allowed in the castle
The castle is an ideal location for a picnic

you may see evidence of whitened cement on the exterior. The castle was started by King Stephen in 1184, but most of the present building dates from the early 13th century. With the neighbouring castles of Grosmont and Skenfrith it formed the 'Three Castles of Gwent'. This is the most beautiful of the three, with a water-filled moat and impressive round towers at each corner. From the top of the gatehouse tower there is a splendid view.

To the Summit of Twmbarlwm

A hill walk which may be combined with the Cwmcarn Forest Drive (Easter to the end of October only). The views from the summit are just rewards for the effort involved, not to mention the sense of achievement.

START

Leave the M4 motorway at junction 28 and take the A467. Signs for the Cwmcarn Forest Drive will be seen after about seven miles. The walk starts from the car park (Pegwn-y-Bwlch) on the Cwmcarn Forest Drive; when the Forest Drive is closed (November to Easter) park at the Visitor Centre and walk up the footpath on the right hand side of the centre. After passing a small lake, take the path to the right over a stile signposted 'Pegwn-y-Bwlch'. Continue up this path, crossing three tarmac roads to reach the car park.

DIRECTIONS

Go over a stile signposted 'Castle Mound' and climb the well worn path. The gradient relents and the walk then crosses the fortification ditch of an Iron Age hill fort. Continue across the summit plateau to reach the 'trig' point. Directly ahead now is a large mound, known locally as the 'Twmbarlwm Pimple'. After taking in the view, follow a broad track down to a stile and then, keeping a

The way up to the summit

forestry plantation on your right, head down to a road. Follow the road for about ½ mile then take a track on the right leading down beside a fence. Cross a rutted track, bear right along fence and head for a stile, signed 'Darren', in the corner of the field. Go over the stile and continue with the fence on your left. Shortly turn left by a public footpath sign and proceed along the bottom of the field to reach a stile in the corner.
Continue beside the fence to later emerge from the trees. The track now descends with a

WALK 112
GWENT
ST237929

Information

The walk is two and a half miles long
Two steep sections
Several stiles
Dogs should be kept on leads
Pub near the entrance to the Forest Drive in Cwmcarn
Toilets at the Visitor Centre

line of pylons on the left. Cross a stile and head down towards some old farm buildings. Turn right and follow a track leading to a gate and then downhill through the edge of a larch plantation and through a gate into a narrow secluded valley. Turn right at the T-junction, cross a stile and ascend a broad track up the side of the valley. At a crossing with a new forest road, keep forward to the top of the pass and the return to the car park.

Cwmcarn Forest Drive

The seven-mile Cwmcarn Forest Drive was the first of its kind to be developed in Britain. It is open from Easter to October and provides breathtaking views, picnic sites, barbecues and play areas. At the entrance to the drive is a visitor centre providing local information, souvenirs, maps and guides.

The view from the top

Twmbarlwm Mound

According to legend, this large mound covers the grave of a great Welsh chieftain who died fighting the Romans some time back in the first century AD. Archaeologists, however, disagree, claiming that it is a Norman motte, upon which a watch tower once stood.
The mound is certainly a prominent landmark, visible from many parts of Gwent, and from its summit the panoramic view extends over Newport, the Severn Estuary, the Quantock Hills and, on a clear day, as far as the Brecon Beacons.

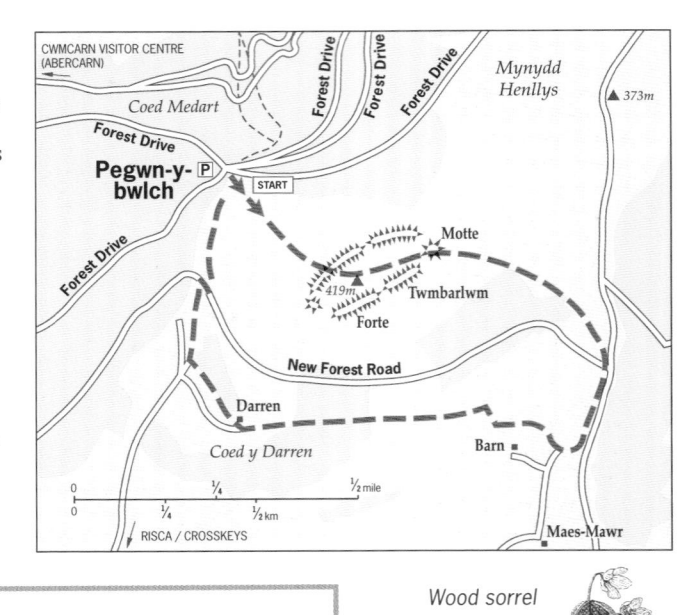

What to look out for

Ebbw Forest is a large area of coniferous woodland including Japanese larch, sitka spruce and Scots pine.
Coal tits and goldcrests forage among the foliage and are easiest to spot in winter.

Wood sorrel

Along the Glamorgan Canal

A pleasant and peaceful walk along a section of a historic canal with so much natural history that it has been turned into a nature reserve.

START

Take the A470 from Cardiff and then follow the A4054 through Whitchurch. Turn down Velindre Road. Go past the hospital and turn down Forest Farm Road. Park in the small parking area on the right, opposite a pylon; an old millstone set in the ground marks the entrance to the Glamorganshire Canal Local Nature Reserve.

DIRECTIONS

Go through the gate, follow the left-hand track and soon cross an iron bridge. Continue along the canal towpath for about ¾ mile, passing between the Melingriffith feeder stream and the old Glamorganshire canal, then pass an old lock, before reaching the remains of a second lock. Here the canal, as such, comes to an end and the water disappears into a concrete pipe.

Turn right and ascend a flight of steps up a bank. At the top, turn right along a shady path that follows a narrow ridge above a wooded slope known as Long Wood – an interesting contrast to the outward journey, with a variety of trees and wildlife. After about 50yds there is a log seat and the course of the now dismantled railway can be seen to the left.

At a junction of paths just below a house, keep to the right and follow a wider track which leads on beside a stone wall and back to the starting point.

Broad-leaved dock

An old – and once well-used – lock on the canal

The shady path that leads through the Long Wood, dappled with sunlight through the leaves

Melingriffith Feeder
This old industrial waterway once supplied water to the Melingriffith Iron Works.

Glamorgan Canal
Completed in 1794 this canal was built to transport iron ore, coal and limestone on a 25-mile journey from Cyfartha, near Merthyr Tydfil, to the mouth of the River Taff in Cardiff. It fell into rapid decline when the Taff Vale Railway was constructed.

What to look out for

The grey heron may be seen fishing in the canal, which is home not only to the fish, but also to a number of marginal and waterside flowering plants including Himalayan balsam with its pink flowers, marsh marigold, purple loosestrife and arrowhead, to name but a few. Long Wood is an interesting stretch of mixed woodland containing beech, ash, elm, alder, oak, holly, sycamore and hazel. In spring the ground may be carpeted with primroses, ramsons and bluebells. Among the trees you may see squirrels and perhaps a great spotted woodpecker.

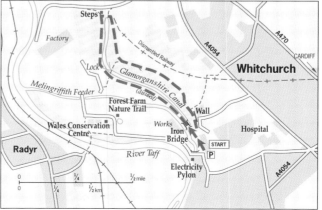

St Donat's Bay

WALK 114
SOUTH GLAMORGAN
SS916683

What to look out for

The wooden valley harbours willow warblers and blackcaps in summer. Along the coast, plants such as sea cabbage and wild carrot are common.

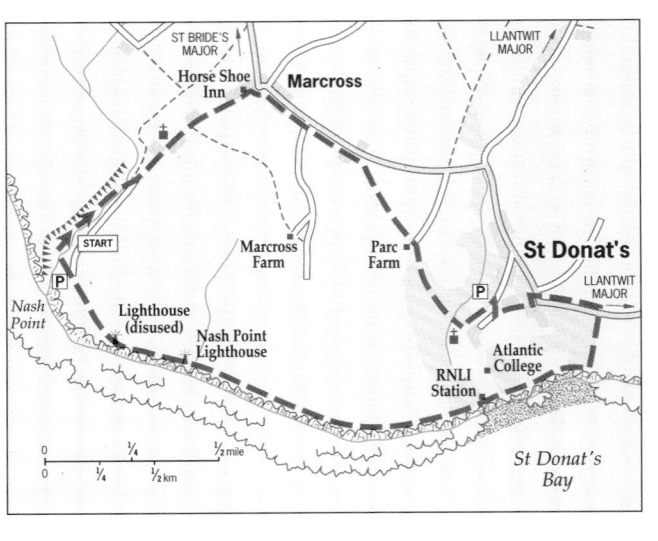

This walk passes two interesting churches and an impressive castle. It also includes stepping stones across streams, a wooded valley, a lighthouse and a final cliff-top section with impressive views.

Information

The walk is four miles long
Care is needed on the cliff-top section
Several stiles
The Horse Shoe Inn is *en route* in Marcross
Ice cream kiosk (seasonal) at the start

START

Head north-west of Llantwit Major, via a minor road – single track with passing places – to St Donat's, signposted 'Atlantic College'. Park at the Nash Point car park (there may be a charge) on the Glamorgan Heritage Coast, where there are good views over the Bristol Channel.

Palmate newt

DIRECTIONS

A track leads from the car park down into a narrow valley where a path continues up the valley, crossing a stream via stepping stones at several points. Continue through woodland to reach a footbridge. Go up steps and through gap in hedge on to the road, turn left past Marcross church and reach a T-junction at the village inn. Turn right here and then bear right at the next junction. After walking up the hill take the second turning on the right, after an old school building on the right.
On reaching Parc Farm, keep straight on and go through a gate to follow a grass track through a wooded valley. Bear left at a junction and on reaching a clearing with derelict building on right, continue straight on to reach a track. Turn right and walk down to St Donat's Church. After visiting the church go back up the track which shortly joins the driveway to St Donat's Castle on your right. With the castle gateway behind you, walk straight ahead on the road with speed humps which passes between college accommodation buildings, to reach a public road. Turn right and after about ¼ mile go through a metal kissing-gate with carved stone sign 'King George's Field' on the right, to follow a path down towards the sea. Go through a gate and turn right over stone stile along the cliff-top path. Before long you will pass a stepped path which leads to a beach, and then the boundary wall of Atlantic College which is housed in St Donat's Castle. Cross a slipway where there is a lifeboat station, and then ascend some steps on the right to follow a path through

The lighthouse at Nash Point, on route of the cliff-top path

the trees that leads you back up to another stone stile and the coastal path.
Continue along the breezy cliff-top, passing Nash Point lighthouse and crossing a few stiles on the return to the starting point.

St Donat's Castle

It is said that this castle has been continuously inhabited since the day it was built. It is a concentric castle with an inner bailey protected by a dry moat and strong curtain walls. The building now houses Atlantic College, opened in 1962 as a sixth form college to accommodate 300 boys and girls from all over the world.

St Donat's Church

Dating from the 11th century, this church contains a Norman font and some very old stained glass which is possibly the oldest in Wales. Members of the Stradling family, who once resided in the castle, are buried in the Lady Chapel.

Around Rhossili

WALK 115
WEST GLAMORGAN
SS414881

A coastal walk on the western side of the Gower Peninsula, providing wonderful vistas out to sea, with the serpent-like promontory of Worms Head a prominant feature.

START

Follow the A4118 from Swansea and about one and a half miles north of Port Einon turn right along the B4247. The road ends at Rhossili where there is a large car park opposite the Worms Head Cottage Hotel.

DIRECTIONS

Leave the car park to follow a tarmac path down to a gate and continue along a broad track beside a stone wall. The ditch and rampart of an Iron Age fort can be seen on the right. At a point where the wall bends around to the left, keep straight on across the grass towards the coastguard station, which doubles as the Gower Coast Reserves Centre. Continue around the headland to the left, keeping well back from the edge of the cliffs. The path leads on through the gorse and soon rejoins the stone wall. In due course the path drops down to Mewslade

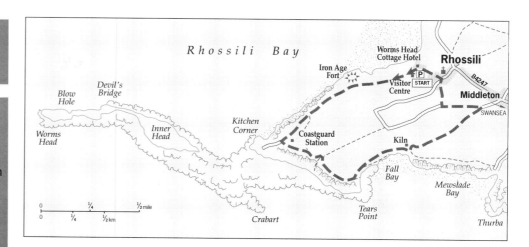

Bay. Where the path divides keep straight on to follow the gently ascending higher route. Continue along the top of the headland for about a mile. On reaching the remains of a lime kiln at the head of a little inlet, follow a track up to the left and climb an iron ladder over a stone wall. Turn right and follow the path around the edge of a field to reach a stile. Continue, crossing three more stiles, then look out for an easily-missed track on the left, between hedges. This takes you through a tunnel of trees to a stile. Cross this and the stile opposite to continue along an avenue of trees. At the end cross another stile and keep forward across the field to another stile. Continue along a broad rutted track to reach a T-junction. Turn right here and follow a cart track back to Rhossili. On joining a road turn left and make your way back to the start, passing Rhossili church on the right.

The curving sands of Rhossili Bay, with the downs behind

Rhossili Bay

Said to be one of the finest unspoilt beaches in Britain, this three-mile stretch of golden sands is half a mile wide at low tide. The *Helvetia* was wrecked in a storm on Monday 31 October 1887 and remains of its timbers can be seen embedded in the sand.

Worms Head

Known as the 'Land's End of Gower', this fascinating promontory is a mile long and it takes its name from the Scandinavian word *Orme* which means serpent. Connecting the inner and outer headlands is a natural rock arch known as the Devil's Bridge. The outer headland is a bird sanctuary where kittiwakes, fulmars, guillemots and razorbills may be seen in the summer. A stepped path leads down from the coastguard station to a causeway.

Rhossili Church

The foundations of this church date back to the 6th century but the present building is of Norman construction. Inside is a white marble tablet commemorating Petty Officer Evans, a local man who died in 1912 with Captain Scott on his ill-fated expedition to the South Pole.

Carreg Cennen Castle

The main object of this pleasant, easy walk is to visit the ruins of Carreg Cennen Castle which is situated in this wild and remote corner of the Brecon Beacons National Park.

START
Leave the A483 at Ffairfach, just before Llandeilo and follow the road for two and a half miles to the village of Trap. From here a lane leads up to a car park just below the castle.

DIRECTIONS
From the car park follow the lane towards the castle, stopping at the farm to pay your admission fee. After exploring this romantic fortress, go back down to access path and follow a broad track leading down into the Cennen Valley, crossing a wooded slope and descending gently to the valley bottom. Turn right here and follow a path beside the Afon (river) Cennen.

Soon the ruined castle will come into view, dramatically silhouetted against the sky on its limestone crag.

Go over a stile on the left, descend some steps and continue beside the river passing below the castle crag. The track in due course joins a lane which is followed past Pantyffynnont farm and uphill to a T-junction. Here turn right and walk back along the road for a short distance to return to the car park.

Carreg Cennen Castle
Perched on the top of a 130ft limestone crag, Carreg Cennen is said to be one of the most romantic castles in Wales.

According to tradition it was originally built for Urien – one of King Arthur's knights – but the present building dates from the time of Richard II. It is a fascinating place to explore, particularly the vaulted passage cut

through solid rock that leads for about 150ft inside the cliff to a well. The steps leading to the vault can be found in the left hand corner of the inner ward – it is a good idea to take a torch along with you, for exploring.

During the Wars of the Roses, the castle was captured by Lancastrian supporters who later had to surrender to the command of Edward IV. In 1462 five hundred men equipped with picks and crowbars were employed to

Carreg Cennen overlooks Trapp (below) from its lofty crag (right)

make the castle uninhabitable and were paid the grand sum of £28 for their work.

Owain of the Red Hand
It is said that in a cavern below the castle Sir John Goch, also known as Owain the Red Hand, is doomed to sleep for a thousand years, and that when this 14th-century Welsh hero and his fifty-one companions awake there will be peace all over the world.

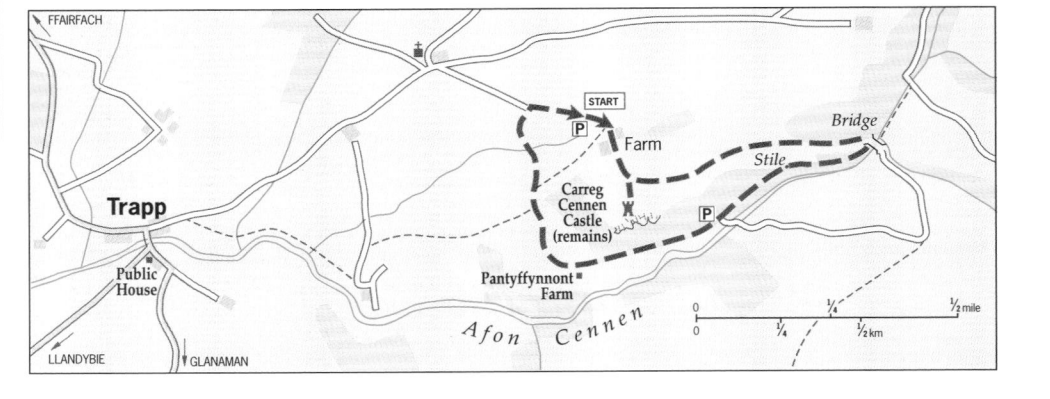

Llanstephan Castle

This is a varied walk along paths and quiet lanes which overlook the Tywi estuary. It includes a visit to a Norman castle which provides dramatic views out to sea.

START

Llanstephan is reached by turning off the A40 just west of Carmarthen and following the B4312. The walk starts from a large car park beside the estuary of the River Towy.

DIRECTIONS

From the bottom right-hand corner of the car park ascend some steps by an information board. Follow a path gently ascending between fences. On reaching a road, turn left. There is a good view of the castle to the left as you walk along the road.

On reaching a junction, bear right and continue up the lane leading to the castle. Turn sharp left just before a house and follow a stony path up to the ruined fortress. An information panel relating the history of the castle will be seen on the right hand side of the path.

After visiting the castle return down the path to reach the lane and turn left, passing the house again. The impressive stone boundary wall on the right surrounds the grounds of a big mansion called Plas. Follow the lane down between high hedges, and opposite the house on the right go left over a stile to follow a gravel track through a pleasant secluded valley which leads down to the sea. Go through a gateway and continue with a stone wall on your right. On reaching a concrete slipway by St Anthony's well, turn left up a shady path beneath overhanging trees. At the top of the rise a seat is conveniently placed on the left.

Continue with occasional glimpses of the estuary through the trees to the right, then emerge from the trees to find some more seats and an open view out to sea. Further on there are more seats, a shelter on your left and, to the right, some stone steps leading down to the beach. You can return to the start that way if the tide is out. Otherwise continue along the path, passing more seats on the way. When the path divides, bear right and descend a flight of steps to a road. Turn right along the road, then a few steps on the left lead to a path which can be followed back to the start.

Llanstephan Castle

Standing on a headland occupied since prehistoric times, this Norman castle was built on the site of an Iron Age promontory fort by one of the de Clares in the 12th century. Its purpose was to guard a crossing point on the estuary and it is one of several castles along Carmarthen Bay from Loughor and Kidwelly to Laugharne. Above the old gateway is a slot down which boiling water or oil would have been poured on the heads of unwanted visitors. The twin-towered gatehouse served as the castle's main living quarters and from the top is a fine view over Carmarthen Bay, stretching to Worms Head in the east and Caldey Island to the west.

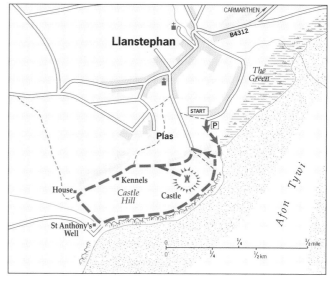

Llanstephan beach and the castle

Sandmartin

What to look out for

Woodland in the area harbours early purple orchids and wood anemones.
Along the coast, watch and listen for linnets and stonechats in the scrub, and you might even be lucky enough to see a peregrine soaring or gliding overhead.

Manorbier Castle

An easy walk taking in a section of the Pembrokeshire coast path with exhilarating views across the sea. Special features include a prehistoric burial chamber, and Manorbier church and castle.

Information

The walk is one and a half miles long

Few stiles

The paths are easy to follow but take care when crossing the top of a deep fissure

Pub in village

Toilets at car park

START

Manorbier is about six miles west of Tenby, turning left off the A4139 onto the B4585 to reach the village. The walk starts from a large car park just below the castle.

DIRECTIONS

On the seaward side of the car park follow a path to the right to reach the beach. Walk across the beach to the left hand corner and go up a flight of concrete steps and cross a stile.

The path then gently ascends with pleasant views across the bay, but take very great care where the path goes around the top of a deep fissure – there is a steep drop below.

Soon reach the King's Quoit, the remains of a prehistoric burial chamber, and follow the path to the left of the burial chamber and ascend through the ferns, dipping in and out of hollows, heading back towards Manorbier. The path follows the edge of a field with a good view of the castle.

In due course reach a gate, continue through the churchyard to the Manorbier church (well worth a visit) on the right. On turn left. Descend, passing Manorbier church and on reaching a pavement, turn right. Cross the road with care and go through a metal gate in a wall to the castle.

To visit the castle, climb some steps in the trees on the right and over a stile into the car park. Rounding a corner, go left

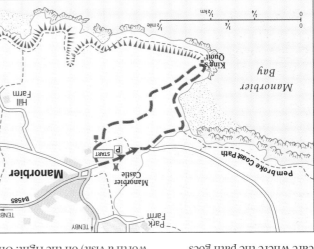

King's Quoit

This is one of many neolithic burial chambers to be found in Wales. The capstone measures 16ft 9in long, 8ft 6in wide and is up to 2ft thick.

Guillemot

Manorbier Church

Dedicated to St James the Great Apostle and Martyr, this church has a tall, square, fortress-like tower and is perched on the hillside opposite the castle.

These tall-towered churches were intended as lookouts and refuges.

The nave predates the castle and in the chancel is a 13th-century effigy of a member of the de Barri family, who built the castle. The 14th-century oak loft leading into the tower is one of the few remaining examples of medieval church woodwork in the county.

What to look out for

There are lots of interesting shells on the beach, and look out for fulmars, herring and great black-backed gulls, guillemots and razorbills.

An assortment of wild flowers includes thrift or sea pink, hemp agrimony, English stonecrop, red valerian and ox-eye daisy.

Manorbier Castle

Constructed of quarried limestone this picturesque castle was established by Odo de Barri, a follower of Gerald de Windsor. His famous grandson was Giraldus Cambrensis, otherwise known as Gerald of Wales. In 1188 Gerald, who was then Archdeacon of Brecon, travelled through Wales with Baldwin, the Archbishop of Canterbury. Afterwards Gerald recorded their travels in a fascinating book *Itinerary Through Wales*. He described his birthplace, Manorbier, as 'the pleasantest spot in Wales'. His greatest wish was to became Bishop of St David's, but King John refused to grant his wish and he died a disappointed man in 1216. He is buried at St David's Cathedral.

The castle is open daily from May to September and for a week at Easter.

The sturdy defensive walls of Manorbier still stand in the leafy valley

St David's (Penmaen Dewi)

This is a very strenuous, but interesting walk on a headland at the extreme west of Wales. It passes a secluded beach and takes in the remains of a promontory fort and a prehistoric burial chamber.

Information

The walk is three and three quarter miles long
Craggy slopes to ascend on return route; can be avoided by returning from the headland along outward route.
A few stiles
The nearest pubs are in St David's
Good picnic spots along the walk
Toilets in the car park at Whitesands Bay

START

To reach Whitesand Bay follow the B4583 for two miles on the north-west side of St David's. Normally you have to pay a small fee for parking here.

DIRECTIONS

From the car park cross the road and go over a stile in a wall to the right of a telephone kiosk. Follow the coastal path beside a fence, keeping to the right as it wanders around through the gorse. As you come over a rise the bay of Porth Melgan is seen below. Keep straight on ignoring two paths to the right. (A detour can be made at this point down to this secluded beach.)
Follow the path on a gentle ascent around St David's headland. The path goes through a rampart of piled up stones, the remains of an Iron Age promontory fortress, which is known as the Warrior's Dyke. Turn right. Further on you will pass a cliff on the left where rock climbers may be seen in action (but not during the nesting season). Detour right here to visit Coetan Arthur, a prehistoric burial chamber, then return to the path.
Go over the next hump and on through the heather and rocks with Carn Llidi silhouetted against the sky on the right. Descend to a junction of paths and follow the broad track to your right down into the shallow valley above Porth Melgan.
Continue go up the other side (the longest uphill stretch on the walk), passing through a kissing-gate on the way. On reaching a junction with a concrete path, you may like to continue to the summit of Carn Llidi (at 600ft altitude, this is a good vantage point – the west coast of Ireland can be seen on a clear day), but otherwise turn right and follow the surfaced path downhill to join a track beside a wall.
Cross a stile beside a gate and pass through Danyardig farmyard. Then follow a metalled lane which brings you down to the Whitesands Road. Turn right and make your way back to the car park.

St Patrick's Chapel

A stone tablet near the start marks the site of a chapel dedicated to St Patrick. He is reputed to have sailed from here to Ireland in the early part of the 5th century.

Arthur's Quoit (Coetan Arthur)

This is a prehistoric dolmen with a capstone 12ft long and 1ft thick. Legend has it that it was thrown here by King Arthur from the summit of Moelfre Hill.

St David's Head

The view from here is particularly fine. To the south is Ramsey Island and westward lie the smaller islands called the Bishop and Clerks. On a very clear day you can look north across Cardigan Bay and see Snowden, nearly 100 miles away.

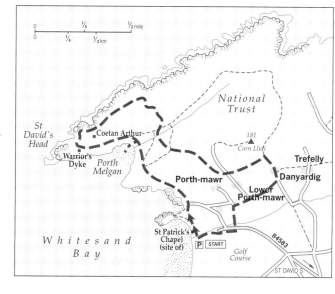

What to look out for

Look for interesting shells on the beach.
Atlantic grey seals may sometimes be seen basking and fishing off this coast. Sea birds may include razorbills, guillemots, kittiwakes, fulmars and gulls.
The wild flowers are particularly beautiful in spring and early summer.

The sandy bay at Porth Melgan is well worth the short detour

Razorbill

A Ramble Around Nevern

WALK 120
DYFED
SN084400

This pleasant walk takes in the historic church of St Brynach and its curiosities, and passes through a beautiful, peaceful countryside following riverside and woodland paths.

START
Leave the A487 at Velindre to follow the B4582 down to the pretty riverside hamlet of Nevern. Park carefully on the roadside by Nevern Church.

DIRECTIONS
From the main gate of Nevern Church turn right to follow a footpath between a stream and the churchyard wall. Turn left by a cottage to cross a small footbridge over the stream and then continue along a stony track. On meeting a road turn right. Go uphill for about 100yds and at a bend keep straight on to follow a path signposted 'The Pilgrim's Cross'. After about 50yds reach the cross, carved on the rock face to your right. The path continues, soon levelling out, and is well shaded by overhanging trees. Go over a stile and proceed through a pleasant wooded valley. Keeping the fence on your left, cross a stile and continue walk on through the trees.

Now following a ledge cut into the hillside, ascend some natural rock steps to reach a stile. Cross a field and then go left through a metal gate. Continue down a stony track for a few yards towards a building and look out for a path descending on the right. This goes down to a little footbridge spanning a stream. Keep straight on to across a concrete drive, passing to the left of a garage and then to the right of a cottage. Continue through the trees just above the river. After passing a derelict cottage the path rises gently. On reaching Pont Newydd farmhouse, turn left to follow a rutted track. Shortly you will cross a stone bridge (Pont Newydd), after which the track ascends slightly. On joining a surfaced lane keep straight on to pass Llangwynnair Manor hotel. Just past the derelict farm buildings turn left up a footpath and go through a gate, beneath a tunnel of trees and through woods alive with birdsong. On reaching three gateways take the middle path, soon walking between high banks with wild flowers. Go over a stile and through a field, cross another stile and turn left along a road to go over a stone bridge and return to the church.

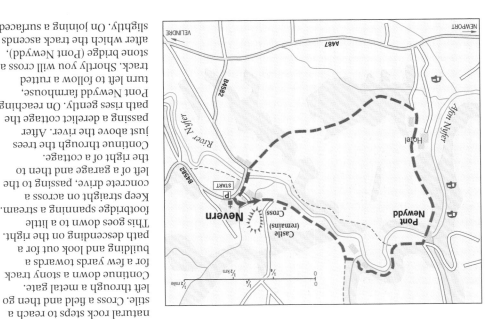

The attractive old bridge leading into Nevern village

Information

The walk is three miles long. A gentle walk along well defined paths and tracks. A few stiles to cross. Pub in village is called the Trewern Arms. Toilets by village school.

Nevern Church

Founded in the 6th century by St Brynach, Nevern church has a squat battlemented tower which once provided the community with a refuge from marauding sea rovers. It is approached through an avenue of ancient yew trees. One is known as 'the bleeding yew' because blood-red sap oozes out of a broken branch – and, it is said, will do so until a Welshman re-occupies the castle on the hill above. In the churchyard stands a beautiful 10th-century Celtic cross. According to legend, the first cuckoo of spring is supposed to arrive in Nevern on St Brynach's day (7 April) and perch on the stone.

Ramsons

What to look out for

It is a good walk for observing wild flowers – and for picking blackberries in late summer. Bluebells and ramsons grow in the woods, and rabbits and squirrels are much in evidence. You can look out for trout and salmon in the River Nyfer, but the fishing is private.

Above Llangrannog

WALK 121
DYFED
SN311542

A very pleasant walk providing stunning views from a fine stretch of coastline that is owned by the National Trust. It is easy to follow and the paths are well maintained. It may be enjoyed at any time of the year providing it is not too windy.

START

Llangrannog is reached by turning off the A487 at Brynhoffnant to follow the B4334. Drive down through the narrow streets of the village to reach a car park overlooking the beach.

DIRECTIONS

At the right-hand corner of the small beach, ascend a flight of concrete steps to a path which gradually ascends, soon giving views down over Llangrannog. Shortly reach a picnic table

The bay at Llangrannog

tucked away in a corner on the right.

Further on, look down on the top of Carreg Bica, the strange rock that can be seen from the beach. Around the next corner is a flat area with a picnic table and a superb view out to sea.

Ignore the stile on the right and continue along the cliff-top path. After about 20yds a stepped path on the left leads down to a charming hidden cove.

Continue along the cliff-top path beside a fence. Cross a stile and the path begins to rise again. Go over another stile and turn left along a broad track. (A detour track leads out to the headland from here.)

Continue around the headland, with new views appearing all the time. On reaching a junction of paths, keep to the right, directed by an erosion control notice. Follow a path up to the col above, and then go over a stile beside a gate. (From here you can follow a concrete road up to the coastguard station on top of the hill of Pendinas Lochtyn, returning the same way and turning right at the gate.)

Follow the coastguard road, then cross a stile beside a gate and head straight down to two more stiles in succession to rejoin your outward route by the picnic table on the platform overlooking the sea.

Llangrannog

Set in a steep green valley, this is a pretty village that is very popular during the

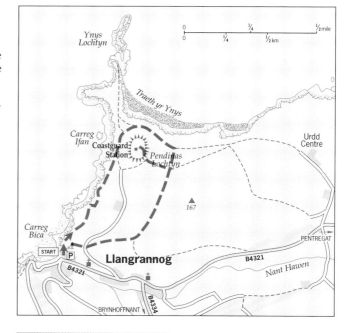

tourist season, when car parking can sometimes be rather a problem.

Carreg Bica

This strange looking crag is 50ft high and dominates the sandy beach. According to local legend, it is actually a tooth that was troubling the Devil. Unable to bear the agony any longer, he yanked it from his jaw, threw it over his shoulder and this is where it landed.

Ynys Lochtyn

It was on this headland that the composer Edward Elgar found inspiration for his *Introduction and Allegro for Strings*. He wrote in his diary:

'On the cliff between blue sea and blue sky, thinking out my theme, there came to me the sound of singing. The songs were too far away to reach me distinctly, but fitting the need of the moment I made the little tune which appears in the introduction.'

WALK 122

DYFED
SN753791

Parson's Bridge

This is a varied route providing several points of interest in a wild and spectacular part of Wales.

START
Ysbyty Cynfyn is on the A4120 about midway between Devil's Bridge and Ponterwyd. Parking is available just in front of the church.

DIRECTIONS
Walk beside the church wall to go through a small metal gate, then continue along a wide track. Soon you will be looking down into a valley and the track in due course descends a wooded slope in a series of zig-zags to reach the metal Parson's Bridge, spanning a deep gorge. On the far side, turn left to follow a track beside a fence leading up to a wooded slope. Two stiles are crossed and you then follow the edge of a field, keeping a fence on your left. Go over another stile and then continue along the top side of the field along a broad track. After crossing another stile, head diagonally up to the right to a ruined building, and then continue to join a gravel track. Bear left along the track, which joins a tarmac road beyond Llwyn Teifi Farm.

Continue for some distance, ignoring track on left, then go over a stile on the left and down to a little footbridge spanning a stream. Head up through a field to a farm. Bear right and follow the road into the hamlet of Ystumtuen. Follow the road to the right, cross a bridge and on reaching a stone bungalow go through a gate on the right and walk past an old mine to follow a track up the right-hand side of a little valley. A pool comes into view ahead of you (a good spot for a picnic), beyond which go over a stile in a fence and continue up to the top of the pass. Cross another stile and continue, with the fence on your right, to subsequently re-cross the fence via another stile. On joining a track keep straight on (a detour to the left leads to a small stone circle). Follow a signposted path down a slope to a stile and then go straight across a field to another stile. From here the path leads steeply down a wooded slope to Parson's Bridge. Retrace your steps back to the start.

The view from the stone circle near Yspytty Cynyfan

Ysbyty Cynfyn Church
Four large prehistoric standing stones in the churchyard wall provide evidence that this was once a pagan site, Christianised by the establishment of a church, probably in the 6th century.

The churchyard contains a sad inscription on a stone opposite the church porch, recording the death of quad-ruplets, all within six days of their birth. Their father died of typhus a month later.

Ox-eye daisy

Parson's Bridge
The first bridge here was built for the benefit of a parson who came from Llanbadarn Fawr, near Aberystwyth, to conduct the services at Ysbyty Cynfyn. One day the rickety old bridge collapsed and he fell to his death. Today's bridge is a metal structure and quite sound.

The Artists' Valley

WALK 123
DYFED
SN685952

Much of this walk is well shaded by trees making it a particularly enjoyable excursion on a hot day. Stunning views and pleasant riverside paths are features of this walk which you will find particularly memorable.

Crossing the shady Furnace

Information

The walk is two and a quarter miles long
There is some ascent involved but it is fairly easy going
One stile
Pub in Talybont further along A487
Toilet in car park

START

This walk starts from the small village of Furnace which is on the A487 about ten miles south-west of Machynlleth. Park in Ynys Hir car park (RSPB), open from 9am to 9pm (or dusk if earlier).

DIRECTIONS

From the car park follow the entrance drive up to the main road. Directly opposite is the Dyfi Furnace. Turn right along the narrow pavement and by the Hen Efail craft shop, cross the road to follow the road up Cwm Einion – 'The Artists' Valley'. After about 400yds leave the road at a bend by a footpath sign and continue up a rocky track beside a stone wall, bearing right with the wall. On reaching a junction turn left then follow the track beside a fence and on through the trees. On joining a lane keep straight on, but shortly leave it to follow a signposted track leading down through the trees to the left. Ignore a track to the right and stay on the main route. Go through a small gate and cross a bridge over the river, then head up to a stile. Do not go over it, but follow the path to the left passing beneath a little yellow cottage. Go through a gate and turn left along a lane. On reaching another lane turn left and shortly follow a signposted path on the right which leads around the hillside of Foel Fawr. Continue along the wide track through the ferns, cross a little stream and then descend to a farm in the valley below. On joining the farm drive, turn left. Pass a memorial to Major General Pugh, then leave the road at a cattle grid and turn left along a signposted path to follow a stone wall on your right. At the end of the wall go over a stile and turn right along a metalled lane. This rises for a short way and then drops down to the A487. Turn left and follow it back to Furnace.

Trailing St John's-wort

What to look out for

The 900-acre Ynys Hir Reserve is home to many breeding birds including redstarts, pied flycatchers and all three species of woodpecker.
Butterflies to be seen include pearl-bordered and marsh fritillaries, and the plantlife includes ling, bog pimpernel and trailing St John's-wort.

Dyfi Furnace

This is the best preserved example of an 18th-century charcoal-burning blast furnace in Britain. It was set up in about 1755 and was in use for about 50 years. It later became a saw mill and the waterwheel which can be seen on the side of the building was installed at this time. This hamlet is known as Furnace but its correct name is Eglwysfach or Ysgubor-y-Coed.

Foel Fawr

The viewpoint on Foel Fawr offers a panoramic vista across the Dyfi estuary, taking in the mountains of southern Snowdonia. There is a legend that King Arthur once leapt across this estuary and his horse left its hoof print on a rock which can still be seen.

The Flooded Village

This is a varied walk in the beautiful Elan Valley – an area often referred to as the 'Lake District of Wales'. It is a particularly scenic walk, with wonderful views from the top of the pass.

START
The Elan Valley Visitor Centre is about three miles south-west of Rhyader on the B4518. The walk starts from the car park.

DIRECTIONS
From the car park walk up the road to pass through the entrance gates and turn right across a Bailey bridge which spans the River Elan beside a now disused suspension bridge. Turn right then left to pass through a gate and follow a broad stony path beside a fence, ascending gradually through the trees, with views down to the river. On reaching a junction turn left and shortly right to follow an old railway track above the Visitor Centre. The track rises gently, soon becoming level with the top of the dam, then passes a quarry on the right which provided stone for the construction of the dam. Beyond the quarry, the track soon becomes a narrow stony path following the edge of the reservoir.
On reaching a stream on the left, the main ascent of the walk begins beside a conifer plantation. After a few yards, when the track divides, keep left and at the end of the plantation keep straight on, ignoring the track to the right.
Less steep now, the broad grass track passes a ruined farm house and leads pleasantly to the top of a col.

Information

The walk is four miles long
A few stiles
One ascent to top of mountain pass
Refreshments in the visitor centre
Several suitable picnic places on the walk
Toilets in visitor centre and in Elan Village

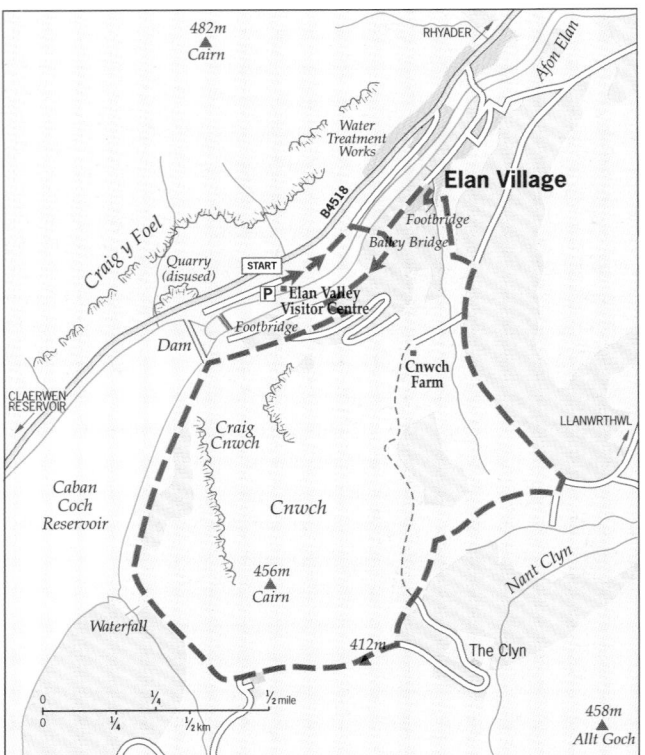

The bridge across the Caban Coch Reservoir, in the drowned Elan Valley

Continue, to reach a gate and join a surfaced lane. On reaching a T-junction, turn left along a road, passing on the right a wooded slope which is part of the Cnwch and Allt Ddu Nature Reserve (RSPB).
After passing Cnwch Farm, continue round a corner and look out for a green track on the left descending through the ferns. Soon turn left on the track leading down to the village (toilets on the left). Turn right over the Bailey bridge and return to the Visitor Centre car park.

Caban Coch Dam
The Elan Valley Reservoirs were built at the turn of the century to provide water for the City of Birmingham, some 73 miles away. The first dam to be constructed was Caban Coch, opened on 21 July 1904 by King Edward VII and Queen Alexandra, and finally completed in 1906. It stands 122ft high and 610ft long, covers an area of 500 acres and is 800ft above sea level at full capacity.

Elan Village
Built in 1906 to house the reservoir maintenance staff, this attractive village consists of a school, a schoolteacher's house, the Reservoir Superintendent's house, and twelve cottages.
The original Elan village was flooded and beneath the reservoir lie several farms, a Baptist chapel, a church, a schoolhouse and eighteen cottages. Also beneath the water are two large houses – Cwn Elan and Nantgwyllt – which had connections with the poet Shelley. They also inspired Francis Brett Young's novel *The House Under the Water*.

What to look out for

Birds that may be seen on this walk include skylark, meadow pipit, dipper, grey wagtail and pied wagtail. In the woods you may see pied flycatcher, wood warbler and redstart during summer months. Look out for buzzards, peregrines and kestrels – if you are really lucky you may see a red kite with its distinctive forked tail. The visitor centre gives a good insight into the valley and its reservoirs.

Twm Sion Catti's Cave

Well shaded for a hot day, this walk is set in wild and dramatic scenery, making a complete circuit of a wooded hill above the confluence of the Tywi and the Doethie.

START
The walk starts at the RSPB car park at Ystradffin, just past the church. From Llandovery take the minor road north to Rhandirmwyn and head towards the Llyn Brianne Reservoir.

DIRECTIONS
Go through a little gate at the end of the car park and follow a board walk across a marshy area. At the end of the board walk follow the path to the right down through the trees towards the river, soon reaching a pleasant riverside glade with seats.
Follow the path up and down steps around the hillside above the river, which now flows noisily through a rocky gorge. The path leads up to a junction where a flat boulder makes a convenient seat. (It is possible to avoid the steep climb to the cave by continuing directions at * below.)
The path leads directly upwards to Twm Sion Catti's Cave, climbing steeply and threading its way between and over moss-covered boulders. Look out for an arrow scratched into the rock ahead of you – pointing left at a spot where you could easily follow a false trail.
The cave is now directly above and a slippery squeeze – on all fours – will get you

Garden warbler

Information
The walk is two miles long.
Well-maintained track with some ascent, particularly up to the cave; take care when the rocks are wet and slippery; the remainder follows an easy gradient
No stiles
Dogs should be kept on leads
Pub in Rhandirmwyn serves bar snacks
Picnic place beside river near beginning of walk

What to look out for

Over 40 species of birds breed in these woods, and between April and July look out for pied flycatchers, redstarts and wood warblers. A wealth of non-flowering plants include mosses and lichens on tree trunks, and ferns such as lady fern and polypody on the ground.

inside. Return then to the main track.
*Continue around the hillside – down steps and around rocky corners to pass through the final section of the rocky gorge. The sound of the river fades as you round the hill and the track surface becomes less rocky and more grassy, leading through the ferns and trees. Eventually return to the board walk and retrace your steps to the car park.

Ystradffin
This chapel, dedicated to St Paulinus, stands beside the ancient road to Strata Florida Abbey, to which it once belonged. It stands on the three-way boundary of the old counties of Cardiganshire, Carmarthenshire and Breconshire.

Dinas Nature Reserve
This reserve, acquired by the RSPB in 1968, is a good example of a Welsh sessile oak wood and is home to the red kite. Some 90 species of bird are recorded in the reserve each year, and over 40 species regularly breed here during spring and early summer; these include pied flycatchers, redstarts and wood warblers, all migrant visitors to Britain.
The centrepiece of the Nature Reserve is the conical hill of Dinas, but though its name suggests the existence of a fortress on the summit, there is no real evidence of one.

Twm Sion Catti's Cave
Born at Tregaron in 1530, Twm Sion Catti (real name Thomas Jones), lives on in legend as a highwayman and a practical joker – often referred to as the Welsh Robin Hood.
Popularly believed to be one of his hiding places, the cave is really just a hollow formed by a large rock leaning against the face of another one. Inside hundreds of names have been scratched and carved with varying skill on every available rock surface, some dating back to 1839.

Historic graffiti in the cave

Porthyrogof Cave

WALK 126
POWYS
SN918105

This is an exciting walk through wild and romantic scenery, including an impressive waterfall and a limestone cavern that boasts the largest entrance in Wales. Not a walk for wet conditions.

Information

The walk is three miles long
Fairly rocky and very steep in places where limestone can be extremely slippery after rain – great care is needed and sensible footwear essential
Virtually no road walking
A lot of stiles
Ice cream shop about 200yds up the road towards Ystradfellte
Pub in village
Area suitable for picnics by 'Blue Pool' towards end of walk
Toilets in Porthyrogof car park

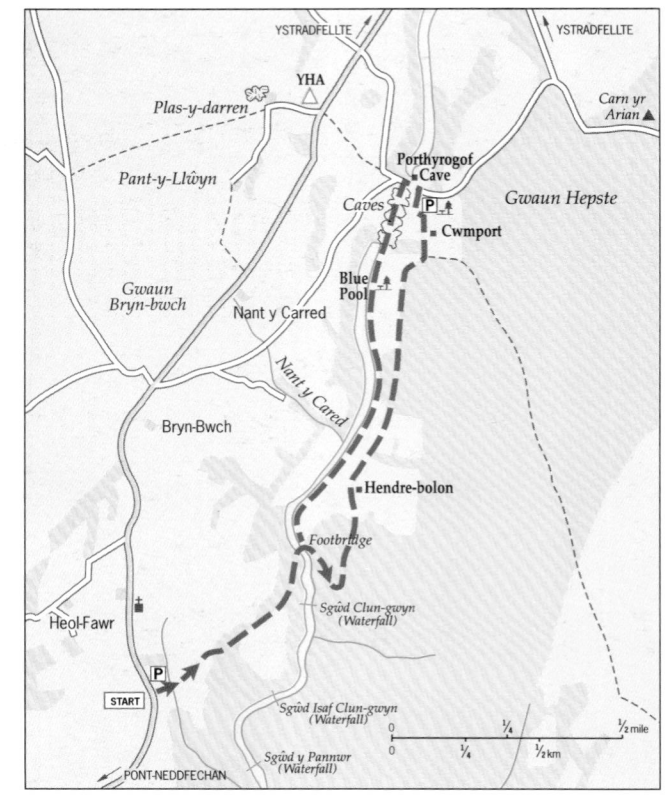

The entrance to the cave

START

West of Brecon, turn south off the A40 at Sennybridge, at Defynnog branch left with the A4215, then turn right onto a minor road to go through Heol Senni and on to Ystradfellte. Continue for about two miles and just beyond a shop on the right and a chapel on the left reach a well-used parking area on the grass verge.

DIRECTIONS

Follow a lane down between fences to go over a stile. At next junction bear right following waymarked path via two footbridges to reach another stile. The path now leads down through trees.

Follow the main path and soon on the right will be seen the Sgwd Clun waterfall. Continue along the path winding through trees to reach a footpath spanning the Afon Mellte. On the other side, turn right and follow a rough, rocky path up a steep slope (note the warning sign), then go right and up again to join a higher path adjoining a fence. Turn left and after about 150yds go right over a stile. Now turn left along a wide track to another stile. Turn left and later reach a stone cottage where an 'advised path' waymark directs you over a stile and on beside a fence, passing through the cottage garden.

Woundwort

The path joins a lane which is followed between tumbled stone walls for nearly ⅜ mile to reach a stile below a white-washed farm.
Soon afterwards the lane meets a road. Turn left, and immediately on the right is the Porthyrogof Cave car park. Go over stile on the left side of the car park and follow a rocky path down into the valley.
Turn left beside the river and the large cave entrance soon comes into view.
After visiting the cavern return to the car park and cross the road to follow a footpath (not the bridleway at the same point). Go over a stile and follow a rocky path down the old river bed.
In due course the resurgence of the river is reached. Keep high here and follow the path over rocks. Soon you can descend to the riverside path where a large flat area overlooks the 'Blue Pool'.
At the end of the flat area the track goes up to a stile and continues beside the river, leading on through the trees and over two more stiles back to the footbridge crossed earlier on the walk. From there retrace your steps back to the start.

Sgwd Clun-gwyn Fall
This is one of three waterfalls on the River Mellte and its name means 'White Meadow Fall'.

The Cave
Situated at the head of a rocky, wooded gorge, this cave has the largest entrance in Wales at 57ft wide. The River Mellte disappears under a wide arch at the base of a cliff and flows underground for about a quarter of a mile.

The Blue Pool picnic area

What to look out for

There is a substantial area of native broad-leaved woodland, including oak, birch, alder, mountain ash and yew. It is also good for ferns, with hart's tongue, brittle bladder fern and green spleenwort much in evidence. Look out in summer for wood warblers and treecreepers, and dippers that bob up and down on boulders in the river searching for food. Kingfishers and grey wagtails may also be seen.

Llyn cwm Llwch

This walk that takes you through a beautiful wooded valley in the heart of the Brecon Beacons, ascending above the tree line to a hidden pool, said to be frequented by fairies and to be of unfathomable depth.

START

Near the western outskirts of Brecon, follow the road opposite the Drovers' Arms, pass under the A40 and continue to drive past Ffrwdgrech Lodge and cross a stone bridge. You face a choice of three roads ahead with signs to Cwmgwdi Camp on the left and ahead, with 'No entry for military vehicles' to the right. Take the road straight ahead. In due course you reach a crossroads. Go virtually straight ahead where the road becomes a very rough track and ends in a clearing where a walkers' car park is found through a gate.

DIRECTIONS

Follow the track up the valley beside the twisting River Llwch. Cross a stream, go through a gate and then continue between stone walls. At the end of the walls turn right and follow the edge of a field to pass behind an old stone cottage.

Cross two stiles in succession and then turn right to follow a well trodden track, now heading towards the twin summits of Corn Du and Pen y Fan. The gradient gradually steepens slightly and after crossing a ladder stile and passing a National Trust sign, continue over undulating ground. Where the track divides, bear left and continue over another rise, beyond which the little lake of Llyn cwm Llwch comes into view. (It is possible to extend the walk here along the track which zig-zags up to the ridge above, then turns left for several hundred yards to reach the memorial to Tommy Jones, with extensive views.) Return to your starting point along the same route.

Llyn Cwm Llwch

This small glacial lake, reputedly bottomless, was described by the 12th-century chronicler Giraldus Cambrensis as a mysterious

WALK 127
POWYS
SO006245

Information

The walk is about three and a half miles long; an extension can be made up to the ridge above the pool
Fairly strenuous walking
A few stiles
No road walking
Nearest pubs and toilets are in Brecon
Picnic place beside Llyn Cwm Lwch (but do not swim in the lake)

What to look out for

Dippers and grey wagtails may be seen in the valley near the stream, and as you ascend higher through the valley buzzards, ravens and curlews may be seen. Ring ouzel are summer visitors.

Above, the start of the walk
Left, the memorial to Tommy Jones

spring that was 'deep but of a square shape like a well and although no streams enter it, trout are sometimes found in it'.

A popular local story has it that long ago some men dug a channel into the edge of the pool to let out the water. Suddenly a huge man in a red coat, seated in a large armchair, popped up to the surface of the lake and bellowed to them 'If you do not give me some peace, I shall drown the town of Brecon!' They fled and never came back.

Poor Little Tommy Jones

The inscription on this sd memorial reads: 'This obelisk marks the spot where the body of Tommy Jones aged 5 was found. He lost his way between Cwmllwch farm and the Login on the night of August 4th 1900. After an anxious search of 29 days his remains were discovered on September 2nd. Erected by Voluntary subscription. W Powell Price. Mayor of Brecon 1900.'
Tommy was staying with his grandparents at Cwmllwch Farm, but wandered off on his own. The search party looked in vain, never expecting that he would have ventured so high above the valley.

Llangattock Circuit

From the attractive village of Llangattock, this is an enjoyable walk along a section of the Monmouthshire and Brecon Canal, usually busy with pleasure boats in the summer. The return is through woodland and fields, with good views of the Black Mountains.

Primrose

START
From Crickhowell cross the old bridge spanning the Usk, turn left and then immediately right along a minor road leading into Llangattock village. Cars may be left in Park Drive opposite the Horse Shoe Inn adjoining a recreation area.

DIRECTIONS
Facing the Horse Shoe Inn, turn left and then shortly go right over a bridge and past old stone cottages to reach Llangattock church. After visiting the church continue along the road and bear left at the next junction.
Go through a metal kissing-gate on the right and walk up through the field, making for the top right hand corner. Cross a stile and turn immediately left under a canal bridge, along the towpath of the Monmouthshire and Brecon Canal.
On the other bank you will pass Llangattock Wharf, which now provides moorings for the Llangattock Boat Club, and a block of old lime kilns.
Walk on, passing beneath stone bridges and over-hanging trees. When you pass beneath bridge 112 (you will need to pass the bridges then look back to see their numbers) go over a stile on the left and continue down a broad track.
On reaching a bend cross a stile on the right and follow the path through a larch wood. Cross a stile at the end of the wood and keep straight on following a line of telegraph poles in the middle of a field. Look out for a footpath sign on the left beside a metal kissing-gate. Go through it and follow a lane back to the start.

Llangattock Church
Dedicated to St Cattwg, this church was founded in the 6th century but rebuilt in the 12th. Inside are a set of stocks and a whipping post.

Monmouthshire and Brecon Canal
Constructed between 1794 and 1800 this canal was used for transporting coal, lime and agricultural produce between Newport and Brecon. It was also connected by various tram roads to local ironworks and carried iron ore and finished products. Commercial use of the canal came to a close with the building of railways, but today it is a very popular leisure amenity, navigable for 32 miles through the Brecon Beacons National Park.

Llangattock Wharf
This wharf was at the end of a tram road which descended from the limestone escarpment on Mynydd Llangattock. Limestone was brought here to be burnt in the lime kilns, then the extracted lime was taken by barge to Brecon and sold for agricultural purposes.

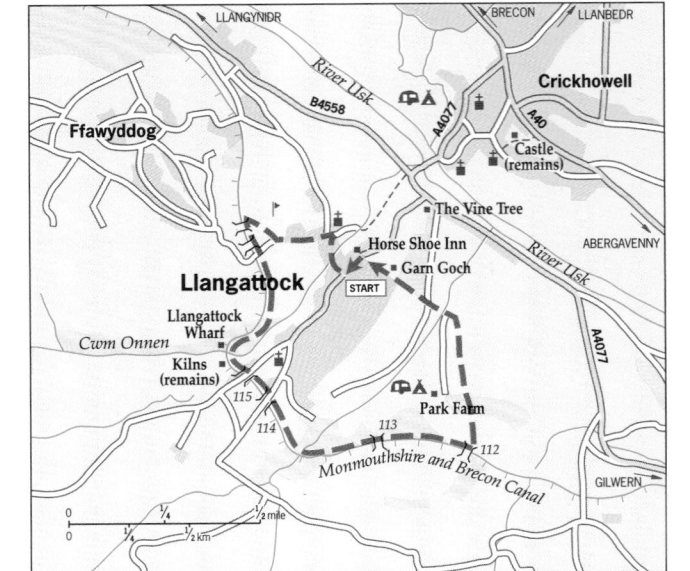

Moorings at Llangattock Wharf

What to look out for

Grey herons and the kingfishers are often seen along the canal, and mallards with their accompanying brood are also an essential part of the canal scene. Primroses and lesser celandines grow along the canal bank in spring.

Garn Goch
A low mound in the recreation field at Llangattock carries a plaque which identifies it as a burial mound, most probably of Neolithic date (4000-2500BC). The stone chamber with its capstone is an Ancient Monument site.

A Walk Around Hay-on-Wye

This walk is a mixture of town and countryside around the fascinating old market town of Hay-on-Wye. The town has an interesting history and is famous for its numerous book shops which attract visitors from all over the world.

START
The starting point for the walk is a large car park near Hay-on-Wye Craft Centre and Information Centre on the south side of town.

DIRECTIONS
Leave the car park, cross the road and turn left along the pavement. Shortly, turn right down Back Fold Lane to pass below part of the Tudor mansion adjoining Hay Castle. The lane snakes around old buildings and meets Castle Street. Turn right and shortly stop to look

Robin

up at the front of Hay Castle. Now bear left and then left again and go down to the Clock Tower. Cross the road and turn right along the pavement, then left by the Three Tuns – 'the Last Free House in Wales'. Follow the pavement down Bridge Street and just before the bridge go right by a footpath signed 'Bailey Footpath and Picnic Area'. Pass a couple of picnic tables on the right and follow the path around to the left, passing under the road bridge before turning left along a path running parallel with the River Wye.

Look out for a path on the left which goes under an old railway bridge and continue beside a stone wall. Go through a gate and then another gate on the left to enter the churchyard of St Mary's parish church. Turn left along the pavement, cross the road and go through a metal kissing-gate to follow a path beside a dingle. Cross a little bridge and continue along the path, over another footbridge and meet a road. Turn left along a pavement and pass the Swan Hotel and Hay Cinema Book Shop. Cross the road and follow the pavement down Peterchurch Road (signposted) and return to the car park at the start.

Hay Castle
The remnants of Hay Castle, consisting of a gateway and a tower, are linked to a handsome Jacobean mansion with tall chimney stacks and gables. The house was badly damaged in a fire some years ago and is gradually being rebuilt. It is not open to the public.

Old Railway
The old railway was originally a tram road, built in 1818 to link the canal at Brecon to Talgarth, Hay and Eardisley in Herefordshire. It was later developed into a railway.

Effigy of Mol Walbee
Inside the church is a mutilated effigy which is reputed to be that of Maude de Valerie otherwise known as Mol Walbee. She was the wife of the wicked Norman Lord William de Braose and

The Cinema Book Shop, one of many

came to a sad end, being starved to death by King John in Windsor Castle.

The King Of Hay
Richard Booth's first empire was as the owner of the

world's largest second-hand book shop. He then decided that, as Hay was in neither England nor Wales, it must be a kingdom of its own and he is now well established as the self-styled 'King of Hay'.

WALK 129
POWYS
SO230422

Information

The walk is one and a quarter miles long
No stiles
Easy, level walking all the way
Plenty of pubs and cafés in the town
Picnic tables and riverside seats on the route
Toilets in the town

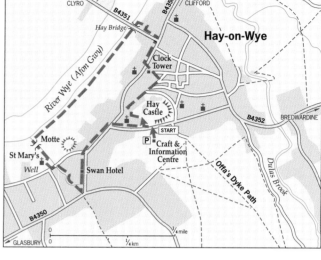

Hay-on-Wye

What to look out for

Overlooking Hay-on-Wye are some superb hanging woodlands, comprising mainly sessile oaks. Redstarts and pied flycatchers are sometimes seen in spring and summer. Woodland flowers to look out for include wood sorrel and wood spurge.

A Circuit of the Sugar Loaf

This short walk, mainly through woods in a quiet and remote corner of Wales, takes in the site of what was once the largest abbey in Wales and the supposed grave of Prince Llewellyn, the last true prince of Wales.

START

Abbeycwmhir is about four miles north of Llandrindod Wells via the A483. Park by the church.

DIRECTIONS

Walk up the road a short way and turn right by a footpath signed 'Owain Glyndwr's Way'. The track passes above the church and then continuess through a farmyard.

Cross a stile beside a gate and continue beside a fence. Shortlyafter this, go through a gate and walk on through the trees.

Passing between two conifer plantations the track gently ascends. Ignore the first turning on the right and bear left at the next junction.

When the track joins a forestry road go straight across and continue down through the trees descending into the valley below, still waymarked 'Owain Glyndwr's Way'.

At a track junction turn left and follow a forest track which leads around the base of Sugar Loaf Hill and back to your starting point.

The forest track, south of the Sugar Loaf

Now follow the road uphill for a short way, then go through a gate on the right, opposite an archway in a wall, and continue down a path through a field to reach the ruins of Abbey Cwmhir. After exploring the ruins retrace your steps to the starting point.

Abbeycwmhir

This isolated hamlet is set among forested hills about five miles east of Rhayader. Opposite the Happy Union Inn is a Victorian church built by the Phillips family. They made their money out of Manchester cotton and lived in the Hall, constructed out of stone from the ruined abbey.

Owain Glyndwr's Way

Linking Knighton with Welshpool, this is a 125-mile waymarked route.

It passes through many locations associated with the Welsh prince Owain Glyndwr, who led a rebellion against the English in the 15th century and became a Welsh national hero.

The Abbey Ruins

Founded in 1143 by a Welsh prince for the Cistercians, Abbey Cwmhir was once the largest abbey in Wales. Its nave, at 242ft long, was only bettered by York, Durham and Winchester cathedrals. The building was badly damaged during Owain Glyndwr's uprising, never to be repaired. It was finally abandoned and its stones plundered for building in the surrounding area.

All that remains to be seen of the abbey today are a few grey stones marking the outer walls, bases of piers, parts of the transepts and the altar steps.

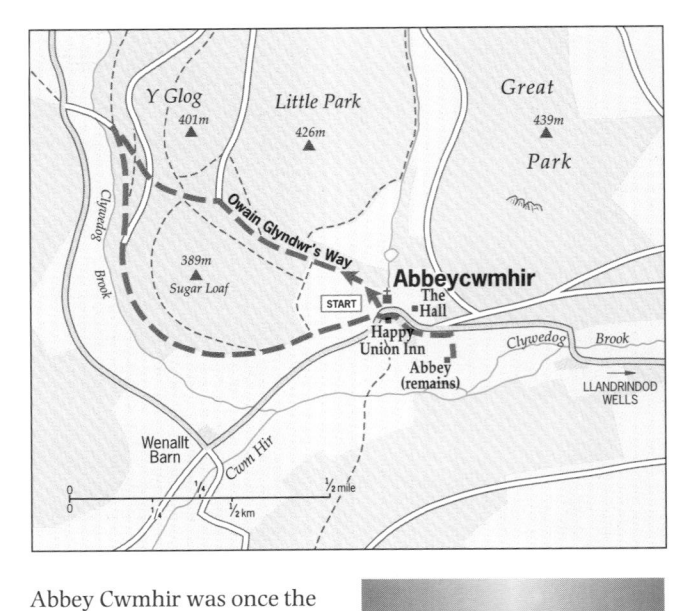

Information

The walk is two miles long
One stile
Pub in village

The Grave of the Last True-born Prince of Wales

Although no original gravestone for the prince has ever been found, and his body has certainly not been unearthed, it is believed that the headless corpse of Prince Llewellyn the Last was carried here for burial after he was killed and beheaded at Cilmeri, near Builth Wells, in 1282. The prince's head was sent to London to be exhibited on Cheapside as a symbol of Edward I's victory and warning to other 'rebels'.

A large slab of slate displaying a carved sword marks the place in front of the high altar where the grave is most likely to have been.

What to look out for

Mixed flocks of woodland birds can be found during the winter months, comprising species such as marsh tits, great tits and nut-hatches. During the spring and summer, look out for redstarts and wood warblers, and keep an eye on the skies for buzzards and the occasional red kite.

The Spectacular Waterfall of Pistyll Rhaeadr

Though short this walk encompasses both the tranquil and powerful aspects of nature, passing through quiet sheep pastures to reach an awe-inspiring waterfall.

START

Llanrhaeadr-ym-Mochnant lies on the B4580 between Oswestry and Llanfyllin; from the village follow a four-mile cul-de-sac signposted 'Waterfall'. Either park in rough lay-bys 200yds or so before reaching the road end, or in Tan-y-pistyll farmyard (small charge).

DIRECTIONS

From just outside the gated entrance to Tan-y-pistyll, take a narrow path uphill to pass through the left-hand of two small gates. Continue to the edge of the wood then turn right on to a broader path. Go through a narrow gate and continue past weirdly exposed tree roots to open country, crossing a ladder stile by a wide gate. Continue up the valley, ignoring a public footpath which ascends steeply left, to where a track slants down from high on the left. Veer right to follow this track down to the stream. Cross the narrow stream on stepping stones and then, beyond a gate, slant rightwards up a green track, soon merging with a broad track which joins from the left. Follow the broad track around the hillside, descending gently (magnificent views of the distant waterfall) to its gated junction with the surfaced approach lane. Here the two routes diverge.

For the shorter walk, turn right and follow the lane back to the start point in under ½ mile.

For the extended route, turn left and follow the lane for a little under ½ mile. Take an initially surfaced track leading down to the right. Go past Tyn-y-wern farmyard and through a gate. Continue along the track over two footbridges to Tan-y-graig

The highest waterfall in Wales

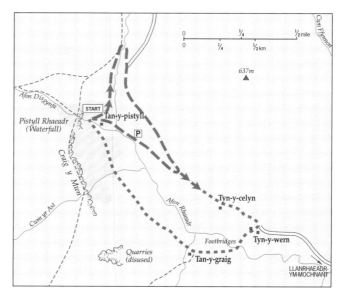

(home to inquisitive sheep dogs). Avoid the farmyard itself by veering slightly right on a track leading to a gate in 100yds.

Beyond the gate the track forks into three. Take the left-hand, uphill fork for 100yds then bear right across the hillside along an obvious slatey path. Beyond mine ruins the path runs alongside a fence with fine views into the valley.

Ignore a stile and yellow arrow on the right and continue straight on, entering woodland at a stile. Within an area of mature trees, the path bends right to the stream and crosses it below the spectacular waterfall by an iron footbridge. The car park is reached soon after.

Pistyll Rhaeadr

The Afon Disgynfa drops almost vertically down a cliff barrier into a pool then spouts beneath a natural rock arch into the lower fall. At 245ft high, the 'Spouting Waterfall' is the highest in Wales. The cliff barrier is a geological feature of the last ice age, having been formed about 10,000 years ago by glacial action.

Bishop William Morgan

Bishop Morgan began translating the Bible into Welsh in 1578 while living at Llanrhaeadr-ym-Mochnant, the village in the valley below the waterfall. His bible played a central role in the survival of the Welsh language.

Dandelion

What to look out for

This is sheep-farming country so, depending on the season, you will see lambs with their mothers, or sheep dogs at work gathering sheep for dipping or shearing. Among the woodland in the river valley below the waterfall you might see a dipper or hear a great spotted woodpecker. More common bird species include coal and marsh tits.

Llangollen Canal and Dinas Bran

Colourful narrowboats and scurrying wildlife enliven this gentle towpath walk, with an option to return via the atmospheric ruins of a hilltop castle.

WALK 132
CLWYD
SJ215423

START

In Llangollen turn off the A5 at traffic lights onto the A539 then turn right after crossing the bridge. Take the first left and soon after crossing the humped-back canal bridge, turn left to car park opposite the school (no weekday parking from September to the end of June between 8am and 6pm; alternative parking by A5/A539 traffic lights).

DIRECTIONS

Return to the humped-back bridge and join the towpath at the wharf café. Pass beneath the bridge to follow the towpath eastwards, soon veering away from the noise of the road below. The canal is bridged by a farm track after about a mile, and by the A539, 500yds or so beyond that. Here the two routes diverge:

On the Shropshire Union Canal

(a) For the canal walk, continue along the towpath for another 500yds or so, then cross by a tiny bridge on to the A539 opposite the Sun Trevor Inn. Return along the towpath to the start point.

(b) For Dinas Bran, pass under the bridge then turn sharp right and cross a stile onto the road. About 25yds after bridging the canal, cross the road and follow a farm track steadily uphill between trees to a surfaced lane known – for good reason – as the Panorama Walk. Turn left to follow the lane, with the hilltop ruins of Castell Dinas Bran soon coming into view. After ½ mile turn left into a narrow lane, then just beyond a cattle grid cross the stile on the right and ascend via a meadow and steeply rising path, over a stile, to the summit.
Descend the far side of the hill by a zig-zag path to gain a green track beyond a grassy hump. Turn left, go through a gate, and descend the track between the trees. Where tracks cross, continue straight ahead and soon pass through a small gate on to a path, which descends steeply at the side of a pasture (seats here). Cross over a narrow lane and follow a surfaced path between fences and finally descend steps to the T-junction of lanes at the start point.

The view from Castell Dinas Bran

Llangollen Canal

Built by Thomas Telford in 1805, this branch of the Shropshire Union Canal was part of a waterways system linking the Mersey, Dee and Severn rivers.
Four miles east of Llangollen the canal crosses high above the River Dee, on the famous Pontcysyllte aqueduct.

Castell Dinas Bran

The hilltop has been fortified since before the Iron Age, but the castle ruins we see today are the remains of a 13th-century fortification.
Legend has it that the beautiful Myfanwy Fechan

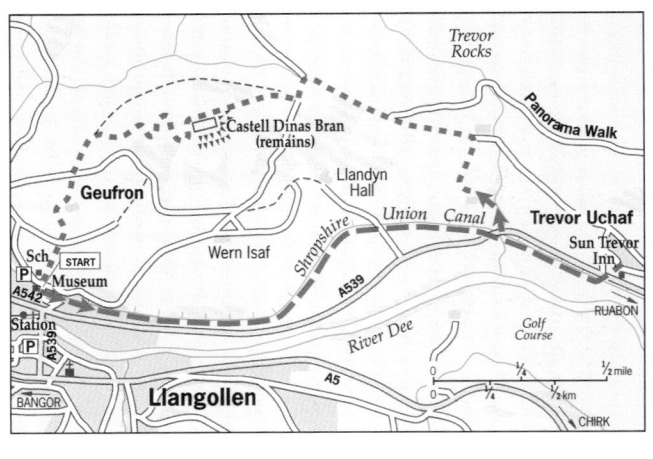

lived here. The young bard Hywel ap Einion, deeply in love with the heiress, would toil up the hill each day to sing her praises, only to be spurned for a wealthier suitor. Broken-hearted, Hywel composed his 'Ode to Myfanwy' which was later famously set to music by Joseph Parry and is now a favourite song for male voice choirs.

What to look out for

On the canal waterbirds such as moorhens, coots and mallards can be seen, often paddling hard to escape approaching boats. Water voles make their homes among tree roots on the banks. Among the waterside plants look for cuckooflower, marsh marigold and monkeyflower.

Information

Information
The walk is three and a half miles long by either route
Level towpath on the canal route, but steep paths on Dinas Bran
Half a mile of quiet road walking on the Dinas Bran route
A few stiles on Dinas Bran
Dogs must be kept on leads on Dinas Bran
Pub with restaurant and outside tables for children on the canal walk; café with outside tables at the canal wharf
Ideal picnic places among the castle ruins or alongside the canal

Clocaenog Forest at Bod Petrual

WALK 133
CLWYD
SJ036511

This is a gentle pine forest walk with a delightful prelude and finale through mixed woodland and around a lake inhabited by ducks. Information boards and displays set out in a restored gamekeeper's cottage add to the interest.

START

Bod Petrual (or Petryal) lies about 400 yards off the B5105, about seven miles south-west of Ruthin, on a narrow lane signposted to Melin-y-wîg. There is a large parking area.

DIRECTIONS

From the parking area, go past the Forestry Commission information board (leaflets available here from the honesty box) on a path soon merging with a good track. Follow the track to a white cottage, the ground floor of which is now a visitor centre. From the back door of the cottage (that is, the entry not the exit door), veer left across the clearing to enter the dark forest on a good path. After passing between stone gateposts, follow the path to the left, then 20yds later swing right on to a broad path bedded with pine needles. The path soon

Information

The short walk is less than a mile long, the full walk about three miles
Good paths or tracks throughout
Almost no road walking
No stiles
No pub or refreshments
Picnic tables near the start point and by the lakeside
Toilets near parking area

narrows and becomes stony as it descends gradually into the little valley of the River Clwyd, and curves to the right. The river, here merely a trickling stream, can be glimpsed through trees or reached from several points by a short detour.

The path soon merges into a broad, slaty track which leads in 50yds to the surfaced approach lane. Here the two routes diverge:

(a) for the short route turn right and walk along the lane for 100yds to the lake. Turn right and follow the lakeside path back to the picnic and parking area.

(b) For the longer walk, go 50yds left along the lane then turn right onto a broad forestry track. After about a mile the track reaches the forest edge then curves right back into the depths. Ignore the track which veers left and continue straight on, along

the obvious track which leads back to the approach lane. Turn right to explore the roadside lake before returning to the parking and picnic area.

Clocaenog Forest

Clocaenog Forest was established in the 1930s, at a time when the need to produce timber as cheaply and quickly as possible superseded any aesthetic appreciation of these uplands – hence the monotonous rows of Sitka and Norway spruce. The trees are now mature and ready for felling, so subsequent planting will be in accordance with the present more enlightened attitude to forestry.

The area has undergone several stages of planting and felling since the natural forests were first cleared by settlers during the Neolithic period, some 3,000 years ago. Information boards in the Bod Petrual visitor centre explain fully the evolving Clocaenog landscape (open daily during holiday seasons).

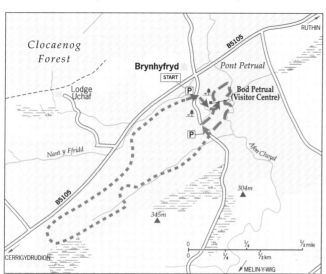

The lake and Cocaenog Forest

What to look out for

You are more likely to hear than see birds of prey in the forest. Bold, inquisitive blue tits and chaffinches may join you at the picnic tables, and mallard on the lake will paddle over at the first rustle of a sandwich bag. Though the sunless forest floor cannot support much growth, the borders of the tracks display a variety of hardy wild plants.

Woodpigeon

The Precipice Walk

WALK 134
GWYNEDD
SH746212

Despite its name, this superbly situated walk is mostly straightforward. Dramatic views on the 'precipice' section contrast with peaceful lakeside scenery.

Information

The walk is three and a half miles long
Some uneven ground which requires steadiness
Short section of road walking on a quiet lane to start and finish
Several stiles
Dogs must be kept on leads
No pub nearby
Many excellent picnic sites, both on the Precipice Path and by the lake
Toilets at car park

Peregrine

START
The walk overlooks the attractive town of Dolgellau on the A470. Five miles north of Dolgellau on the A470, just south of Ganllwyd, take the minor road signposted to Llanfachreth and Abergeirw. Turn right in Llanfachreth towards Dolgellau. In the corner of the second road junction is a convenient car park.
The start point can also be reached via minor roads from the south, leaving the A494 two miles east of Dollgellau.

DIRECTIONS
From the car park, walk down the minor road of the T-junction for about 100yds then turn left on a track among trees (signposted 'Llwybr Cynwch' and 'Precipice Walk'). Veer right from the track on a good path around a cottage, and cross the wall by a ladder stile. Beyond a second ladder stile is a wonderful view of Llwybr Cynwch, backed by the distant mountain of Cader Idris.
Resist the shore for a little while and instead fork right on a grassy path to begin an anti-clockwise circuit of the little hill above the lake. The path, though narrow and uneven in places, has been well maintained and is perfectly obvious to follow. Information boards at intervals briefly describe the natural history of the area. The so-called 'Precipice' section appears about halfway round the walk, where the path twists across a steep hillside – exhilarating rather than worrying, but keep a tight hold of fearless youngsters.
Five stiles must be crossed before the path eventually circles round to arrive at the southern end of the lake. Follow a good track on the left side of the lake to rejoin the approach path for the return to the car park.

Nature versus Industry
Initial impressions gained from the Precipice Walk are of nature at its most unhurried and unsullied: of rugged mountainsides sweeping down to a glistening river estuary.
Yet the view to the north is dominated by severe blocks of conifers and ugly gaps where felling is taking place. In the far distance rise the sinister twin towers of Trawsfynydd nuclear power station, while beneath your feet you can see the scarring evidence of road improvements and, noting derelict cottages, of rural depopulation. What pleases the eye of the visitor may stick like a thorn in the side of the inhabitant.
Yet now that tourism has become an integral part of rural life, natural beauty in this area of the country is being protected not only on aesthetic grounds but, increasingly, as a valuable economic resource.
Evidence of this change of attitudes can be seen on the Precipice Walk, in the tangible form of the more acceptable mixed planting and selective felling methods being used in the forests.

Looking north from Foel Cynwch

What to look out for

Buzzards and ravens utilise the updraught on the hill for spectacular soaring. Undisturbed by people on the path below, kestrels can often be seen hovering over the hill crest, scanning for some unsuspecting small mammal. Water fowl will be seen or heard bustling among the reeds on the lake shore, and grey squirrels may be seen in the wood.

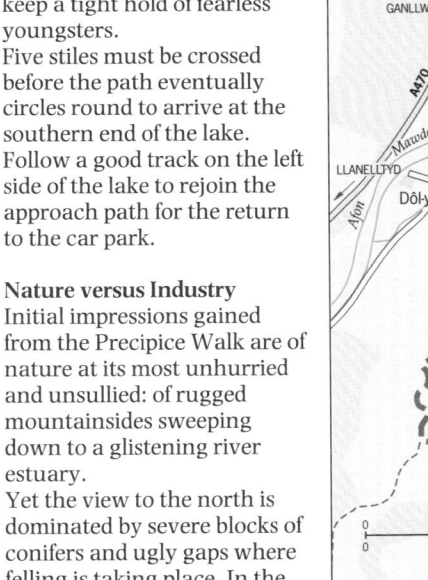

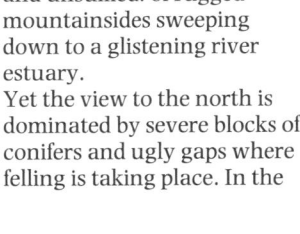

The Lakes of Crafnant and Geirionydd

Though rough in places, this walk among the forested uplands of Snowdonia rewards with beautiful lake scenery and an exciting diversion into an old slate quarry. Less energetic walkers can enjoy a gentle stroll around the more picturesque of the two lakes.

START

From the village of Trefriw on the B5106 between Betws-y-Coed and Conwy, follow the lane signposted 'Llyn Crafnant' for two miles to a Forestry Commission car park.

DIRECTIONS

For the less rugged walk, turn right out of the car park along the lane, then circle Llyn Crafnant using forestry tracks and paths and the continuation of the surfaced approach lane.

Otherwise, take the rising forestry track opposite the car park entrance, crossing a ladder stile by a gate after 50yds. At its end continue by a stony path, crossing a stile after 10yds, to mine spoil in open ground beyond trees. From 30yds beyond the stile, the adventurous could detour to the right, through a short tunnel leading to the entrance to a huge quarried chamber (torch essential). It is also possible to walk across the top of the tunnel.

Return to the main path and fork right 70yds beyond a ruined mine building on to a stony path which curves round the hillside and eventually descends into the Geirionydd valley. Continue through a gap in a stone wall and veer right 50yds beyond the gate in a second wall (ignore a minor path which joins from the left). Pass through a gap in a collapsed stone wall to a rocky knoll topped by a stubby monument with splendid views of Llyn Geirionydd. Take the path on the forested right shore of the lake. Protruding tree roots make rough going, and one short descent requires care when covered in pine needles, but this is a delightful section of the walk. At the lake end, turn right to follow the forestry track uphill for about 300yds. Leave the track 50yds before a sharp right bend for a steadily rising path through trees. Twice cross over the winding track to

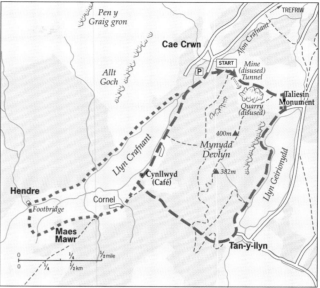

maintain your direction on the uphill path. The path emerges on the track a third time where it bends left.

Follow the track for 50yds then leave it at a right bend for a steeply rising path on the left. This soon levels then begins a steep descent. Where the lake of Llyn Crafnant comes into view, fork right, crossing a stile after 10yds into open fields, then gain the surfaced lane near the lakeside café. Turn right to follow the lane back to the car park in a little over ½ mile.

Taliesin

The monument on the rocky knoll overlooking Geirionydd commemorates Taliesin, perhaps the greatest of the Welsh bards, who lived here in the 6th century.

Mines and Quarries

Evidence of old lead, copper and zinc mines abound in this part of Snowdonia. The old workings visited on the walk

On the shore of Llyn Crafnant

WALK135
GWYNEDD
SH756618

Information

The walk is three miles long by either route
Frequently uneven ground on the full circuit; easy, level walking on the Llyn Crafnant option
Half to one and a half miles of road walking on dead-end lane
Several stiles to cross on the full circuit; one on the Crafnant option
Dogs may be allowed off the lead on forestry sections
Idyllic lakeside café
Several excellent picnic sites on the lake shores

What to look out for

Unlike near-sterile Geirionydd, the waters of Crafnant are not polluted by drainage from lead-bearing rocks or from the noise of speedboats. Birdlife is plentiful: you may see mallards, tufted duck and great crested grebes here, and mute swans in winter.

are in fact part of the Clogwyn y Fuwch slate quarry. Note how the slanting roof of the chamber matches that of the tilted strata of the rock.

Common
mouse-ear

What to look out for

Along the wooded rivers you
may see grey wagtails and
possibly a dipper. Great
spotted woodpeckers,
nuthatches, tree creepers
and tits also inhabit the
valley. The great oak tree
just before Nant Rheadr
cottage dates to about
1765. Experimental fenced
plots nearby contain plants
protected from the sheep.

Aber Falls

An impressive waterfall provides the incentive
for this pleasant stroll through pasture and
woodland. River bridges and varied wildlife add
to the charm of the approach.

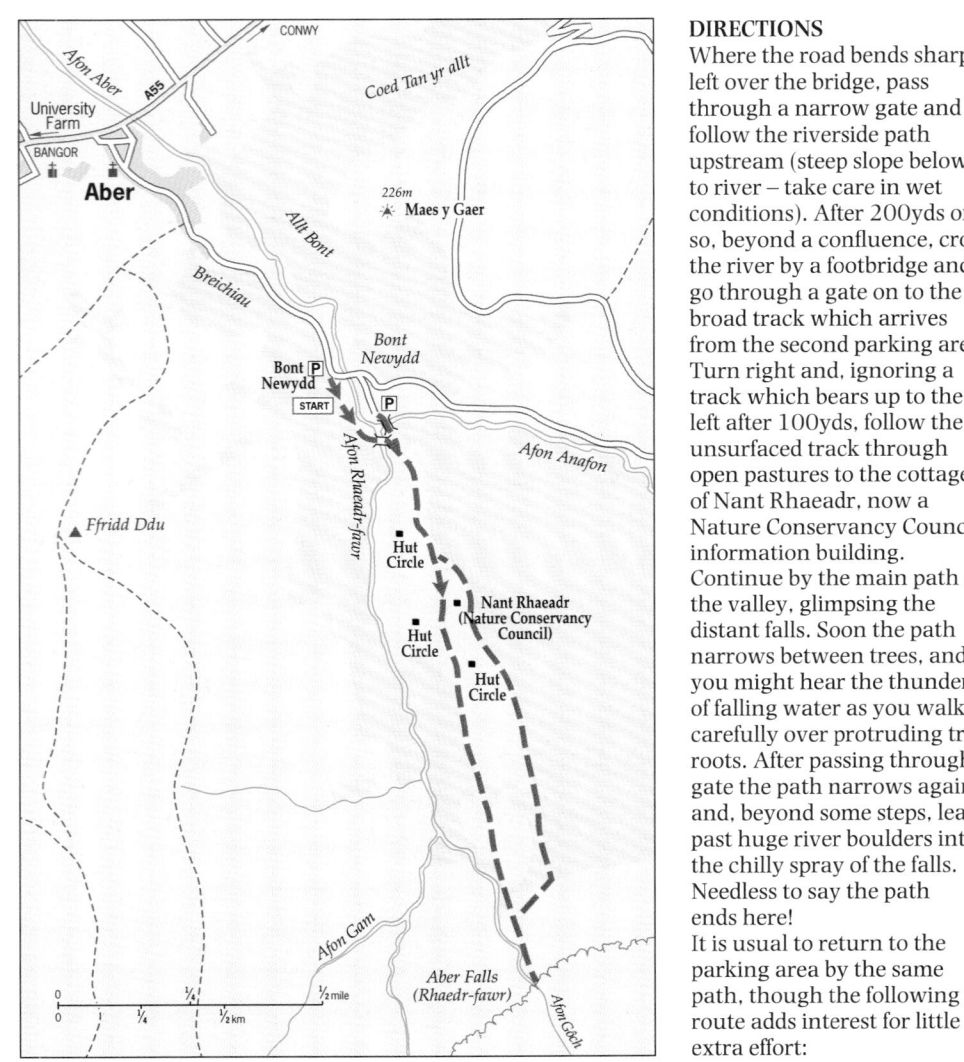

START

The tiny village of Aber lies
near the A55 coast road,
roughly midway between
Bangor and Conwy. From the
village, follow the minor road
signposted 'Aber Falls' for a
little over half a mile to a
parking area at Bont Newydd
(if necessary, cross the bridge
to a second parking area).

DIRECTIONS

Where the road bends sharp
left over the bridge, pass
through a narrow gate and
follow the riverside path
upstream (steep slope below
to river – take care in wet
conditions). After 200yds or
so, beyond a confluence, cross
the river by a footbridge and
go through a gate on to the
broad track which arrives
from the second parking area.
Turn right and, ignoring a
track which bears up to the
left after 100yds, follow the
unsurfaced track through
open pastures to the cottage
of Nant Rhaeadr, now a
Nature Conservancy Council
information building.
Continue by the main path up
the valley, glimpsing the
distant falls. Soon the path
narrows between trees, and
you might hear the thunder
of falling water as you walk
carefully over protruding tree
roots. After passing through a
gate the path narrows again
and, beyond some steps, leads
past huge river boulders into
the chilly spray of the falls.
Needless to say the path
ends here!
It is usual to return to the
parking area by the same
path, though the following
route adds interest for little
extra effort:

Return along the narrow,
stony path to the gate, then
cross a ladder stile on the
right. Follow a steeply rising
path across the open hillside
of boulders, grass and stunted
hawthorn (blue-topped stake
markers) to the forest edge.
Enter the forest at the stile to
gain a narrow path. Ignore a
path which ascends to the
right after 10yds and
continue straight on by the
level or gently descending
path carpeted with pine
needles. After about ½ mile the
path emerges from the forest

at a stile by a gate. Continue
in the same line, passing
through a gap in a stone
enclosure and following the
slight path alongside the
fence at the forest edge. Enter
woodland above the cottage
of Nant Rhaeadr, and follow
the path by the fence which
leads down to the main track
of the approach, to return to
the parking area.

*The Red River tumbling down the
rock face is a magnificent sight
from far or near*

Aber Falls

The Afon Gôch ('Red River')
drains a moorland bowl
below the high domes of the
Carneddau mountains, the
second highest range in
North Wales. At the falls,
where a rare band of hard
granophyre rock arrested the
eroding action of the stream,
the river plunges 120 feet
over the cliffs of Creigiau
Rhaeadr-fawr in a
mesmerising series of chutes
and foaming deflections into
the swirling pool beneath.
The north-facing aspect of the
cliffs, their inaccessibility to
grazing sheep, and the
perpetually misted
atmosphere, promote growth
of mosses and liverworts.

Beddgelert and the Aberglaslyn Gorge

This walk follows the progress of a river as it slides quietly through green pastures then thunders down a rock gorge. A disused railway tunnel and a legendary dog add adventure and intrigue. Less energetic walkers can enjoy the more peaceful river scenery of a shorter walk from the village.

START

The village of Beddgelert is 15 miles south-east of Caernarfon, at the junction of the A4085 and A498. From the junction, at the little hump-back bridge, take the road towards Porthmadog. After about 200 yards you will see signs for a large car park on the right.

DIRECTIONS

Return to the hump-back bridge, then follow the narrow lane on the right to its end. Cross the footbridge at the river confluence then turn right to follow the riverside path downstream to an iron bridge in about ½ mile. This is where the two routes diverge. (For the short walk via Gelert's Grave, cross the bridge then turn right to follow the path upstream; directions continue at * below). For the extended walk through the Aberglaslyn Gorge, do not cross the river at the iron bridge but continue downstream along a broad track (the bed of the dismantled Welsh Highland Railway), passing through two short tunnels.
When about 50yds from the entrance to a long tunnel, descend to the riverbank and follow the exciting path through the gorge until overlooking a road bridge. Turn sharp left and follow steps uphill through woods to where the path levels. Beyond a gate the tunnel track will be seen on the left. Go through the 350yd tunnel to rejoin the approach track and follow it to the iron bridge.
*Continue upstream and at the second gate Gelert's Grave can be seen beneath a large tree on the left, but to protect

grazing land continue a little further until a signed slate path leads back left over pastures to the fenced grave. Return to the riverside and continue upstream along the gravel and slate path. Go through a final gate to arrive in the lane by the toilets.

Gelert's Grave

An inscription at Gelert's Grave tells the tragic tale of a faithful hound fatally misjudged by his master. The story is entirely within the tradition of poignant Welsh legends, in which this part of Snowdonia – closely associated with Arthur and Merlin – is especially rich. One does not enquire too deeply about factual support for these enthralling tales.

Welsh Highland Railway

This narrow-gauge railway carried passengers and goods between Caernarfon and Porthmadog until its closure 1937. Recent attempts to resurrect the dismantled line as a tourist attraction have so far been resisted.

WALK 137
GWYNEDD
SH590481

Information

The full walk is just over three miles long; the short walk just over a mile
Easy, level walking on the short route; the long route includes a rough, rocky section
Almost no road walking
A torch is useful in the long tunnel
No stiles
Dogs must be kept on leads on the short walk
Several pubs in Beddgelert
Many excellent riverside picnic sites
Benches on the path to Gelert's Grave
Toilets near start of walk

What to look out for

As you follow the progress of the river, watch out for grey wagtails and dippers, both of which perch on boulders in the fast-flowing water.
Moss and ferns grow in profusion in the gorge, and beside the water – look out for polypody fern, hard fern and oak fern in particular.

Yellow pimpernel

The rocky bed of the River Glaslyn

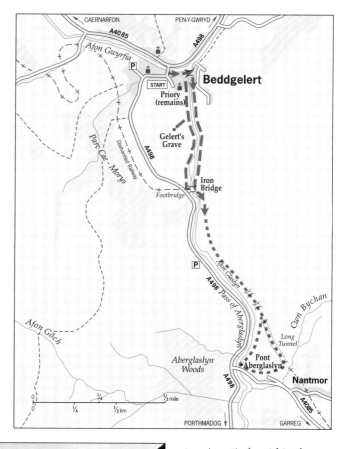

Newborough Forest and Llanddwyn Island

This varied coastal walk contrasts the dark pine forest with the dazzling glare of a sandy beach, with an old lighthouse and lots of sea birds to observe along the way.

START
Newborough (Niwbwrch) lies near the southern tip of Anglesey, on the A4080 about 12 miles south-west of Bangor. At the crossroads in the village centre, take the minor road signposted 'Traeth/Beach' and 'Llanddwyn' to a large car park (small fee).

DIRECTIONS
Take the broad forestry track from near the car park entrance and follow it westwards, parallel to the beach, for a little over ½ mile. Turn left at a T-junction of tracks to arrive at a car park. A path on the right now leads through a depression between trees (sometimes deeply drifted with sand) and out onto the wide sweep of the sandy beach.
Follow the curve of the beach to the right and cross the neck of sand – briefly impassable only during the highest tides – onto Llanddwyn Island. Pass the information board and continue along a broad path, passing a ruined church, to the southern tip of the island (there are several lovely beaches to the right off this path).
After viewing the disused lighthouse (no entry) and other relics, return along the same path, or via detouring paths on the east side of the island, to the connecting neck. (Note that some of the rocky prominences of the tip of the island are cut off by the rising tide.)
Veer right onto the beautiful sweep of dune-backed beach and walk along it for about ¾ mile to the gap in the dunes which leads back to the car park.

Newborough
The 'New Borough' was initially inhabited by reluctant villagers evicted from the site of the proposed Beaumaris Castle by Edward I. In attempting to cultivate the land, they succeeded only in exposing their homes and land to the inexorable drift of windblown sand. Marram grass was planted to stabilise the dunes, which then became home to the rabbits which at one time provided the villagers with their major source of income. Half the huge dune area of Newborough Warren has since been planted with Corsican pine, managed by the Forestry Commission.

Llanddwyn Island
There are several constructions on the southern half of the island, including a stubby marker tower which predates the disused lighthouse. The ruined abbey, of 15th-century origin, stands on the site of the 5th-century chapel of St Dwynwen, the Welsh patron saint of lovers. St Dwynwen is commemorated by the nearby Latin cross; the nearer Celtic cross is of recent origin. The row of cottages near the little harbour were once the homes of pilots employed to guide boats through the treacherous entrance to the Menai Straits.

What to look out for

Oystercatchers, with their distinctive black and white plumage and long, red beaks, can be seen around Llanddwyn Island, while colonies of shags occupy the smaller islands offshore. Other seabirds lay eggs among the thin scrub which covers the ancient rocks of the island, so avoid straying from the paths. These rocks are of pre-Cambrian origin – over 600 million years old.

The sandbar link to Llanddwyn Island

South Stack and Holyhead Mountain

WALK 139
ANGLESEY
SH211819

Information

The walk is three miles long
Rough ground on the
(avoidable) final ascent to
Holyhead Mountain; otherwise
generally good paths and
tracks
Very little road walking on a
dead-end lane
One stile
Café/shop (seasonal) near
start
Picnic possibilities on
Holyhead Mountain
Ice cream van often parked
above lighthouse steps

Though of modest length, this walk takes in the site of an Iron Age settlement, a rocky summit, winding lighthouse steps with unequalled cliff scenery and an RSPB observatory with telescopes trained on nesting sea birds.

START
Follow the A5 through Holyhead, almost to the ferry terminal, then turn left onto the harbour front (Prince of Wales Road). Take the second left, signposted 'South Stack', then turn right at a T-junction. Follow this lane for about one and a half miles then turn right, also signposted. There is a large car park on the left after another half mile.

DIRECTIONS
Cross the stile almost opposite the car park entrance to

arrive at the Iron Age hut circles within 100yds. After exploring these, return to the lane and turn right, passing the café, and climb the hill to reach a small car park. Turn right here to follow a stony path inland, later merging with a surfaced lane. Pass the old radio relay station (to avoid the climb to the top of Holyhead Mountain, continue at * below). Where the lane veers left towards the new radio station, head towards the hump of Holyhead Mountain on the main track.
Continue for a while until another path merges from the right, then fork right and ascend steps. Where the path crests the skyline, turn right to ascend a steep path to the triangulation point and remains of a Roman lookout tower at the summit of Holyhead Mountain.
Retrace your route back to the old radio station, * then take the narrow path which passes on the right side of the fenced compound to a disused lookout tower with views of South Stack Lighthouse far below. Continue along the

path, descending to the road ahead.
(South Stack Lighthouse is now automatic, so access is prohibited. However, it is worth descending at least halfway down the winding steps for tremendous views of sea cliffs and the birds which nest precariously on their ledges. Return to the top of the steps.)
Follow the lane to the café car park then take the path leading down to Ellin's Tower observatory, perched on the cliff edge. Either return to the café and turn right along the lane, or follow a broad path leading directly back to the car park.

What to look out for

On a fine day the mountains of Snowdonia can be seen from the summit of Holyhead Mountain; in exceptionally clear conditions Ireland can also be seen. Below and to the east look out for car ferries plying across the Irish Sea between the port of Holyhead and Dublin or Dun Laoghaire.
During the nesting season (February to July) the South Stack sea cliffs are vibrant with bird life – puffins, fulmars, razorbills and guillemots among them; and choughs are present throughout the year.
At other times you may see rock climbers creeping slowly up the 400ft high vertical cliffs.

The view from South Stack

The Iron Age Settlement of Cytiau'r Gwyddelod
The circular stone bases of more than a dozen Iron Age huts can be clearly seen here. When in use, the huts had conical roofs supported by a central pole, and in some of the circles you can still see evidence of hearths. When raids were imminent, the settlers sought refuge within the stone fortifications built on nearby Holyhead Mountain.

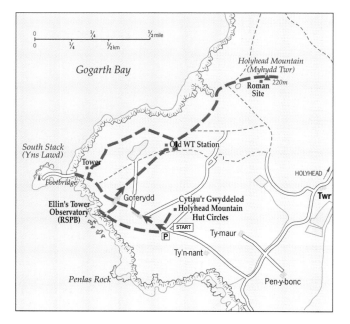

Puffins

NORTHERN
ENGLAND

Castles Above the Plain

WALK 140
CHESHIRE
SJ540591

Two fairy-tale castles, perched on high sandstone crags, are the highlights of this easy stroll around the well-wooded Peckforton Hills. From the ramparts of Beeston Castle the views are outstanding, extending across the fertile patchwork of fields of the Cheshire Plain.

START
Beeston is about two miles west of the A49 from Bunbury. The walk starts from the car park of Beeston Castle.

DIRECTIONS
From the car park (or after visiting the castle) turn right along the lane following a wall round to the right. Soon, by a second car park, join a narrow footpath signposted 'Sandstone Trail' and continue to a stile. Turn left and descend through a conifer plantation to another stile by a cottage.

Turn right into the field by the cottage and go half-left across this field, crossing a footbridge and a stile.

After another 25-30yds, cross another stile and turn right, ascending to the top of the field, heading for another stile. At the stile, turn right into a lane and just past a cottage on the right, turn left through a gate and into the trees. This woodland track skirts the grounds of Peckforton Castle (private). After a gate, a path crosses

Beeston Castle stands in a dramatic setting above the Cheshire Plain

Information

The walk is three miles long
Easy walking
Some road walking on a country lane
Several stiles
Dogs should be kept on leads
Refreshments available at Beeston Castle and the Pheasant Inn at Higher Burwardsley

from the right. Turn left and follow the signposted path straight ahead up the hill. Keep left through the trees, then turn right, following the high walls which enclose the Peckforton Castle estate to reach the pinnacled gatehouse of the Castle Lodge. From the Lodge turn left and follow the lane for about a mile to return to the village of Beeston and the start point.

Beeston Castle
Built by Randulph de Blundeville, Earl of Chester, on his return from the Crusades in 1220, Beeston Castle stands on a commanding red sandstone knoll some 500 feet high, overlooking the Cheshire Plain.
The castle, an English Heritage property today, played an important part during the Civil War and was

'slighted' by Parliamentary forces after the Battle of Rowton Moor. There are tales of hidden treasure in the Upper Bailey well, and there is a small museum in the castle grounds.

Peckforton Castle
This is a mock medieval castle, built in 1844 by Antony Salvin for Lord Tollemache, and is not open to the public.

What to look out for

Chestnut trees, thought to have been introduced to Britain by the Romans, are a feature of the woodlands which surround Peckforton Castle. Sessile oaks and other trees clothe the slopes of the Peckforton Hills, which rise steeply out of the Cheshire Plain. They were formerly part of the Royal hunting ground of Delamere Forest. The woodland harbours wood sorrel, ground ivy and early purple orchids in spring.
The hills are of red sandstone, laid down during the Triassic period about 200 million years ago. The views from the hills extend across eight counties, from the Pennines in the east to the Welsh hills in the west.

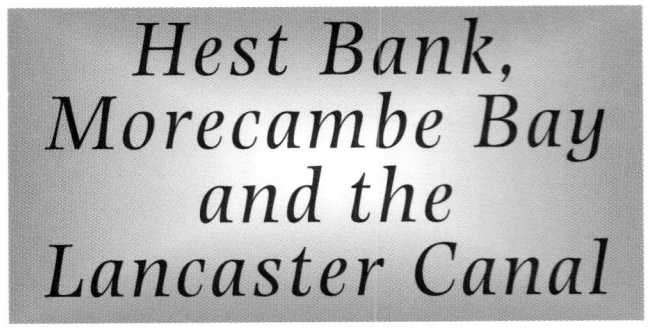

Hest Bank, Morecambe Bay and the Lancaster Canal

This walk features contrasting scenes, from the open shores of Morecambe Bay to the enclosed towpath of the Lancaster Canal, with plenty of water and wildlife.

A stretch of the canal

START

Hest Bank is on the A5105 between Morecambe and Carnforth. Look out for the Post Office, then immediately go over a level crossing to reach the car park on the shore.

DIRECTIONS

Follow the shore road which quickly becomes a gravel track for about 200yds, then pass to the left of a fence and keep to a line between the level saltmarsh and a steep slope of hawthorn scrub. (If walking out on the saltmarsh, keep well away from the dangerous mud flats and tidal channels of Morecambe Bay.) Continue, staying near the edge of the saltmarsh, to eventually go through a narrow stile in a wall, by a sign 'All dogs must be on a leash'. Walk gently uphill and enjoy the extensive views. Walk down the field to a tiny yellow gate where a stile leads into a small field containing a few caravans. Pass Jumbo Rock and keep to the left of Red Bank Farm and cross a high, narrow stone step-stile. A minor road leads along the shore, passing a toilet block and a row of houses. Avoid walking on the road by following a grassy bank on a parallel route overlooking the marshes. Where the road veers inland, continue on, to pass a row of houses. On reaching some seats overlooking the bay, turn inland and proceed to Bolton-le-Sands, past a caravan site, climbing over a rise and going over a level crossing before reaching a pavement. Cross the A6 road (pedestrian crossing nearby) and head straight up a minor road to reach a canal bridge. Do not cross the bridge, but turn right and use a stile to get on to the towpath. Pass a wide bridge carrying a busy road; next is a low-level swing bridge; then a small stone bridge; and finally another small stone bridge with boats and barges moored on either side.
There is a signpost beyond the bridge which gives various canal destinations. One arm points to the shore at Hest Bank. Walk straight down Station Road, passing the shops, then cross the road at a pelican crossing. Use the level crossing to return to the car park.

The Lancaster Canal

The canal from Preston to Tewitfield was opened in 1797. By 1819 it had been extended to Kendal, but the northern section is now derelict. Traffic along the canal declined with the construction of a railway on a parallel route. Today the canal is used purely for leisure.

WALK 141
LANCASHIRE
SO468665

Information

The walk is nearly four miles long
Mostly level ground with half a mile of road walking
A few stiles
Dogs must be kept on leads through first field beyond salt marshes – see directions text
Restaurants at Boulton-le-Sands
Seating at a few points along the route
Areas suitable for picnics along the shore
Toilets near car park at the start

What to look out for

Many species of gulls, waders and wildfowl can be spotted around the shores of Morecambe Bay, with ducks to be seen on the Lancaster Canal. An information board at the start of the walk gives more information. Take binoculars to look across the bay to the Lakeland Fells – there is a view indicator at the start to help identify them. The canal towpath is kept clear of vegetation, but many wild plants flourish alongside garden boundaries. Look out for canalside milestones.

Lever Park, Rivington Reservoir and Rivington Barns

Looking across the peaceful waters of Rivington Reservoir

WALK 142
LANCASHIRE
SD629139

This is a walk for any season, although autumn, with all its glorious colours, is perhaps the best time to explore the woodland tracks around Lever Park. There is an information centre which gives an insight into the wildlife and historical interest of the area.

Information

The walk is three miles long
There is a short ascent which can be muddy
No stiles
There is a café, information centre and play area at the start of the walk
Plenty of places for picnics
Toilets at start point

START

There is no direct access to Lever Park from the nearby M61. Make an approach from Horwich or Chorley, following signposts for Great House Barn, where there is a car park.

DIRECTIONS

From Great House Barn, follow a track towards the wooded shores of Rivington Reservoir. Turn left to follow a wide path which runs roughly parallel to the reservoir shore and continue to the ruined folly known as The Castle.
Walk away from the 'front door' of the castle along the most prominent track. This is quite broad and is lined with oak and sycamore. The track leads to a road, but just before reaching it, turn left along a lesser track. Now cross straight over the road. (To cut the walk short, follow a footpath parallel to the road, which leads straight back to Great House Barn.)

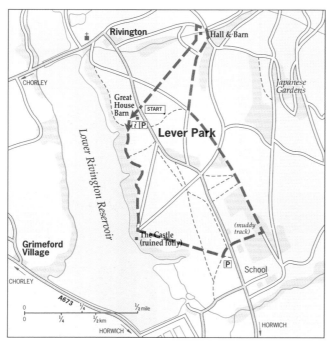

A narrow path, which can be very muddy, climbs gently uphill from the road. It is lined with holly at first, then bends to the left as it levels out in a wood.
On reaching a wide track turn left, continue to a crossroads of tracks and keep forward. At the next junction, turn right and follow a track gently uphill. Later, start walking downhill and keep left to follow a fenced track out of the wood.
Rivington Hall comes into view ahead. Keep to the right of the Hall, then turn left around Rivington Hall Barn. Walk downhill and cross a bridge over a pond.
A narrow road with speed ramps (Hall Drive) leads straight through a beech avenue to return to Great House Barn.

The Reservoirs

There are five reservoirs near Rivington and three more at Roddlesworth, all are connected to the same system which pipes water mainly to Liverpool. Construction of the reservoirs began in 1847, but the work wasn't completed until 1875. The total capacity of the system is 4 million gallons.

Lord Leverhulme

William Lever was born in Bolton in 1851. He entered his father's wholesale grocery business and expanded it considerably.
In 1884, Lever ordered soap from manufacturers and stamped it 'Sunlight Soap' at a time when few brand names were in use. He later moved into soap manufacture, built the village of Port Sunlight and became a leading industrialist. He died in 1925.

Lever Park

Lord Leverhulme bought most of the Rivington Estate and developed it as a home and parkland. The two ancient cruck barns were converted into refreshment rooms and a Japanese Garden was established on the higher slopes. The Castle – a copy of Liverpool Castle – was built overlooking Rivington Reservoir. The park was opened to the public in 1904 and is now managed as a country park.

What to look out for

Visit the information centre first, which offers a fine range of books and leaflets about Lever Park and the West Pennines moors. A small exhibition details the history and wildlife of the park. The information centre is in Great House Barn – a building supported by an enormous oaken cruck-frame. Rivington Hall Barn is a similar structure; both barns have been rebuilt, but the cruck-frames are original. There is a wide variety of birds to see in the woods, including treecreepers, tits and chaffinches.

Wycoller Village, the Beck and the Moors

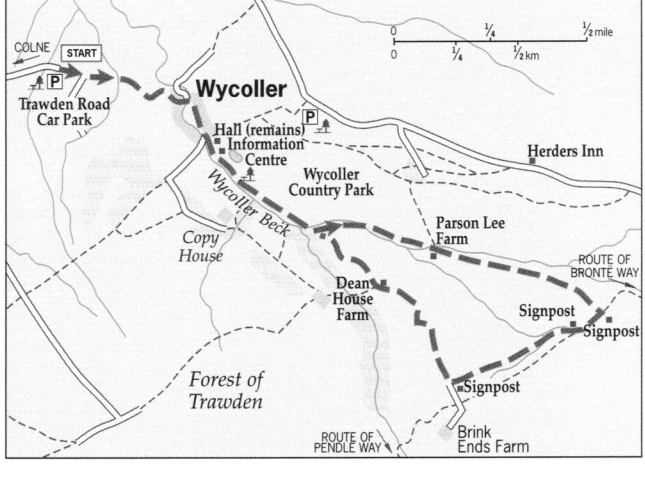

This pleasant walk rises gently from a beautiful village in a wooded valley and touches the fringes of open moorland (best avoided in cold, wet weather though). The walk is strong on both heritage and views.

Information

The walk is three and a half miles long
There is a gradual climb to the moors
A few stiles
Dogs should be on leads through farms and fields
Café, museum and picnic site at Wycoller

START

There is access to Wycoller from Colne or Laneshaw Bridge on the A6068 – both approaches being signposted. The roads are narrow and access to Wycoller itself is restricted to locals and disabled visitors. Everyone else must park 600 yards from the village at the Trawden Road Car Park.

DIRECTIONS

Follow a tarmac path parallel to the narrow road to reach Wycoller. Go straight through the village passing in turn the café, cottages, bridges (cross the beck here), Wycoller Hall, the museum, toilets, duckpond and picnic/play area.

Walk along the track with Wycoller Beck on the right, heading uphill very gently. At a signpost for Dean House Farm bear left, crossing the beck, and soon pass Parson Lee Farm on the right. Stay by the beck, below the farmyard, going through the gate or crossing adjacent stile. Continue uphill rather more steeply along a grassy track, where dogs should be kept on leads.

On reaching a drystone wall, cross a stile by a gate and turn right at sign for Brontë Way and Pendle Way. Go downhill a short way on a good track, then branch to the right along a less clear rushy track where there is a signpost for Wycoller. Follow the track through two gates, then cross a wooden step-stile on the right. There is another signpost for Wycoller. Walk downhill through a field, following a fence, a wall, another fence and another wall. Go through gate (or cross the adjacent stile, rather awkward), then go through another gate into the yard of Dean House Farm. Look for yellow marker arrows and follow the access track away from the farm, downhill to a gate near Wycoller Beck. Simply retrace your steps through Wycoller and return to the car park.

Wycoller

This was a small handloom weaving village dating from the 16th and 17th centuries, pre-dating the larger mill towns nearby.
When plans to flood the valley for a new reservoir were announced, all the inhabitants were evacuated, but when the plan was shelved they did not return and the village fell into ruins. It became a noted beauty spot and was subsequently restored and the surrounding area became a country park. The Brontë Way and Pendle Way both pass through the village.

Wycoller Hall

The building dates from the 16th century and was considerably extended by Squire Cunliffe in the hopes of attracting a wealthy wife. His real passion, though, was cockfighting and he died bankrupt.
The Hall once stood three stories high, though the ruins suggest there were only two. Charlotte Brontë used the Hall and its setting in her famous novel *Jane Eyre*, where it featured as 'Ferndean Manor'. Note the enormous stone fireplace, curious keyhole-shaped wig powdering cupboard and stone mullioned windows.

The old stone bridge over the beck

The ruins of Wycoller Hall

What to look out for

Three types of stone bridge – arched, clapper and clam are encountered.
Look for moorland birds such as meadow pippits and golden plovers, as well as woodland and meadow wildlife at lower elevations. On the higher parts there are views of Pendle Hill, famous for its stories of witchcraft. The excellent small museum, with its various handlooms and old agricultural implements, also has countryside information.

Oakwell Hall

Large bindweed

Though close to the roaring traffic of the
M62, this walk enters a different world – of an
Elizabethan stone and timber country house
with a lovely walled garden, amidst the open
spaces and pleasant footpaths of a modern
country park.

START

There is a large, free car park
on the A652 between
Bradford and Dewsbury,
reached from the M62
(junction 26) via the A58.

DIRECTIONS

From the Country Park
entrance and car park, take
the wide track ahead beyond
the Information Centre, by
the wooden gate.
This path crosses a broad field
(part of a reclaimed colliery)
and leads steeply down to a
bridge over Oakwell Beck.
Cross, and walk up the steps
towards the garden in front of
Oakwell Hall with its little
statue of a ram.
Unless you are going into the

hall, take the path to the left
of the house, alongside the
walled garden behind the hall
and past the wildlife garden.
Continue past the arboretum
to reach the old railway, and
go up a fenced path back to
the old railway bridge.
Turn right along the footpath
alongside the old railway
cutting (avoid the horse
track). After 50yds climb
steps, at the top of which is a
seat with a fine view across
Oakwell Hall and Country
Park and the Spen Valley,
with the tall television mast
on Emley Moor a notable
landmark.
The path soon descends past
birch trees. At a cross roads
take the narrow path

Oakwell Hall, set at the centre of a delightful country park

descending to the right,
parallel with the stream, past
oak and birch woods, soon
crossing a wooden footbridge
to the woods.
Keep on the main path, but
soon take a crossing path to
the right, which leads to
another footbridge over the
stream, then cross the
bridleway (watch out for
galloping horses). Cross the
field ahead on the pathway,
but keep inside the next field
wall before bearing left into a
picnic area, and up a stone
ramp into the car park.
Keep straight ahead towards
Oakwell Hall and Visitor
Centre. Return along the path
in front of the Hall, taking
the steps down to Oakwell
Beck and back along the
same route to return to the
car park.

Oakwell Hall

The Hall, which has been
faithfully refurnished in
period style, began as a mid
15th-century timber
yeoman's house which was

later encased in stone by a
prosperous local landowner,
John Batt – look for the date
over the door. The house has
remained largely unchanged
for 350 years.

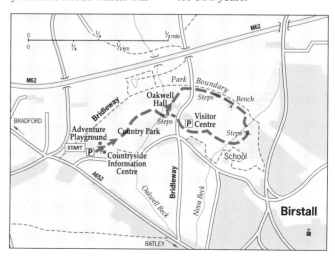

Newmillerdam

WALK 145
WEST YORKSHIRE
SE331157

Gentle paths wind through attractive woodland and around a lake, home to a variety of ducks and other wildfowl, and all along the route the observant walker will be rewarded with interesting flora and fauna.

Information

The walk is two
and a quarter miles long
Broad, easy and
reasonably well surfaced
paths throughout
Lots of lakeside benches
Dogs should be kept on leads
Pubs, cafés, restaurants
and usually an ice cream van
in Newmillerdam village
Countryside Rangers on duty
at weekends
Toilets on the Wakefield side
of the dam

START
The country park is immediately off the A61 between Wakefield and Barnsley and provides free parking. Start the walk at the Barnsley side of the dam, from the car park opposite the Fox & Hounds pub.

DIRECTIONS
Take the path along the lakeside for just over ½ mile, to reach a bridge on the left leading to a long path over the top of the lake (the walk can be shortened here). Continue on the main path along the right-hand bank of the lake, crossing over a small, low, hump-backed bridge over a stream. Pass another bridge on the left. Continue to the next junction and take the left-hand track, which becomes rougher as it rises slightly through the trees. After about another 250yds, at a junction of paths, bear left and in another 150yds, turn left again on to another track, which descends slightly.
The track crosses a stream by a fenced bridge with a clearing on the right, and soon bends sharply left to form a wider path as it meets other incoming paths. After a slight ascent at the next junction (just under ¼ mile) take the left fork, descending to a clearing by the stream and the bridge passed on the outward walk. The track becomes wider again, and joins the lakeside track. Continue by the lakeside to an exit marked by large gates on the Wakefield side of the dam and return to the car park.

Newmillerdam Country Park
The park, opened to the public in 1956, covers 237 acres of woodland and water and provides various leisure and recreation facilities, including orienteering, fishing, walking and a number of special events. The variety of woodlands, open water and marshlands are carefully managed, and the conservation value has resulted in its designation as a Site of Special Scientific Interest. The name Newmillerdam dates back to medieval times when the first corn mill was constructed beside the Owler Beck. A 17th-century mill, in use until 1960, was later damaged by fire before being restored and converted into a restaurant in 1979.

Below, the path beside the dam

Mute swan

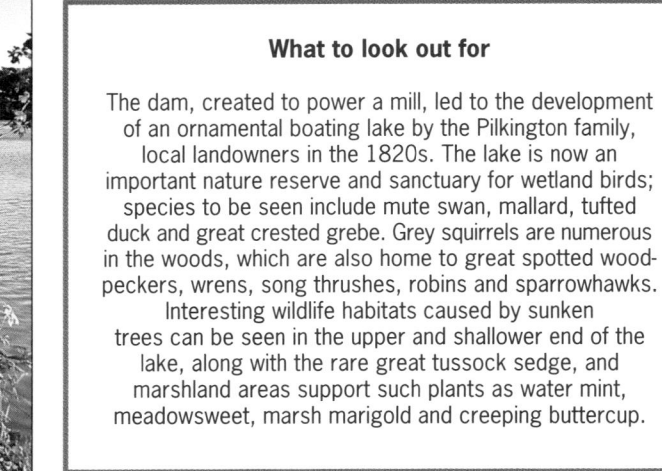

What to look out for

The dam, created to power a mill, led to the development of an ornamental boating lake by the Pilkington family, local landowners in the 1820s. The lake is now an important nature reserve and sanctuary for wetland birds; species to be seen include mute swan, mallard, tufted duck and great crested grebe. Grey squirrels are numerous in the woods, which are also home to great spotted woodpeckers, wrens, song thrushes, robins and sparrowhawks. Interesting wildlife habitats caused by sunken trees can be seen in the upper and shallower end of the lake, along with the rare great tussock sedge, and marshland areas support such plants as water mint, meadowsweet, marsh marigold and creeping buttercup.

Bradfield Dale

The route links the twin villages of High and Low Bradfield, idyllically set in a steep Pennine valley. Fine views of the surrounding moors, an interesting church and the story of the worst dam-burst disaster in British history make this a walk to remember.

START

Low Bradfield is off the B6077, about seven miles west of the centre of Sheffield. The walk starts from the car park on the western side of the village recreation ground.

DIRECTIONS

From the car park turn right, following the narrow path signed 'Path to High Bradfield', parallel to the stream on your right and a wall on your left. Turn right at the second footbridge, and up a steep flight of stone steps. At the top cross a track and climb five more steps. Keep ahead between a fence and a wall to reach the road. Turn left along the road which leads up and alongside the wall of the Agden Reservoir. When the road curves round to the right, follow the footpath signed 'Bailey Hill', which winds steeply up to the right by the side of a plantation. Continue to climb up steeply until you reach a path junction by a stile on the right. Directly ahead and partly overgrown by trees is Bailey Hill, a Norman motte and bailey castle (no access).

Turn right over the stile and follow the path across to the churchyard, entering through two gates. Walk through the churchyard to the main gate, with the Watch House on your left. Keep forward into Towngate and into the hilltop village of High Bradfield.

Now turn right into Woodfall Lane, signed 'Low Bradfield and Dungworth'. Soon after

The parish church of St Nicholas

the lane bends to the left, turn left at a stone stile following public footpath signed 'Low Bradfield'. Keep to the edge of the field by a stone wall, and follow it as it curves right. Continue across several walls and stiles to cross the fields, keeping a line of electricity poles 20yds to your right, and later descend another uneven flight of stone steps onto a lane (care needed) near the upper end of the Damflask Reservoir.

Cross the footbridge over the River Loxley almost opposite the steps, and continue along School Lane, which leads via a walled path to another lane, emerging by the police station. Turn right here back towards the village, and right again at The Plough pub into Mill Lee Road for the return to the car park.

St Nicholas Church, High Bradfield

This lovely parish church built mainly in the 15th century has fine views across the green, reservoir-filled dale to the moorlands beyond. The Gothic-style Watch House on the edge of the churchyard was built in the days when body snatching was rife.

The Bursting Dam Disaster

Just after midnight on 11 March 1864, the newly-completed Dale Dike Reservoir west of Low

Information

The walk is two miles long
Mostly easy lane and field walking, with one steep climb
Several stone squeeze-stiles
Dogs should be kept on leads
Pubs in Low and High Bradfield

Bradfield burst its walls following a landslip. About 700 million gallons of water surged down Bradfield Dale and on as far as the outskirts of Sheffield. A mill at Low Bradfield was swept away and a total of 244 people died. Another 20,000 were made homeless.

What to look out for

Despite their usual retiring nature, weasels are seen fairly regularly in the area, feeding among the stone walls. Watch for agitated meadow pipits perched on the stones. Foxes are sometimes observed crossing the open moors, which are the haunt also of red grouse. The reservoirs harbour waterbirds in autumn and winter.

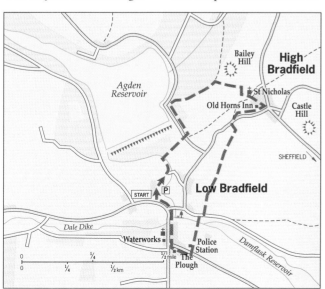

Barton Clay Pits

Under the shadow of the Humber Bridge, along the south bank of the river, lie a series of fascinating lagoons created by the digging of clay for tiles and bricks. It now forms the focal point of a remarkable riverside conservation area full of interesting things to see.

START
Barton is on the south bank of the Humber, alongside the Humber Bridge (A15). The walk starts from the main car park and picnic area of the Barton Clay Pits Country Park.

DIRECTIONS.
Facing away from the river, make your way out of the top right-hand corner of the car park and picnic area. Pass the ponds along a narrow path which leads parallel with houses and the

The Humber Bridge

WALK 147
HUMBERSIDE
TA026234

Information

The walk is around four miles long
Level, easy ground
A few stiles
Dogs are not permitted into the LSHTNC Nature Reserve (alternative route provided) and should be kept on leads elsewhere
Barton Clay Pits Country Park Project Information Centre by the foreshore
Cafés and pubs in Barton; Westfield Lakes Hotel at the foreshore caravan site; light refreshments kiosk weekend and holiday times
Picnic area at the Humber Bridge Viewing Area
Toilets close by

What to look out for

The River Humber is one of Britain's busiest inland waterways and boats of all sizes can be seen, some coming from as far as Southern Europe or the Baltic.
Different wildlife habitats, including the Far Ings Nature Reserve, provide a variety of natural history. During the winter brent geese and ducks, gulls and waders occupy the foreshore.
The larger lagoons harbour birds such as goosanders in winter; reed-fringed margins are the haunt of reed warblers during summer and water rails in winter.
A traditional clay tilemakers yard is passed towards the end of the walk. Special visits are arranged in the summer months to see the pantile makers at work.

Humber Bridge to Far Ings Road. Turn right here along the road up to and beyond the Humber Bridge. Immediately beyond the bridge, a narrow gap stile on the left leads into a permissive footpath through an attractive plantation of trees and shrubs.
This emerges at Dam Road, a narrow, traffic-free lane. Turn right, past allotments, as far as the junction. Cross, and almost directly ahead a stile leads down into a field. Follow the edge of the field straight ahead to a stile by a

footbridge over a stream. Turn left around the edge of the field, having gone past Blow Wells Plantation, then turn right along the hedge.
At the broad gap in the hedge continue in the same direction, keeping the hedge on the left, to a stile in the field corner leading into another narrow lane. Turn right here to the Humber foreshore.
Turn right along the foreshore dyke through a

gate, but look for a stile near by on the right, which leads through into the Far Ings Nature Reserve. (No dogs are allowed in here, so if you have a dog with you, you should continue along the foreshore.)
Follow the path past pools and bird hides curving round to the left, ignoring the stile on the right back into Far Ings Road. At a gate on the right leading into a field, cross through two more gates to the Visitor Centre and

Information Point opposite. From the Visitor Centre head back along the track which leads to the foreshore, climbing some wooden steps and turning right onto the dyke, and continue past a hotel, a caravan site and a water sports area along the dyke. Keep ahead through gates, back along the foreshore and past brickworks to the car park.

Far Ings Nature Reserve
Old hawthorn hedges and deep reed beds around the clay pit lakes form a wonderful, sheltered natural habitat and area to view waterfowl. The Reserve is owned and managed by the Lincolnshire and South Humberside Trust for Nature Conservation. Please keep to the footpaths in the Nature Reserve.

Common poppy

Sewerby Park & Danes Dyke

WALK 148
HUMBERSIDE
TA197687

This walk includes some superb cliff-top and coastal scenery, woodland and a prehistoric dyke. There is also a lovely country house museum and estate, complete with a small zoo.

Information

The walk is under three miles long
Level throughout, except for steep steps at Danes Dyke, but care needed on cliff-top section
A few stiles and kissing-gates
No dogs in Sewerby Park
Refreshment facilities at Sewerby Park (admission fee) or in Bridlington
Toilets about 200 yards from the start of the walk, and in Sewerby Park

START
From the centre of Bridlington, follow Sewerby signs. Just past the railway level crossing, by the model village, turn into the Limekiln Lane car park (pay and display).

DIRECTIONS
From the rear of the car park cross into the overflow field and head towards the sea to pick up the cliff-top path. Turn left along the path, past conveniently placed benches, enjoying the superb views across the Bay.
Where the tarmac ends beyond beach access point, almost opposite Sewerby, continue along the narrow cliff-top path by the edge of fields – keeping well away from the edge. Follow the path towards the woods ahead until you reach a steep gorge – part of Danes Dyke.
Follow the path (signed) to the left. Unless you want to go down to the beach, avoid the steep steps on the right, keeping alongside the field until you reach a wooden stile on the left with a wooden signpost indicating Sewerby. (The path directly ahead soon drops down steps and over a footbridge before ascending Danes Dyke and leading to the car park, toilets and start of the Danes Dyke Nature Trail).
Follow the well-used path back to Sewerby which bears slightly left across the field in front of a red pantiled building, the site of a new golf course. Continue to the woods ahead. The path leads between the cricket pitch and the edge of Sewerby Park estate to the entrance to the Park. Continue along the path past the paddocks and back to Limekiln Lane car park.

The steep cliffs of Sewerby Rocks (left), and Sewerby Hall (right)

What to look out for

Small fishing boats as well as pleasure craft are usually active in the bay, and large tankers and container ships can be observed crossing the horizon. There are magnificent views back along the town or up to Flamborough Head with its lighthouse. The chalk cliffs (part of the Flamborough Heritage Coast) are rich in wild flowers and birdlife. Birds to be seen include herring gulls, kittiwakes, shags, razorbills, guillemots, kestrels, and on the return walk, meadow pipits.
The walk passes the paddocks of Sewerby Park which contain deer, ponies and llamas.

Sewerby Hall, Park and Zoo
The house, built around 1714–20, is now an art gallery and museum, including the Amy Johnson Trophy Room, dedicated to the famous pioneer aviator, who born in Hull. The gardens are full of interest, especially the delightful walled gardens, and there is also a miniature zoo and aviary. The park is open all year, the art gallery and museum from Easter to September.

The York–Selby Cycle Path

This walk is along part of what used to be the east coast main line railway – the Flying Scotsman once passed at 100mph *en route* from London to Edinburgh. It is now a designated cycle path.

A clear path for walking – or running

WALK 149
NORTH YORKSHIRE
SE617419

Information

The walk can be as long as you wish to make it, by simply continuing along the track
Easy walking on ash and gravel paths, but look out for passing cyclists
No facilities on the walk, but toilets and two inns in Riccall (three miles south) and an inn at Escrick
Concrete benches at various points along the route

START
The walk is about six miles south of York via the A19, turning right just south of Escrick on a minor road to Stillingfleet. Park at the car park by the old railway bridge on the site of the old station.

DIRECTIONS
Go down from the car park, through the gate and round to the bridge onto the cycle track. The Maze is about 200yds along the cycle path to the left: follow the track up along the side of the cutting and steps lead down from the top. From the Maze return along the cycle path, under the

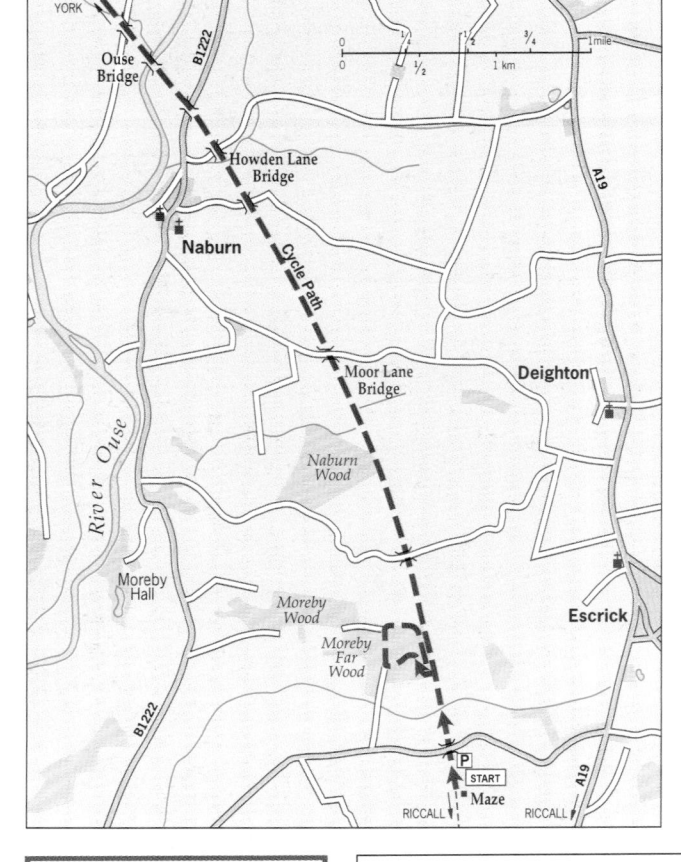

bridge in the direction of York. After about 100yds you pass a mounted coal cutting machine erected as a monument to the coal mining tradition of the area. Ahead is Moreby Far Wood, a plantation of fir trees with various paths, which can be explored before continuing on the cycle route or returning along the track to the car park.

The York–Selby Cycle Path
When the huge Selby coal field – Europe's largest – was being developed in the 1970s, it was realised that the main London-Edinburgh railway could be affected by subsidence and so a new high speed line, to the west of the present route, had to be built. Part of the old railway has been used for the Selby bypass but the remainder has been developed into a cycling and walking way from Bishopthorpe, south of York, to Riccall. It is hoped the route will soon be extended directly into Selby.

The turf maze, near the start

What to look out for

There is a maze is a short distance south of the car park, and a fine view of the River Ouse from Bishopthorpe bridge, with river craft and a fascinating boatyard nearby. Mileposts along the route include some interesting and unusual 'sculptures'. From the more elevated sections of the path there are splendid views across the Plain of York.

Pickering Castle

Pickering's romantic 12th-century castle provides the focal point for this walk on the edge of the North York Moors National Park; additional attractions which can be combined with the walk include a steam-hauled trip on the North Yorkshire Moors Railway or a visit to the delightful Beck Isle Folk Museum.

START
The walk starts at the crossroads and bridge below Pickering Station. There are plenty of well signed car parks in Pickering and at the castle, but all can be busy on summer weekends.

DIRECTIONS
Cross the bridge to the Beck Isle Museum and picnic area, then go through gate along the track to the left of the museum (marked 'Riding Stables'). Go through a gate to the left and along the broad, grassy track past the stables. Soon the path veers right to continue beside the beck and over a stile – ignore a concrete footbridge on the right.

Turn left, away from the beck, over rough pasture towards a wood ahead. Enter the wood by another stile, crossing a track into a caravan site, before following a narrow path between trees to exit at a stile. Bear half-right across a ridged field, and at the top go through the right hand of two field gates onto a stony track.

Follow the track by woods, crossing a stile beside a gate (waymarked) and a farmhouse (now a pottery). The way narrows between hedges to a metal gate, then a second gate, before curving right over an open field towards cottages.
Turn right through the gate by these cottages

(waymarked) and right again to a path leading to a pedestrian gate across the railway line (look out for trains) and a footbridge over the stream. Follow the path to the road.
Cross the road and bear right to a path into the woods, which climbs the embankment parallel to the road. It soon joins a broader path from the left, passing limestone cliffs on the left. At a fork keep left, joining another track parallel to the road, and avoiding a path bearing right to the road. Keep to this path, with more cliffs on your right, to reach another fork. Bear right here to join the road with care, and cross to the other side. Pass a trout farm on the beck. Turn left for 250yds

The ruins of Pickering Castle

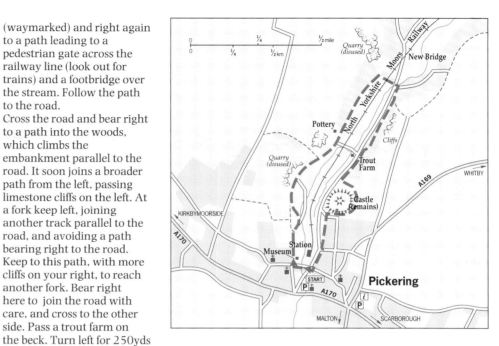

to a wooden barrier and footpath sign, taking a path on the opposite side of the road. Follow an old wall away from road up an incline by the edge of the wood. Where the wall ends go left for 10yds, then right to where paths split below the castle walls. Head right then left up to the castle walls, circling left to the main entrance, then bearing right down steps. Turn left down Castle Road to return to Pickering centre.

Pickering Castle
Enjoying a superb position on a limestone bluff overlooking the town, Pickering Castle (English Heritage) dates from Norman times. It is said that most kings of England between 1100 and 1400 visited the Castle, mainly to hunt in local forests. It is open daily in summer; closed Mondays in winter.

Beck Isle Museum
Collections of domestic bygones, including a room of children's toys, old shops, farm implements and a moorland kitchen bring the past to life in this fascinating museum. It is open daily from Easter to October.

What to look out for

The woods include oak, ash, rowan and whitebeam, with wood anemones and yellow pimpernel on the ground below.

Robin Hood's Bay

WALK 151
NORTH YORKSHIRE
SE950055

Information

The walk is two miles long
Steep terrain
Several stiles and lots of
steps to climb up or down
Choice of cafés, tea shops,
pubs, ice cream stalls and
fish and chip shops in Robin
Hood's Bay village
Picnic site above town,
towards end of walk
Toilets at the car park
entrance

Shag

Dramatic cliff and coastal scenery, a long-lamented clifftop railway line, a foreshore filled with rockpools and a picturesque former smugglers' village of narrow, twisting streets make up this testing walk.

START

Robin Hood's Bay is about five miles south of Whitby. Turn off the A171 onto the B1447 and continue towards the village. Park at the higher coach and car park (charge) at the old station.

DIRECTIONS

From the car park walk past the old station, now the village hall, taking the walkway on the left above the drive down to the Fylingthorpe road. Turn right along the road for 60yds, following the signs 'Railway Path', cross the road and go through a gate on the left onto the old Whitby–Scarborough railway line,

now a footpath and cycle trail. Follow the old railway line for a little less than ½ mile until you reach a large, old concrete stile on the left. The path goes in front of the stile along a hedge to another stile. Cross, turning left along the edge of the fields, crossing several stiles. The path bears right above a shallow wooded ravine.

A stile leads into a wood. Keep on the path now descending above the ravine to yet another stile, leaving the wood along a path which curves steeply down onto the road. Turn right to the cobbled slipway and foreshore at Way Foot.

(From Way Foot fork right up

King Street (cul de sac), turning left at the top into Chapel Street to see this lovely, narrow alleyway of shops and houses. Return down King Street.)
Take the opening just above the Dolphin Inn leading to the sea wall. Steps lead down past the viewing area to the sea wall itself. Continue left along the little promenade along the wall, going up the steps behind the town to reach the picnic site.
Follow the path back up to the The Bank (main street), turn right up the steps, and continue along to the roundabout and lower car park; 300 yards beyond this is the Station car park.

Robin Hood's Bay

Robin Hood's Bay

What to look out for

There are many seabirds along the coast
and the foreshore – mainly gulls, but also terns in summer
and cormorants in winter.
In the bay and beached by the slipway you will see
fishing boats (the traditional North Sea coble is based on a
Viking design), nets, and crab and lobster pots.
Life on the foreshore
and in the rock pools is abundant, and includes crabs, sea
anemones, limpets, periwinkles and small fish
such as blennies.

Robin Hood's Bay

This is one of the most fascinating fishing and tourist villages along the east coast. With its winding, traffic free streets, narrow houses and old pubs, the village is full of atmosphere. A tunnel carries the Mill Stream, emerging by the slipway, and it was along here that smugglers carried their contraband – brandy, gin, silk, tobacco – at the dead of night, out of sight of the excisemen. The huge sea wall was built in 1975 to protect the town from the erosive power of the sea.

Swinsty

A lovely lakeland and woodland walk, with picnic areas, attractive waterside paths, two dams, views and reflections.

START

The Swinsty and Fewston Reservoirs are south of the A59 about ten miles west of Harrogate. Turn off southwards for Fewston village just west of the A59/B6451 junction. There is a well-screened Yorkshire Water car park (free) on the Fewston–Timble road just to the west of Fewston Embankment. There is an alternative car park and picnic site on the minor road to the south of Fewston.

DIRECTIONS

From the car park take the track which runs through the wood immediately opposite the information board, closed to cars by a single wooden barrier. This becomes a broad, stone track through a dense

coniferous plantation (Swinsty Moor Plantation) with fire breaks. After just over ½ mile this emerges opposite Swinsty Hall. Turn left alongside the overgrown garden wall to the rear of the hall, down to the track at the side of Swinsty Reservoir, and turn right

towards the dam. Cross the dam and follow the reservoir road past the lodge for nearly ¼ mile, then bear left along a woodland path which goes close to the reservoir side. At a gate this path joins the lane. Turn left along the lane, crossing the bridge over the eastern arm of the reservoir.

At the far side, a path leads back into the woodland by a car park and attractive picnic site. Keep ahead along the water's edge, following a beautiful path through woods at the reservoir side (fine views through the trees). This eventually emerges in open grassland past a small

wildfowl reserve and climbs the embankment of the Fewston Dam to a gate. Turn left into the Fewston Embankment road, keeping along the pavement to the end of the dam, to reach the car park 100yds beyond the end of the dam.

Swinsty Reservoir

In 1876 the construction of the great dam across the little River Washburn created Swinsty Reservoir to supply

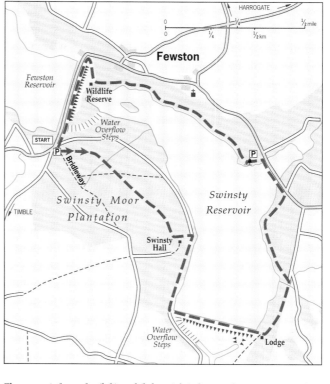

Information

The walk is just over three miles long
Level walking, except for logged slope up to Fewston Reservoir Road; half a mile of rough track at start of walk
No stiles
Dogs must be kept under control
Timble Inn about three quarters of a mile from the start/finish of the walk serves food and light refreshments; it has a family room
Picnic areas at the start of the walk and on east side of reservoir
Toilets and small information point at start of walk

The reservoir from afar (left), and (below right) about as close as you can get!

the city of Leeds with fresh water. It is one of a chain of reservoirs – Thrushcross, Fewston, Swinsty and Lindley – and many billions of cubic metres of water come through it each day. Some of the water in Swinsty has been collected in the valley, but much comes from as far away as the River Laver Leighton Reservoir at Masham, about 20 miles away.

Swinsty Hall

This beautiful Elizabethan house dates back to 1570. An old Dales legend maintains that the hall was built from the ill-gotten gains of a once poor London weaver called

What to look out for

Though this is an area of commercial woodland, the variety of trees is not confined to the usual coniferous spruce, larch and pine, but also includes rowan, sycamore, willow, alder and beech – and the edge of the woods has lots of wild flowers.
Large-scale reservoir works include two dams and outflows.
Both woodland and lakeland birds can be seen, including finches, blue tits, wood pigeons, woodpeckers, mallard and teal.

Robinson who, during the Great Plague, stole gold from plague victims. There is not a shred of truth in this story – it was, in fact, built by one

Ralph Wood, a local landowner, for his newly married son, Francis. It is all so overgrown now that it is easy to miss.

Bolton Priory

This is a walk with lots of variety – a ruined 12th-century priory, riverside areas with a footbridge, stepping stones, stretches of sand and pretty woodland paths with fine views. It is also relatively sheltered, making it an ideal winter walk.

START

Bolton Abbey village can be reached from Skipton (six miles west) on the A59, turning north at Bolton Bridge along the B6160, or from Ilkley via the A65, joining the B6160 at Addingham. There is a large, well signed car park (charge) at Bolton Bridge.

DIRECTIONS

From the top end of the car park, pass the Information Board, turning right into the village. Cross the B6160 (very busy at times) to the hole in the wall opposite, which is the footpath into the Bolton Abbey Estate.

Go down the steps towards the riverside and head towards the wooden footbridge and stepping stones. Cross the bridge (the stepping stones should be avoided unless river is very low) and ascend the hillside to reach a higher level path

Information

The walk is about two and a half miles long
Mainly on woodland or riverside paths, with two short but easy climbs and a section high above the river
No road walking
A few stiles
Refreshment facilities in Bolton Abbey village; cafeteria, restaurant, snacks and ice cream at Cavendish Pavilion (seasonal)
Extensive grassy picnic areas by the priory footbridge and along riverside
Toilets at Bolton Abbey car park and Cavendish Pavilion

The priory, seen across the river

through the woods.
Keep on the main path through the woods, eventually descending to a stile and rounding the hillside to join the lane from Storiths. Keep ahead to cross the stream at Pickles Gill by the footbridge to the right (or stepping stones ahead). Turn left alongside the stream to a stile which leads to the riverside path and then a second stile to cross the wooden bridge at the Cavendish Pavilion. (The walk can be extended at this point into the Strid Wood Nature Trails; free map available at entrance.)

From the Cavendish Pavilion, go back along the riverside past the parking areas, following the curve of the river to the right where, on the hillside, a narrow path leads to steps and a stile then meets the road by the Cavendish Memorial. Keep left along the path parallel to the road and go through a gate to the entrance of Bolton Priory Church.
Maintain your direction along the church drive, past the rectory, taking the stile left to a path over the field, rejoining the path to the hole in the wall for the village centre.

Bolton Priory

The priory was founded by a group of Augustinian canons, who moved here from Embsay, near Skipton, around 1154. The church (still in use) and most of the ruins date from the 12th to

the 15th century, the newest part being Prior Moone's western tower which was never completed. The roof is a very recent addition. Bolton Hall was converted from the former gatehouse in the 18th century; the rectory was once a grammar school, endowed by the 17th-century scientist, Robert Boyle (of Boyle's Law fame).

The Legend of the White Doe of Rylstone

During Elizabethan times an abortive rising against the Queen spelled disaster for the Nortons of nearby Rylstone Hall, resulting in imprisonment or death for most of the family. A surviving sister, Emily, would walk six miles across the moors to visit her brother's grave in Bolton Priory churchyard, taking with her the little white doe that had been a gift from her brother. Long after her death the white doe would still be seen wandering around the gravestones.

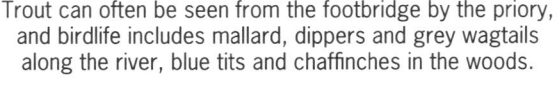

What to look out for

Trout can often be seen from the footbridge by the priory, and birdlife includes mallard, dippers and grey wagtails along the river, blue tits and chaffinches in the woods.

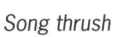

Song thrush

How Stean Gorge and Tom Taylor's Cave

A dramatic walk with splendid views, a streamside section, a footbridge over a gorge and a pathway under a steep overhang. Torches are essential for exploring the cave and can be hired at the café at the start.

WALK 154
NORTH YORKSHIRE
SE092743

Information

The walk is one and a half miles long
An undulating route, with a steepish climb at the end
Several stiles
Dogs must be kept on leads
Nearest pub in Middlesmoor
Cafeteria, restaurant and ice creams at How Stean Gorge
Toilets at How Stean

The gorge (above), and the path

START
How Stean is about seven miles north of Pateley Bridge. At Lofthouse turn left on no-through-road to Stean. Park at small car park (charge) in the quarry on the left.

DIRECTIONS
From the car park walk westwards along the lane to the café which is the entrance point to How Stean Gorge. Ahead across a small field, now used as an additional car park, is Tom Taylor's Cave, which is signposted and is in a small walled enclosure. From the cave, head for the far left-hand corner of the field to a gate, where orange arrows indicate the way ahead. In the next field keep forward to the barn. Turn left through a gate, then keep ahead across the next two fields, through clearly marked gates. In the next field veer right to reach the 'Nidderdale Way' signpost at the field boundary. Pass through a stone stile and bear diagonally left across the field to reach a wooden gate in the fence. Descend steps to cross a footbridge then ascend steps to reach a small enclosure with a caravan. Keep right here to reach a lane, passing the caravan on your left. At the lane turn left for the return to the car park.

How Stean Gorge
This limestone gorge dates from the Ice Age, the stream carving out a deep ravine. It is 80 feet deep in places, and forms natural rock gardens with mosses, ivy, and a variety wild plants growing out of the crevices. In the bottom of the gorge, the stream forms a series of impressive cascades and whirlpools. In dry weather, the really adventurous walker can take the steps down to the limestone bed of the stream at the bottom of the gorge to explore How Stean Tunnel. The tunnel is some 170 feet long and goes under the road – but it is usually very wet.

Tom Taylor's Cave
This beautifully formed cave is reached from the Gorge footpath by a little ladder stile in the entrance. It is 530ft long and reasonably dry, but torches are essential and care must be taken on the uneven ground. It eventually emerges at The Cat Hole, a depression in the ground in the field which is used as a car park and children's play area. The cave is named after Tom Taylor, a notorious local highwayman. In 1868 two boys found 32 Roman coins which had been hidden on a high ledge. They are now displayed in the Yorkshire Museum at York.

What to look out for

The upper gorge has attractive mixed woodland of ash, hazel, thorn and birch trees. Trout can usually be seen lazing in the peat-brown waters of Stean Beck in the first part of the walk. How Stean Gorge offers fantastic water-carved limestone formations, cave systems and elevated walkways. A visit to the cave is the highlight of the walk.

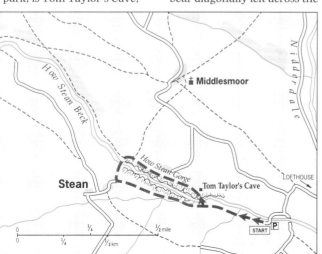

Aysgarth Falls

A series of creamy white waterfalls formed by the River Ure falling down gigantic steps creates one of the most spectacular natural features in the north of England. But this is also a waterfall that can be enjoyed from close quarters from broad, limestone shelving rocks.

Early purple orchid

START
Aysgarth is at the heart of Wensleydale on the A684, about seven miles west of Leyburn. There is a car park (charge) at the National Park Centre.

DIRECTIONS
From the centre of the National Park car park, almost opposite the Information Centre café, climb the steps which lead onto the embankment of the former railway. Turn left along the embankment and walk to the end before turning right through a metal kissing-gate. Go up the pasture to a stile, keeping straight ahead to cross another a stile and head for the trees ahead. Bear right just before the trees and continue to a stile in the wall at the corner of the field, emerging onto a lane. Turn right and, taking care with traffic, go down the lane for 120yds. Where the lane bends right, take a narrow pedestrian gate on the left, beside a field gate leading to a track into the woods.
Continue for 300yds through the trees, then bear right across a clearing to where the path forks just before the railway cutting. Take the left fork to go over stile next to a gate and turn right alongside the old railway line. The path climbs alongside the top left-hand side of the railway cutting, before descending to a stile by a gate beside a railway bridge and crossing of paths. (Turn right for a short cut back to the Falls).
Turn left along a track, but as the track bends left, take the signposted footpath right across pasture to a stile. Go over the stile and continue ahead across scrubland until you reach a track. Turn right on the track, cross a cattle grid by the old railway line and continue on the track to Hollins Farm.
Pass in front of the farm, going left through the farmyard (follow the yellow waymarks). Bear left along the path, signposted 'Aysgarth 1 mile'. Continue in the same direction, avoiding Landrover tracks bearing left, passing through any farm gates, and continue straight on to another stile. Cross over and continue for about 50yds, following the path beside the fence. Directly opposite a wooden footpath sign on the fence marked 'footpath to Castle Bolton', the path bears left towards the waterfalls.

One section of the Aysgarth Falls

Cross a stile. Directly ahead a narrow, slippery path leads down to the Lower Falls (not suitable for young children). Return to the main path and continue past the Lower Falls viewing area. Follow the 'return path' sign and walk on through the gates into Freeholders' Wood. Continue on the path past Middle Falls viewing platform to the road. Cross carefully, and take the path opposite back into the car park.

Aysgarth Falls
The total ddrop over the three sets of waterfalls is about 160ft and the steps have been formed by huge limestone blocks. The viewing platforms give excellent views of the Lower and Middle Falls. The best place to enjoy the Upper Falls is from the far side of Aysgarth bridge, which dates back to Tudor times.

Tarn Hows

Tarn Hows is one of Lakeland's pearls. Its beauty is legendary: still waters reflecting tall stands of firs and larches and rocky islets topped by pines.

START

The walk starts from Glen Mary Bridge on the A593 between Skelwith Bridge and Coniston. There is a small car parking area among the trees on the east side of the road, just south of Glen Mary Bridge and Yew Tree Tarn – look out for National Trust signs 'Tom Gill' and 'Glen Mary' next to the pull-in.

DIRECTIONS

From the car park, cross the stream by the footbridge and turn right, along a stony path. Continue uphill on this path, through oak woodland with the tumbling gill to your right. The path bends round to the left. Several paths appear and disappear up the slope and it is not always easy to follow the right one, but this is not critical; keep heading up with the cleft of the gill just to your right. Eventually the path leads to a wicket gate. After this the ground begins to level off. The series of waterfalls is the Glen Mary Falls. Continue uphill with the stream still on your right. Soon the trees end and the path leads out on to the lake shore. Turn right along the wide track and go through the gate, then simply keep to the smaller gravelled path above the lake shore. The south side of the lake has open grassy places; these give way to birch groves and conifers in Rose Castle Plantation on the east side, whilst the north and west sides are heavily wooded with ornamental plantings of tall conifers. Keep to the main path. (For a challenging detour, a path to the right leads to the ridge of Tom Heights. This is the peak to the west of the lake and offers spectacular panoramic views.) The main path soon leaves the shore, but if you want to explore the marshy inlets there are side-paths which link up eventually with the main path again. Continue along the main path to the starting place just before the gill and the gate, then turn right to follow the path back through the wood.

Old Trees, New Trees

The trees of the Lakeland valleys were once an important resource, managed in coppices and cut down to their bases every ten years or so to provide crops of sturdy poles. The poles were then used either to make bobbins in local factories or to make charcoal, the fuel needed to smelt iron. Although they were coppiced regularly the trees were never removed or killed. Trees have stood on this spot for at least 8,000 years. Some, such as the small-leaved limes which grow among the oaks close to the gill, are rare and are only found in ancient woods. The impressive stands of conifers around Tarn Hows were planted in Victorian times and have added greatly to the drama of the place.

Tarn Hows from Sawrey viewpoint

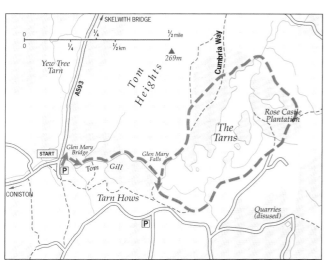

What to look out for

The pedunculate oak of Southern England is replaced in the Lake District by the sessile oak. If you look carefully at the leaves you will see that they taper at the base and have a long stalk, unlike the southern oak which has lobes and a short stalk. Three species of bird – wood warbler, pied flycatcher and redstart – are summer breeding visitors to these woods.

Muncaster

At the head of Eskdale lie the highest mountains in Lakeland, and at its foot are the dunes and estuary of Ravenglass. This walk incorporates a trip on a miniature railway, a water mill, a castle and a Roman ruin.

START
Ravenglass is just off the A595 about five miles south of Gosforth. Park at the Ravenglass and Eskdale Railway and catch a train. There is an hourly service up the valley (for times and charges, tel. 0229 717171). Alight at the first stop, Muncaster Mill, and the walk starts here.

DIRECTIONS
From Muncaster Mill station go through the mill yard and up the track, past the old wheel machinery and chicken sheds, then turn right along a bridleway, signposted 'Castle' and 'Ravenglass'. Walk along the bridleway for about 20yds.
Two paths lead off to the left. Take the first of these, signposted 'Castle'. Walk up the rather steep path, through woodland, until this levels off and meets a track. Go straight on following a dip between wooded ridges for about ½ mile. At the end of the woodland, go through a gate and turn left.
At the road (A595) go through a gate and straight on, downhill along the pavement, then cross the road with care and go through the

gates of Muncaster Castle. Walk down the drive signposted 'Muncaster Church' and 'Footpath to Ravenglass', past the stables, garden centre and café. At the end of the drive, go straight across the lawns, with waterfowl pens to your right, to meet another drive. Cross this and follow a track uphill, signposted 'Ravenglass via Newtown'. At the end of this wooded track, go over the stile and out on to the open hill top.
The route is signposted but the path is not obvious; follow the direction indicated by the signpost, to the right of the hill crest. At isolated gate posts, continue ahead to the

plantation with the rooftops of Newtown just beyond. Cross the stile and walk downhill through the plantation to go through a gate and turn along a broad track, passing a house on the left. On reaching a metalled private road, turn right past

What to look out for

The woods of Muncaster Castle contain some very exotic trees. The castle itself is only a century old, built on to fragments of a 14th-century tower house.
Walls Castle has a much better pedigree but is no more than a ruin. In fact it began as a Roman bath-house, associated with the fort of Glannaventa which lies buried on the other side of the track.
From the top of the hill there are fine views, of Ravenglass Dunes (a nature reserve) and the Esk estuary. In the distance to the north is Sellafield Nuclear Power Station.

Roman bathhouse ruins on the right, then continue to the end of the road, passing Walls Caravan Park. Just after the gates is a footpath on the left which leads to Ravenglass station.

The Ravenglass and Eskdale Railway
The Eskdale narrow gauge railway was opened in 1875 to carry iron ore from Boot to Ravenglass, beginning as a 3ft gauge but converted to 15in gauge in 1915. The railway is now a popular tourist attraction.

Muncaster Castle and Owl Centre
Diverse attractions are offered at this castle, the seat of the

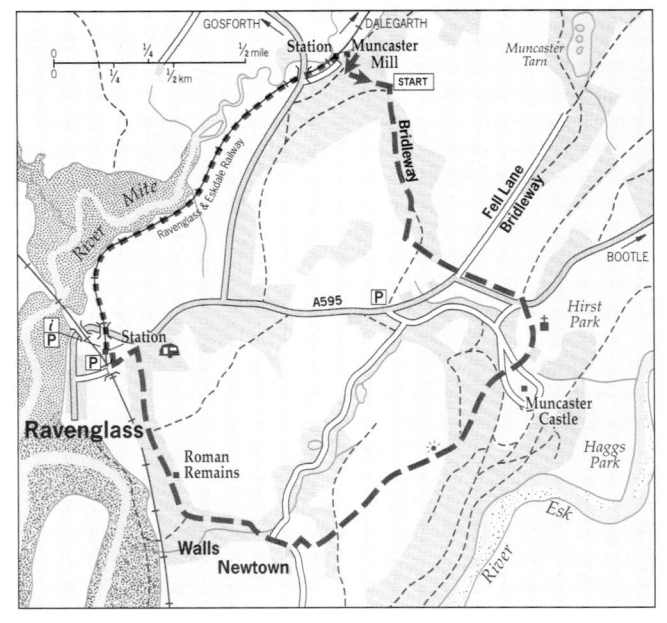

Pennington family since the 13th century. Inside is a fine collection of 16th- and 17th-century furnishings and portraits, whilst the lovely grounds include a nature trail and commando course. Muncaster Castle is also the headquarters of the British Owl Breeding and Release Scheme. The garden and Owl Centre is open all year daily; the castle is open April to November, Tuesday to Sunday and Bank Holiday Mondays.

Muncaster Mill
There has been a mill on this site since the late 15th century, and flour and oatmeal are still ground on the premises using water power from the 13ft waterwheel. The mill is open from April to September.

Muncaster, first stop for the train

Derwent Water

Badger

Making use of the regular boat service, this walk provides the opportunity to enjoy Derwent Water to the full without expending a great deal of time and energy. This is Beatrix Potter country – Squirrel Nutkin was created here and red squirrels are still a feature of the beautiful lakeshore woods.

START

Keswick is off the A66, about 15 miles south-east of Cockermouth. There is a large lakeside car park off the B5289 (the Borrowdale road). Alternatively, park in one of the town centre car parks and follow the signs to the lakeshore. Walk down to the landing stages and purchase tickets for the launch. Boats leave every hour, calling at various points on the way around the lake. The walk starts at the Lodore landing stage and finishes at Hawes End.

DIRECTIONS

Take the boat from Keswick to the Lodore landing stage, then walk along the track and through a wicket gate to meet a road, turning right to pass the Lodore Swiss Hotel. (Just after the hotel on the left is a path to the Lodore Falls.) Continue along the pavement until there is a footpath on the right, signposted 'Manesty'. Cross the stile or go through the gate to follow this stony path, over a low bridge spanning a clear stream, then across marshland to a foot-bridge over the River Derwent. Cross the Derwent and follow the boardwalk over more level marshland to a knoll with oak trees. Cross the knoll and continue over more boardwalks to a gate. Go through this and follow the path over hummocky ground, bearing right with the lakeshore to your right, and the mountain ridge of Cat Bells beyond the woodland to your left. The path now leads through Manesty Park, cutting across marshy inlets by high, narrow boardwalks and leading to Manesty Wood. Go through the gate and continue on the main path. With views of the lake to your right, follow the clear path through the woods and out on to a metalled track beside a

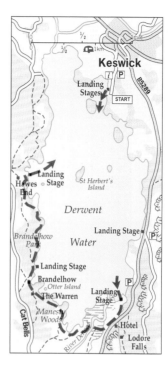

slate-built cottage called The Warren. Turn right down this track, signposted 'Brandelhow', to a little bay. Go through the wicket gate to Brandelhow and bear to the right of the house along a stony path. Bear left, uphill, then right through a gate and into Brandelhow Park. Drop down to the lakeshore. (There is a landing stage here should you wish to cut short the walk.)
Continue along the shore and through the woodland of Brandelhow Park for several hundred yards. At the edge of the wood, go through a wicket gate. The path meets a field here. Bear left beside an old wall, then right into another field. Walk along the path, through a gate and to the right of the house. Bear immediately right down to

Derwent Water, lovely in any season

the lakeshore, and continue to the Hawes End landing stage for the boat back to Keswick.

The Lakeland Oaks

Most of the trees around Derwent Water are sessile or Durmast oaks. The Lakeland oaks were once cut to make bobbins or pencils, or were burnt to make charcoal.

What to look out for

Birds on the lake include greylag geese, tufted duck and mallards, with the occasional family of whooper swans in winter. The woods harbour nuthatches, treecreepers and woodpeckers. Badgers and red squirrels are more numerous than you might think. Views of the surrounding mountains are excellent.

Gelt Woods

WALK 159
CUMBRIA
NY520592

Towering cliffs of orange sandstone, hanging woodlands, gorges and white-water rapids make this walk exciting. There is also a hint of history – battles were fought here and the Romans took stone for Hadrian's wall from the riverside quarries and left their names engraved in the rock.

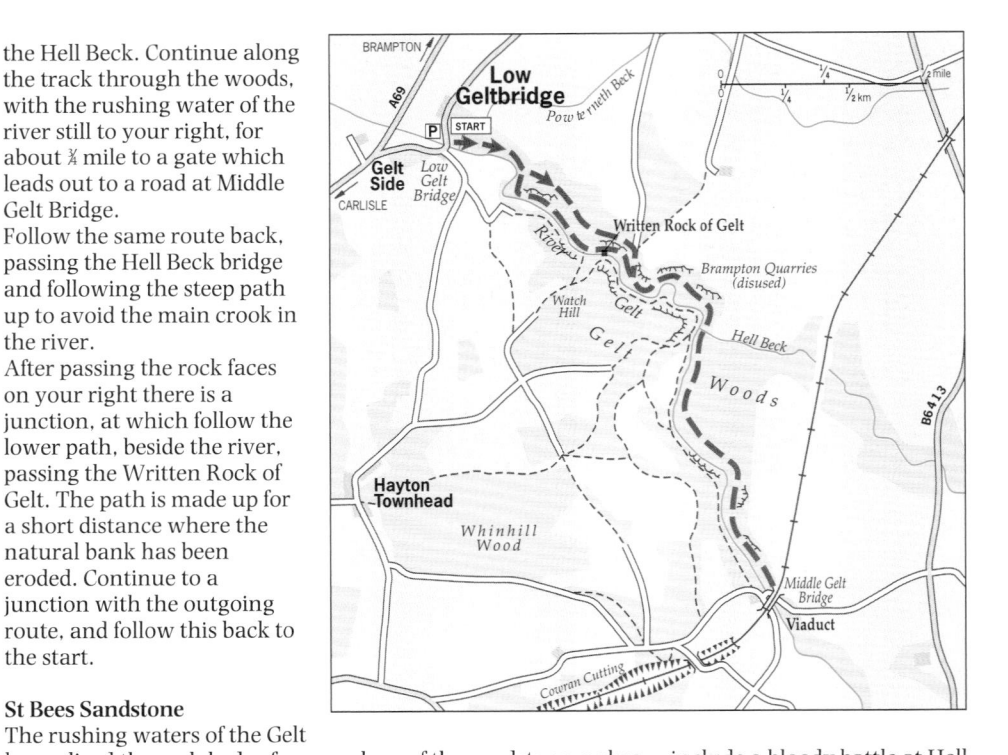

START
There is a small parking area on the north side of Low Gelt Bridge, reached by following the A69 a mile south of Brampton (ie avoiding the new by-pass) and turning off at Gelt Side, signposted 'Hayton Town Head'.

DIRECTIONS
Beyond the parking area and RSPB notice, cross the bridge over the Powterneth Beck and go through the fence gap to follow a woodland track. The track rises up a slope, levels out and then forks. Take the upper track, left, past a seat; the track rises by a series of low steps through beech trees and up some further low steps. Continue to the edge of the woods and then bear right to meet a sunken lane.
Follow this downhill by more shallow steps, either of boulders or branches, and continue past a sandstone cliff on your left. Turn left at a junction and follow the track, with the rushing river down to your right and a high sandstone cliff, behind tall trees, to your left.
Keep on the main path, which rises then bears right and descends via steps to the riverside at a little bridge over

The path through the woods

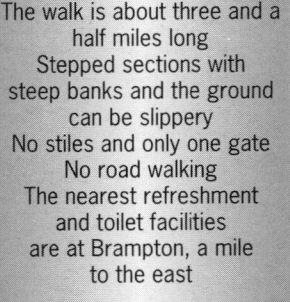

Information

The walk is about three and a half miles long
Stepped sections with steep banks and the ground can be slippery
No stiles and only one gate
No road walking
The nearest refreshment and toilet facilities are at Brampton, a mile to the east

the Hell Beck. Continue along the track through the woods, with the rushing water of the river still to your right, for about ¾ mile to a gate which leads out to a road at Middle Gelt Bridge.
Follow the same route back, passing the Hell Beck bridge and following the steep path up to avoid the main crook in the river.
After passing the rock faces on your right there is a junction, at which follow the lower path, beside the river, passing the Written Rock of Gelt. The path is made up for a short distance where the natural bank has been eroded. Continue to a junction with the outgoing route, and follow this back to the start.

St Bees Sandstone
The rushing waters of the Gelt have sliced through beds of red St Bees sandstone, creating rushes and rapids over harder bands of rock and creating cliffs up to 50 feet high. The beautiful warm

Long-tailed tit

colour of the sandstone makes it easy to identify as the building material for local villages. It was quarried here for Hadrian's Wall (there was nothing suitable any closer) and can be seen at its best at nearby Lanercost Priory.

Royal Battles by the Gelt
Historical events in the area include a bloody battle at Hell Beck Bridge in 1570, when 3,000 rebels supporting Mary, Queen of Scots were defeated by Elizabeth's cavalry. Bonnie Prince Charlie also visited the area – he took his army of highlanders over Low Gelt Bridge, marching on his way to Carlisle in 1745.

What to look out for

The woodland is in the care of the RSPB, and bird life includes a special trio of northern birds – pied flycatcher, redstart and wood warbler.
The lofty viaduct above Middle Gelt Bridge was built in 1835 and carries the Newcastle–Carlisle Railway.
The 'Written Rock of Gelt' is a rock face above the river where Romans carved graffiti while they were quarrying stone for Hadrian's Wall. A secret path leads up from the river.

The Eden Valley

Langwathby

River Eden

Station

A686

PENRITH

Rosehill
Cottage

P Hotel START

Cross

Edenhall

St Cuthbert's
Church

0 ¼ ½ mile
0 ¼ ½ km

Field scabious

The Eden Valley, between the Lake District and the North Pennines, is one of the most beautiful pastoral landscapes in Britain. The fact that it is often by-passed by visitors helps to maintain its unspoilt quality. This walk is a gentle introduction to the river and one of its most interesting villages.

START
Edenhall lies just off the A686, two miles south of Langwathby. Park either in the village or close to the Edenhall Hotel, from where the walk begins.

DIRECTIONS
Walk out of the village past the children's play area. Just before the red-brick Rosehill Cottage turn right and go through the gate, signposted 'Langwathby and River Eden'. Walk along the track with a fence to your right and sheep pasture to your left. Ahead in the distance is the village of Langwathby. Continue to a wicket gate, between narrow conifer plantations, and keep forward along the path. On reaching the river turn right, signposted 'Edenhall and Church' and walk along the river bank on a raised path to go through a gate. Proceed uphill, past the end of the conifer plantation to your right, then follow a line of beech trees, with a steep slope and the river to your left. Continue along the path (which can be overgrown in summer), passing the high wall of the Edenhall estate deer park on your right, and go down some steps to follow the edge of the park until the river veers away to your left. Go through a wicket gate to join a track, and bear sharp right to follow this over the parkland, past a lone oak and towards the stone Plague Cross. (Here you can detour to the left to see St Cuthbert's Church, retracing your steps to the cross.) Bear right along the metalled track, past the East Lodge and into the village. Turn right on the main road to return to the start.

What to look out for

Otters still inhabit the Eden, though they are rarely seen. Most daytime sightings are cases of mistaken identity, usually referring to mink which have become quite common here over the last decade.
Birds of the river include goosander and cormorant during spring and summer; dippers and grey wagtails are residents and kingfishers come and go. In winter, skeins of greylag geese fly up and down the valley, filling the air with their contact calls.

St Cuthbert's Church (above), and the Plague Cross, Edenhall (left)

Edenhall
Edenhall is an estate village, created by the Musgrave and Gibson families. The hall itself no longer exists, but there are some beautiful buildings in soft red sandstone, characteristic of the Eden valley. 'Homefield', close to the tall farmhouse, was a tithe barn and the church tower was once used as a pele, a refuge from raiding Scots at the time of the Border Wars.

The Plague Cross
The stone cross towards the end of the walk is called the Plague Cross and dates back to four hundred years ago, when an epidemic struck the village and killed a quarter of its inhabitants. As no tradesman would risk entering the stricken village or making any kind of contact with its people, villagers paid for their food by placing money in a sink of vinegar beneath the cross.

Information

The walk is about two miles long
Generally very easy underfoot with one short incline
A few gates and no stiles
There is some road walking in Edenhall, a very quiet village with only light traffic
The Edenhall Hotel provides bar meals and there is a children's play area opposite

Bowlees

High Force, two miles to the west of Bowlees, is the highest waterfall in the country, but it is impossible to explore it in safety. This walk uses the excellent parking/picnicking area of Bowlees as the pivot for two short walks, leading beside the tumbling waters of the River Tees and Bowlees Beck to more accessible waterfalls.

START

The little hamlet of Bowlees lies three miles north-west of Middleton-in-Teesdale on the B6277. The entrance to the large car park and picnic area lies just to the east of the scatter of farms and cottages, on the east side of the beck.

DIRECTIONS

There is a wardens' office at the back of the car park with a nearby notice for orientation. For the walk upstream of the Bowlees Beck, follow the path between the beck and the office, bear left at a fork and continue past the toilet block to a footbridge. It is possible to cross to the far side here and explore the shallow, stony stream at its safest point.

There are cascades and pools and the banks are covered with wild flowers. Cross back and continue upstream, up a series of steps with a pretty waterfall on your left, then with woodland to your right. You are on the land of the Raby estate and the path is accessible with their permission. Through a gate, the path is broad and passes a grassy bank before entering trees again and leading eventually to Summerhill Force. Behind the waterfall is Gibson's Cave. Retrace your route back to the car park.

For the walk along the Tees, start at the car park and cross the back by a low concrete bridge, then go up a flight of steps to the Visitor Centre (the old Methodist Chapel). Left of the Centre, walk down the track straight ahead, with a meadow on your right, to the road. Turn right and cross the road, then go through a gate on the left side of the pasture. Cross two fields, with a gate between, then cross a stone stile and drop down a path through woodland. The path leads to the Wynch Bridge, a little suspension bridge over the River Tees. On the far side turn right. The waterfall to your right is called Low Force. The current can sometimes be fierce here and some of the pools are deep,

Pied wagtail

Low Force Waterfall on the River Tees

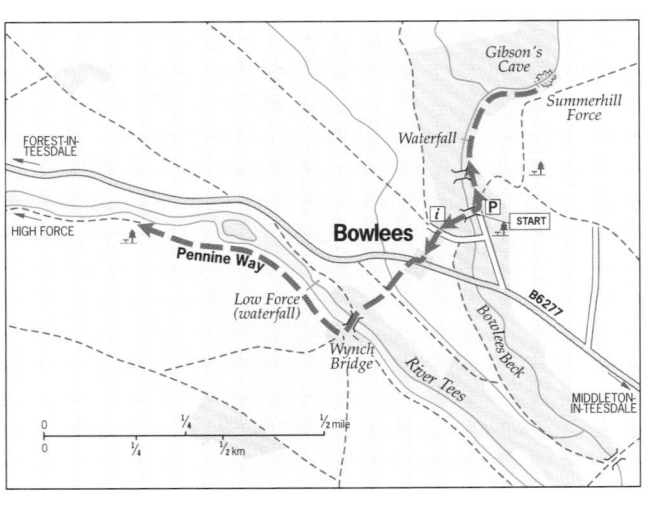

Information

There are two halves to the walk, each a mile long
Both walks have some steps and stiles, but the Gibson's Cave walk is easier
The Tees walk crosses a road
Refreshment facilities at the Visitor Centre
Picnicking is possible at many places on the banks of the streams
Toilets at start of the first walk

but by continuing upstream along the clear gravel path you soon reach quieter waters with good picnic places. Return by the same route.

Hay Meadows

In July the meadows of Teesdale are cut for hay. These days most British farmers make silage, putting fertiliser on their fields and cutting their grass when it is still very green and juicy. This means that wild flowers can never compete with the grass or set their seed. Farmers in the Pennine dales still use more traditional methods and cut hay a little later, by which time the wild flowers have finished their growth, and though the grass crop is not so heavy, this has kept the countryside colourful.

Gibson's Cave

Gibson was on the run from the law in the 16th century when he found the perfect hiding place – behind a waterfall!

Stanhope

Weardale is one of the most attractive of the North Pennine valleys, criss-crossed by drystone walls, swathed in flower-rich meadows and pastures, and dotted all over with barns and farm cottages. Once the land of the Prince Bishops and heart of the lead-mining industry, this hotch-potch of history has turned a walk around the village of Stanhope into an adventure.

Information

The walk is just over four miles long
Mainly level, but with a descent in the town and an ascent up the wooded bank beyond
Several wicket gates
Stepping stone crossing of the river best undertaken in dry conditions; can be avoided by using the bridge downstream
Stanhope has a full range of facilities and places to eat

START

Stanhope is five miles west of Wolsingham on the A689. Park at the Durham Dales Centre, off the main road and just to the west of the Market Place.

DIRECTIONS

From the Centre turn left, along the pavement to the Market Place. Cross the road towards the Pack Horse Inn and bear left, down Butts Crescent. Before the river, turn left down The Butts beside a terrace of cottages, then cross a level crossing. (Trains are few here, but take care.)
Follow the path across a pasture, away from the river, to a wicket gate. Go through the wicket gate and past some tall beech trees with a barn away to the right.
Cross the next field and go through another wicket gate, then over a sports field to meet the river and another level crossing. After the gates and crossing, follow the path

Above, stepping stones over the Wear, and left, St Thomas's Churchyard at Stanhope

over a meadow, with the river to your right. This leads to another wicket gate and out on to a side road.
Turn right along this quiet little road and cross a bridge over the river, then another bridge over the railway, and turn right along a metalled track through a caravan park.
At the end of the caravan park, beyond some old cottages, continue straight on, over a stile and along a woodland path with the river down to your right.
After the wood the path bears right, downhill and beside a wall. Turn left at the end of the wall and follow the path between a fence and a row of trees, over the crossing, then beside tennis courts and another fence with meadows to the left.
Go over a stile and past the buildings of Unthank Mill, with the river now beside you

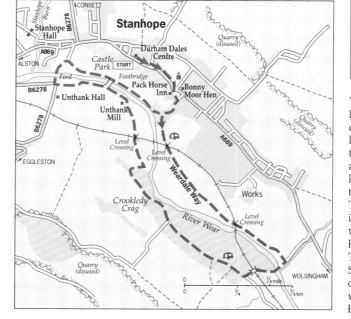

on the right. Follow the riverside track, past a bridge (which can be used as an alternative route across the river if it is in flood) and on to the ford, crossing via the impressive stepping stones. Walk up the road and turn

right just after the playing field, following a metalled track with the walls of Castle Park on the left and the river on the right. On reaching The Butts, turn left to return to the Market Place and Durham Dales Centre.

What to look out for

There are some interesting buildings along the walk, including Stanhope Hall and Unthank Mill. The Butts was the archery range, dating back to the days when practice was compulsory. The Bonny Moor Hen still has the cellar where poachers were imprisoned. Woodland flowers along the walk include primroses, bluebells and cowslips, at their best in May.

The Battle of Stanhope

In the early of the 19th century many of the Pennine lead-mining towns resembled the wild west; the law was not always easy to enforce and local villains were often treated as heroes.
The story goes that one night in 1818, a gang of miners were caught poaching on the Bishop of Durham's land. They were brought to Stanhope and imprisoned overnight in the cellar of what was then called the Black Bull Inn. However, a rescue party of miners attacked the keepers and there was a brief and bloody fight. In the struggle, the miners got clean away.
The Bonny Moor Hen, on the site of the Black Bull, is named after the red grouse that the miners were poaching.

Castle Eden Walkway

WALK 163
CLEVELAND
NZ402243

An old railway line has been converted into more than a walkway and nature trail, and is a small paradise for children, with play areas, picnic sites and even a model railway.

START
The walk starts at the car park of the Station House Visitor Centre at Thorpe Thewles, signed off the main A177 Stockton to Durham road.

DIRECTIONS
From the car park take the wooden gate at the exit, cross the hollow and walk up the steps on the other side to the station platform by the Visitor Centre. Turn right and follow the Castle Eden Walkway – a surfaced path along the old railway trackbed – for a little over ⅛ mile, passing the entrance to the Nature Reserve.

Just past the third bridge turn left, go up the steps and at the top turn left again, crossing the bridge.

The path, signed 'Circular Route', enters a field and follows the field edge, curving round between a small group of trees before bending right to cross the fields. Continue to the right of more trees, passing a sign 'Footpath Loop'. The path now descends alongside a hedge where the two tracks converge. Turn right, descending slightly, then turn right again opposite garage buildings to go through a wooden gate and enter Thorpe Wood (Nature Trail). Continue along a surfaced path and pass Thorpe Pond.

Information

The walk is about two and a half miles long
Mainly level, easy walking with one steep slope which can be avoided
Excellent for dogs
Countryside Warden service available at most times
Picnic sites but no refreshment facilities
Toilets close by (may be closed)

Above, on the route of the walkway, and left, the Station House centre

Where the path forks, keep straight ahead (or bear left to rejoin the railway path at an earlier point, avoiding the steep climb to come). Before a gate take a right fork up some steps and a short steep slope. Continue straight ahead past another gate. After a few yards the path bends left before going through a kissing-gate to rejoin the old trackbed. Turn left to return to the station and car park.

What to look out for

The railway embankments contain a wide range of butterfly species. Birdlife to be seen and heard includes mistle thrushes, coal and great tits, treecreepers, willow warblers, cuckoos, woodpeckers and birds of prey. Thorpe Pond has great crested newts, frogs, toads and dragonflies.
Wood anemones and bluebells (not for picking) flourish in the wood in spring, and giant bellflowers are at their best in July.

Frog

Marsden Rock

There are coast walks in either direction from Marsden, both of unexpected richness considering the closeness of industrial Tyneside – sea cliffs, islands alive with seabirds, miles of clean golden sands, rock pools, smugglers' caves, and a lighthouse at Lizard Point.

START

The village of Marsden lies on the coast just to the south-east of South Shields and two miles north of Whitburn. Start in the large car park (pay-and-display in summer) at Marsden Bay, on the seaward side of the A183.

DIRECTIONS

Facing the sea from the car park, turn right along the clear cliff path. (The walk can be extended along the cliff path to the left.) It is impossible to get lost, but don't be tempted off the path, which could be dangerous.

The rocky coast near Marsden

What to look out for

The islets, arches, pillars and stacks are impressive, composed of magnesian limestone 245 million years old. The main island is 91 feet high. Most of the islands throng with nesting seabirds in the spring. Rocky cliffs are chosen by many species because they are inaccessible to predators and give easy access back to the sea. Marsden provides some of the closest and safest viewing of their nesting sites – and the noise and the smell are unique!

Kittiwakes, ocean-going gulls, are the most numerous, making nests of seaweed which they manage to stick to vertical clefts and crevices on the rock. By contrast, herring gulls – seaside scavengers which rarely go far from land – make much bigger nests, usually on the grassy cliff-tops of the islands. Cormorants are inshore specialists too, roosting on the islands, safe from foxes. Fulmars are the most aerial of the Marsden cliff-nesters, sailing on the updraft of air along the cliff edge, often eye to eye with walkers on the path. Out to sea, gannets, skuas, shags, terns, guillemots, eiders and a host of other birds can be seen passing to and fro, following the rhythm of tides and seasons.

The clifftop vegetation includes thrift, sea plantain and scurvy grass, with rock rose, thyme and autumn gentian on the limestone outcrops.

Fulmar

The main features to look for along the way include the rock stack called Lot's Wife, Marsden Grotto, then the main seabird island of Marsden Rock, after which come the smaller stacks of Pompey's Pillar and Jack Rock, and finally the Souter Lighthouse on Lizard Point. The return route is by the same path.

Marsden Grotto

What looks like an ordinary pub perched on the clifftop is just the start of an adventure. The grotto was established in 1782 by a character called Jack the Blaster and was intended to service the needs of tourists and smugglers, who used a cave to the south of the grotto. Access to the foot of the cliff is much easier today than it was in Jack's time; he built the flight of steps but there is now an electronic lift which, for a very modest charge (you only pay on the downward journey), takes you down to the beach and the pub which is set into the base of the rock face. At low tide it is possible to walk out to Marsden Rock, which dominates the sea view.

Souter Lighthouse

Though no longer a working lighthouse, this red-and-white striped tower is open to the public.

Hadrian's Wall

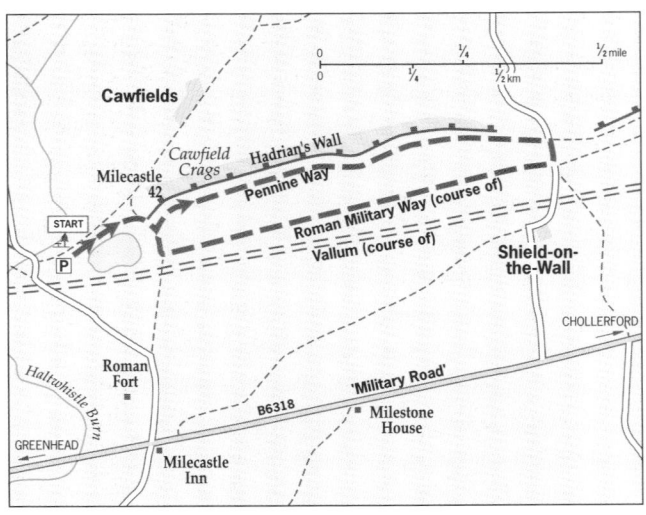

This walk, though fairly short, takes in a spectacular section of Hadrian's Wall, with splendid views stretching away to the east over Windshields Crag, its highest point. We return along the Roman Military Way.

START

The starting point of the walk is 14 miles west of Hexham and 22 miles east of Carlisle. From the B6318 'Military Road' take the unclassified road, signposted 'Whiteside', leading north, opposite the Milecastle Inn. In one mile reach the Northumberland National Park car park by the lake at the reclaimed Cawfields Quarry Picnic Site.

DIRECTIONS

Leave the car park on the path alongside the lake, heading east, with Hadrian's Wall rising up on the ridge ahead. (The water may look inviting on a warm day, but heed the warning notices – it is not safe to swim.)
Turn right after the first kissing-gate, go through another and join the Pennine Way as it bears left uphill beside the wall. Milecastle 42 lies at the foot of the slope, and the highest point of the walk comes after a short steep pull 500yds later.
Descend, keeping near the wall. Go through a kissing-gate, and turn right on to a tarmac road. In a few yards cross a stile over the wall on the right. Go straight across the field and over the ladder stile opposite, then follow the straight green path, the course of the Roman Military Way. This heads directly towards a small pointed hill, the other side of which is the face of the quarry. At its foot,

At Cawfields Crag

turn right and continue, to rejoin the outward route at the gate below the Milecastle. From there go back past the lake to the car park.

An Outpost of the Empire

The remarkable construction of a defensive wall from coast to coast, built by the Romans under the rule of Hadrian, has a world-wide reputation. The part within Northumberland National Park, utilising the natural defences of the crags of the Whin Sill, is the most dramatic and best preserved. On all sides there are wide open views of a wild countryside which is not very different now from how it must have looked in those days. It speaks volumes for the military authority and the organisation of the Roman Empire that such a 'boundary wall' could be conceived and implemented over many decades, then garrisoned and defended for nearly 400 years at such a distance from the seat of power in Rome.

Heather flowers

Hareshaw Linn

Linn is the Northumbrian name for a waterfall and exciting though the whole walk is, the most impressive sight (and sound) is saved for the very last moment when water bursts forth over a shadowy rock face in a bower of trees high overhead.

START
Bellingham is in the North Tyne valley, 18 miles north-west of Hexham on the B6320. From the town centre take the road signposted 'Redesmouth', and in 50yds turn left opposite the Police Station. The Northumberland National Park car park is 200yds along this lane beside the Hareshaw Burn.

DIRECTIONS
The path heads upstream from the car park on the left

Just one of the waterfalls in Hareshaw Dene

Information

The walk is two and a half miles long
Mostly easy walking but some ups and downs; paths are mainly good, but there is a cobbled section
Pubs and café in village
Good picnic areas near start

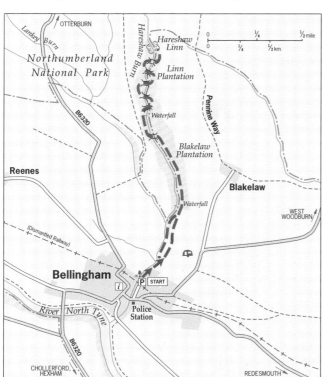

of the fence, then on through the farm gate or kissing-gate past Foundry Farm. Walk uphill to the next kissing-gate and bear right where there is a choice of paths. One branches left, keeping to the edge of the riverside alders, and allows glimpses of the burn below. The other climbs on to the ridge of an overgrown spoil heap with good all round views. (As both paths come together again below a waterfall, choose one for the outward journey and one for the return.)
The path then winds through an area of small hillocks, once spoil heaps in the iron-making days. At the edge of the wood a kissing-gate leads on to a cobbled path, gradually gaining height before arriving, after 800yds, at the first bridge. A little way upstream is the first of a series of falls, cascades and deep pools that are typical of a hill burn. Just above the falls there is a second bridge, then a third

where the gorge becomes narrower and steeper. After the fourth and fifth bridges it becomes narrower still, with huge boulders in the burn, fallen from the rock walls above. A wooden walkway along a steep bank leads to stone steps and then to the sixth and last bridge where the roar of the Linn can be heard. Through a glade the first glimpse appears; up the steps the Linn comes into full view. A path passes under a huge overhang to allow a closer look at the tumbling water, but an arc of vertical rock wall prevents any further progress. Return by the same route.

Hareshaw Ironworks
Hareshaw was a hive of industrial activity in the 1840s. Both iron ore and coal were mined and many spoil heaps are still there, though now reclaimed by nature. Part of a dam, built for waterpower for the furnace bellows, still exists above Foundry Yard.

Competition from other ironworks, nearer to the big towns and railways, sounded the foundry's death knell and it closed in 1848. Ironically the railway came to the town in 1862, passing right by the Yard, but too late to save the ironworks. Now the railway too has gone.

The Dene
Now owned and managed by Northumberland National Park Authority, there is unrestricted public access to

Hareshaw Dene and the Linn. It has been a popular spot for more than a century and the six bridges were originally built by the people of the town.

Mistle thrush

What to look out for

Wild flowers are abundant, with primroses everywhere in the woods in spring, marsh marigolds along the burn, and the meadows blue with harebells in the late summer. In the autumn a wide variety of woodland fungi flourish among the fallen leaves. The deep sheltered dene is a haven for wildlife too. Dippers and grey wagtails nest along the burn, the woodland birds include redstart, wood warbler and pied flycatcher. Roe deer may be seen, especially early or late in the day, and there is at least one badger sett.

Dunstanburgh –
The Castle Above the Sea

The harbour at Craster

From the tiny little harbour at Craster, Dunstanburgh Castle away to the north is perched high on a hill, with sheer cliffs on the seaward side. Its keep and towers, although fairly battered, seem just about capable of withstanding one more siege.

WALK 167
NORTHUMBERLAND
NU256198

Information

The walk is three miles long
Mainly level, easy walking on grass
No stiles but several kissing-gates
Dogs must be kept on leads over grazing land
Pub in Craster serves bar meals and there is also a restaurant
Lots of grassy areas for picnicking along the coast near the castle

START

Craster is on the coast six miles north-east of Alnwick. From the A1 Alnwick bypass take the B1340 then follow signposts to Craster on unclassified roads. There is a large National Trust car park in the old quarry at the western edge of the village.

DIRECTIONS

Turn right out of the car park and walk to the harbour, then turn left along the sea front. Go through a kissing-gate and follow the path north along the edge of the rocks. There are two more kissing-gates. After the second, take the path to the right round the head of an inlet. Surprisingly, although so tiny and now partially marsh-filled, this used to be a port from which warships sailed. The path then winds uphill to the castle entrance.

From the castle retrace the outward route as far as the second kissing-gate, after which turn right and follow the fence uphill and through a gate. Turn right along the edge of the field to another gate, then left along a track through a shallow gap in the ridge. At the bottom of the slope turn left through a kissing-gate and follow the path running below 'The Heughs', the craggy ridge on the left. The best route keeps to the left immediately below the slope, arriving at another kissing-gate. The path then goes through a short stretch of woodland to emerge at the road opposite the car park.

Dunstanburgh Castle

Thomas, second Earl of Lancaster, founded the castle in the early 13th century. In the 1380s its defences were strengthened by John of Gaunt, Baron of Embleton, who led an invasion of Scotland from here, but his action did not stop constant raiding by the Scots. His son, Henry of Bolingbroke, succeeded him in 1399 and later that year usurped the throne to become King Henry IV. Thus Dunstanburgh became a royal castle and was a Lancastrian stronghold during the Wars of the Roses. Seiged, counter-seiged, captured and recaptured, in 1464 it finally fell to the Earl of Warwick to be held for Edward IV. The poundings taken during many battles wrought great destruction which was never fully repaired. Now an English Heritage property, the castle is open to the public and has a small information centre in the grounds.

Craster Kippers

Craster has long had a fine reputation for its kippers (still smoked in the traditional way over oak chippings), which are sent far and wide from the smokehouse near the harbour.

Herring gull

What to look out for

Look out for seals and cormorants offshore. Many other seabirds can be seen from the coast path, particularly eider duck. In the nesting season, the cliffs on the north side of the castle are alive with kittiwakes, fulmars and shags.

A lovely display of wildflowers includes thrift and bird's-foot trefoil, and lots of butterflies may be seen along the coast and on the return route. The scrub along the Heughs provides a landfall for exhausted incoming birds, especially in autumn. Birds such as warblers and chats rest and feed here, recovering from their flight across the North Sea.

Bamburgh and Budle Bay

WALK 168
NORTHUMBERLAND
NU184349

Bamburgh is a pretty seaside village and its huge Norman Castle dominates the landscape for many miles around. The walk starts at the Castle, crosses a lovely stretch of heathland to a serene sheltered bay, taking in one of the best stretches of coast in the country.

Bamburgh Castle

Information

The walk is three and three quarter miles long
Mostly level on grass or beach with some easy rocks to cross; at some high tides it may be difficult to get past Black Rock – see alternative in route directions
Pubs, cafés and restaurants in Bamburgh
Good picnic sites along most of the route, although the dunes in Budle Bay are probably the best

START

From the north, Bamburgh is reached via the B1342, leaving the A1 just beyond Belford. From the south, 12 miles beyond Alnwick, the B1341 leads to Bamburgh. There is a large car park at the east end of the village opposite the castle entrance.

DIRECTIONS

From the car park turn left, walk back along the road and take the path along the edge of the cricket field below the castle crag. At the end of a ruined wall bear left, then right beside a fence, to join a road leading north from the village. Follow it, turning right at the top of the hill,

through an informal parking area and down through the dunes. Go left along the beach, heading for the inland side of the lighthouse at Stag Rock, and take the path up the bank past a lifebuoy to the golf course entrance.
Take the path westwards across the golf course and, 50yds before reaching a drystone wall, bear right on the green path winding along the edge of the heath above the dunes. Continue along the edge of the fairway then descend to a ruined concrete gun emplacement overlooking Budle Bay. Go left behind it and descend again towards the caravans, then bear right through the dunes to the old pier.
Follow the beach to the right, skirting Black Rock below Budle Point (if tide is very high, use the path running just above the beach instead). Continue along the beach then head towards the north end of the castle, keeping just to the right of a lifebuoy. A path then runs south along the seaward side of the castle beside a fence. At the south end fork right, away from the fence up towards the castle entrance. Start down the access road then fork left on to a path leading directly back to the car park.

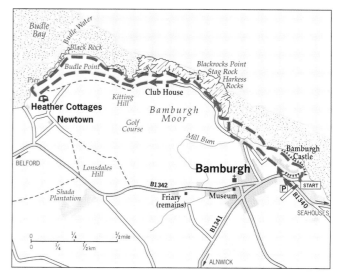

Bamburgh Castle

For 900 years the great Norman Castle of Bamburgh has towered above the sea on its basalt crag, and for 500 years before that it was the royal centre of the Kingdom of Northumbria. But the 'golden age' of Bamburgh began in the 7th century with the arrival of Christianity, when King Oswald established the monastery on nearby Lindisfarne (Holy Island) which would become a great centre of learning.

The Victorian Heroine

In 1838 Bamburgh again became famous, courtesy of Grace Darling, daughter of the keeper of the Longstone Lighthouse. During a storm which had driven the *Forfarshire* on to Harcar Rocks, she and her father risked their lives to row a fishing coble to rescue the survivors. Her bravery caught the imagination of the whole nation and inspired many songs and stories; people flocked to the area from all over the country to catch a glimpse of her – she even became a national heroine in Japan! The cottage in which she was born is now a small museum, and among the exhibits is the rescue boat.

What to look out for

Northumberland is the only English county where eider ducks nest and there are usually great flotillas of them around Stag Rock, as well as many other seabirds and waders along the coast. At low tide Budle Bay has a fantastic display of lugworm casts. In spring and summer the heathland near the golf course has a beautiful array of wild flowers, and is alive with butterflies including grayling and common blue.

The Town Walls of Berwick

WALK 169
NORTHUMBERLAND
NT997531

This is a short and easy walk along the ramparts that defended Berwick for centuries during prolonged border disputes between the English and the Scots .

START

Berwick-upon-Tweed is just off the A1 in northern Northumberland. Follow the signs for the town centre and park in the large car park in the old cattle market, immediately north of the Scots Gate.

DIRECTIONS

From the car park go back to the road, left through Scots Gate, cross over and walk along the south-east side of the Walls. With a statue (of Lady Jerningham) in view turn sharp right up a ramp then left up steps to Meg's Mount, the start of the circuit. Go back down the steps and north-east over Scots Gate. The higher path on the left gives the better views. At the next great bulwark, Cumberland Bastion, the tunnels in the walls which gave access to the flankers for men and ammunition can be seen below. Continuing

around the ramparts, Brass Bastion at the north-east corner provides a splendid viewpoint from which most of the fortifications can be seen.

The walls run south-east now over Cow Port, the only gateway through the walls surviving in its original form. There is a path down to it on the town side and the Barracks are only a few yards away.

Still heading south-east, Windmill Bastion stands at the most easterly point in the defences. (It did originally have a windmill on top, but in Victorian times and in both world wars guns were sited there for coastal defence.) Now go due south to Kings Mount. From this point the

planned Elizabethan fortifications along the riverside were never completed and the medieval walls are joined.

The path descends along the sea wall past Black Watchtower, and over two more access points, Ness Gate and Fisher's Fort, to Coxon's Tower above the river. The arched doorway on the town side of the tower leads to a tunnel inside the walls. The tunnel is not open to the public.

Continue upstream along the Quay Walls to the 300-year-old river bridge. Cross the road and go along Bridge Terrace. After the gun emplacements at the next corner bear right uphill, passing under the new road bridge to arrive back below Meg's Mount.

Above, the river bridge, and left, the bastion

Turn right, and head back towards the Scots Gate and the car park.

A Battleground

Berwick has had a turbulent history, and was for centuries a major prize in the struggle between the English and Scots. During countless battles over about two hundred years, Berwick changed hands thirteen times, but has been part of England since 1482.

The immensely strong battlements constructed in the reign of Elizabeth I clearly illustrate the continuing strategic importance of the town.

Peel

This energetic walk climbs steadily to give impressive views of Peel Castle, continuing upwards to a height of some 500 feet above sea level at Corrin's Folly. There are spectacular views of the rocky coastline, which is a haven for sea birds.

START
Follow the road round the harbour towards Peel Castle. On the left before the causeway is the fairly large car park.

DIRECTIONS
Go up the steps to the right of the car park entrance. At the top of the steps follow the track straight up the hill. It joins a wider gravel track which swings round to the right. Follow this round the headland. Continue, passing two shallow but quite dramatic disused slate quarries. The track runs out by the second of these, but you will see a steep path up the hill to the right. (Children and dogs should be strictly supervised at this point.)

Head up towards the summit of Thistle Head. When you reach three large blocks of granite, take the right-hand track. Follow this until you reach the wall, go through the gate, signposted 'Raad Ny Foilian' (coast path). Continue along the path, which becomes rocky with a severe drop to the right (spectacular views of the coastline). When the track divides, take the right fork. Continue until it divides again, go left this time. Head towards the dry stone wall (view of the south of the island, the Milner Tower on Bradda Head, and the Calf of Man). Keep left at the next two divisions, with the walls on your right (view of Corrin's Hill and Folly). Where the path divides, keep right, climbing steadily up towards the tower. From up here you can see Peel, Port Erin and the Calf, St Johns, and to the north-east, Jurby Head.

Follow the wide grass track north, descending towards Peel. Head towards the wall, go through the kissing-gate and continue straight on to the crest of the next hill, where you will find the remains of three tumuli (breathtaking aerial view of Peel Castle, the harbour and bay). Follow the path straight down the hill to rejoin the original gravel track, and retrace your footsteps to the car park.

To extend the walk, a footpath starts near the castle entrance and goes round the exterior of the castle walls. There are good views of Peel Hill and the coastline, and the path will bring you round to the harbour wall.

WALK 170
ISLE OF MAN
SC248844

Information

The walk is about three miles long
Steady climbing, steep in places
No road walking, except on extended walk
No stiles, but some kissing-gates
Snack bar near castle
Picnic area by car park, also grassy area by tower
Toilets near castle

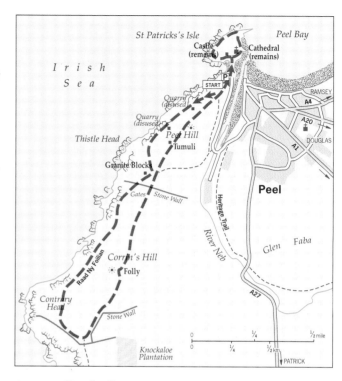

The view over Peel

Corrins Hill and Folly
Constructed in 1806 by Thomas Corrin as a memorial to his family, the tower is 50ft high and built on the highest point, some 500ft above sea level.
The four corners of the tower are aligned with the four points of the compass. Corrin, his wife and their child are all buried nearby.

Peel
Though primarily a fishing port, Peel is, in fact, a city with two cathedrals: one in the centre and one within the castle. The castle was built to protect the cathedral of St German's, possibly founded by St Patrick, and is said to be haunted by a black dog. The castle is open from Easter to September.

What to look out for

St Patrick's Isle is a popular haunt for grey seals which escort the fishing boats into harbour, and look out in summer for the harmless basking sharks.
Stonechats and meadow pipits haunt the coastal scrub.
There are many butterflies, and among the wild flowers are harebells, self heal, ling and thrift.

SCOTLAND

Balcary Cliff Tops

This is an invigorating walk across the cliff tops of the Solway coastline, an area rich in ornithological interest. The views take in the beautiful Galloway Hills, an offshore island and the distant peaks of the Lake District. Care must be taken on the cliffs.

START
Balcary Bay is part of Auchencairn Bay on the Solway Firth and lies about two miles south-east of the Galloway village of Auchencairn, on the A711 Dumfries to Kirkcudbright road. Start the walk from the car park opposite the Balcary Bay Hotel.

DIRECTIONS
Follow the road from the car park round past the holiday homes to the left and take the signposted track for Balcary Point and Rascarrel. Turn left after passing through the wooden kissing-gate near the house and walk along the edge of the field to another kissing-gate which takes you through a small copse along a gravel path. Continue through the copse and fork right where you can see a derelict lifeboat station below on the left. Proceed through bracken and gorse to Balcary Point, where there are excellent views of the huge, sharp rocks and the dramatic seascapes beyond.
Follow the path through the metal kissing-gate, down from Lot's Wife to Rascarrel Bay (about a mile) with a

WALK 171
DUMFRIES & GALLOWAY
NX821495

dry-stone wall on the right. Continue down to and along the shoreline across stones. Walk behind the holiday homes at Rascarrel Bay and take the path to the right, passing through two wooden kissing-gates, parallel to Rascarrel Moss Plantation. At Loch Mackie pass through

Information

The walk is three and a half miles long
Hilly, and very muddy in places
No stiles, but several kissing-gates
Hotel at Balcary Bay

another kissing-gate and turn right, following the edge of the field with a wall on your

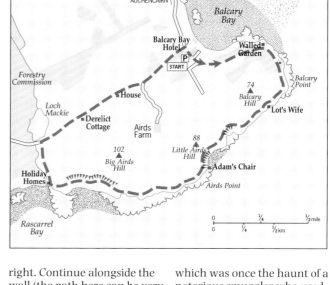

right. Continue alongside the wall (the path here can be very muddy). Pass through a gate next to a derelict farm cottage and continue along a farm track (with fine views of the Galloway Hills of Bengairn and Screel).
Return to the car park down the farm track, past a house on the right.

Smugglers' Haunts
The Balcary Bay hotel was built by Manx smugglers in the year 1625 as a trysting-place for freebooters. It was the headquarters of the smuggling syndicate of Clark, Crain and Quirk, and was raided by Customs Inspector General Reid in 1777. A private house until 1948, it then became a hotel, and still has secret underground chambers with walls five feet thick and doors opening onto the sea.
Along the coast is Adam's Chair, a natural rock seat

which was once the haunt of a notorious smuggler who used a lantern up here to guide smugglers' vessels to shore.

Hestan Island
This island, now a wildlife sanctuary, is accessible only at low tide and has caves once used as hiding-places for contraband whisky and brandy.
The island was immortalised as 'Isle Rathan' by Samuel Rutherford Crockett in his novel *The Raiders*. Once worked by copper-miners, it is also the site of a manor-house built in the 14th century for Edward Balliol.

The cliffs at Balcary

Black-headed gull

The River Annan

Information

The walk is three and a half miles long
Level, easy ground
About three quarters of a mile of road walking
A few stiles
Blue Bell Inn serves snacks, but does not allow children
Plenty of cafés and ice-cream shops in Annan
Picnic area near car park

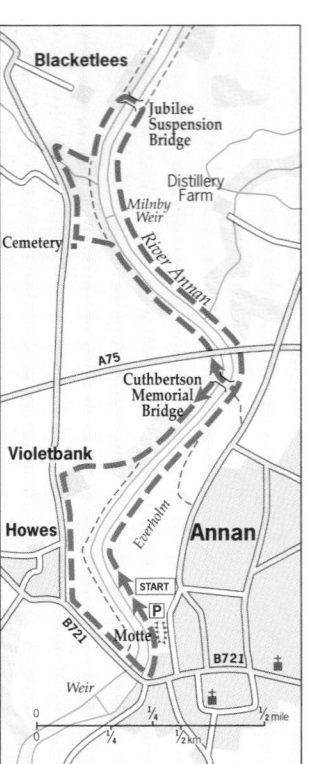

This is an easy and very popular walk along the wooded banks of the River Annan. The river is noted for its wildlife and for the number of deciduous trees which line its banks.

START
Annan is off the A75 Gretna to Stranraer road, 17 miles north-west of Carlisle, and the same distance from Dumfries. The walk starts from the Everholm car park, just outside the town, next to the Motte.

DIRECTIONS
Follow the riverside path on the edge of the Everholm playing fields. Go through the gate at the end of the path, where it becomes a rough track. Follow the track, pass through a kissing-gate and continue down to the Cuthbertson Memorial Bridge. Cross the footbridge and turn right. Proceed along the riverbank passing under the road bridge until you come to a footbridge.

Turn left up the steps onto a path which leads to the cemetery. There is a seat about 50yds from the steps. Cross the metal stile into the cemetery. Go straight ahead across the cemetery to the left side of the gatehouse. Turn right at the main gate along quiet Brydekirk Road, through a wood and turn right at the old bridge. Go down to the river again, turn left and follow the path at edge of the field to reach Jubilee Suspension Bridge.

Cross and turn right to continue back along the river. Cross a stile at the edge of the field. Cross Cuthbertson Bridge again and turn left along the river, later taking the track up to Violetbank on the Brydekirk road.

Turn left and follow the road to the outskirts of Annan. Turn left immediately after the Blue Bell Inn to return to the car park.

The Everholm
The nearest thing that Annan has to a public park is The Everholm playing field and sports complex. The athletics track was opened by Steve Ovett, who lives nearby, and the centre has hosted a number of international athletics meetings.

The complex also has a rugby pitch, gym and conditioning room, outdoor table-tennis (during the summer) and a putting-green. There is a trim-track with a number of wooden exercise aids, such as monkey bars and leap-frog.

The Annan Bridges
The metal Cuthbertson Bridge, recently upgraded, was built as a memorial to Captain William Graham Cuthbertson and to the men and women of Annan who gave their lives during World War II. It provides an ideal point from which to watch the bird life on and around the river.

The Jubilee Suspension Bridge is an even finer vantage point, providing a panoramic view to the north, taking in the small wooded islet which splits the Annan in two and is known by the locals as 'Rabbit Island'.

Beside the River Annan

Yellow loosestrife

Traquair House

Information

The walk is around a mile
long; one and a half miles if
you include the maze
Easy ground
No road walking
One stile
Cottage tearoom at
Traquair House
Picnic area near the car park
Toilet facilities at
Traquair House

Weasel

This is a lovely short walk through woodlands within the grounds of Scotland's oldest inhabited house. Other attractions here include a maze, a brewery, historical displays and a delightful old tearoom. The walk is only accessible from April to September.

START
Traquair House is off the B709, six miles south-east of Peebles, near Innerleithen. Start the walk just outside the courtyard gates next to the garden. There is a car park next to the 'wineglass lawn' (charge for entry to house and grounds).

DIRECTIONS
Come out of the courtyard and turn left. Proceed through a stone doorway straight ahead, past garden and beech hedge and a croquet lawn on your left. Turn left after the wickerwork summerhouse and two huge horse chestnut trees. When you reach the Quair Burn, veer left through some lovely old yew trees and massive firs. Continue left along the bank of the river. Go through a swing gate and bear left diagonally across the meadow until you come to a stile (across the meadow on your right you can see where Quair Burn flows into the River Tweed). Cross the stile and turn right. Walk up the side of the fence with the River Tweed on your right. After about 50yds turn left into woodland. Follow the path through woodland across three footbridges. After crossing the third footbridge turn left. On reaching the drive by the house turn right, passing the brewery on your left and the Well Pool on your right. At the junction turn left, back towards car park.

Traquair House
Romantic Traquair House, dating from the 10th century, is steeped in history. This is where Alexander 1 signed a charter, and William the Lion held court here in 1209. It was visited by 27 kings and queens, among them Mary, Queen of Scots. Many kings and nobles used to visit the estate for fishing, hunting and hawking. The house has a splendid library and a fine collection of tapestries, family relics, antiques and paintings. There is a restaurant, a tearoom, gift shop, art gallery and craft workshops.

Traquair's 18th-century brewery produces up to 60,000 bottles of beer each year and is open to visitors. There is also a maze to explore and a fascinating collection of toys. The house is open daily from the end of May to September; limited opening Easter to May. The grounds are open April to September.

Above and left, the house and grounds

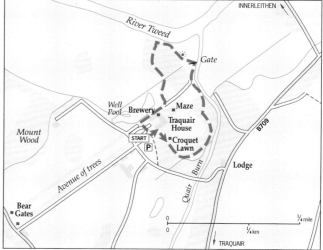

Gullane Bay

Seaside walks are always fun and this one is no exception. It goes along an excellent sandy beach beside the broad Firth of Forth, with views across to Fife, and returns beside the famous Muirfield golf course.

WALK 176
LOTHIAN
NT476831

Information

The walk is about two and a half miles long
Good paths, but soft going across the sand dunes
Dogs can run on the beach, but should be kept on leads by the golf course
Pubs and cafés in Gullane
Toilets near the car park

START
Gullane is 15 miles east of Edinburgh. Turn off the A198 in Gullane at the sign 'To the Beach' and park at Gullane Bents car park.

DIRECTIONS
From the car park walk down the tarmac path to the beach, reached by a gap through the dunes. There is a play area to the left.

Turn right and walk along the beach on the firm sand. The view extends from Edinburgh over to the Fife Hills and round towards the Bass Rock.
When you reach the rocks go up to the right and walk along the shore path, passing concrete blocks placed here in World War II as tank traps, then over a shingle beach. The path goes through the dunes (soft sand and harder going) then improves to run outside a fence to reach the scant remains of an old chapel.

The dunes at Gullane Bay

The path winds inland following the line of a stone dyke. Continue up a broad grassy path, keeping the wood on your right. The path swings right to start the return journey, passing along the edge of Muirfield golf course. Pass through a fence beside a gate (note the warning about keeping dogs under close control because of rabbit snares).
Cross the end of the road over the golf course and pass to the right of a green shed. Turn left at wooden gatepost and continue with the fence on your left. At a junction fork left, at the next junction go left, and at an open area head for a signpost about 50yds ahead. Turn right on a broad grass path to wind through the dunes and return to the beach.

Gullane Bents
Considerable work has gone on here to restore the dune system, which suffered in the 1920s and 30s from vehicles being driven down to the

What to look out for

This is a superb area for nature study. Over 200 species of birds have been recorded here and at Aberlady Bay to the west, including many waders and seabirds. In winter thousands of common and velvet scoters and brent geese are seen. The area is also rich in interesting plants including autumn gentian, burnet rose and northern marsh orchids. Grey and common seals are often seen offshore, especially near the Hummell Rocks, at the west end of Gullane Bay.

Muirfield golf course

beach, and between 1941–5 from military training – the area was used as a practice ground for the Normandy Invasion in 1944. Information boards give details of how the restoration has taken place.

Muirfield Golf Course
Muirfield is one of the famous 'links' courses on which the British Open is played, when the world's best golfers pit their skills against the natural hollows, knolls and traps.

Pentlands Reservoir

This easy walk below the Pentland Hills, just outside Edinburgh, takes in woodland and an attractive reservoir with plenty of birdlife. The walk starts and finishes at a visitor centre with wildlife displays and a children's play area.

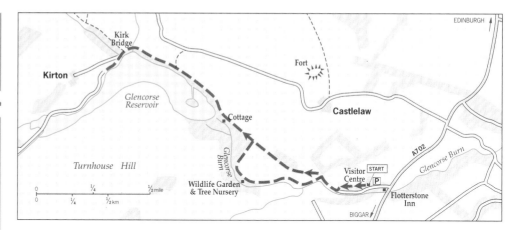

Information

The walk is about three miles long
Easy going on good paths or tracks
Some road walking
Dogs should be kept on leads
The Flotterstone Inn, open all day, serves bar meals; children are welcome
Toilets at visitor centre

START

Flotterstone is on the A702, south of Edinburgh, easily reached from the city or the ring road. Drive past the inn for about 100yds to reach the Visitor Centre car park.

DIRECTIONS

From the Visitor Centre, follow the path that runs parallel to the road, then join the road and continue straight on. On the right is a military training area. Reach Glencorse Reservoir and continue along the road beside the water, returning the same way. (You can, of course, continue along the road as far as you wish before turning back.)
On the return, just before the end of the wood, where there are some fine old pines, turn right through a gate and walk down a track beside a burn. On the right is a wildlife garden and tree nursery. Continue along the track, through two gates, and eventually rejoin the road and path back to the Centre.

Glencorse Reservoir

Glencorse is known as the 'Queen of the Pentland Reservoirs' – there are 11 such stretches of water around the hills, providing for the needs of thirsty Edinburgh. The reservoir was built in 1822 and has a maximum depth of 71 feet; it holds 367 million gallons. All this area is now part of the

Glencorse Reservoir

Pentland Hills Regional Park, a large stretch of country managed on a co-operative basis by landowners, local authorities and voluntary bodies for conservation, recreation and agriculture.

Wildlife Garden and Tree Nursery

Down by the burn on the return walk is an interesting small wildlife garden and a tree nursery, cultivating many different species, which helps to replenish stocks in the woodland.
You will also find here a small enclosure called 'Forever Green', with trees planted in September 1990 by John Gibsone and his wife Margaret in celebration of their golden wedding anniversary.

What to look out for

You should see a variety of waterfowl on the reservoir, especially in winter – look for tufted duck, pochard, goosander and wigeon.
You may see squirrels as well as birds in the woods.

Beecraigs and Cockleroy

On the summit of Cockleroy

Information

The walk is about three and a half miles long
Tracks and paths mostly have good surfaces, with one short stretch of open grassy hill
Two sets of steps at the deer farm
Dogs should be kept on leads
A range of information is available at the Park Centre
Refreshments available at the centre
Cafés in Linlithgow
Picnic tables at Balvormie near an attractive pond
Toilets at the park centre, at Balvormie and in Linlithgow

Fox

Beecraigs Country Park offers a wide range of activities, including a climbing wall and target archery course. The walk takes in a wonderful viewpoint, a trout farm and a deer farm.

START
Beecraigs Park Centre is two miles south of Linlithgow. Take a minor road from the west end of Linlithgow, signed 'Beecraigs Country Park', then follow signs for Beecraigs Loch, turning left then right to reach the Park Centre.

DIRECTIONS
From the Centre, return past the entrance, cross the road and take the track opposite, signed 'Balvormie Walk'. In 100yds take left fork past a gate on to a forest track. Follow the track for nearly ½ mile to reach the 'trim track'. Just beyond this is the Balvormie car park. Cross the road, signed 'Cockleroy Walk' and take the path immediately in front of the toilet block to re-enter the woods. About 250yds after the toilets, where a blue waymark points back the way you have come, turn right onto a narrower path down across a small stream and continue to a junction. Turn left to reach a road, cross over (the Cockleroy car park is on the right) and continue on the path opposite (another blue waymark).

At the edge of the wood, cross a stile and walk up to the summit of Cockleroy (cairn and a viewpoint indicator). When you have enjoyed the view, return to the stile and retrace your steps to the Cockleroy car park, across the road, and back to Balvormie. Cross the car park and from its right side cross the stream and turn left along a wide track fringed by fine broad-leaved trees. Keep on this track for about ½ mile, to reach the next road. Turn left for 50yds and turn right on the road to the trout farm. Pass the anglers' lodge and reach the trout farm, leaving it by crossing the bridge and climbing the steps to the top of the dam. Turn right along the dam and then left in the woods, keeping the loch on your left. Part way along the loch at a junction, turn right, signed 'Deer Farm'. Climb and descend steps to enter the walkway through the deer farm, continuing round to the left, then climb and descending more steps to return to the Park Centre.

Cockleroy
Cockleroy, which has remains of an ancient fort, is only 912ft high, but commands an exceptional view. On very clear days you can see Goat Fell on Arran, the Bass Rock to the east, Edinburgh, and across the Firth of Forth. The viewpoint indicator will help you to identify all the places you can see.

The Trout Farm
The fish bred here are used for stocking rivers and lochs in the area, providing sport for anglers, and trout can also be bought for the table.

The Deer Farm
Red deer, our largest native mammals, are bred here for their meat, which can be bought at the park centre. The stags have been 'de-antlered' to save them injuring themselves or the hinds. Young are born in June, and in October during the 'rut' the stags can be heard roaring as they prepare to mate.

What to look out for

The Cockleroy view stretches from coast to coast. In the woods you may see roe deer, rabbits, brown hares and perhaps a fox, and birds include great spotted woodpeckers.

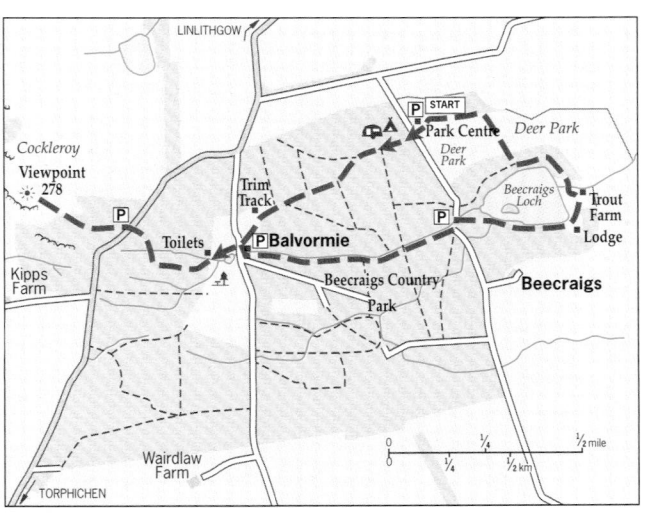

Strathclyde Country Park

This is a satisfying walk along even paths, through scrubland which is brimming with wildlife. Along the way are views of a lovely loch and a little bit of Roman history.

Information

The walk is just over two miles long
Mostly even ground, with some hilly sections
No stiles
No pub; cafeteria close by (seasonal)
Good picnic places all along the walk

The Roman fort

START

The country park, 1,650 acres which is split by the M74, is in the Clyde Valley between Hamilton and Motherwell, about ten miles south of Glasgow. Leave the M74 at junction 6 and follow signs on the A723. The walk starts from the Sandy Beach car park at the south-eastern edge of Strathclyde Loch.

DIRECTIONS

From the car park cross the road, turn left and continue uphill along the pavement. At the first junction, after a row of houses on the right, turn left back downhill across the road. Continue along the path with Viewpoint car park on your right. Pass picnic tables and walk downhill through scrubland towards the loch. Keep right at the first junction, continue down and cross a footbridge. After the second footbridge, veer left into the open ground along the edge of the loch (several seats along here with good views).

Continue along the loch until the path swings right and takes you along the bank of the South Calder River. Visit the Roman Bath House here, then cross Spine Road to see 'Roman Bridge' (actually of 18th-century construction). Return to the pavement and turn right towards the north of the park.

Take the path before Orbiston Spur to visit Orbiston Park. Walking past the swings with the golf course on your left, continue straight ahead at the junction and proceed downhill for about 80yds, taking a narrow path on the right into the woods to find the remains of Orbiston Tower. Retrace your steps to the swings and back downhill to Spine Road, turning left to rejoin the main route.

After a short distance cross over into scrubland again. Take the path between the Bath House and the road and follow it past the site of the Roman fort, past Viewpoint car park. The path now runs alongside the road. Follow the path across the road, turn right and continue back down to the starting point beside the loch.

A view across the loch

What to look out for

Strathclyde Park was the site of a Roman fort and the remains of their bath house is an attraction.
Watch for stonechats and linnets in the scrub; their song is especially noticeable in spring.

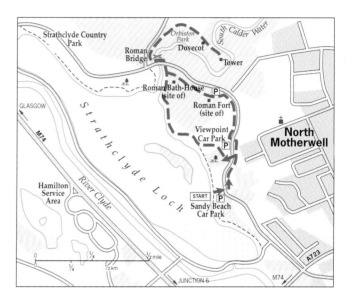

Roman Bath House and Fort

The hill on the eastern side of Strathclyde Loch is the site of a Roman fort. Only faint traces remain, but in its day it would have housed a garrison of around 500 troops.

The bath house, discovered in 1973, would have been a kind of Turkish bath for the soldiers, to soothe away the stresses of life on the frontier.

Orbiston Park

The park is centred on the remains of Orbiston Tower or Castle. Historians are baffled about who occupied it, but evidence shows that they ate well. Mussel-beds were kept for the table, there is a dovecote nearby, where some 400 pigeons would have been bred for food, and there is a solidly-constructed ice house.

Culzean Country Park

Set in Scotland's first country park, in the grounds of a fine castle, this walk takes in some splendid scenery and covers a variety of terrain – cliff tops, sandy beach, a walled garden, woodland, ponds and a disused railway line.

START
Culzean Country Park is off the A719, four miles west of Maybole and 12 miles south of Ayr. There is an admission charge to the park. Start the walk in the car park next to the walled garden at the heart of the park.

DIRECTIONS
From the car park turn downhill towards Happy Valley, with the walled garden on your left. At the southern point of the walled garden bear left following the line of the wall. At the first fork turn right. Continue to Happy Valley pond and bear left. Turn left again onto a gravel path and then take the first path on the right through woodland. Where the woodland path joins a track, turn left and continue to a crossroads. Turn right and go uphill along a drive. Turn sharp right after a row of cottages and down past Sunnyside Mill, an old meal-mill.

From the mill continue uphill under an old railway bridge and then right up onto the disused railway line. Follow the line for ½ mile to Morriston Bridge. Take the steps up onto the bridge and turn right onto a track. Continue down the track through the 'Cat Gates',

WALK 180
STRATHCLYDE
NS230098

Information

The walk is just under three miles long
Mostly easy ground
No road walking
No stiles
Dogs must be kept under control
No pub, but there is a tearoom (seasonal) at Swan Pond Cottage and a coffee house at the visitor centre
Picnic places at Swan Pond and Port Carrick

where an impressive old beech hedge forms an attractive canopy overhead. In about 50yds fork left. At junction turn left, following the path with Hogston Burn on the right. At Carse Pond turn left along Piper's Brae towards the Swan Pond Cottage and Aviary.

From the cottage go to the edge of Swan Pond and turn left, following the edge of the pond. Pass the play area in the trees and take the path on the left, signposted 'Port Carrick'.

From the coast retrace your steps to the pond-side path and turn left over a footbridge. Turn left again

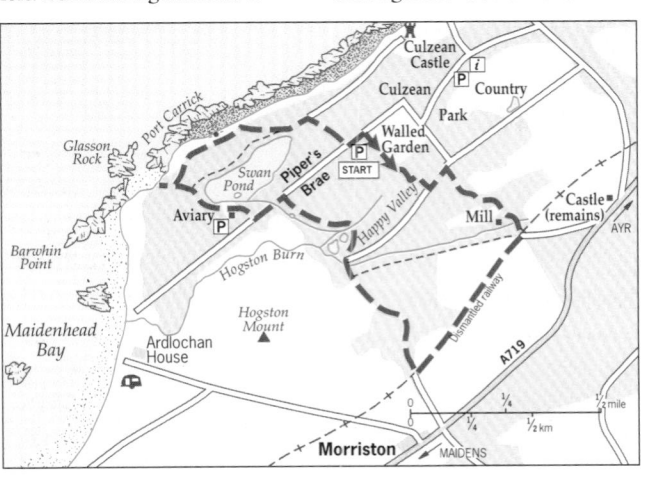

up along the cliff-top path, then cross the next old estate road, back onto Piper's Brae. Turn left and then take the first right to return to the start point.

Culzean Country Park
Culzean (pronounced 'Kullane') Country Park and the nearby castle, both in the care of the National Trust for Scotland, together provide one of Scotland's most popular days out. The park covers 563 acres and has a wide range of attractions, from beautiful woodland walks to an adventure playground. There is a visitor centre with various facilities, and this is also the base for the ranger naturalists who provide guided walks. A number of events are held in the park each year.

The Walled Garden
The garden is in the shape of a blunt diamond to allow the fruit trees to enjoy maximum sunshine. The kitchen garden was established in 1815 and the pleasure garden is over 200 years old.

Looking down the coast, with Ailsa Craig in the distance

What to look out for

The cliff-top path affords superb views of the Clyde, the Isle of Arran, Ailsa Craig and the Mull of Kintyre.
Given the range of habitats, the Country Park is a great place for wildlife of every description. The heathy cliffs support flowers such as thrift, sea campion, ling and formentil. At low tide, search the rock pools for sea urchins, anemones and limpets, and great northern divers, eiders and long-tailed ducks are seen offshore in winter.
The Happy Valley woodland has many old, gnarled trees and exotic shrubs, including fine specimens of western hemlock, wellingtonias and Scots pines. Two mighty sitka spruces ('Adam and Eve') are among the oldest in Britain.
The old railway line, which ran from Maidens to Dunure, also has plenty of wildlife. In the cliffs are two cave systems where herald moths hibernate.

Glenashdale Falls

Glenashdale Burn

The island of Arran has been called 'Scotland in Miniature'. It is a very popular holiday area and contains superb mountains, lovely coastline, historic buildings – and Glenashdale Falls, justly famed for their beauty. The walk also visits the Giants' Graves, an ancient chambered cairn.

WALK 181

STRATHCLYDE
NS047253

Information

The full walk is about four miles long; about three miles if Giants' Graves are missed out

Good paths and tracks, but steep, sometimes slippery climbs to Giants' Graves and the upper part of the path to the falls

Dogs must be kept on leads

Cafés and pubs in Whiting Bay

Toilets in Whiting Bay

START

The ferry from Ardrossan on the Clyde coast (daily service all year round, several boats a day) arrives at Brodick. The walk starts from the village of Whiting Bay, ten miles south of Brodick. In summer, with Arran's excellent bus services, the walk could easily be done on a day trip without taking your car on the ferry; buses are less frequent out of season. If you do take the car, park opposite the youth hostel in Whiting Bay.

DIRECTIONS

From the youth hostel follow the path signposted to the falls up beside the Glenashdale Burn. Go through a gap in the fence and in another 100yds turn left up the path signposted

'Giants' Graves'. Climb up a long flight of steep steps and at the top turn left along a broad path. Part way along this section there is a seat with a lovely view back across Whiting Bay to Holy Island. Reach the clearing containing the Giants' Graves (there is some 100-year-old carving on the stones – Victorian graffiti). Return down the (slippery) steps to the path in the glen and turn left. The path climbs steadily towards the falls, crossing two bridges over side streams. At a sign go right and down to a viewpoint below the falls, which tumble impressively over a series of rock steps and are deafening when the falls are in spate. Return to the main path and continue up to the top of the falls, crossing the burn above them by a footbridge (with a rather different but still impressive view of the falls).

Follow the path right to start the return journey. At a wall go through the gap and turn right, continuing along the path through a gap in another wall, and follow the sign 'Iron Age Fort'. The path then twists sharply back up to the left, through the wall again, and turns right on a broad track. Leave the forest at a gate and continue down the track, passing through two kissing-gates, to South Kiscadale. Carry on downhill to reach Whiting Bay and at the main road turn right to return to the start of the walk in 400yds.

Glenashdale Falls

The falls are the highest on Arran, tumbling for over 120ft in a triple cascade over rock steps into a narrow, wooded gorge. Above the falls the stream is called the Allt Dhepin; below them it becomes the Glenashdale Burn.

The Giants' Graves

Arran is very rich in prehistoric remains, including standing stones, circles and cairns. The chambered cairns, early tombs, follow a common pattern, with a shallow grave in a chamber, originally topped with a large rock slab. The whole grave was often covered with a cairn of boulders several yards high. Sometimes groups of tombs occur in rows. Most of the cairns date from about 2500–3000BC.

Turnstone

What to look out for

In spring and summer the trunks and branches of the trees are festooned with lichens and mosses. A variety of woodland birds such as garden warblers and chiffchaffs may be seen in summer, as well as year-round residents such as squirrels and deer.

The Banks of Loch Lomond

Loch Lomond is famed for its beautiful scenery and excellent wildlife. This walk crosses fields and goes along quiet lanes to reach a secluded corner of the loch.

Information

The walk is about three and a half miles long

Quiet roads and paths

A few stiles

Dogs are not allowed in the nature reserve so are best left behind

Pub and café in Gartocharn

Toilets in Gartocharn

START
The village of Gartocharn is on the A811, three miles north of Balloch and 20 miles north-west of Glasgow. At the public toilets turn left if coming from Balloch (right if coming from Drymen), then turn right past the police station. There is a small parking area by the church.

DIRECTIONS
Walk past the church and turn left down the track immediately past the community centre. Go through a gate and walk down the field, keeping the hedge on your right. Further down there are sections of boardwalk. Reach a small stream and turn right through a kissing-gate, keeping the stream on your left. Turn left through another

The view over the loch

gate and cross the stream by a sleeper-bridge. Turn right, then left at the junction. In about 100yds there is a post box. Turn right here, signed 'Private Road'.

Go round two bends and at a junction continue straight ahead signed 'Nature Reserve' (good view of Duncryne, the hill above Gartocharn, on the right). At the next junction fork left and, keeping left, follow the track to the loch shore. Pass through a gate and go right with the track

and at a junction turn left, then left again at the public toilets to return to the start point.

Follow the footpath through Shore Wood as far as the second stile. Retrace your steps from this point as far as the post box in the road. Turn right here and follow this road. The first two houses are Townhead of Aber and Aber Cottage ('aber' means estuary, and is found in Welsh as well as Scottish placenames). The road curves round past Ross Priory, an outstation of Strathclyde University, and gives a fine view back over the loch and its islands. Continue along the road for about ¾ mile, then at the main road turn left, then left

Shore Wood
The wood is part of the Loch Lomond National Nature Reserve, which also includes the islands, and is carefully managed to maintain its character and conserve the wildlife and the fine trees. The woodland has a rare atmosphere of great tranquillity, and in spring the floor of the wood is a rich carpet of bluebells.

Loch Lomond
This is the largest sheet of inland water in Britain and is over 23 miles long. The southern part is broad with a number of islands – from the walk you can see at least five. The wooded island called Inchcailloch ('the old woman's island') can be visited by boat from Balmaha on the east side of the loch. The islands are on the Highland Boundary Fault, which continues eastwards over Conic Hill, seen from the loch shore. The whole Loch Lomond area is now a Regional Park.

What to look out for
The lake is a good area for birds – black-headed gulls and teal are found in summer, and look for parties of whooper swans and goldeneye in winter. Loch Lomond dock has its only British site here.

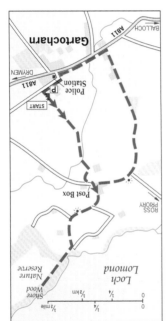

Dùn na Cuaiche – an Inveraray Viewpoint

Dùn na Cuaiche is a noted viewpoint high above the town of Inveraray and is part of the estate of the famous Inveraray Castle, which can be visited before or after completing the walk.

WALK 183
STRATHCLYDE
NN097093

Information

The walk is about four miles long
Good tracks and paths, steep in places
No stiles but some steps
Dogs should be kept on leads
Café at the castle (seasonal) and in Inveraray
Toilets at the castle (seasonal)

The spectacular view down Loch Fyne from the hilltop

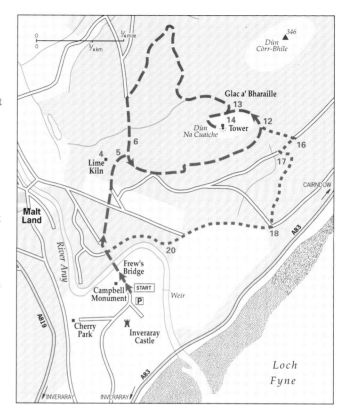

START

Inveraray is 24 miles north-east of Lochgilphead and 25 miles west of Arrochar. Park at the castle car park, reached by turning off A83 at the signed entrance at the north end of the village.

DIRECTIONS

The walk is one of the three waymarked routes on the hill. For this walk follow the blue waymarks from the car park, passing a monument marking the execution of 17 Campbells by the Marquis of Atholl in 1685, then crossing the River Aray by Frew's Bridge (designed by John Adam and built in 1758). Over the bridge fork right, following the blue waymarked path up through woodland. Pass through a kissing-gate and continue uphill across open meadow to a gate, then follow a track through woodland, passing the remains of an old lime kiln (point 4) and a huge western red cedar tree (point 5), believed to have the largest girth of any such tree in Scotland. About 50yds after the tree turn right and continue climbing steadily.

Where the path meets a track turn right and later turn left up a flight of steps with a rope handrail.

The path crosses a rock fall (fine view down Loch Fyne over Inveraray) and a little care is needed at this point. The path then turns left to climb steeply towards the top of the hill (point 12). This section of path may well be muddy and quite slippery. The hollow before the summit (point 13) is Glac a'Bharaille ('hollow of the barrel'). From here a good track leads to the summit and its little lookout tower, at a height of 813ft. The view over the castle, town and loch is quite superb and well worth the effort of the climb. The easiest way down is to return to point 13 (see * below) and turn left down a broad grassy track which takes you back to point 6 on the trail. From there retrace your steps to the car park.

*It is possible to extend the walk from point 13 by turning right (take care on the slippery section between points 13 and 14). At point 12 fork left downhill. At point 16 turn right and continue down the track to point 17 then turn left. On reaching the main track again at point 18 (at the 'Sweetie Seat') turn right. Between points 18 and 20 the walk follows 'The Grand Approach', constructed around 1775 as the principal entry to the castle. Continue until you meet the outward route and turn left to retrace your steps to the start point.

Inveraray Castle

The castle is the seat of the Duke of Argyll, Chief of Clan Campbell. It was built in the late 18th century to replace an older castle and at the same time the entire town of Inveraray was replanned and moved to its present position. Castle and town were planned together by Roger Morris and form one of the best preserved groupings of their kind anywhere in Britain. The castle is open from Easter to October (closed on Fridays).

The Lookout Tower

Dùn na Cuaiche means 'fort of the cup', possibly from the hollow near the top of the hill. The tower was designed by Roger Morris and William Adam and was built in 1748 for the grand sum of just £46. The roof was restored in 1989. The tower is sited so that it appears in silhouette when viewed from below, and is a popular local landmark.

Cherry Park

The block of buildings known as Cherry Park, in the castle grounds, holds an exhibition on the work of the Combined Services Operations unit that was based at Inveraray during the years of World War II.

What to look out for

The woods on Dùn na Cuaiche contain many fine trees: the excellent walks leaflet available at the castle will help you to identify them. There are woodland birds and also ravens and buzzards, and mammals include rabbits, squirrels and foxes. From the hilltop on a very clear day you can see the dam on Ben Cruachan, 20 miles away to the north.

The Fairy Hill

This is a short walk to the top of a hill long associated with fairies, passing through pleasant woodland along the way. On the busiest summer weekend, when Aberfoyle is full of visitors, you may well find yourself alone up here.

Information

The walk is about one and a half miles long
Good paths and tracks to follow
No stiles
Dogs should be kept on leads until away from the houses
Inns, cafés, toilets and a tourist information centre may be found in Aberfoyle

START
From the A821/B829 junction in Aberfoyle, turn down Manse Road to cross the infant River Forth to a small parking area by the side of the road at Balleich.

DIRECTIONS
From the parking area follow the 'Fairy Trail' markers along a road which soon becomes a track leading to Doon Hill (good views of Aberfoyle, the forests and the former quarry above the village). Continue past a low wooden barrier and at a track junction go straight on.
In a further 70yds or so turn left on to the hill, following little toadstool signs. The path winds up the hill, passing lichen-covered boulders.
At a junction near the top, go right as indicated and climb up to the summit to find a cleared area. The tall pine tree is said to be the spirit of Robert Kirk.
Follow the toadstool markers off the hill and curve round with the path as it weaves through the woods, eventually depositing you on a side track. Turn left and in 50yds regain the outward route to retrace your steps to the parking area.

The Man the Fairies Stole
The Reverend Robert Kirk practised his ministry in these parts in the latter part of the 17th century. A Gaelic scholar, he was very interested in stories of the 'little folk' and it is said that he managed to gain communication with them, learning many of their secret ways and lore.
However, he could not resist broadcasting this information and his book, *The Secret Commonwealth of Elves, Fauns and Fairies* was published in 1691. The little people were, understandably, extremely annoyed at his betrayal of their trust, so while he was out walking on Doon Hill they spirited him away and he was never seen alive again. He did appear once at a relative's funeral, crying out that if a knife was thrown over his head, he would become flesh again, but his relatives and friends hesitated and the chance was lost forever.

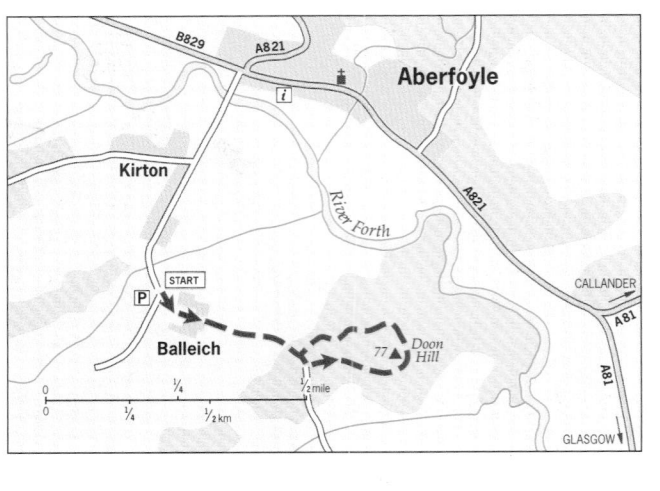

A toadstool signpost

Red squirrel

The wooded slopes of Doon Hill

What to look out for

Apart from the possibility of fairies, less fanciful residents of the woods to look out for include squirrels and roe deer, and woodland birds such as great tits, coal tits and nuthatches. Wood warblers are summer visitors.

The Highland Edge

This walk is from a forestry visitor centre near Aberfoyle, in an area where massive geological forces produced a major fault line millions of years ago. The walk uses forest tracks and paths, passing a fine waterfall.

WALK 185
CENTRAL
NN521014

Information

The walk is about four miles long
Good paths and tracks, with some steep sections
No stiles
David Marshall Lodge has good displays and an audio-visual show
Café at David Marshall Lodge
Picnic sites at the Lodge and at various places on the walk
Toilets at David Marshall Lodge

Down the rocky valley

START
David Marshall Lodge is on the A821, a mile north of Aberfoyle.

DIRECTIONS
From the left of the main entrance to the lodge follow the path signposted 'Waterfall Trail'. Go left at the first junction and right at the next. After crossing the raised wooden walkway turn right and soon cross the line of an old droving trail (Rob Roy operated around here, holding people to ransom for the original 'black mail'). The path winds down to the

'Waterfall of the Little Faun', 55ft high. As you approach the burn turn right. Turn left over the footbridge, then right and immediately left along a forest track (note information board on the production of slate in this area). At the next junction turn left, climbing steadily. Turn left onto a path for a short distance to see another waterfall, and soon rejoin the forest track. Continue uphill along forest track, with the burn on your right. At a junction of tracks turn right and contour round the hill, climbing again to a fine viewpoint, and continue along the track up the west side of a deep gully which is right on the fault line. On reaching the clearing at the top where the track ends, turn right on a delightful path, descending steeply. This is the route of a former 'inclined railway' used to take limestone from the quarry on Lime Craig to the kilns below. Continue downhill crossing one forest track, then meeting another. Turn right, with Dounans Camp below and the site of the lime kilns nearby. Cross the fault line again and in a further ¼ mile, at sign 'Trail End', turn left. Follow the path across a footbridge over the burn and turn right. Continue for 120yds with the burn on the right, then follow path to the left alongside a wooden handrail for the return to the lodge.

The Highland Edge
This great fault runs right across Scotland from the Clyde estuary to Stonehaven and it is possible to see how the rocks were shaped and

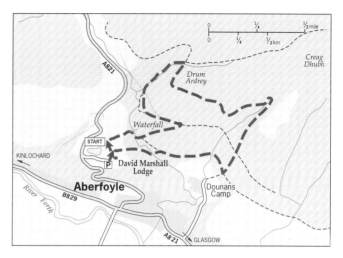

The bridge over the burn

bent by immense forces. The types of rock which can be seen include leny grit, sandstone, dolerite and slate.

David Marshall Lodge
The lodge is the main visitor centre for the Queen Elizabeth Forest Park and has a great deal of informative literature, including a leaflet on the Highland Boundary Fault Trail. Among the displays are items showing how writers such as Wordsworth and Scott attracted early tourists here and ensured the lasting fame of the Trossachs.

What to look out for

The information boards along the trail give lots of information about the geology, history and wildlife of the area, showing how the forest has evolved and what birds you can expect to see and hear, including buzzards.

Bracklinn Falls

WALK 186
CENTRAL
NN637083

This is a very straightforward out-and-back walk leading to a fine series of waterfalls and passing lovely woodland on the way.

Information

The walk is just over
a mile long
The path has a good surface
and is level nearly as far as
the steps leading down
to the falls
No stiles; one kissing-gate
Dogs should be kept on leads
No facilities at site, but
Callander has a full range of
hotels and cafés, and a
tourist information centre
Picnic place by the falls

Corn bunting

START

From the eastern end of Callander take the minor road signposted 'Bracklinn Falls'. The road becomes single-track, winding uphill – please drive with care. In about a mile the Bracklinn Falls car park is reached.

DIRECTIONS

From the car park follow the clear path which heads towards the falls. On the right is fine woodland with birch, oak and other trees. After a while the path comes into the open at a convenient bench with a superb view.

What to look out for

There are lovely old beech trees near the car park, and other fine trees in the woodland. You may see brown hares, and, if you are lucky, moorland birds such as lapwing and curlew. Dippers may be seen around the falls.

Bracklinn Falls

Their proximity to Callander has made these falls among the best known in Scotland, and they are always worth a visit. After a period of heavy rain the falls are at their most impressive, crashing over the rocks as Keltie Water fights its way through the narrow pass. There are several separate falls and the spot below the bridge is the best place to see the full drop and to appreciate the power of the water.

A Fine View

From the open stretch of the path there is a tremendous panorama. It takes in the Ochil Hills, with the peak of Dumyat prominent, and in clear conditions you can just see Stirling Castle. The view continues round eastwards to the Gargunnock Hills and Campsie Fells, at the furthest extremity of which you will see the stubby peak of Dumgoyne, one of a number of ancient volcanic plugs in central Scotland.

The tumbling waterfall

Left, a panoramic view

Go through a kissing-gate and descend the hill, with the noise of the falls now apparent. A flight of steps leads down to the Bridge of Brackland, from where the spectacular falls can be seen (at their best after rain). There are paths either side of the water above and below the falls. Continuing over the bridge a little way leads you to an excellent viewpoint high above the gorge. Return by the same route.

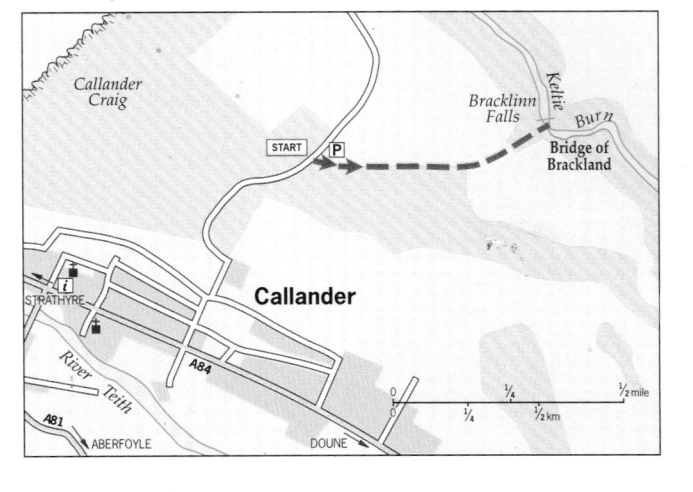

Dollar Glen and Castle Campbell

WALK 187
CENTRAL
NS964989

This is an exciting walk up a dramatic glen with waterfalls rushing down between cliffs, leading to a superbly sited castle.

START
Dollar is about 12 miles east of Stirling on the A91. Follow signs from Dollar to Castle Campbell, and park in the car park part way up this minor road.

DIRECTIONS
From the car park cross the road, pass through the gate and take the path and then steps down into the glen. Turn right up the glen and after the first stretch of boardwalk, go down left to the Long Bridge. Cross the bridge and follow the path through a narrow gap between cliffs, with several

Information

The walk is about a mile long
Rough in places, and some boardwalk; fairly steep climb up to the castle
No stiles
Dogs should be kept on leads
Café (seasonal) at the castle; pubs and cafés in Dollar
Grassy area around castle suitable for picnics
Toilets at castle

fine waterfalls. Follow the path to the left and then up steps on the right as it winds up the glen. Recross the burn higher up and climb up to Castle Campbell.

After visiting the castle, return by turning right through the gate by the castle drive and going down a long flight of steps into the glen. Keep to the path, to rejoin the outward route at the steps leading up to the path back to the car park, signposted 'Lower (quarry) car park'.

Dollar Glen
Dollar Glen is the most dramatic of the steep-sided glens that thrust into the southern scarp face of the Ochil Hills, east of Stirling. Two streams – the Burn of Sorrow and the Burn of Care – rush down the glen, crashing over rocks in tumbling waterfalls. The path twists and climbs up the glen, winding excitingly under cliffs and close to the falls.
The glen has been in the care of the National Trust for Scotland since 1950. In the lower, open part is a grassy area with children's play equipment.

Castle Campbell
Castle Campbell has everything a castle should have: battlements, a tower with winding stone stairs and dark underground rooms. The castle is documented as far back as 1426 and was used by the Earls of Argyll as an eastern lowland stronghold until the 17th century. The name dates from 1490, before which it was called Castle Glume or Gloom, supposedly named by a princess who was imprisoned here; the two burns – Care and Sorrow – would seem to have been named at the same time. True or not, it is a good story!
The castle's importance waned after the mid-17th century, and it passed through various ownerships until acquired by the National Trust for Scotland in 1948. It is cared for by Historic Scotland on behalf of the Trust and is open all year. The view south from the castle is extensive.

The imposing Castle Campbell, above Dollar Glen

What to look out for

The glen is geologically very interesting – indicator boards give more information. Fine oak trees support a varied birdlife, and beneath them grow wild flowers such as lesser celandine.

From Coalmine to Country Park

This walk in Fife is in a figure-of-eight, taking in the shores of an attractive man-made loch, an old cultivated area and the big wheel of the former pit.

START

Lochore Meadows Country Park is about four miles north of Cowdenbeath on the B920, accessed from either junction 3 or 4 of the M90 north of Edinburgh via the Forth Road Bridge. The entrance to the park is at Crosshill, between Lochgelly and Ballingry. The walk starts at the Visitor Centre.

DIRECTIONS

For the first loop, walk down towards the sailing club ('The Lodge') and turn left on to a path to pass behind the building and its car park. The path swings left beside the outflow burn from the loch. Turn right over the bridge and at the far end turn right again. Go through a gate on to the Clune. Walk along the shore and continue round a small inlet. Scramble up on to the rocky knoll (with excellent views across the loch and its islands). Drop down on the west side of the knoll and turn right on the lochside path to rejoin the outward route back to the Visitor Centre.

For the second loop, walk up the main path from the Visitor Centre northwards to

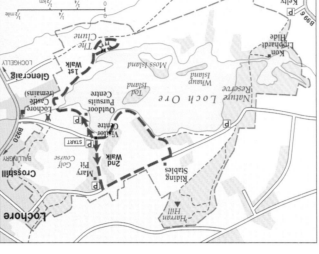

the huge pit wheel of the former Mary Pit and the nearby colliery locomotive. Turn left, pass through a gate and turn left on to the rough road and walk along to the riding stables.

Just past the stables, turn left on a path fringing woodland back to the lochside. Turn left again and walk round the loch to the visitor centre.

Lochore Meadows

The country park has been reclaimed from former mining ground and now

offers a range of recreational facilities including watersports, horse riding, golf and a 'trim trail'. Countryside events are also a regular feature.

At the heart of the park is Loch Ore, surrounded by woodland and open areas. The area south of the loch is on the 'Breaking the Ground' trail (leaflet from the visitor centre), which shows how the area was inhabited and cultivated centuries ago. The ring of stones on Clune Craig may be the remains of a hillfort.

Mary Pit
At one time 350 men worked here, mining the coal deep under the ground; another 2,000 worked in pits near by. The mine-shaft was over 2,000 feet deep, beneath what is now the golf course. The colliery locomotive, called a 'pug', came from the former Michael Pit near Kirkcaldy.

Around lovely Lochore

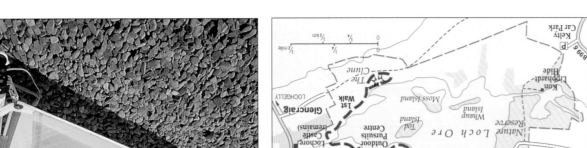

What to look out for

The loch has water birds such as coots, mallards and tufted ducks, all year round, and these are quite commonly seen. However, in winter there are many more species to observe on the water here – goosander, scaup and long-tailed ducks are among the more unusual of these.

The woodland is also home to many birds and small mammals. Watch out for flocks of siskins and redpolls during the winter months.

WALK 188
FIFE
NT171961

Information

The walk is about two and a half miles long
Mixed ground with good paths or tracks
No stiles
Dogs must be kept on leads
The visitor centre has displays and interesting leaflets
Café at visitor centre
Plenty of picnic tables, both by loch and in pit wheel area
Toilets at visitor centre

A Ramble on the Lomond Hills

Information

The walk is about five and a half miles long
Steep in parts; stout footwear is essential
Dogs must be kept on leads at all times
Wide selection of pubs and tearooms in Falkland
Toilets at car park
Picnic sites at the Craigmead and East Lomond Relay Station car parks
Large groups should contact the Ranger Service in advance (0592 741212)

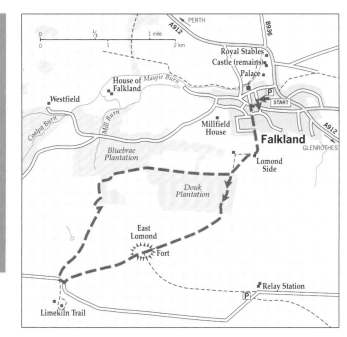

A moderately energetic walk to the summit of East Lomond Hill, site of a prehistoric fort, starting from the delightful village of Falkland.

START
The car park in Falkland, situated near the centre of the village, is signposted from the A912.

DIRECTIONS
Leave the car park at the entrance, passing the public toilets to your right. Turn left at the T-junction, then almost immediately right, up Horse Market. At the end of the street turn left. Go straight on at the crossroads, signposted 'Footpath to Lomond Hills' and proceed up the road and onto the gravel track. At the fork bear right, and after about 50yds turn left, up the wooden steps.
Follow the path up through the wood, going straight on at the crossroads (between two stone markers) and eventually through a wooden horse barrier. Continue climbing towards the edge of the wood. From the end of the wood follow the path south-west (diagonally right) towards the summit. Aim for the gate in the fence and on reaching it cross the stile. Continue straight on up the steep hill until you reach the summit.

A pepperpot tower of Falkland Palace can be seen behind the church in this view of the village

From here continue south-west and regain the path, leaving the summit roughly in line with the right-hand end of the distant reservoir. Follow the path as it winds down the hill (quite steep in parts; may be slippery) until you come to a gate. (Take the Limekiln Trail opposite for a 20-minute detour, returning to the gate.)
Don't go through the gate, but bear right down a grassy track. Turn left at the fork and continue to a ruined wall. Follow the wall until it ends at a corner with another wall. From here descend diagonally left, bearing for a radio mast on the next ridge of hills until you meet a clear path again. Turn right along this, passing a spring on your left, and through old quarry heaps. Soon the path passes between two stone markers. Follow the path diagonally right towards an unfenced spit of trees which projects from the main plantation below. When you

reach the trees turn left and walk around the edge. Shortly before the main plantation (and just before a large mass of boulders in your path) turn right into the trees. Once through the trees, cross the stile to your left, and turn right.
Follow the path down, passing a ruin to your right. When you reach the rough road, turn right and proceed to the junction with your outward route. Turn left and retrace your steps back to the car park.

East Lomond Hill
This is the site of a prehistoric fort, dating from between the late 1st millennium BC and the early 1st millennium AD. The summit is crowned by a large Bronze Age cairn, and there are remnants of the ramparts lower down. Once part of the hunting forests of Falkland Palace, a 'Ranger' was appointed in 1605 to protect deer and discourage the public. Now the area is part of Fife Regional Park, and a modern day Ranger Service operates.

What to look out for

Roe deer and red and grey squirrels are found in the woods. The moor is home to red grouse (the only site for them in Fife), and curlews, skylarks, meadow pipits, wheatear and whinchats may also be seen on the hill.

The Earl's Tower

WALK 190
TAYSIDE
NO136235

This walk near Perth visits a tower set high on a cliff with superb views, and takes in fine woodland with excellent wildlife.

The Earl's Tower is in a superb cliff-top setting

What to look out for

The woods are rich in bird life and many species, from chaffinches to tawny owls, have their homes here. There are also roe deer and you may see the flash of a white rump as one bounds across the path.

Information

The walk is about two and a half miles long
Mixed paths and tracks, with some climbing and rough ground
No stiles
Nearest refreshment and toilet facilities are in Perth
The Stone Table area is excellent for a picnic

START

From Perth, cross the Tay by the old Perth Bridge (A85) and at the traffic lights on the far side go straight ahead up a steep hill. Follow signs for Kinnoull Hill Woodland Walks to go right at the hospital, and right again to the Corsiehill car park.

DIRECTIONS

From the car park take any of the small paths up the hill to the indicator at Corsiehill viewpoint (superb panorama of mountains). Turn half-left towards the cottage, walk up beside the fence and at the end of the fence turn left on a small path which soon broadens. At a cross path go straight over.

Just past a brown waymark turn left on to a path with a yellow waymark and continue through fine open woodland for about ¼ mile to a broad track (marker 13).

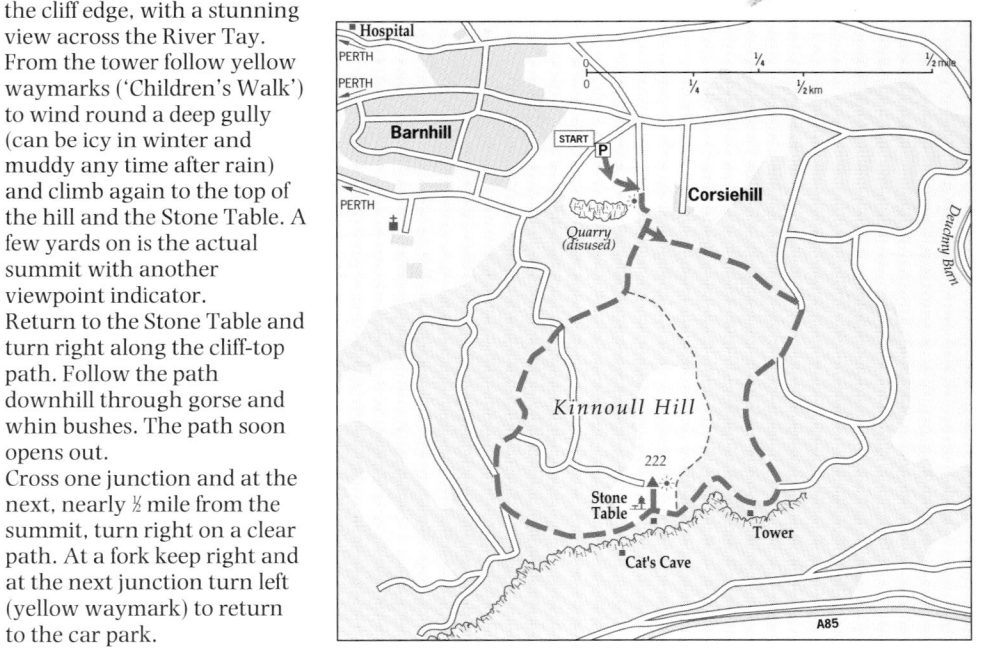

The stone table

Turn right and continue on this track below tall pines, then at a fork in about 600yds go right, signposted 'Tower'. Follow the track round to the right and uphill to reach Kinnoull Tower on the cliff edge, with a stunning view across the River Tay. From the tower follow yellow waymarks ('Children's Walk') to wind round a deep gully (can be icy in winter and muddy any time after rain) and climb again to the top of the hill and the Stone Table. A few yards on is the actual summit with another viewpoint indicator.
Return to the Stone Table and turn right along the cliff-top path. Follow the path downhill through gorse and whin bushes. The path soon opens out.
Cross one junction and at the next, nearly ½ mile from the summit, turn right on a clear path. At a fork keep right and at the next junction turn left (yellow waymark) to return to the car park.

Kinnoull Tower

Contrary to its appearance, the tower is not a real ruin, but was built this way by the Earl of Kinnoull in the 18th century. He was inspired to build the folly, so the story goes, after visiting Germany and seeing the romantic castles on cliffs above the Rhine. There is another similar tower on Binn Hill a mile or so to the east.

Stone Table

This feature of the hill was also built for the earl, so that he and his friends could sit here and enjoy the view, just as we do today. He did not, of course, have the M85 motorway interchange directly below.

Rook

Around Glen Lednock

An attractive and varied walk which includes fine woodland and a lovely waterfall. A diversion can be made to a viewpoint tower. The walk is particularly good in spring and autumn when the colouring is at its best.

WALK 191
TAYSIDE
NN773221

START

Comrie is seven miles west of Crieff. The walk starts from the car park just off Dundas Street (the A85).

DIRECTIONS

Walk up Dundas Street and where it swings left go straight ahead into Monument Road. Shortly take the signposted path on the right. Continue along the path, keeping the fence on your right, through fine woods of beech, oak, larch and birch. Cross a small burn. The path enters the woods proper and broadens out to give excellent walking. In ¼ mile fork right to the Little Caldron viewpoint, continuing to rejoin the main path, which narrows, and runs alongside the road. The path becomes a wooden boardwalk before plunging in flights of steps to the Deil's Caldron (Devil's Kettle) waterfalls. Climb steps to join the road, and continue carefully along it. (In 200yds a diversion can be made to the left to climb the hill to Lord Melville's Monument.) Carry on with the glen opening up. At a left-hand bend in the road go ahead on a track signposted 'Laggan Wood' and follow yellow waymarks to the Shaky Bridge (its far end is ingeniously balanced in the fork of a sycamore tree). Over the bridge turn right along the path beside the river. Cross a stile and climb steps to join a lovely grassy path with a good view of the monument. The path climbs gently above a wet meadow to enter Laggan Wood by a stile, and before long starts the descent towards Comrie. Ignore the sign 'Forest Walk' on the right.

At a fork turn right down steps (a short diversion left leads to a viewpoint with a splendid panorama of Comrie and Strathearn). The path continues down to rejoin the burn and passes a weir before re-entering Comrie by the cricket ground. Turn right over the bridge and follow the path right and left (now following an old railway line). At a cross path go straight on between fences to return to the car park, or divert left into the village to visit the Scottish Tartans Museum.

Information

The walk is about four miles long
Good paths with some boardwalk and steps; some climbing, especially to the Melville Monument
A few stiles
Dogs must be kept on leads
Nearest refreshments and toilets are in Comrie
Good picnic areas in the woods and by the Shaky Bridge

Looking across the glen

What to look out for

There are lots of different trees to identify, and woodland birds such as finches, tits and treecreepers. Moorland birds can also be seen on the open stretch. Mammals include rabbits and possibly roe deer and foxes in the woods.

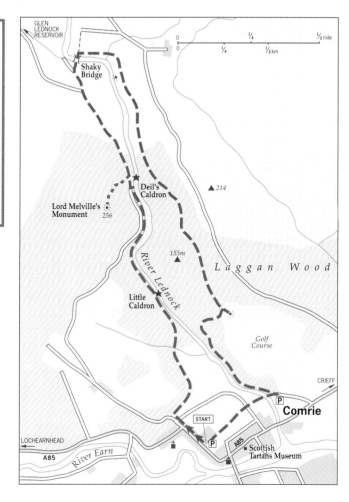

The Deil's Caldron

The falls are an impressive sight, tumbling out of a narrow gorge between cliffs and over rock steps to a deep pool (the Caldron) some 100ft below.

Lord Melville's Monument

The monument, 73ft high, was built in 1812 in memory of Henry Dundas, first Viscount Melville. He was Lord Advocate of Scotland for many years and had an estate at Dunira, west of Comrie. From the monument there are superb views all around.

Scottish Tartans Museum

In the main street of Comrie, the museum includes displays on the history of tartan, how it evolved, how dyes were made from plants and vegetables, and much more. There is a reconstructed weaver's cottage and a special children's corner. The museum is open Easter to October daily.

The Hermitage and Ossian's Cave

This short walk visits Ossian's Cave and The Hermitage, both built in the 19th century for one of the Dukes of Atholl and now owned by the National Trust for Scotland. The Hermitage is above the splendid Falls of Braan.

WALK 192
TAYSIDE
NO013422

START
The National Trust for Scotland car park is off the A9, one mile north of Dunkeld (signposted).

DIRECTIONS
Rather than heading directly for The Hermitage from the car park, take the forest track that heads uphill beside the main road, signposted 'Craigvinean'. (Across the A9 is the prominent cliff of Craig y Barns, used by climbers.) At the top of the rise the track swings left by a field. (The Perth to Inverness railway

Wren

runs under your feet in a tunnel here.)
Continue through fine woodland for about ½ mile. At a junction of tracks a sign points left to The Hermitage. Follow this path and in 30yds take the right fork onto a slightly rougher path.
You soon reach Ossian's Cave, in an area of huge boulders with the River Braan rushing past below. Turn left along the riverside path and in a few yards reach a viewpoint on the right above the river. Continue through a Norway spruce plantation to reach the main falls and the Hermitage.

(From here a longer signposted route leads through woods to Inver and back to the car park.)
Our walk returns over the bridge and along by the river on the main path, back to the car park.

Ossian's Cave
This is a folly built in the 18th century and named after the legendary Celtic bard. It is well made, with a corbelled roof, and it is quite safe to go inside.

The Hermitage
Another folly, set high above the waterfall, the Hermitage

The Falls of Braan

is also called Ossian's Hall. It was built in 1758 by the third Duke of Atholl before he succeeded to the title – apparently as a delightful surprise for his uncle, the second Duke.
In those early days, visitors would have entered to see a painting of Ossian on the far wall. When a hidden pulley was operated, the painting slid into a recess, giving entry to a smaller room. Here, the walls and ceiling were covered with mirrors and coloured glass, and the reflections of the waterfalls below were truly amazing. The bridge dates from the same period.

What to look out for

The woods contain many fine trees including old Douglas and silver firs. If you are lucky you may see Britain's smallest bird, the goldcrest, and other woodland birds include long-tailed tits, wrens and willow warblers.
Wild fruits include blackberries and bilberries in season.

The Pass of Killiecrankie

The Battle of Killiecrankie in 1689 was one of the first victories for the Jacobite rebels. Learn about the battle at the National Trust for Scotland visitor centre, and then walk down into the lovely pass to see the site for yourself.

START

The National Trust for Scotland Visitor Centre is at Killiecrankie on the B8079, three miles north of Pitlochry. The car park is open all year; the centre is open daily from Easter to late October.

DIRECTIONS

Walk round the back of the Visitor Centre, following signs 'Pass and the Soldier's Leap'. Go down steps and across a wooden bridge over a burn. This is Trooper's Den, where the first shot of the battle in

The view from the bridge

1689 was fired. Continue down the path (a seat gives a splendid view of the pass), descending a long curving flight of steps to turn sharply left for a few yards and then right, signposted 'Soldier's Leap'.

Return to the signpost and continue on the riverside path, soon passing Joseph Mitchell's fine railway viaduct of 1863 – 510ft long and 54ft high at its highest point.

The path continues through splendid mature woodland, with the River Garry below. This stretch is particularly fine in the autumn when the trees are at their most colourful. In about ½ mile pass Balfour's Stone, where Brigadier Balfour, a Dutch commander in the government force, is said to have been killed in the retreat after the battle.

Join the old road from Tummel Bridge to Blair Atholl, noting the fine milestone on the left, and soon turn right on the footbridge over the Garry. Look back here for a splendid view up the pass, framing the soaring peak of Carn Liath, part of the Beinn a'Ghlo massif. Return by the same route to the Visitor Centre.

The Battle of Killiecrankie

The aim of the Jacobite rebels was to overthrow the Hanoverian William of

The Soldier's Leap, where a desperate man jumped to safety

Orange and restore the Stuarts to the British throne. Here, on 27 July 1689, they met government troops. Led by John Graham of Claverhouse – 'Bonnie Dundee' – the Jacobites won a rapid and total victory. Unfortunately Graham was killed and without its charismatic leader the rebellion fizzled out.

The Soldier's Leap

The story here is that one Donald MacBean, fighting on the government side, ran into the pass in an attempt to escape. Coming to this point, as he told, 'I laid down my gun and hat and jumped, and lost one of my shoes in the jump'. At 18 feet across, it would be a very respectable distance for a trained athlete of today, and shows what a desperate man can do.

What to look out for

Look out for birds such as great spotted and green woodpeckers among the oak and birch. Ferns grow in profusion on the forest floor. Regular guided walks from the Visitor Centre.

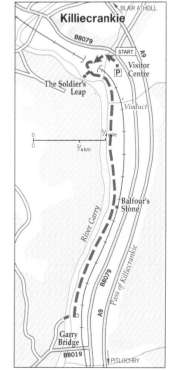

Dunnottar Castle

WALK 194
GRAMPIAN
NO8788855

This splendid short walk goes from the attractive harbour at Stonehaven to one of Scotland's most dramatic castle ruins, standing on a cliff-top promontory, and returns across a pebble beach.

Information

The walk is about three miles long

Good paths, but a long flight of steps at the castle, and pebble beach on the return

Some road walking

Several stiles

Dogs should be kept on leads

The Marine Hotel at the harbour is open all day and welcomes families

Cafés in Stonehaven

Ladies toilets at Dunnottar Castle; others in Stonehaven

DIRECTIONS

START

Stonehaven Harbour is 15 miles south of Aberdeen, reached by turning off the A94 into Stonehaven and following signs to the harbour. There are parking spaces at the harbour.

From the harbour walk up Wallace Wynd (a wynd is a lane) and turn left into Castle Street. Where the road ends, continue ahead on a path which climbs steeply to the left to meet another road. Turn left and in a few yards, where the road bends sharply right, go ahead on the path between fences, with a fine view back over the town, harbour and the cliffs beyond. (The war memorial on the prominent knoll to the right is worth the short diversion through a gate and over the grass. An imposing rotunda, it is inscribed around the inside: 'One by one Death challenged them. One by one they smile in his grim visage and refused to be dismayed'. Return to the gate and turn right.)

Continue along the cliff path. Cross two stiles, walk across a field (usually of turnips), cross

Right, Dunnottar Castle and below, Stonehaven Harbour

path ascending the grass of the beach climb up the Castle Haven. At the far end on to the pebble beach of back by turning right, down After visiting the castle, start entrance and ticket booth. steps and go across to the Dunnottar, turn left down the the castle. On reaching winds round the bay to reach reach Castle Haven. The path field. Cross one more stile to along the edge of another two more stiles and walk

Dunnottar Castle

The castle was started in the late 14th century and has 15th- and 16th-century additions. It was besieged several times, notably in 1652 when it held out for eight months before surrendering to Cromwell's forces.

The considerable remains are very impressive, both on the approach towards the castle and on closer inspection. A guidebook can be bought on

Stonehaven

Stonehaven is an attractive town with a good sandy beach beyond the harbour. On the old pier is the Tolbooth Museum of local history. It is housed in the oldest building in Stonehaven, which was built in the 17th century, and it was used in Zeffirelli's recent remake of Shakespeare's *Hamlet*. The castle is open daily (but limited hours in winter).

entry, and all the main buildings are clearly labelled. Its dramatic setting has made Dunnottar a popular choice as a film location, and it was

slope on the left (not the very steep gully just left of the cliffs) to regain the cliff-top path. Retrace the outward route back into Stonehaven.

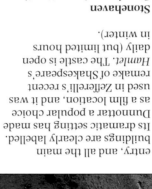

built as a store for Dunnottar about four hundred years ago.

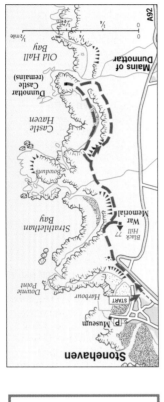

What to look out for

This is a very good area for seabirds, with an RSPB reserve at Fowlsheugh, to the south. From May to July, watch for razorbills, guillemots, fulmars, kittiwakes and great black-backed gulls. Puffins and eiders also come to Fowlsheugh to breed.

Keep a look-out for peregrines, which may be glimpsed hunting along the cliffs.

Duff House and Bridge of Alvah

Duff House, near the attractive seaside town of Banff, is considered to be one of William Adam's very finest works. This walk follows pleasant tracks through the woodland of its extensive policies, passing an 18th-century refrigerator, a mausoleum and a beautiful old bridge.

Information

The walk is about four miles long
Good track or path all the way
Dogs should be kept on leads
Cafés and Tourist Information Centre in Banff
Toilets at the Duff House car park and in Banff

START

Duff House is just off the southern outskirts of Banff, signposted from the A98. The walk starts from the car park.

DIRECTIONS

From the car park turn left and walk around the edge of the sports field to reach the Fife Gates, named for the second Earl Fife, who was largely responsible for laying out the park in the mid-18th century. Pass through the Fife Gates and follow the track south. At a fork keep left (the right fork goes to 'The Orchard' where honey can be purchased). In a further 100yds take the small path on the left,

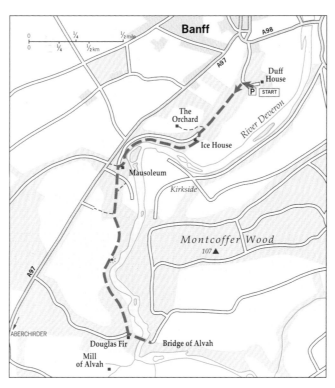

The imposing Duff House

signposted 'Woodland Footpath'. Immediately on the right, down a few steps, is the former ice house for the estate. Continue along the winding path, with the River Deveron on the left. The path rejoins the main track at the Duff Mausoleum, built on the site of a former Carmelite chapel. Turn left along the track and at the next fork go straight ahead.

At a triangular junction keep left, with fields on the right and, at one point, a fine view of the river through a gap in the trees on the left. Reach a junction with a fine old Douglas Fir ahead (said to be a 'wishing tree' – if you stick a coin in the tree, spin round three times and make a wish, your wish should come true). Turn left here, steeply down the track to reach the Bridge of Alvah. Return to Duff House by the same route.

Duff House

The house was designed by William Adam for William Duff, who became the first Earl Fife. Work began in 1735, but for various reasons, including a protracted lawsuit over Adam's fees, was never completed. The house fell into disrepair, but considerable restoration work is now under way. It is open to visitors in the summer.

The Mausoleum

There was a mausoleum in the original plans, but it was not until 1791 that work started at the instigation of the second Earl Fife, then aged 62. The mausoleum is in rococo Gothic style and contains a monument to the first Earl, whose body was brought here when the building was completed. The second Earl was so proud of his Banffshire roots that he had soil from the area taken to London and spread on the ground where he was building a house, so that he could say that he 'lived on Scottish soil'.

The Bridge of Alvah

The bridge was rebuilt in 1772, replacing an even older crossing of the river. A graceful single-arch structure, it complements its fine setting perfectly. The section of our walk which leads to the bridge was originally a carriage drive, intended to show off the fine park of Duff House to visitors. The scenery was considered at the time to be an ideal representation of how the landscape should be 'arranged'.

What to look out for

The woods and fields here have interesting birdlife. Look for pheasants and grey partridges, and grey herons down by the River Deveron – a fine trout and salmon stream. There are plenty of rabbits and you may spot deer if you are lucky.

The Bow-Fiddle Rock

A short walk on the lovely Morayshire coast linking two attractive towns, passing a famous offshore landmark and crossing a superb stretch of sandy beach.

WALK 196
GRAMPIAN
NJ513671

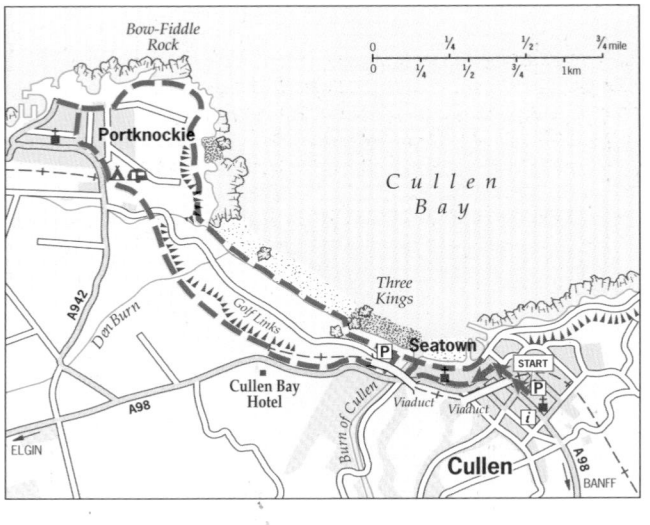

START
Cullen is on the A98, 20 miles east of Elgin. Park in the square.

DIRECTIONS
From the square, walk downhill towards the sea, passing under the railway viaduct (fine view over Cullen Bay) and continue left with the main road above Seatown. Turn right at the Royal Oak Hotel, overlooked by the viaduct. Pass a row of houses and turn left down a slip road, back towards the viaduct. Cross the footbridge over the Burn of Cullen, pass under the viaduct and turn right onto the main road. Continue along the road to the Cullen Bay Hotel. Leave the road here to join the old railway track, now a footpath, and walk towards Portknockie, with the golf course and beach below to the right.
Continue into Portknockie. The path rises to Bridge Street. Walk down it and continue down either New Street or Victoria Street, passing the Victoria Hotel. At the end, turn left along Patrol Road for a short way to see Portknockie's picturesque harbour.
Return along Patrol Road. At the end fork left. Pass a small boatyard and turn left onto a track towards the sea. In a further 50yds turn right to find a path running alongside a fence on the cliff top. (There is soon a superb close-up of the Bow-Fiddle Rock.) Follow the cliff-top path (fine views) until Cullen Bay comes into view. Where a path joins from the right, go left down the steps to reach the shore.
The path reaches the broad, firm sands of Cullen Bay. Once across the sands, go right up steps to a small promenade. Cross the Burn of Cullen by the footbridge, just below the railway viaduct, and enter Seatown. Either walk along the front or explore the maze of lanes between the houses. At the harbour turn right and left to reach a path climbing up to the main road and return to the square.

What to look out for

There is plenty of birdlife offshore here, including cormorants and eiders. Look for birds on the beach such as oystercatchers and a variety of gull species. Turnstones and purple sandpipers appear in the winter months.

The Cullen Viaducts
The railway viaducts are here because the Countess of Seafield refused to allow the line to cross the policies of Seafield House, a little way inland.

The Bow-Fiddle Rock
This large rock stack has been eroded by the sea, forming the natural archway from which it gets its name, though from the Cullen side it looks rather more like a whale's tail. A large number of sea birds can usually be seen on the rock.

Cullen Seatown
The houses of the former Invercullen are mostly 18th- and 19th-century, and are tightly grouped in a maze of narrow lanes. The famous smoked fish soup, Cullen Skink, originated here.

The distinctive Bow-Fiddle Rock

Loch an Eilein

WALK 197
HIGHLAND
NH898085

This is a beautiful walk around what is considered to be one of the most picturesque lochs in the Highlands, set amid one of the finest remnants of the ancient Caledonian Pine Forest with the massive Cairngorms as a dramatic backdrop.

Information

The walk is just over three miles long
Mainly level, easy ground
Dogs should be kept on leads as this is a Nature Reserve
Lovely picnic areas around the car park and Information Centre, and at the north end of the loch

START
Loch an Eilein is three miles south of Aviemore. Follow the B9152 from Aviemore turning left to Inverdruie, then right on to the B970. After a mile or so turn left, signposted 'Loch an Eilein'. Park in the car park at the end of the road.

DIRECTIONS
Leave the car park by the footpath and after 100yds or so reach the information centre. Go straight ahead to join a footpath which encircles the loch. Head anti-clockwise around the loch. Go left at the first fork and continue on the footpath, passing the ruins of Loch an Eilein Castle on its island on your left. Soon you will pass Loch an Eilein Cottage on your right and pass through a gate into ancient Caledonian Pine woodland.

Loch an Eilein Castle

Keep to the main path with the waters of the loch on your left. Beyond some fallen trees, where the path splits, take the left branch, passing the head of the loch and climbing a short steep hill. From the top of the hill continue through more woodland and cross a small wooden footbridge over the stream. Once over the footbridge, continue to the left, slightly downhill, crossing some stepping stones over another narrow stream and continuing on the obvious footpath.

Continue on the footpath with Loch an Eilein still on your left for about 1½ miles, ignoring a narrow path which turns left towards the loch.

At the next path junction, keep ahead across a footbridge. Continue on the main path, up a long, easy hill, through a gate, and past a cottage on the right. Continue through woodland. Take the next left fork downhill over a footbridge and return to the car park.

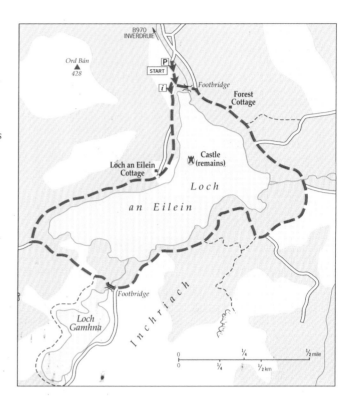

Loch an Eilein Castle
Dating from the 14th century, local legend claims that the castle was once the lair of the notorious 'Wolf of Badenoch', otherwise known as Alexander Stewart, the grandson of Robert the Bruce, who was eventually excommunicated by the Church for burning down Elgin Cathedral. The castle was once reached by a causeway of flagged stones, now covered by the waters of the loch, and only rarely is the water level low enough to reveal the stones.

The Loch
At the east end of the loch, near the car park, there is a broad bay offering fine views of the castle island and the hill beyond. The waters are safe, but bathers beware – they stay very cold until well into July.

What to look out for

The castle ruins were used by one of the last native pairs of ospreys to breed in Scotland, before the old Scottish stock became extinct earlier this century. The re-introduction of the osprey to Scotland is one of the great environmental success stories, and you can often see these magnificent fish-hawks hunting over the waters of the loch, although none now breed on the castle ruins. The loch area is part of the Cairngorms National Reserve, and many rare species of birds and mammals live and breed here, including red squirrels, crested tits, Scottish crossbills and capercaillie. More about the history and wildlife of the area can be learned from the Information Centre.

Neptune's Staircase

This is an easy and interesting walk with a mixture of attractions – boats on a canal, the site of an ancient castle and marvellous views to the highest mountain in Britain.

START
Banavie is about four miles north of Fort William via the A82 and the A830. In Banavie turn right onto the B8004 and soon reach the large car park at the foot of a series of canal locks known as Neptune's Staircase.

DIRECTIONS
Leave the car park passing to the right of the Moorings Hotel on to the canal towpath. A series of eight locks ('Neptune's Staircase') lifts vessels over 70ft at the head of Loch Linnhe.
Cross over at one of the lock gates to the far side of the canal and turn left to follow the easy towpath for almost two miles.
Where you see a row of cottages down a steep bank to the right of the towpath, turn right down a narrow path and then left onto a track which leads to the ruins of Torcastle.
From the castle, return to the canal and go through the tunnel below it. Where the track joins the B8004, turn left to return to Banavie and the start of the walk. All along this road there are superb views of Ben Nevis, Britain's

highest mountain, and the surrounding peaks.)

Banavie
In 1948 the parish priest of Glenfinnan, the Rev Father P J O'Regan published a small book in which he claimed that Banavie was the birthplace of St Patrick. He was quoting a 10th-century writer who said that 'St

The view on a brilliant day of Ben Nevis, from Banavie

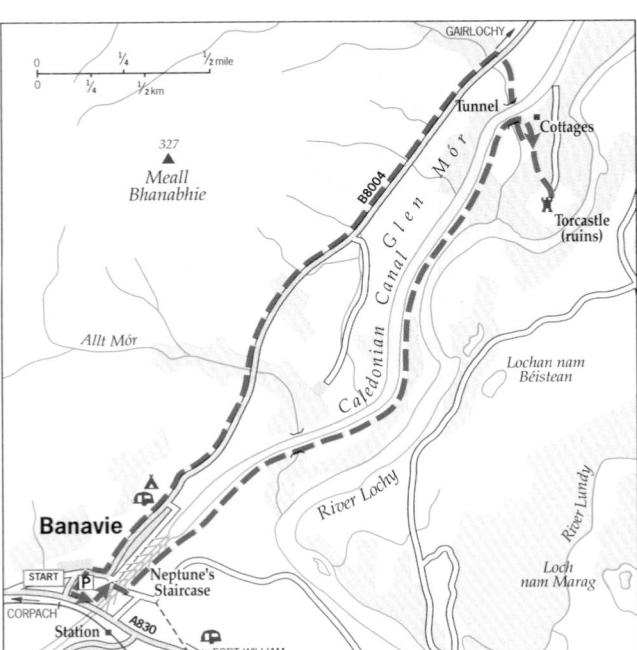

Patrick belonged to the village of Bannavie, not far from the western sea'.

Torcastle
The ruins of the 19th-century Torcastle stand on the site of a very ancient fort, Tor Castle. In 1630, an anonymous author wrote, 'There was ane ancient castle builded whaire this Torcastle is which was called Beragonium and this Torcastle was builded last by ane which is called Ewen MacAllane the Chief of Clan Cameron'. It has also been suggested that this is the site of Torc Castle, the capital of the Dalriadic Scots. In 1947 Torcastle opened as a hotel, but it was destroyed by a fire in 1950 and never rebuilt.

The Caledonian Canal
Thomas Telford's Caledonian Canal, running from Corpach, just north of Fort William, to Inverness, was completed in 1847. Its purpose was to provide a navigable waterway between the Firth of Lorne on the west coast and the Moray Firth on the east, saving shipping the long journey all around the north coast of Scotland. It is still used by some commercial boats and fishing boats, but is largely used nowadays by pleasure craft. The waterway also takes in Loch Linnhe, Loch Lochy, Loch Oich and Loch Ness. The series of locks on the canal at Banavie was christened 'Neptune's Staircase' by Telford, and the name has stuck.

The Fabulous Falls of Foyers

Of the Falls of Foyers, the poet Robert Southey once said, 'everything is beautiful, and everything – woods, rocks, water, the glen, the mountains and the lake below – in proportion'. The walk also offers tantalising glimpses across the deep and mysterious waters of Loch Ness.

START

Foyers is about 13 miles east of Fort Augustus via the B862, turning onto the B852 just north of Whitebridge. Park at the car park or layby on the roadside, close to the telephone box and post office (Foyers Stores).

DIRECTIONS

Pass through the gate opposite the post office and shop and turn left down the footpath. After about 40yds turn right down to a wooden fence and then left again. The path winds steeply downhill. At the next junction turn left and proceed downhill, later taking the narrow path around the left side of a large rock to the falls viewpoint. Retrace your steps uphill. At the junction go straight ahead across a footbridge and along the cliff edge. Follow the path alongside the fence. At the next fork, bear right on the path through the trees. Turn left at the next junction and continue along this path, crossing a car track and descending a steep narrow path towards houses and the road. Turn left onto the road. On reaching a tight right-hand bend, turn left onto the 'no through road' and cross the river on the old road bridge. Continue straight ahead past the telephone box and follow the road past the entrance to Foyers Burial Ground. Continue along the road to reach some farm buildings. Go through the farm and bear left through a gate onto a track up towards the forest. Pass through another gate and turn right onto the forest track. Continue straight on, climbing uphill. In about ½ mile, at a junction on the brow of the hill, go straight ahead.

After about another ½ mile reach a junction of forest roads and turn left, then go through the gate onto a track leading out of the forest. Cross a bridge (view of Upper Falls) and continue past some cottages uphill to the road. Turn left and return to the starting point.

What to look out for

The Loch Ness Monster, of course – but there is a great deal of wildlife in this area which is more easily seen.
You may spot a buzzard circling above the forest, and on the bridge over the River Foyers look out for salmon jumping – especially when the river is in autumn spate.
Roe deer can often be seen in the fields, particularly in the early morning and evening.

The view from the path to the Falls of Foyers

Loch Ness

The longest loch in Scotland, Loch Ness extends for 21 miles from Inverness to Fort Augustus. Its great depth – 754ft at one point – of dark peaty waters has encouraged the legend of 'Nessie', the Loch Ness monster. The story is not new – it is claimed that a sighting was made by St Columba in the 6th century. Since the 1930s, monster spotting has become something of a boom industry in the area, with Nessie museums and visitor centres doing great business.

Falls of Foyers and the River

The Falls are particularly dramatic after heavy rain. From a narrow rocky lip, the main fall drops about 100 feet down a steep cliff into a dark pool below.

To the right of the stone bridge over the River Foyers you'll see the remains of British Alcan's original hydro-electric scheme, used in the making of aluminium. The flow of water was diverted above the bridge into pipes which fed the factory turbines at the bottom of the hill.

(map)

Loch Ness
Foyers Bay
Piers
Works
School
B852
Foyers Burial Ground
Foyers
Telephone
Farm
Police Station
Store / Post Office
P START
220 ▲
Lower Falls
Glenlia Farm
Upper Falls
Weir
241 ▲
Creag Bhreac
River Foyers
B852
0   ¼   ½ mile
0   ¼   ½ km
FORT AUGUSTUS

Durness and Balnakeil

Starting from the most north-westerly village on the Scottish mainland, this walk includes impressive limestone cliffs, a beautiful beach of sparkling white sands and, on a clear day, a view of the Orkney Isles.

Information

The walk is about four miles long

Mostly flat and easy, with a section along the sands; care needed close to the cliffs

Some road walking

No stiles

Dogs should be kept on leads where there are sheep in the fields

Tea shops in Balnakeil and Durness

START

The Sutherland village of Durness is some 15 miles north of Rhiconich on the A838. The walk begins at the car park just opposite the Parkhill Hotel in the village.

DIRECTIONS

Leave the car park opposite the Parkhill Hotel and turn left. Follow the road and after ½ mile pass the Balnakeil Craft Village. Continue along the road for about another ¼ mile. At a churchyard wall, the road turns left. At this point bear right onto the beach and continue along the sands with the sand dunes on your right. After ¼ mile rejoin the road and continue, turning right just before a cattle grid and crossing grassland towards the cliffs, with a stone wall on your left. Walk uphill, bearing right towards buildings on the headland. On the cliff top, bear right towards the next group of buildings. After ¼ mile turn right on to a broader track and keep left at the junction with another track. Go through a gate in a wall and then follow the wall on your right.

Just past the corner of the field, turn right through another gate and walk across the field. Go through another gate and walk across the rough road between the fences. Go through a final gate onto the road and turn left to return to the starting point.

Balnakeil Craft Village

This was established in 1964, with Sutherland County Council funding, on the site of an old radar station. The Craft Village uses the former radar station buildings, and a community of craftspeople and artists have gathered here. There is a pottery, an art gallery and many other attractions, including a tearoom.

Balnakeil Churchyard

Celtic monks established a monastery here in the 6th century – Balnakeil means

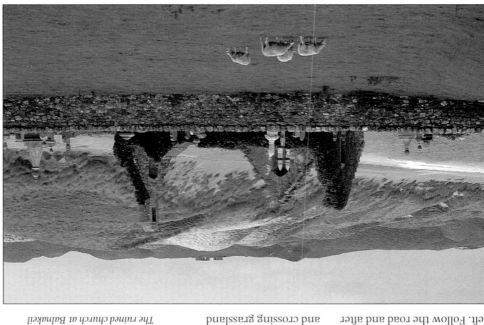

The ruined church at Balnakeil

'the place of the kirk'. Ancient Vatican records show that the church here donated 14s 8d towards the cost of the Crusades in 1274!

The graveyard has some fascinating and very old graves, including one, inscribed in Gaelic, Latin and Greek, to the Gaelic poet Rob Donn Mackey, the Bard of Reay. Another tomb contains the remains of one Donald McLeod who reputedly committed at least 18 murders. He bought his way in by contributing some money towards the construction of the present building, in 1619, on the condition that he would be buried in the graveyard.

Sango Bay

This bay, just below the caravan site in the village of Durness, boasts one of the finest beaches in the area. Brilliant white sands, limestone cliffs, deep green seas and the constant cry of fulmars and herring gulls make it a place to linger, especially when the sun shines. At low tide several limestone skerries appear, and on the outskirts of the bay there are lots of rock pools.

What to look out for

Puffins breed on the cliffs just south of Durness and there are thousands of fulmars nesting on ledges on the limestone cliffs of Sango Bay. Also between April and July you are likely to see guillemots, razorbills and kittiwakes. Sango Bay has lots of rock pools which are always worth exploring.

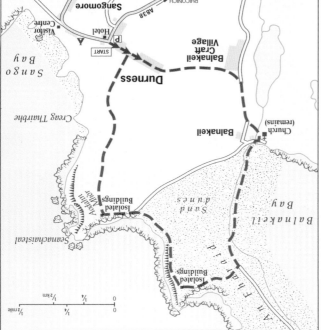

Index

Note: all numbers refer to walk numbers